The University of Cincinnati

THE UNIVERSITY
OF CINCINNATI :

A Success Story in Urban Higher Education

by Reginald C. McGrane

HARPER & ROW, PUBLISHERS

New York, Evanston, and London

To the Memory of Lenore
and
To the Students and Alumni
of the
University of Cincinnati

Contents

Acknowledgments

At the suggestion of President Walter C. Langsam, the Board of Directors commissioned me, following my retirement, to write a comprehensive history of the University of Cincinnati. The initiation of this work was due to President Langsam, and he has been my constant counselor in the preparation and completion of the manuscript. Notwithstanding his other arduous duties, President Langsam has meticulously read the entire manuscript, suggested improvements in the style and content, and, in innumerable other ways, has encouraged and assisted me. Two members of the Board of Directors and a member of the Administration have also read the entire manuscript and have drawn upon their intimate knowledge of various aspects of the University and its operation in order to make the account as inclusive as possible.

I have also been fortunate enough to have had access to valuable manuscript material. The sons of former President Raymond Walters—Raymond Walters, Jr., Everett Walters, and Philip G. Walters—placed at my disposal the illuminating daily diary kept by their father that shed much new information on the problems of his long and distinguished administration. The two daughters of former President Charles W. Dabney—Mrs. Alexander Thomson and Mrs. John W. Ingle—supplied useful data in personal interviews and intimate correspondence relating to their father's administration of the University. Louis Nippert, the son of the late Judge Alfred K. Nippert, made available the latter's valuable collection of correspondence which illuminated many aspects of the early history of the University. Russel Eaton of Urbana, Illinois, the great grandson of John H. James, the first graduate of Cincinnati College, graciously presented to the University the diploma of Mr. James and documents illustrative of early student activities.

Professor William D. Schwarberg, Associate Director of Athletics, rendered invaluable aid in tracing the various stages of the athletic history of the University. The Clerk of the Supreme Court of Louisiana, New Orleans, Louisiana, supplied manuscript documents relating to the historic Louisiana court decision pertaining to the estate of Charles Mc-Micken in that state. Dean Herman A. Moench of Rose Polytechnic Institute of Terre Haute, Indiana, and the American Council on Education, Washington, D.C., supplied information, on request, pertaining to the history of one of the early Presidents of the University and on the development of higher education in the United States.

The author also wishes to acknowledge the valuable assistance rendered by the following officials, alumni, and students of the University: Roscoe L. Barrow; A. H. Davis; Mrs. Joyce G. Agnew; John P. DeCamp; G. A. Ginter; Carter V. Good; Jack Grieshaber; Robert Heuck; Paul Herget; Robert Hoefer; C. Albert Joerger; Mrs. J. S. Montague; William R. Nester; Frank R. Neuffer; Garland G. Parker; Rabbi Abraham I. Shinedling; J. B. Silverman; John E. Small; R. A. Van Wye; Charles K. Weichert; and Cornelius Wandmacher.

Finally, the author is under deep obligation to the staffs of the University Library, the Library of the Medical College, the Library of the Law College, the Public Library of Cincinnati, the Ohio Historical and Philosophical Society Library, the Ohio State University Library, the Library of Miami (Ohio) University, the Bucks County Historical Library of Pennsylvania, the Historical Society of Pennsylvania, and the Library of the Louisiana State University, for their courtesy and assistance.

REGINALD C. McGRANE

Cincinnati, Ohio
May 1963

Introductory Note on
Municipal Higher Education

The University of Cincinnati is the second oldest and the second largest of the municipal universities in the United States. The year in which the first unit of a university or college is established is generally accepted as marking the founding date of the institution. The two oldest units of the University of Cincinnati—the Cincinnati College and the Medical College of Ohio—were established in 1819. The Board of Directors of the University, accordingly, have selected the year 1819 as the founding date of the University. Another date often cited in connection with the establishment of the University is 1870. It was in that year that the University of Cincinnati was chartered as a municipal university under the provisions of a law by the General Assembly of Ohio enacted April 16, 1870, entitled "An Act to enable cities of the first class to aid and promote education."

The College of Charleston, Charleston, South Carolina, was the first municipal *college* in the United States. It was opened in 1790 and came under municipal control in 1837. Later it reverted to private status.

Jefferson Seminary of Louisville, Kentucky, which was the original antecedent of the University of Louisville, was opened in 1798. The University of Louisville claims that it is the oldest municipal *university* in the United States.

The University of Cincinnati, therefore, is the second oldest municipal university in the United States; and, in 1962, with a net enrollment of more than 20,000, it is the second largest municipal university. The largest municipal university in the United States is the City University of New York.

The rise of urban universities can be traced back to the period of the revival of learning during the Middle Ages. Groups of students were attracted to great teachers such as Abelard at Paris. Many of the continental universities were located in cities, for example, in Paris, Bologna, Vienna, Prague, and elsewhere. The citizens of these cities frequently complained of the presence of the boisterous, often impecunious, students in their midst; but they realized these educational institutions brought prestige as well as more income to the city in which they were located. Hence, the cities began to grant subsidies to provide better educational facilities. This encouraged teachers to remain there and caused more students to be attracted to these localities.

The idea of a municipal university—an institution of higher learning controlled by municipal authorities and supported in whole or in part through city taxes—began in the United States in the middle of the nineteenth century with the founding of the College of Charleston and the University of Louisville. The movement then lay dormant for a number of years, but in the last two decades of the nineteenth century, it developed great momentum as the United States became highly industrialized and urbanized. By the turn of the century, leading educators expressed the belief that the municipal university would probably be "the most important movement of higher education in the next generation." United States Commissioner of Education P. P. Claxton prophesied in 1917 that "probably within a quarter of a century most cities of 200,000 or over and some even smaller," would have "such institutions at the head of their system of education; organizing all other agencies, directing their energies, and inspiring the people to strive for higher and better things." Perhaps the first intimation even to many educators of the genuine importance of this effort in popular education came with the formation at Washington in 1914 of an Association of Urban Universities.

According to the American Council on Education in 1961, there were seventeen municipal universities and colleges in the United States. They were established as a result of a variety of motives and a diversity of local conditions. Some, such as the University of Cincinnati, owed their origin to a bequest to the city for educational purposes with which other educational foundations were from time to time combined. The desire on the part of parents to have their children educated at home in order that they might have more parental control over them was an important motive in the founding of some of these universities and colleges. Another impelling factor in the creation of these corporations was the opinion that they would have a beneficial effect on the local public schools and would greatly improve them. Also, the vocational needs of the commercial and industrial classes of the population which wanted a more practical education than that afforded by colleges that stressed the importance of a classical education, was frequently urged as a reason for their creation. It was also hoped that the diffusion of knowledge might break down the prejudices against agricultural and mechanical occupations and result in more respect for all types of labor. Irrespective of all these motives, however, the most urgent reason advanced in behalf of such universities and colleges was the democratic desire upon the part of the American public to provide educational opportunities for those who otherwise might not be able to go to college.

Throughout the history of public education in America there has been a constant demand that it be made more democratic; that the opportunities for education be afforded to all the people. First came the demand for free, tax supported, non-sectarian elementary schools to give training in the 3 R's; then for high schools—the "people's colleges"—to train young people for citizenship; then for normal schools to train teachers for the lower schools; and then for colleges to train for the higher callings in life. As America became highly industrialized it became evident, as Charles A. Beard said, that industrial democracy could not endure without a sound and efficient public service. The colleges, therefore, had to assume new responsibilities and had to train young men and women for public service in many new professions. But this was an expensive process. Since many parents could not afford to send their children to old established colleges, there was a growing demand that the colleges come to them by creating municipal institutions wholly or partially maintained by public funds in which all the youth of the land might be given an opportunity to obtain higher education. As Thomas Jefferson had said: "If all the people are to rule, all the people must be educated"; and he believed and significantly pointed out that there was "a mass of talent which lies buried in the poverty of every community."

The municipal university was thus the logical outgrowth of the American idea that all the youth of this country shall be educated to the best purpose irrespective of the position or wealth of their parents; that education for all should not be limited to childhood but should be continuous throughout life. The rise of the municipal university marked an era in the development of American education second only to the establishment of the free public school system.

The ideal of a municipal university should be an institution which serves the whole community. The city university should be the brains and directing force of its schools, the natural capstone of the city's educational arch. It should be closely related to, and indeed be the directing force of, the intellectual, scientific, and industrial life of the city. It should aim to help assist every citizen in the community who has an urge for intellectual and spiritual advancement to satisfy this desire. To what extent the University of Cincinnati has tried to realize these ideals is recorded in the history of its origin and development.

The University of Cincinnati

1

Prelude to a University: Early Efforts and False Starts

From the beginning, the University of Cincinnati was a "city university." Under an earlier name it came into being (1819) at Fourth and Walnut Streets, in what was then the heart of a river town of about nine thousand people.

Cincinnati was founded by some twenty-six settlers in 1788 and incorporated as a city in 1802, a year before Ohio became a state. Within three years of its incorporation, there were civic leaders eager to establish a college. They looked to the state legislature for authority to act, but they relied on themselves and their neighbors to provide the initiative and the money.

Despite various physical moves and changes of name, the University and its antecedents were always urban in location, atmosphere, and purpose. The University of Cincinnati was municipal in character long before it became a municipal university in formal law. Its contribution to American higher education over 150 years is above all notable for the great stimulus it has given to the urban concept that was to have such a spectacular growth in mid-twentieth century.

CINCINNATI UNIVERSITY

The people of Cincinnati always have had an appreciation of and a desire for collegiate education. As early as 1805, two years after Ohio was admitted to the Union and when the population of Cincinnati was less than a thousand, the community tried to obtain one of the colleges which was to be financed through "college townships" granted by Congress in fulfillment of the promise of the Ordinance of 1787 that "schools and the means of education shall be forever encouraged" in the Northwest Territory. When there was a long delay in securing this grant because of the difficulty with Judge John Cleves Symmes over the particular township

1

that was to be reserved in the Miami Purchase for this purpose, a group of disgruntled Cincinnatians determined through their own efforts to establish a university.

A school association was formed in 1806; subscriptions were solicited; a tract of land was procured; and a brick building was erected. On January 23, 1807, the General Assembly of Ohio authorized forty-nine persons of Cincinnati to form a corporation to establish Cincinnati University. The corporation was to elect as officers nine trustees, a treasurer, a clerk, and a collector. By a subsequent act (February 3, 1807) John Riddle, Joseph Van Horn, William Stratton, Ethan Stone, Stephen Wood, Samuel Hilditch, Luke Foster, Matthew Nimmo, and Daniel Symmes were appointed commissioners to raise by means of a lottery a sum not exceeding $6,000 for the use of the trustees of Cincinnati University. The commissioners were instructed to publish the scheme of the lottery in three or more newspapers in Ohio and were each bonded to the sum of $50,000 to apply the money so raised for this purpose. At least three of the commissioners were to attend the drawing and, when the lottery was completed, to publish the names of the fortunate numbers in one of the newspapers of Cincinnati or Chillicothe. The drawing was to commence on or before the first day of September 1809, and was to be completed within ninety days. Ten days after the drawing of the lottery all prizes were to be paid. Two years later (February 17, 1809) this act was amended, permitting the commissioners to modify or reduce the lottery scheme, and four new commissioners were appointed: William Ruffin, Martin Baum, William Ramsay, and Jacob Burnet in place of Ethan Stone, Samuel Hilditch, Matthew Nimmo, and Daniel Symmes who had refused to act as commissioners.

As required by law the commissioners published the scheme of the lottery in the *Liberty Hall* and *Cincinnati Mercury* and the *Western Spy*. They advertised "a fortune for $5.00," offering one prize of $15,000, one prize of $5,000, five prizes of $1,000 each, three thousand prizes of $5.00 each, and the last drawn blank was to be entitled to $5,000, a total of $45,000 in prizes. These terms were later modified as permitted by the amended act; and in order to encourage the sale of the tickets, the friends of literature were urged to join companies or clubs and allowed to purchase the tickets on credit. The commissioners pointed out "the benefits and advantages resulting from such an institution to society; every citizen is sensible of its utility." The commissioners, therefore, hoped that the public would realize that by encouraging the sale of tickets "they not only had a chance of bettering their circumstances, but at the same time would render an essential service to their country." From the rapid sale of the tickets the commissioners expressed the belief they might be able to commence the drawing of the lottery at a much earlier date than at first contemplated.

Soon, however, the commissioners began to encounter many difficulties owing to the extreme scarcity of money caused by the depression of 1807 resulting from Jefferson's embargo policy. They also met much opposition, since many persons did not approve of the idea of establishing a university by means of a lottery. The commissioners grew discouraged and began to contemplate the abondonment of the whole business. They fully realized the serious and unpleasant consequences that would result from giving up the idea of holding the lottery. It would necessitate the sale of the building erected in order to pay the workmen, and many individuals would lose the money they had already paid for its construction. In addition, the commissioners were fearful of ever succeeding again in establishing a university in the locality. As a matter of fact, the lottery was never held, and little of the money obtained from the sale of tickets was refunded to the purchasers. Finally the whole scheme collapsed when, on May 29, 1809, Cincinnati experienced "the most violent tornado ever known by the oldest inhabitants of the town." Trees were twisted and torn up by the roots, and among the houses wrecked was the University's new brick building. Thus ended the first effort to found a university in Cincinnati.

THE CINCINNATI LANCASTER SEMINARY

Seven years after the Cincinnati University project (1814), the Methodists in Cincinnati attempted to establish a Lancasterian school. Such a school employed the Lancasterian method of instruction. This was a system of education based upon the ideas of Joseph Lancaster, an Englishman, who had more advanced students act as monitors or teachers for the younger pupils. Shares of stock of $25.00 were sold to build a schoolhouse. But the organization meeting was broken up by the secession of a large number of the shareholders who objected to a school controlled by any single religious group. The seceders established the Cincinnati Lancaster Seminary. The populace so enthusiastically supported the new school that in a few weeks the Methodist school was merged in the Seminary.

In February 1815 an act was passed by the General Assembly of Ohio granting a group of prominent citizens of Cincinnati corporate rights under the name of the Cincinnati Lancaster Seminary. The first directors of this corporation were: Jacob Burnet, Nicholas Longworth, Charles Marsh, William Corry, Davis Embree, and Daniel Drake. The First Presbyterian Church leased to the new Seminary a lot on Walnut Street for ninety-nine years upon which to build a schoolhouse, reserving the privilege, however, that each year twenty-eight poor children should be educated free of cost. Since the subscriptions were paid in installments there was some delay in erecting the frame school building. The banks of

Cincinnati agreed to lend the institution an extended credit, the sums necessary for the completion of the edifice. The building was located at the corner of Fourth and Walnut Streets in the rear of the Presbyterian Church. The Seminary began operations in April 1815, when the building was only partially roofed.

Within a fortnight over four hundred students were admitted. The classroom was heated on the principle of an oven, since the brick floor was laid over flues that were fired from the outside. The pupils learned their letters as the monitor called them out by tracing them in a shallow trough filled with sand. By the charter the Seminary consisted of a junior and senior department subdivided into a male and female school. After operating for three years the school began to decline and was temporarily closed. In 1818, however, new life was fused into the sinking concern by chartering of the Cincinnati College into which the Lancasterian school was merged.

2

After the Indians, Before the Canals

In 1819, two decades after its first settlers had come ashore from their flatboats and rafts and had broken them up to build rude huts, Cincinnati was already a busy little trading and manufacturing city. It was huddled close along the Ohio River, a place of sawmills and brickyards, of five banks, many woodworking shops, of boat-building yards, grist mills, distilleries, bookbinderies, tanyards, and foundries. It had had one or more newspapers since 1793. Steamboats were rapidly replacing the old flatboats and keelboats, and were being built at yards along the river. Cincinnati businessmen were caught up in the "canal fever," and were agitating for construction of the Miami & Erie Canal. This, however, was not to be started until 1825.

It was a time of stupendous enthusiasm and limitless optimism, of lavish and imposing plans for future growth. But it also was a time of shaky credit, of capital scarcity, and of financial instability. Cincinnati banks suspended specie payments in 1818, and by 1820 all the banks in the City had shut their doors. The panic of 1820 lasted five years. It was not an auspicious time to found a university, however modest. The Indians were gone, the canal was yet to come. A great river city was burgeoning, and with it the primitive educational institutions on which a great university would be built in God's good time.

CHARTERING THE CINCINNATI COLLEGE

When the Cincinnati Lancaster Seminary was projected, it was intended for the instruction at small expense of a great number of children. As a matter of fact, in it were gathered the children of the City long before the public schools were established. At that time there was no classical academy or grammar school of a permanent kind in the town. But the Seminary did not satisfy many Cincinnatians. They declared

5

there was a real need for a college. As the building for the Seminary was not large enough to afford recitation rooms for college classes, General William T. Lytle proposed to his fellow directors of the Seminary that they appeal to the citizens of Cincinnati to subscribe to a fund to finish and enlarge the building "which had been begun for the Lancaster Seminary, endow it, and procure a college charter."

Accordingly, on December 22, 1818, Ephraim Brown of Hamilton County presented in the Senate of the General Assembly of Ohio a petition from sundry citizens of the county who were shareholders in the Cincinnati Lancaster Seminary requesting that a college be established in connection with the Seminary. The Senate quickly passed an act to incorporate the Cincinnati College. This bill was referred in the House to a select committee which reported it with two amendments. One amendment was that the property of the corporation both real and personal should be "exempt from taxation"; and the other amendment provided that "it shall not at any time be lawful to attach the Cincinnati College to the Miami College, nor shall any part of the Miami Purchase given by Congress for the support of a university ever be applied to the use or benefit of the Cincinnati Lancaster Seminary or the Cincinnati College." Both of these amendments were rejected by the House.

On January 22, 1819, the General Assembly of Ohio created a new corporation under the name of "The President, Trustees, and Faculty of the Cincinnati College," and repealed the act incorporating the Lancaster Seminary. The capital stock of the new college consisted of 5,000 shares of $25.00 each which were to be subscribed by the public. Twenty-nine hundred shares were subscribed within a week. The total amount subscribed was nearly $40,000 by about forty persons. The largest contributor was General William T. Lytle with a subscription of $11,500. The next largest subscribers were Jacob Burnet and J. H. Piatt.

The affairs of the College were to be managed by a Board of Trustees to consist of not less than thirteen nor more than twenty members who were to be elected annually by ballot by the shareholders on the last Friday of March. Each shareholder was entitled to one vote for every share of $25.00, until the number of shares amounted to five, and one vote for every five shares above this number he or she might hold. The Board of Trustees was empowered to elect a President and Vice-President of the College and appoint members of the Faculty. The principles of morality and of the Christian religion might be taught, but the act stated that the "religious tenets that may be peculiar to any particular sect or denomination shall never be taught or enforced in the college."

Jacob Burnet, Joshua L. Wilson, Oliver M. Spencer, Daniel Drake, Levi James, Samuel W. Davis, William Corry, Francis Dunlavy, Spencer Johnston, William Lytle, Zaccheus Biggs, John Thompson, William H. Harrison, Joseph H. Crane, Joshua Collett, Jesse Hunt, Samuel Burr,

John Reynolds, James Galloway, and Martin Baum were appointed the first trustees of the College. In 1824 several new names appeared in the list of trustees: the Reverend William Burke, G. T. Torrence, D. K. Este, J. S. Lytle, P. S. Symmes, Daniel Gano, William Greene, Joseph Benham, T. Graham, Charles Hammond, Nathan Guilford, E. S. Haines, and A. Mack.

The news of the incorporation of the Cincinnati College was acclaimed in Cincinnati by the local press. "At no place in the western country," said the *Cincinnati Inquisitor,* "have greater exertions been made for the promotion of literature and science." Cincinnati was situated in a "populous and flourishing district." The new institution ought always to have a respectable number of students, provided it was managed well. The incorporators were congratulated on having laid the foundation of a school that promised "to be of lasting benefit to the state."

RULES AND REGULATIONS OF THE COLLEGE

The Board of Trustees drew up a set of rules and regulations for the management of the College. The duties of the President and Vice-President, professors, and tutors were outlined. It was the duty of the officers of the College to visit the boardinghouses and the rooms of the students at least once a week. This was to assure the parents of out-of-town students that there would be careful supervision of the morals and welfare of all those who matriculated in the College.

The price of boarding and rooming in respectable families was estimated at from $2.50 to $3.00 per week. The tuition was $20.00 a session or $40.00 per year, and an entrance fee of $5.00 was required of each student at the commencement of his first session. It was claimed that the necessary expenses of a student, exclusive of clothing and books, ought not at the highest rate of boarding, exceed $150 or $170 per annum.

Candidates might be admitted into any class which on examination they were judged by the Faculty qualified to enter, but no person who had studied at any other college or university could be admitted into the College without producing a certificate from the President or Faculty of such college or university that he had left it without censure. No person was admitted into the College unless he had passed an examination set by the Faculty which showed that he was able to translate from Latin into English Sallust, Caesar, Virgil, or other authors equivalent to these; to make in grammatical Latin an exercise in the well-known text of Mair's *Introduction to Latin;* and to translate into English passages from the Evangelists in the Greek Testament and be able to do arithmetic to the rule of three.

The College year was divided into a winter and a summer session. The winter session was from the second Wednesday in November to the first

Wednesday in April. The summer session commenced on the first Wednesday in May and terminated with the annual commencement which was held on the last Wednesday in September. This gave the student a spring vacation of four weeks and a fall vacation of six weeks.

The courses studied by the various classes as set forth in the rules and regulations were somewhat modified by the time the College began to operate. As finally decided upon, the freshmen studied at least two books of the *Aeneid*, including prosody, the Greek grammar, one or two of the Evangelists in the Greek Testament, the accurate construction of Latin, and arithmetic through the rule of three. The sophomore class paid particular attention to Virgil, the odes of Horace, Lucian, the book of Xenophon, and arithmetic through fractions. The studies of the junior class were geometry, algebra, practical mathematics—including surveying and navigation, conic sections, spherics—natural philosophy, composition, and occasionally the languages. The studies of the senior year were natural philosophy, astronomy, belles-lettres, moral philosophy, logic, chemistry, composition, speaking, and the languages.

Particular emphasis was laid upon religious worship and moral conduct. Every student was required to attend prayers in the College Hall, morning and evening, and public worship on the Sabbath. The due observance of the Sabbath, or the Lord's Day, was indispensable for every student, and all practices inconsistent with it were expressly prohibited. No student was allowed "to possess or read any indecent, impious, or irreligious books"; and if any student was convicted of this offence or "of lying, profaneness, drunkenness, theft, or playing at unlawful games," he was to be punished "according to the nature and heinousness" of his crime. Any student found guilty of fighting a duel was expelled from the College. No student should have or keep in his room any spirituous or fermented liquors "without express permission" from the teacher of the class to which he belonged. Nor should any student "go to a tavern or tippling house, for the purpose of entertainment or amusement, without permission from some member of the Faculty; nor shall he on any occasion keep company with persons of publicly bad character under penalty of admonition, and, if the practice be continued, of expulsion." All students were admonished to dress plainly and to appear neat and clean. Every student was required to possess a black gown that he should wear at church or any public ceremony. Members of the literary societies were required to submit their compositions for orations to the Faculty for inspection five days before they delivered them on the public stage.

The use of the Cincinnati Public Library, containing more than 2,000 volumes, and the cabinet of the Western Museum, were placed in the College at the disposal of the students. It was claimed that the philosophical and chemical apparatus of the College was sufficiently complete to perform the usual experiments.

The founders of the College boasted that they could see no reason why the institution they were establishing "should not shortly vie with other seminaries of a similar grade in the Atlantic states." The wealth and population of the western country seemed sufficient to justify their high hopes. By the census of 1820 the population of Ohio was over a half-million, and one-fifth of it was concentrated in Hamilton County. The states bordering on the west were growing so rapidly that the founders were confident that the period was "near at hand when the youth on this side of the mountains will equal in numbers those that are now in the Atlantic states."

The Board of Trustees inserted an advertisement in the local papers announcing that the College would be opened for the reception of students on the first Monday in May 1819, at which time a freshman and sophomore class would be formed out of the Grammar School and neighboring academies. However, it was not until the following September that the College was organized; and it was not until November 9, 1819, that the first session commenced with a freshman, sophomore, and junior class. As the ringing of the College bell at six o'clock in the morning and eight in the evening apparently alarmed some of the citizens, a notice was published in the press informing them that the bell would be rung during each session of the College at "six, eight, and one-half before nine o'clock in the morning and twelve, two, five, and eight in the afternoons." The bell was tolled when rung for College purposes, but in cases of fire it would be rung violently so that every citizen might take his assigned fire post.

The First Faculty

The first Faculty of the Cincinnati College consisted of the Reverend Elijah Slack, the President; the Reverend Thomas Osborn of the Episcopal Church, professor of languages; and Mr. David Taylor, a tutor. The Grammar School attached to the College was under the direction of the professor of languages.

The first President of one of the two oldest units of the university of Cincinnati, the Reverend Elijah Slack, was born in Bucks County, Pennsylvania, the same county from which later came the founder of the University of Cincinnati, Charles McMicken. On his father's side the Reverend Dr. Slack was descended from an old Dutch family from near Leyden, Holland, who came to New York City when it was called New Amsterdam. On his mother's side he was a descendant of a Presbyterian family from Belfast, Ireland. In 1805 young Slack entered Princeton College, from which he was graduated three years later with high honors. He then taught for three years in an academy at Trenton, New Jersey, meanwhile pursuing his theological studies at Princeton. In 1812 he was elected Vice-President of Princeton College and appointed professor of mathematics, natural philosophy, and chemistry. In the fall of 1817 he was elected President of the newly founded Lancaster Seminary in Cincinnati. When this institution was merged with the Cincinnati College the Board of Trustees unanimously elected him President and to the professorship of mathematics, natural philosophy, and chemistry. The same year he was ordained a Presbyterian minister.

The Reverend Dr. Slack was President of Cincinnati College until 1822, and at the same time he was also registrar and treasurer of the Medical College of Ohio. Philander Chase, Episcopal Bishop of Ohio, the uncle of Salmon P. Chase, was President of Cincinnati College from October 1822 to July 25, 1823. He found "the duties fell heavy on the President" and resigned at the end of the year. The Reverend Dr. Slack once more assumed the management of affairs of Cincinnati College, not as President, which he declined, but as Vice-President. In 1837 he moved to Brownsville, Tennessee, where he took charge of a high school for girls. In 1851, when the Cincinnati College of Medicine and Surgery was organized, the Reverend Dr. Slack, "then a venerable septuagenarian with a wealth of flowing white hair," was appointed professor of chemistry; there he taught until his death in 1866.

Dr. Slack (who received an honorary doctor of laws degree from Princeton in 1863) took an active and influential part in the educational life of Cincinnati. In addition to his Presidency of the Cincinnati College, he helped found, with Daniel Drake, the Medical College of Ohio, was its first registrar, and for eleven years was on the Faculty of that institution. He was also the President of the first medical society of Cincinnati, called the Cincinnati Medical Society, and also one of the founders of the Historical and Philosophical Society of Ohio.

Dr. Slack was a scholar who was fond of teaching. He was not a successful lecturer, being too pedantic, too diffuse in his remarks, and totally lacking in a sense of humor. His awkwardness in the classroom frequently caused much hilarity. On one occasion, when he was lecturing to a mixed class of young men and young women, he endeavored to show the chemical composition of water. He picked up a pig's bladder, which was to serve as the receptacle, and remarked, "I shall now fill my bladder and proceed to make water." His audience burst into hysterics of laughter much to his astonishment.

EARLY COMMENCEMENTS

The first Commencement of the Cincinnati College was held in the morning of September 26, 1821, in the north wing of the College building. "A numerous and notable audience" was reported present. President Slack began the ceremonies with prayer. Frederick A. Kemper then delivered a Latin salutatory oration. He was followed with an oration by

Joseph Junius James, and another oration on "Slander" by Richard Spencer. The oration on "Eloquence" by William H. Harrison, Jr., the son of General William H. Harrison who was one of the trustees of the College, was "an impassioned, glowing harangue" delivered "with his characteristic impetuousity." John H. James, to whom was awarded the First Honor, acquitted himself with "great credit" with an oration on "Literature and Science" and "a chaste, appropriate, and highly affecting valedictory address." The President addressed the graduates, "the first fruits of the institution" in "a solemn, impressive, and affectionate style" and the ceremonies were concluded by prayer.

The degree of Bachelor of Arts was conferred upon three graduates—Frederick A. Kemper, William H. Harrison, Jr., and John Hough James—at this Commencement. It is interesting to recall that Mrs. Walter C. Langsam, the wife of President Langsam of the University of Cincinnati, is the great-great-granddaughter of Thomas James, the younger brother of Levi James, who was the father of John Hough James. Three years later these same young men were awarded the honorary degree of Master of Arts. At that time any graduate of the College was entitled to a master's degree upon application to the Faculty the third year after he received his first degree.

STUDENT LIFE

There were two literary societies in the College—the Philomatic and the Erophoebic. The Philomatic Society was organized on January 18, 1818. The catalogue of the College in 1840–1841 stated the influence of these societies promoted "the ultimate objects of the institution—developing the mind and adding incentives to a generous emulation for literary excellence." This may have been true by that year, but records of the early years of the Philomatic Society reveal numerous incidents of ungentlemanly conduct and the use of vulgar and immoral language by its members. In the spring of 1821 a contest between these societies threw the whole College into an uproar. George Wilson and William Lytle started a fist fight, but were stopped by the intervention of the Faculty. Wilson was frequently the cause of trouble in the Philomatic Society. On one occasion the President of the Society called him to order for talking. Wilson said that he had only asked Robert T. Lytle "to go wh——ing with him." For using such immoral language Wilson was fined one dollar. Another time Wilson was fined the same amount for using immoral and profane language in the Chapel. C. Ramsey, another member of the Society, was fined one dollar for disorderly conduct. He had defied the President of the Society with "fine and be damned"; whereupon he was fined again. The Philomatic Society did publish a literary magazine, the *Olio*, "the first issue of which appeared on May 26, 1826; it contained literary essays, historical articles, poetry, and occasionally a humorous essay." The Society offered a gold medal valued at $50.00 for the best original poem written by a citizen of the western country. It had to contain at least four hundred lines. The first prize was won by Thomas Peirce for "The Muse of Hesperia," which was published in December 1822.

In 1840 the second chapter of Beta Theta Pi, which had been founded the preceding year by John Reilly Knox and eight other men at Miami University, was established at Cincinnati College. This chapter ceased to exist after 1844. The Phi Delta Sigma Society was also founded in 1840, but it did not last very long.

The manners of the students were criticized both by citizens of the City and by visitors to the College. Articles appeared in the local press written by residents of Cincinnati stating they had seen "students of the College crowding a tenpin alley every hour of the day, blaspheming and drinking spirituous liquor" and complaining about noises at night when "a considerable number of these students assembled in the College edifice to the great annoyance of the neighborhood." An English traveler who visited the College in 1823 predicted that it would not be well attended until better regulations were established. He attended a lecture and "was much shocked at the want of decorum exhibited by the students who sat down in their plaids and cloaks and were constantly spitting tobacco juice about the room."

DECLINE OF THE CINCINNATI COLLEGE

The dark period in the history of the Cincinnati College began in 1824 following the holding of the fourth Commencement. Up to that year the College seemed to have been moderately successful largely due to the energetic efforts of President Slack. The College had a Faculty consisting of three professors and a tutor; there were four hundred pupils regularly enrolled in the Lancasterian department; and the average number of pupils in the College was sixty. Most of the subscriptions to the institution, however, had been made in town lots. The hard times following the Panic of 1819 caused the value of property to drop and little income was derived from this source as these lots could not be sold. Yet the debts of the institution had to be paid, and they were increased as a result of a fire which almost destroyed the College building. About the same time Miami University, founded upon an extensive land grant from the Federal government, began in full operation; and as it drew students from the same area as the Cincinnati College, the revenue from tuitions dropped. The lack of funds to maintain the establishment compelled the trustees in 1825 to cease collegiate instruction. The Lancasterian department was at length suspended, and by 1827 all operations of the Cincinnati College were discontinued. The Presbyterian Church commenced a suit for the recovery of the property on the ground that the suspension of that school was a violation of the lease. The lawsuit was, at length, terminated in favor of the College, but it contributed still further to the financial troubles of the institution.

During a period of ten years the rooms in the dilapidated College edifice were rented to various societies. When some of these could not be cleaned and refitted for this purpose, part of the building was used as a stable, and pigs wallowed in the cellar. In 1832 the building was utilized as a cholera hospital.

In that year the trustees resolved to make an effort to redeem the institution from decay and degradation. Morgan Neville, the President of the Board, issue an eloquent appeal to the citizens of Cincinnati to re-establish the Institution; but the appeal was of no effect. The Board then entered into negotiations with the Mechanics Institute to transfer the building, or, at least one-half of it, to the association on condition that it be repaired; but the negotiation failed.

By 1835 the public had apparently lost all interest in the project of establishing an institution of higher learning in the City. The dilapidated building, erected under most flattering auspices, was a ghostly reminder of the sanguine hopes of its founders.

3

The Heyday of
Daniel Drake

In many ways Daniel Drake may be thought the all-time first citizen of Cincinnati. Certainly he was the most colorful and energetic of its leaders in the most formative and dynamic decades of its history. Drake was a kind of "frontier Leonardo"—a man of diverse talents and stupendous energies. In a busy, contentious life he was physician, scientist, author, educator, and civic leader. And just as he did much to shape the contours of Cincinnati as a City, so he did much to lay the foundations of higher education in the community.

Despite recurring financial panics Cincinnati nearly tripled its population from 1820 to 1830 and just about doubled it again from 1830 to 1840. It was an ebullient age in the Queen City of the West, and nobody quite so much as Drake typified that lively, imaginative, optimistic climate of enterprise. Later on Charles McMicken was to provide the initial endowment from which the University of Cincinnati was to emerge. Drake might equally well be regarded as the father of the University, for his labors, talents, dreams, and inexhaustible energy were poured into the building of a medical college that became the nucleus of a university to come.

Three days before the Cincinnati College was incorporated, the General Assembly of Ohio, on January 19, 1819, passed an act establishing the Medical College of Ohio. The founder of the College was Daniel Drake. In 1800 he began the study of medicine in the office of William Goforth in Cincinnati. Goforth held no degree. Like many other physicians of his day he had studied medicine in the office of a physician, although he had grown up in New York City, one of the few American cities that could boast of a medical college. The Medical Department of King's College, which later became Columbia University, had been established in 1769, but suspended its operations during the Revolution and was not reorganized until 1792. Goforth began his study of medicine

14

in 1783 when the Medical Department of King's College was not functioning. He studied medicine in the office of Joseph Young, a prominent New York physician who was a graduate of the Medical Department of the University of New York. Later Goforth studied anatomy and surgery under Charles McKnight who was a graduate of Princeton and an army surgeon during the Revolution.

In 1788, Goforth left New York City in company with his brother-in-law, John S. Gano, and the family of Isaac and Elizabeth (Shotwell) Drake who were migrating to Kentucky. The Drake family consisted of Mr. and Mrs. Drake, young Daniel Drake who had been born October 20, 1785, on a farm near the present town of Plainfield, New Jersey, his infant sister, and an unmarried sister of Mrs. Drake's. The Drakes settled in Limestone (Maysville), Kentucky. Goforth settled in Washington, Kentucky, where he remained until 1799 when he joined other members of his family who were living in Columbia, near Cincinnati. The next year (1800) Goforth moved to Cincinnati.

After studying and working with "Dr." Goforth for five years, Drake decided early in 1805 to seek further training in medicine at the University of Pennsylvania. "Dr." Goforth, unsolicited, gave Drake a certificate of proficiency signed, "William Goforth, Surgeon General, 1st. Division, Ohio Militia." This was probably the first medical "diploma" issued west of the Alleghenies. Drake was the first medical student in Cincinnati and later became the father of western medicine.

After a five-month course at the University of Pennsylvania, Drake returned to the home of his parents in Maysville, Kentucky. He remained there until 1807 when, upon the invitation of "Dr." Goforth, he returned to Cincinnati to take charge of the latter's office.

Drake took an active part in the professional, civic, and commercial life of the City; and in 1810 published *Notices Concerning Cincinnati, Its Topography, Climate and Diseases*. Five years later he published a classic description of the population and resources of Cincinnati and the Miami Country entitled *Natural and Statistical View, or Picture of Cincinnati and the Miami Country*. He was at this time thirty years of age.

Drake's *Picture of Cincinnati* won for him a national and international reputation, as parts of his book were translated on the continent of Europe for the benefit of people who contemplated emigrating to America. His reputation as a physician, scientist, and author was established.

Upon the completion of his book Drake left Cincinnati in October 1815 for Philadelphia, accompanied by his wife. In 1815–1816 he attended medical lectures at the University of Pennsylvania, and then with his wife went to West Point. He found upon his return to Philadelphia that he had failed to receive notification of the exact date set for the final examinations and the Commencement. But the Medical Faculty of the University, in view of his "unavoidable absence" from the final examinations, examined and approved him; and on May 14, 1816, at a special Commencement conferred the degree of Doctor of Medicine on him. It is claimed that this is the only special investiture ever conferred in the long and distinguished history of the University of Pennsylvania.

After receiving his coveted degree Drake returned to Cincinnati; and the next year (1817) was invited to become a professor in the medical department of Transylvania University, Lexington, Kentucky. This was the first medical college west of the Allegheny Mountains and was created in 1799, but it was not until the fall of 1817 that all the medical chairs were filled and courses began. At the close of the session, early in March 1818, Drake returned to Cincinnati and resigned his professorship at Transylvania University.

On his return to Cincinnati, Drake conceived the plan of establishing a medical college in the City. The project was well received by the general public, but many of the physicians opposed the plan. Some were jealous of the young man of thirty years, because he was already famous as the author of *Picture of Cincinnati,* and because he had held a chair in Transylvania University. Others did not like the scheme, as they did not want well-trained physicians in Cincinnati to compete with them and hurt their own pocketbooks.

Drake wrote the charter of the Medical College of Ohio, took it up to the Legislature at Columbus, and procured its passage. The bill passed the Legislature without a dissenting vote. By the act of January 19, 1819, Daniel Drake, Coleman Rogers, Samuel Brown, and Elijah Slack were the incorporators and also constituted the first trustees and the first Faculty of the College. One provision of the law specified that no professor or lecturer could be appointed or dismissed without the concurrence of three-fourths of the Faculty. By the law Daniel Drake was appointed President of the College; Coleman Rogers, Vice-President; and Elijah Slack, Registrar and Treasurer. At that time there were seven medical colleges in the United States. The Medical College of Ohio was the second medical school established in the western country.

It was expected that the College would be put into operation that fall. But this was found impossible, as Dr. Samuel Brown, formerly of Kentucky, then residing in Philadelphia, did not accept his appointment. Before the act was passed Drake had offered Brown the chair of anatomy, and Brown had given Drake the impression he would accept it. It was because of this that Brown was named in the law a member of the first Faculty. Immediately after the enactment of the law Drake wrote to Brown outlining the plan of organization of the new College and requested his views on the subject. Brown did not reply to Drake for eight months, and then sent him a letter declining the offer and stating that he had obtained a much better position at Transylvania University. Drake promptly published a letter in the newspaper, *Liberty Hall*, censuring Brown's conduct for not having replied sooner indicating his refusal of the position. Drake declared that the affair was no longer between Dr. Brown and himself but between Brown and the State of Ohio with whose dignity Brown had trifled and whose interests he had betrayed. The organization of the Medical College of Ohio, therefore, had to be deferred, unless the people of Cincinnati awakened to the importance of establishing such an institution which would make the City the chief seat of medical science for the western country.

This was the great dream of Drake throughout his entire life. He wanted to make Cincinnati a great medical center. He realized that for the Medical College of Ohio to endure and become a successful school, it was necessary for the Faculty to have access to an abundance of clinical material for purposes of undergraduate instruction. He also realized that with the growth of the City's population there was a great need for a hospital in which the sick poor might receive medical attention. Drake's idea of a hospital in the City encountered much opposition because of the fear of increased taxation. With the help of General William H. Harrison, then a member of the State Legislature, an act was passed by the General Assembly, on January 22, 1821, to establish in the township of Cincinnati a public infirmary to be known and called by the name of the Commercial Hospital and Lunatic Asylum for the State of Ohio.

The law appropriated $10,000 for the establishment of the Hospital. The township was to furnish a suitable site, and its trustees were to superintend the erection of the building. The current expenses were to be defrayed by one-half of the duties on sales at auction in the City, and as far as it might be necessary afterward, by the ordinary poor taxes. Paupers and Ohio boatmen when sick at Cincinnati were to be treated gratuitous. The lunatics of the state who were paupers were to be sent to the Asylum by the different counties, and they were to pay for each two dollars a week, "the price that is now paid for keeping them in jail."

The act provided that it should be "the duty of the Faculty of the Medical College of Ohio to give to all of the patients . . . the medical and surgical advice and service which their cases may require, without charge, in consideration of which they shall be at liberty, under such regulations as they may choose to prescribe, to introduce the pupils of said College into the said Hospital and Asylum to witness the treatment of patients there assembled. The moneys that may accrue to the said College from admission of students into the said Hospital and Asylum shall be employed exclusively in the purchase of books, anatomical preparations, and . . . apparatus for said College."

Drake was far in advance of his time in foreseeing that a hospital was a necessary part of medical education. As he told his pupils:

The time has passed by when students will flock to men of genius for the purpose of listening to expositions of theory, or to be amused with creations of imagination. The school which is not based on a hospital may have learned and able professors; but the results of their teaching can never be satisfactory to the student who seeks to make himself a good, practical physician, and surgeon.

As a consequence of Dr. Brown's refusal to accept his chair, Drake obtained an amendment to the charter by an act passed by the Legislature on December 30, 1819, making the creation or abolition of a professorship or lectureship dependent upon a two-thirds instead of a three-fourths vote of the Faculty. The purpose of this amendatory act became apparent at the first meeting of the Faculty on January 14, 1820, at which Drake and Slack were present. Drake exhibited a letter from Dr. Brown stating that he would not accept the appointment as professor of anatomy. Drake likewise produced evidence showing that Dr. Rogers approved of the course pursued by Dr. Brown of intriguing against the welfare of the College. Consequently Rogers was dismissed from the Faculty by the vote of Drake and Slack. Upon Drake's recommendation, Dr. B. S. Bohrer was elected to the vacant chair of materia medica and Dr. Jesse Smith to the vacant chair of anatomy and surgery.

The Opening of the College and Student Life

On November 1, 1820, the first session of the College began with a class of twenty-four students. Drake, Bohrer, Smith, and Slack constituted the first Faculty of the College.

The first home of the College was located at No. 91 Main Street just below Pearl. It was a two-story brick building. All the lectures were given upstairs in an ordinary room over an apothecary shop kept by Drake's father and brother. The Faculty subsequently voted that Drake should be allowed for the rent of the room to the Medical College the sum of $100 a year.

The first Commencement of the College was held on April 14, 1821, in the Chapel of the Cincinnati College. William Barnes, David Dyer, James T. Grubbs, Isaac Hough, Samuel Monett, Ichabad Sargeant, and James Wooley were awarded the degree of Bachelor of Medicine.

When the Alumni Association of the Medical College of Ohio was organized, James T. Grubbs was present and was elected the first President of the Association. He gave a brief talk in which he discussed the first Faculty of the College and the character of the student body. Each one of the professors, he said, lectured every day, some of them twice; one of them, Smith, even three times a day. They had to lecture so much in order to cover the material in their subject. He said Drake was "a gentleman of the old school"; Bohrer "a gentleman of the Southern school." Both were "very pleasant and affable to all the students." Smith was "very positive and immovable in his opinions." Slack was "a rather slow, heavy man" but a good chemist. The students considered Drake their best teacher. This was also the opinion of Samuel D. Gross, the foremost surgeon of the century for four decades, who was one of Drake's colleagues in the Medical Department of the Cincinnati College. Drake loved to teach, and because he loved it was a great lecturer. His voice was clear and strong and "so powerful that when the windows of his lecture room were open he could be heard at a great distance." Sometimes he read his lectures, but usually he lectured without any notes. The better students were fascinated and thrilled by Drake's ardor and animation, his eloquence, scintillating wit, and infectious enthusiasm; the weaker students, however, complained that he was too abstruse and too argumentative in his discourses. Some of the students at a later date complained of the way some of the professors lectured, especially those who used notes and had to hunt through their "pieces of paper of varied sizes and shapes" as they lectured.

According to Grubbs the students were "all deeply in earnest. I never heard any noise or saw any disturbance of any kind in my student life." Perhaps the rigid rules adopted by the Faculty governing student conduct helped somewhat to produce this state of affairs. During lecture hours students were required to uncover their heads and observe silence and not be late for their classes. Any student who fought a duel or sent or accepted a challenge to fight a duel was expelled from the school. Likewise any student who wantonly or maliciously disclosed anything concerning the dissections or anatomical pursuits carried on in the institution, or engaged without the knowledge and approbation of the professor of anatomy in procuring any anatomical subject, was debarred from all classes. In 1829 two students were accused by their classmates of theft. One was exonerated as no evidence was found to substantiate the charge. The other one, however, was dismissed from the school as it was definitely proved that he had "stolen and sold a waistcoat"; and "had tried to pass a fifty dollar bank note of Mississippi which he knew to be counterfeit" and had given a servant girl in his boarding house "a copper coin as a gold coin."

To be a candidate for the degree of bachelor of medicine the student had to attend two full sessions in the institution, or one in the Medical College of Ohio, and one in some other medical college. The Medical College of Ohio was the first in the United States to extend the curriculum to five months. Later the course of study was shortened to four months as was the custom in the other medical schools. The candidate had to pass a satisfactory private examination before the Faculty; and prepare a thesis written in English, Latin, or French which he had to defend publicly. Each student had to pay a graduation fee of $3.00 to each professor. The diploma awarded by the first Faculty was almost an exact copy of that of the University of Pennsylvania. The student purchased tickets for each professor to attend his lectures. At the first session the price of these tickets was $20.00 per professor. Subsequently the price of these tickets was raised and students were permitted to pay for them on a credit basis, but it became so difficult to collect delinquent debts that in 1842 the credit system was abolished. The matriculation fee, including the use of the library and admission to the hospital, was $5.00. In the beginning the students assisted the professors in obtaining anatomical material which meant robbing the graveyards of bodies of deceased persons. In 1828, however, the Faculty decided that it was expedient to abolish this method of procuring anatomical subjects through the agency of the students and arranged to pay a resurrection man (a professional grave robber) $10.00 per subject.

The Expulsion of Drake and Its Consequences

Three days after the second Commencement was held the internal friction in the Faculty resulted in the expulsion of Drake from the College. On March 7, 1822, the professors met in a solemn council with Drake presiding. Smith moved the dismissal of Drake from the Faculty, and Slack seconded it. Drake put the question which carried in the classic language of Smith, *"nemo contradicente"* (without a dissenting vote). The founder of the College was driven out of the institution which he had created. The two-thirds rule had turned out to be a two-edge sword. The great defect in the charter was that it had made the professors also the trustees. Thus a majority of the Faculty could force out the other and elect whomever they wanted. The Faculty adjourned for half an hour. After the adjournment on the motion of Slack, Smith was elected President pro tempore. Thus Drake's first connection with the Medical College of Ohio came to an end.

The expulsion of Drake created a storm of public indignation. A committee of the citizens of the City requested the Faculty to reinstate Dr. Drake to his professorship in the College. The panic-stricken Smith and Slack quickly rescinded their vote dismissing Drake and again reinstated him as a member of the Faculty. Drake, however, refused to accept the appointment and immediately sent in his resignation.

The expulsion of Dr. Drake may be said to have terminated the first period in the history of the Medical College of Ohio. During the following winter Dr. Jesse Smith attempted to carry on a course of lectures in a room in the rear of his residence on Walnut Street, between Third and Fourth Streets. The College brought suit against Drake to recover some of the property in his possession, but he refused to surrender it. Bellamy Storer and William Greene were the attorneys for the College in this case, which finally was amicably adjusted.

Late in 1822 an effort was made to resuscitate the College. A committee appointed by a medical convention visited Cincinnati and recommended to the Legislature the appointment of a Board of Trustees composed of laymen to take over the entire control and management of the institution. In accordance with this recommendation the Legislature passed an act, December 13, 1822, appointing the following thirteen persons as members of the first Board of Trustees of the Medical College of Ohio: William Corry, William Henry Harrison, Samuel W. Davies, Vincent C. Marshall, Jeremiah H. Brower, Joseph Canby, Joseph Gest, Ethan Stone, Jacob Burnet, Truman Bishop, William Burke, Martin Ruter, and Alexander Campbell. They appointed the following faculty: Jedidiah Cobb, professor of the theory and practice of medicine; Jesse Smith, professor of anatomy and surgery; Elijah Slack, professor of chemistry; and John Moorhead, professor of materia medica and obstetrics. Drake was offered a chair in the new organization, but refused it and instead accepted a chair in Transylvania University.

During the next four years, while Drake was away—up to 1827—there was peace and quiet in the Medical College of Ohio. In 1824 the school moved to the building once occupied by the Miami Exporting Company and Banking House on Front Street near Sycamore. The following year, on February 5, 1825, the General Assembly passed a new act reducing the number of trustees from thirteen to seven and gave the College for a period of four years the taxes and penalties upon sales at auction in Hamilton County. By a subsequent act, passed in the same year, on December 31, 1825, the Legislature changed this law; the number of trustees was increased to eleven, and the College was given one-half of the taxes and penalties upon sales at auction for a period of five years instead of four years, and the College was given the privilege of introducing pupils or students to witness the treatment of patients in the hospital. During the next four years the College derived from this source of revenue over $24,000. This enabled the College to purchase ground on Sixth Street between Vine and Race Streets and to erect in 1826 a College edifice which contained two spacious lecture rooms and eleven other apartments suitable for the accommodation of a class of 350 students. The act of 1825 also made it obligatory on the part of the College to educate one indigent pupil to be selected by each district medical society in the State who was to be instructed free of cost, except the payment of the matriculation fee. The Board of Trustees by this act were required to report annually to the General Assembly on the condition of the College.

The College began to flourish. The number of students increased from eighteen in 1823 to 101 in 1828. In 1825, Moorhead was chosen Dean by a majority of the Faculty. The following year the Faculty passed a rule rotating the Deanship annually at the beginning of each session from one professor to another in the order in which their chairs had been established with the right of any professor of declining it in favor of the person next after him in line of succession.

BEGINNING OF THE WAR OF EXTERMINATION

But the war within the College was renewed. The "outs" were not satisfied with the "ins," and in 1828 the medical convention, consisting of delegates from the district societies, passed a resolution requesting the General Assembly to do something for the improvement of the institution. As a matter of fact the College was growing prosperous. Nearly the whole debt of the institution, with the exception of a small sum borrowed from the Bank of the United States, was paid off; the number of students increased; and an additional lot of ground was purchased in order to enlarge the College building. In 1830, Charles E. Pierson, professor of materia medica, verbally resigned the Deanship and for the ensuing session Slack was Dean.

In that year Drake returned to the City from the Jefferson Medical College at Philadelphia where he had been lecturing. He brought with him Dr. John Eberle and Dr. Thomas D. Mitchell to form the nucleus for a new medical college, the Medical Department of Miami University. This was the commencement of what was called the "war of extermination" of the Medical College of Ohio.

The proposed Miami Faculty, as it was called, created consternation in the ranks of the adherents and Faculty of the Medical College of Ohio. They yielded the citadel, and Drake dictated an amalgamation of the two Faculties. After much wrangling Drake finally accepted the chair of clinical medicine.

The arrangement did not last long, however. Drake was not satisfied with his chair, and his enemies wanted to get rid of him and the Miami contingent. The Board of Trustees reduced the number of chairs and rearranged them so as to get rid of Drake's friends. Drake found himself isolated and on January 19, 1832, resigned his chair.

To make matters worse, cholera broke out that year in Cincinnati. The City Council appealed to the Faculty of the Medical College for aid. They recommended that all the streets, lanes, and public landings be cleaned of all filth, the cellars ventilated, and the privies purified by the use of chloride of lime. As a consequence of the epidemic the opening of the College had to be postponed to November 12.

In 1833 the war of extermination was again renewed. The enemies of the Medical College of Ohio brought charges against both the Faculty and the Board of Trustees. They were accused of favoritism and of filling the professorships with unknown men; of gross negligence in the management of the funds of the College; and of failing to attract students to the College even though the tuition was lower than that in many schools in the United States. The Faculty members were accused of neglecting to perform their duties at the Hospital and of incompetency. The Commissioners were in session in Cincinnati for three weeks and examined between forty and fifty witnesses. In December they submitted their report to the General Assembly recommending a larger Board of Trustees and a new organization of the Faculty. This report was referred to a Select Committee which disproved the charges and sustained the Faculty and the Board.

It might well be said that *mutatis mutandis* would have been a good motto for the Medical College of Ohio during this twenty-year period. The next move in the war of extermination was the creation by Drake in 1835 of a Medical Department in the revived Cincinnati College as a rival school to the Medical College of Ohio.

4

The Uphill Road of the 1830's

In the summer of 1835, Dr. Drake conceived the project of organizing a Medical Department in the Cincinnati College. The proposition was given serious consideration by the Board of Trustees of the College. Ten years had elapsed since collegiate instruction had been suspended in the Cincinnati College. The College edifice was in a dilapidated condition; yet it was susceptible to being repaired and used again. It was evident that the medical profession of the City and the General Assembly of Ohio were thoroughly disgusted with the state of affairs in the Medical College of Ohio. There was the danger that the Medical College, because of its depressed condition, might be compelled to close its doors. This would leave the State of Ohio without any medical institution. Since the charter of the Cincinnati College empowered the Board of Trustees to appoint professors and grant and confer "all and any of the degrees conferred in any college or university in the United States," the trustees declared they deemed it their duty to create a Medical Department in the College.

The Board of Trustees, accordingly, proceeded to appoint a medical Faculty. In the hope, however, that the Medical College of Ohio might be able to clean its house, the trustees of the College decided to take three of the professors of the new medical department from that institution and the remainder to consist of Drake and newcomers. This left the way open for the Medical College of Ohio to accept this Faculty and complete its own reform without necessitating the establishment of a new school. The Board of Trustees of the Medical College, however, refused to accept this way out of their dilemma; and so the Board of Trustees of the Cincinnati College proceeded to organize a medical Faculty. Some of the professors in the Medical Department contributed $800 towards the repair of the College edifice, and $3,500 was obtained by subscriptions from citizens of Cincinnati.

THE FACULTY

The Faculty of the Medical Department of the Cincinnati College was undoubtedly the best in any western medical institution at that time. They were all able men, eminent in their respective fields. It included such men as Samuel D. Gross, regarded as the doyen of American surgeons. Gross was professor of general and pathological anatomy, physiology, and medical jurisprudence. The chair of pathological anatomy which Gross occupied was the first of that kind established in the United States. Dr. Willard Parker, who filled the chair of surgery, was a matchless surgeon. Dr. James B. Rogers, professor of chemistry and pharmacy, was a chemist of national reputation and an excellent lecturer.

With such a Faculty the Medical Department of the Cincinnati College became a formidable rival of the Medical College of Ohio. The enmity between the two schools was extremely bitter. There were frequent clashes between the students of the two institutions.

RIVALRY BETWEEN THE MEDICAL DEPARTMENT AND THE MEDICAL COLLEGE

The great bone of contention between the schools was admission to the Commercial Hospital. The Medical College of Ohio by law had a monopoly of the instruction and care of patients in the Hospital. Drake set up a small hospital opposite his College, and the Eye Infirmary he established with Jedidiah Cobb in 1827 became the clinical department of the new school. Finally, in 1839, an act was passed by the Legislature allowing students of the Cincinnati College to attend clinical lectures in the Commercial Hospital, and some of the professors of the Medical Department of the Cincinnati College became members of the staff of the hospital.

The new school, the Medical Department of the Cincinnati College, succeeded in drawing more students than the Medical College of Ohio. At its first session the Medical Department of the Cincinnati College had a class of 66 students and at the second, 125, considerably more than the Medical College of Ohio, and the second largest enrollment among the western medical schools. The Medical Department of the Cincinnati College was unquestionably a success and the crowning achievement of Drake's career. During the four years of its existence, 1835–1839, the school educated nearly 400 pupils.

HANDICAPS OF THE MEDICAL DEPARTMENT

The Medical Department of the Cincinnati College operated under a serious disadvantage—the lack of an endowment. But what contributed to its dissolution in 1839 more than anything else was the resignation of

Dr. Parker, who accepted the chair of surgery in the College of Physicians and Surgeons in New York City. The vacancy of the surgical chair was soon followed by the retirement of Dr. Gross and by that of other members of the Faculty; Dr. Drake being the last to withdraw. He accepted a position at the Louisville Medical Institute, which later became the University of Louisville.

The Establishment of the Law School

Having established a Medical Department, the Board of Trustees of the Cincinnati College decided to institute a Law Department in the College. A private law school had been founded in the City in 1833 under the name of the Cincinnati Law School. There were at the time only three law schools in the United States: the Harvard Law School, established in 1817; the Law Department of the University of Virginia, founded in 1824; and the Yale Law School, created in 1826. The Cincinnati Law School, now an integral unit of the University of Cincinnati, is the oldest law school west of the Alleghenies, and, with the exception of the session in 1841–1842, has been in continuous operation since it was established.

The man most responsible for the early success of the Cincinnati Law School was Timothy Walker. Through his paternal grandmother he was descended from William Brewster, who came over in the *Mayflower* in 1620 and became the spiritual guide of the Pilgrims of Plymouth. Walker was graduated from Harvard College and the Harvard Law School where he had as one of his professors, Judge Story. Since Massachusetts at that time required three years exclusive law reading for admission to the lowest grade of the bar and four more for admission to the highest, and one could be admitted to the bar in Ohio after one year's residence, Walker moved West and in 1830 located in Cincinnati. The year of probation, required by the laws of the State, was spent in the office of Bellamy Storer and Charles Fox. At the end of the year Walker opened an office for himself and soon afterwards formed a partnership with Edward King and Salmon P. Chase.

Edward King was the son of the distinguished Federalist, Rufus King, Senator from New York, and the last candidate of the Federalist Party for the Presidency. He attended the celebrated Litchfield Law School, Litchfield, Connecticut, founded by Judge Tapping Reeve in 1784, which ceased to exist in 1833. Moving to Ohio, King married a daughter of Thomas Worthington, Governor of Ohio, and first located in Chillicothe where he won an early success at the bar as an eloquent and accomplished lawyer. When the State capital was moved from Ross County to Columbus, the Kings moved to Cincinnati, where there were greater opportunities for a lawyer of recognized power.

In the spring of 1833, Walker and King conceived the idea of starting a private law school. Walker was probably the prime mover, as he had been greatly impressed by the benefits he had derived from his instruction under Judge Story at Harvard. The discontinuance of the Litchfield School that year was probably one of the reasons which prompted King to assist Walker in the undertaking. They succeeded in inducing Judge John C. Wright, then a member of the Supreme Court of Ohio, who had moved from Steubenville to Cincinnati to join them in the enterprise.

In May 1833 an announcement of the School appeared in the local press. It contained the name of J. M. Goodenow, Judge of the Court of Common Pleas of the North Circuit, as a member of the Faculty, but for some unknown reason he never was a member of the Faculty. The announcement stated that the course of instruction would embrace "lectures on general and local law; practice in moot courts organized on the work of the several courts of Ohio; and frequent examinations upon the books read."

OPENING THE LAW SCHOOL

The School began on October 7, 1833. The lectures were given in rooms above the office of King and Walker on the north side of Third Street, east of Main Street. The tuition for regular students was $60.00 per year; for those studying in a law office, $100 per year. There were seventeen students in the first class, one of whom was Charles D. Drake, the son of Dr. Drake, who afterwards was Senator from Missouri, Chief Justice of the Court of Claims, and the author of *Drake on Attachment*. As a private school it had no power to confer degrees; so in the summer of 1834 an arrangement was made with the Cincinnati College by which it became a department of that institution and took the name it still bears, The Law School of the Cincinnati College. As a symbol of the historical heritage of the Cincinnati College, the President of the University of Cincinnati always becomes the President of the old Cincinnati College, and all members of the Board of Directors of the University become trustees of the College. The same persons continued nominally members of the Faculty, but due to severe illness, Edward King was incapacitated and was unable to resume his chair. He died in February 1836. "Edward King," as Charles D. Drake said, "was an astute advocate and a brilliant orator."

The first Faculty of the Law School of Cincinnati College consisted of Timothy Walker, professor of the law of real estate; John C. Wright, professor of practice, pleading, evidence, and criminal law; and Joseph S. Bennam, professor of criminal law and the law of personal property, who filled the chair vacant by the death of King. He was an able Kentucky lawyer of great eloquence, a large and portly man of imposing appearance. The next year Edmund S. Mansfield, who for more than half a century was closely connected with the literary, educational, and religious life of Cincinnati, was added to the Faculty as professor of constitutional law and equity.

In his introductory lecture in 1837, Timothy Walker spoke on "The Dignity of the Law as a Profession." "No one," said Walker, "should enter the profession as a sinecure. . . . Nothing great or good in any calling was ever achieved without corresponding effort." His maxim as a lawyer and one which he endeavored to impress upon his pupils was: "No principle can justify us in doing, or our clients in requiring us to do for them, what we should blush to do for ourselves."

The First Commencement and the First Graduates of the School

The first Commencement of the Law Department was held at the end of the session, 1835–1836. The following students were graduated: Herman J. Groesbeck, William Rankin, Jr., Clement B. Simonson, Benjamin Hoffman, James W. Ryland, William S. Starr, George F. Emmons, James Gilmore, and Augustus Boyd. They were the first graduates of the Law School of Cincinnati College, but no degrees were conferred at this Commencement. On March 3, 1837, the second Commencement was held. At this Commencement the degree of Bachelor of Law was conferred upon the above-mentioned students (already alumni of the College) and in addition upon the following students: Roswell S. Howard, Joseph McCormick, John S. Davis, Royall T. Wheeler, John L. Miner, Samuel F. Carey, Theodore S. Parvin, John Dillon, Algernon S. Grigg, Alexander Duncan, James E. Boyle, John Flinn, and Nelson R. Rairden.

Revival of the Academic Department of Cincinnati College

Besides the Medical and Law Departments, Dr. Drake wanted to revive the literary department of the College and establish a Faculty of arts. He wanted to make Cincinnati College "a great and useful university." The Board of Trustees decided to test by actual experiment the possibility of maintaining a Faculty without an endowment fund. They issued a circular soliciting from the citizens of Cincinnati a sum of $10,000, payable in two years, on the condition that the Reverend William H. McGuffey would accept the Presidency of the College. A preparatory grammar school would be established under the supervision of the President. The salaries of the professors were guaranteed for the first two years, and all those who subscribed and paid $50.00 or more should be permitted to send one pupil either to the College or grammar school for one year free of tuition. The medical professors subscribed some $800, and the public contributed $3,500 more. Although the subscriptions amounted only to $4,300 the Board of Trustees decided to go ahead with the venture. A committee of the Board recommended that not all the professorships be filled during the first year, but that instruction should be given in the following subjects: intellectual and moral philosophy, the ancient languages, mathematics, natural philosophy, astronomy, civil engineering, mechanics, and machinery; and that the courses in chemistry, anatomy, and physiology be given by the professors of those branches in the Medical School; and the course in constitutional law be given by the professor of that branch in the Law Department.

The Faculty

In these circumstances in the fall of 1836, the Academic Department began to function with an enrollment of forty students. The Faculty consisted of William H. McGuffey, President and professor of intellectual and moral philosophy; Ormsby MacKnight Mitchel, professor of mathematics, philosophy, astronomy, and civil engineering; Asa Drury, professor of ancient languages and Greek and Roman antiquity; Edward D. Mansfield (of the Law Section), professor of constitutional law, political economy, and the philosophy of history; James B. Rogers (of the medical section), professor of chemistry in its application to the Arts, agriculture, mineralogy, and meteorology; James N. McDowell (of the medical section), professor of descriptive and comparative anatomy; Samuel D. Gross (of the medical section), professor of physiology, physical education, and mental philosophy; Charles L. Telford, professor of rhetoric and belles-lettres; and Timothy Mason, professor of vocal music. "Cincinnati College," wrote Mansfield in the *Cincinnati Chronicle*, December 9, 1837, "was the first institution of the kind in the United States, so far as known, to establish a professorship in music. It was an experiment of the success of which some members of the Board of Trustees and many patrons of the College entertained serious doubts. Those doubts no longer exist. The progress of the pupils in learning to sing leaves no doubt that the day is not distant when the universities and colleges of the Country will have music taught in them as regularly as mathematics." Although Professor Mason's course in the science and practice of music was optional, it was extremely popular with the students.

This was an interesting Faculty. The President, William Holmes McGuffey, had been a professor at Miami University where he had acquired a high reputation as a successful teacher. He was offered the Presidency of Cincinnati College by a group headed by Dr. Drake who hoped to direct the income of Miami University to Cincinnati College. Whether McGuffey was involved in this movement is not known. It is known, however, that while McGuffey was President of Cincinnati College he advised parents not to send their sons to Miami "where it is more likely they would be made drunkards and gamblers than good scholars." Mc-

Guffey knew when he entered Cincinnati College that it was an experimental career. During the three years he was President of Cincinnati College, McGuffey grew in popularity both with the students and with the townspeople. He was the intimate friend of the most distinguished citizens of the City: the Beechers, the Mansfields, and the Drakes. As a member of the Institute of College Teachers, McGuffey took an active part in the promotion of the common schools. He made many public addresses urging the General Assembly of Ohio to create a State educational office. As a consequence of the public demand, Samuel Lewis was elected State Commissioner of Common Schools, March 30, 1837, three months before Horace Mann became Secretary of the State Board of Education for Massachusetts.

McGuffey's lecture rooms were always crowded. It is recorded that "a group of citizens eager to hear him and unable to gain admission to the lecture hall cut a hole in the ceiling of the hall and gathered there every Sunday to hear him expound the scriptures." His course on intellectual and moral philosophy was popular with the students. One of his colleagues analyzed McGuffey's ability in teaching: "McGuffey had discovered a method for himself and had learned to use it with matchless skill. His method was to illustrate every abstract proposition with some concrete example. His felicity and fertility in the application of his method was quite wonderful. He was rich in pungent anecdote, apt in citation from history and literature and life, skilful in analogy. The one phrase you would hear from all his students was 'He makes us think'." The Board of Trustees accepted his resignation with "deep regret" when, in 1839, he resigned to accept the Presidency of Ohio University. They declared he had presided over the institution "with acknowledged ability and zeal." One of his biographers claims that "even the failure of the College was forgotten in the admiration for its President as a man valuable in stimulating an entire City to aspire to the ideals of noble living." It is asserted that McGuffey as President of Ohio University, was not successful as an administrator. It is claimed that he was unable to get along with his colleagues at that institution. "His rugged independent spirit made it impossible for anyone to fill a professorship during his administration except upon McGuffey's terms." Apparently, the Board of Trustees of Cincinnati College did not think he displayed these qualities in Cincinnati. His Presidency of Cincinnati College is remembered especially as the time the Cincinnati publisher, Truman and Smith, brought out the *McGuffey Eclectic Readers*. His brother, Alexander H. McGuffey, who later was for many years a member of the Board of Directors of the University of Cincinnati, was the active collaborator with President McGuffey in the compilation of the *Readers*, the most popular series of schoolbooks published west of the Allegheny Mountains. It is understood the *First Reader* was wholly the work of

Alexander H. McGuffey, as was the *Speller* which completed the series.

Ormsby MacKnight Mitchel was a graduate of West Point, an eloquent lecturer on astronomy, and an inspiring teacher. Mitchel was not only professor of mathematics and philosophy in the Academic Department of the College, but was likewise in charge of the instruction in civil engineering. This was one of the first collegiate courses in civil engineering in the Country. Other members of the Faculty were: the Reverend Asa Drury, an excellent teacher and an ordained Baptist minister; and Charles L. Telford, a tall, dignified man; a distinguished writer, and a graceful orator.

HANDICAPS OF THE ACADEMIC DEPARTMENT

Cincinnati College revived under President McGuffey and with such men on the Faculty as Drake, Gross, Mitchel, Walker, and Wright; it flourished for three years. At one time as many as 160 students were enrolled in the institution. But it was handicapped by the lack of an endowment, and after the resignation of President McGuffey, the medical and literary departments declined; the Law Department alone continuing to operate.

THE CINCINNATI OBSERVATORY

While teaching astronomy in the Cincinnati College, Professor Mitchel came to realize the need of an adequately equipped observatory to acquire an intimate knowledge of celestial phenomena. An opportunity was afforded him to set forth his idea when during the winter of 1841–1842, Mitchel was asked by the Cincinnati Society for the Diffusion of Knowledge to give a lecture as one of a popular course. He chose as his subject "The Stability of the Solar System." His lecture aroused considerable curiosity and interest, and he was requested to continue the series with a few lectures on astronomy. "At the first evening," Mitchel recorded in his diary, "the audience was respectable; on the second evening my house was full, and on the third it was over-flowing." His lectures were enthusiastically received, and he was asked to repeat the last lecture in a larger room in the Wesley Chapel. At the close of this lecture, Mitchel proposed that a society be organized and that $7,500 be raised by the sale of shares $25.00 each, for the purpose of erecting an observatory and equipping it. Each shareholder was to be entitled free access to the observatory. Mitchel personally canvassed the community for subscriptions and within three weeks 300 shares had been subscribed. On May 23, 1842, the Cincinnati Astronomical Society was organized. The Society instructed Mitchel to proceed to Europe to procure suitable instruments and to learn how to conduct an observatory.

In the summer of 1842, Mitchel set out on his journey. He tried to get the national government to accredit him with a foreign mission, but was unable to interest either Daniel Webster, Secretary of State, or President Tyler. He sought the aid of John Quincy Adams, who in 1825 had proposed the erection of a national observatory, only to be ridiculed throughout the country for such a scheme. Adams was greatly interested in the enterprise and gave Mitchel a letter of introduction to Sir George Airy, Astronomer Royal, at Greenwich Observatory, England.

Sir George welcomed Mitchel and gave him free access to the Greenwich Observatory. But neither in London nor Paris did Mitchel find the kind of telescope he wanted. In Munich, Germany, however, at the institute founded by Frauenhofer, Mitchel found a refractor telescope made up of two lenses, "juxtaposed but not cemented, twelve inches in diameter, that cost $9,000." Although the price seemed prohibitive, Mitchel, undaunted, made a provisional contract that the firm should not sell the instrument until they had heard from him after he had consulted the Society.

When Mitchel returned to America the country was in a business depression. Nevertheless, the additional funds were obtained largely through Mitchel's tireless efforts and his offer to serve as director of the Observatory for ten years without pay. Nicholas Longworth generously donated the site for the building; on November 9, 1843, the cornerstone was laid by the venerable John Quincy Adams, then seventy-seven years of age. The hill on which the Observatory was located was named Mount Adams in commemoration of the revered ex-President of the United States.

Mitchel hired the workmen and personally supervised the construction of the building, meanwhile teaching five hours a day in the College. He had to build a limekiln, a sand pit, and a dam across one of the ravines while it was actually raining and so obtain an abundant supply of water for the mixing of the mortar. In February 1845 the telescope arrived and was mounted. Just as the building was nearly completed, Mitchel received his severest setback. The Cincinnati College edifice burned down, and every dollar of his income was cut off. To earn an income Mitchel delivered public lectures which won for him national reputation as an orator. In 1859, Mitchel became director of the Dudley Observatory at Albany. He entered the Union Army during the Civil War, rose to the rank of major general, and died of yellow fever in 1862. It was due to the indomitable energy, persuasive oratory, and the perseverance of Professor Mitchel that the Cincinnati Observatory, "the first astronomical establishment worthy of the name in the United States," was erected.

CLEVELAND ABBE

The activities of the Observatory lay dormant during the Civil War, and for a number of years the instruments and the library were in the charge of a caretaker. In January 1868 the Astronomical Society elected Cleveland Abbe director of the Observatory. He was born in New York City, December 3, 1838, the son of George W. Abbe, a merchant of New York City, and Charlotte (Colgate) Abbe. His early education was acquired in private schools there and in the New York Free Academy, later the College of the City of New York. In 1857, Abbe received his Bachelor of Arts degree from this institution and three years later his Master's degree. During 1857–1858 he was a tutor in the Trinity Latin School, New York. In 1859 he was appointed assistant professor of engineering in the Michigan Agricultural College and the next year tutor in engineering at the University of Michigan where he came under the influence of Professor Brunnov and became an enthusiastic student of astronomy. When the Civil War broke out Abbe tried to enlist as a volunteer but was rejected after a few weeks at a training camp because of excessive myopia. Consequently, from 1861 to 1864, he assisted Dr. B. A. Gould of Cambridge, Massachusetts, in his work for the United States Coast Survey. Then for two years (1865–1867) he studied under the famous Otto Struve at the Observatory of Pulkowa in Russia. In 1867, Abbe returned to the United States and accepted the position of assistant in the United States Naval Observatory, from which institution he came to Cincinnati. Professor Abbe, the second director of the Observatory, was a trained astronomer and a worthy successor to Mitchel.

In April 1868, Abbe came to Cincinnati to assume his duties. But he soon began to complain of the handicaps which he encountered in carrying on his work. He declared that the buildings and grounds needed to be repaired, and that the rolling roof of the equatorial gave a great deal of trouble as it had done for many years past. He found the telescope was extremely sensitive to the least wind. He reported that it was hard to make observations. The object glass was quickly covered with dew; the adjustment of the telescope was disturbed by the slightest wind; the smoke from the Observatory's chimneys blew into the eyes of the observer; when the roof was rolled back, the person of the observer was exposed to the elements; and the astronomer's chair was not convenient.

As a result of the difficulties encountered, Abbe turned his attention to meteorology. He suggested that the Observatory issue a system of weather reports. Such reports would be of great use to the astronomer and could be made the basis of weather prediction that would be valuable to the country. He knew that for the past twenty years much work had been done in Europe in predicting the weather. In 1860 a British Admiral began to send out storm warnings, and ten years later a French astronomer began to publish a bulletin for the Royal Observatory at Paris giving daily weather reports. This bulletin became valuable, not merely in giving news of the weather, but in giving seamen and merchants a possible basis for forecasting the weather of the next day.

The Western Union Telegraph Company should be given the credit for publishing the first weather maps in the United States. As early as 1864 the chief operator of all the large telegraphic offices received each morning a brief telegram from various places giving the state of the weather, the temperature, and direction of the wind. Two years later F. A. Armstrong, local manager of the Western Union Telegraph Company in Cincinnati, suggested to his employer, George T. Williams, the division superintendent, that these reports be kept in such a form as could be utilized by the public. Armstrong prepared a crude map with probably not over a dozen or fifteen plates and drew a circle at each place locating the stations with an arrow indicating the wind and figures below giving the temperature. H. W. Smith, an old telegrapher, helped prepare these maps. As a result of the efforts of these men a bulletin called "The Western Union Telegraph Company Weather Report" was issued which was furnished to subscribers at $1.00 a month.

Professor Abbe became interested in these maps and was a daily visitor to the Cincinnati office of the Western Union. He took part in the preparation of the maps, but he was more interested in forecasting the weather. To this end he wrote a letter on July 29, 1868, to Mr. John A. Gano, President of the Cincinnati Chamber of Commerce, in which he proposed that a group of volunteer observers at different points make weather reports at specified times and telegraph their observations to the Cincinnati Observatory where they would be classified by him and arranged for publication in the daily press. He pointed out that the Cincinnati Observatory was well fitted to carry on such work because of its central position with reference to the railroads and telegraph systems of the country. He felt confident that the requisite number of experienced observers could be found, and if no one could be found at any desirable place, then the telegraph office should be supplied with the proper instruments and an employee of the company be instructed in their use; the company being responsible for the cost of these instruments.

After much consideration of this proposition, Mr. Gano requested Professor Abbe send him a second letter that could be presented to the Chamber of Commerce. The requested letter was sent along with a sketch showing some of the stations from which reports were desired and a sample dispatch. In the letter Professor Abbe enlarged upon his plan to include in addition to forecasts of the weather predictions regarding the status of the river stage.

The subject was brought to the attention of the Cincinnati Chamber of Commerce, and that body in June 1869, authorized Professor Abbe to organize a system of daily reports and storm predictions. Experienced observers at distant points offered their services without pay. The Western Union Telegraph Company offered the use of their line at a nominal price. The Cincinnati Chamber of Commerce in the interest of science and progress generously agreed to pay for three months the cost of extra telegrams for reports from points other than those received by the Western Union. Upon the basis of all these reports Professor Abbe was able to issue daily bulletins giving forecasts of the weather. These bulletins were written on manifold carbon paper by clerks in the Western Union offices and delivered by their messengers and were known as "creasers." As a result of his predictions Professor Abbe was given the nickname, "Old Probs" (Probabilities), a sobriquet that originated with the clerks in the Western Union engaged in the weather business.

In October 1869, Professor Abbe secured the support of five principal jewelers of the City in adopting the Observatory mean time as their standard. The correct time was given to these persons on the first Saturday of each month. Later the Observatory supplied the standard time to the City for a compensation of $1,000 a year, and the City Council agreed to provide the necessary public clock and telegraph wires.

Professor Abbe was most enthusiastic over his experiments. In a letter to his father he said, "I have started that which the country will not willingly let die." This was true for from these modest beginnings at the Cincinnati Observatory were laid the foundation for the Federal Weather Bureau. In 1870, Congress appropriated $20,000 for a national weather bureau under the direction of the Signal Service Corps. Professor Abbe, alone in the United States, was already experienced in drawing weather maps from telegraphic reports and in making forecasts from them. Naturally, he was appointed to an important position in this service. This he accepted in 1871, and as professor of meteorology was often the official forecaster of the weather. Before he left for his new duties, he married Frances Martha Neal of Cincinnati.

Professor Abbe, says his biographer, W. J. Humphreys, was not essentially "a creative scholar. He made no important discovery and published but little that contained anything new and original. He was primarily a teacher and a propagandist. . . . He was also one of the most active of those who worked for the adoption of standard time." He was later the recipient of a gold medal by the Royal Meteorological Society of Great Britain for eminence in meteorology and was awarded a medal by the Natural Academy of Sciences for contributions to human welfare. With the departure of Professor Abbe from the City the separate activities of the Observatory came to an end, for shortly thereafter the institution was absorbed by the University of Cincinnati and moved to a new location on Mount Lookout.

5   *Two Turbulent Decades*

The roar of the "Roaring Forties" was heard in Cincinnati as plainly as anywhere in the land. Henry Ward Beecher was editing the anti-slavery *Cincinnati Journal,* and on occasion wore a pistol in his belt to aid the special deputies protecting Negroes. A promising young lawyer named Salmon P. Chase was no less active in the abolitionist cause. But Cincinnati's trade was in good part with the South, and local sympathy for the slaveholding states across the Ohio River brought many days of race riots. Disorder and tension, however, were not barriers to growth. Cincinnati in 1840 had a population of 46,000. In 1850 it was 115,000, an increase of 150 per cent. By 1860 it reached 161,000.

To some the Queen City was above all an important station on the underground railroad for runaway slaves. For others it was a subversive center of pro-slavery sympathy and agitation. But to all Cincinnati was the "City most likely to succeed" in all the western country. It was the greatest publishing center west of the Appalachians. The *McGuffey Readers* were pouring from a Cincinnati press and were to continue until 1901, when a total of 100 million copies had been printed. Cincinnati gained fame in these decades as "Porkopolis"; it was the nation's chief meat-packing center. But it still had no stable institution that could with confidence be called a university. There were only beginnings. However, there also were men of vision and energy, intent on giving this booming river city the university it wanted and needed.

There also were by this time men with money. Nicholas Longworth, the City's first millionaire, was not only growing superb wines on the south-facing hills near the basin of the City; but was also making money by canny purchases of land—in a City growing by 35 to 150 per cent in each decade. One such man of new-found wealth was to give the University of Cincinnati its breakthrough before long.

THE CINCINNATI COLLEGE ACADEMIC DEPARTMENT

In 1839 the Reverend Thomas J. Biggs was chosen President of the Cincinnati College and professor of intellectual and moral philosophy and rhetoric on the resignation of President McGuffey. The new President was a Philadelphian by birth, a graduate of Princeton College, and had studied for the ministry at Princeton Theological Seminary. He had taught at Princeton College and had been pastor of various Presbyterian churches. In 1832 he accepted a professorship in Lane Seminary, Cincinnati, which had been endowed by his friends on the condition that he accept it. As a result of religious dissensions in the Presbyterian Church, Reverend Mr. Biggs resigned his professorship and was elected President of the Cincinnati College. He was a painstaking student, and his administration was successful. When, however, on January 19, 1845, the College building burned down and the Faculty were forced to secure temporary private apartments for the College classes, President Biggs resigned. He was immediately chosen President of Woodward College in Cincinnati which position he held until the College in 1851 was reorganized.

When President Biggs submitted his annual report to the Board of Trustees after the fire, he raised the question at the suggestion of the academic Faculty whether it was practical and expedient to attempt to revive collegiate instruction. A committee of the Board to whom this question was referred reported that it was impractical at that time to reestablish the Grammar School and academic instruction in the College for the following reasons: (1) The establishment of the public school system in Cincinnati rendered it quite unnecessary to continue the primary department; (2) since Woodward College had been founded and was amply endowed and intended to maintain college classes it was useless to revive academic training in the Cincinnati College as it would obtain but a part of the patronage of the City. In the absence of an endowment for the Cincinnati College, the Board of Trustees were financially unable to pay the salaries of the requisite number of capable professors required to give collegiate instruction. Furthermore, the Committee pointed out that the experience of the College in both eras of its collegiate practical existence, as well as that of Woodward College, convinced them that "no considerable number of college pupils could be obtained." Since, however, it had been the purpose of the founders of the College to advance education, the Committee recommended that lectureships be established in various branches of learning and science. These lecturers should be permitted to use the College Hall gratuitously and be allowed to sell tickets for admission to their lectures.

This plan was adopted by the Board of Trustees. The Academic Department was discontinued, but public lectures were given by some of the academic Faculty, such as Professor Mansfield and Professor Mitchel, and by other scholars and scientists from the East.

Although the Academic Department was suspended in 1846, the idea of making the Cincinnati College a real seat of learning was not entirely forgotten. In 1857 the Board of Trustees considered a proposition to request Professor Mitchel to accept the Presidency of the College and to reorganize a literary and scientific department. After a "spirited discussion" a Committee of the Board was appointed to study the problem. This Committee brought in a plan, drawn up by Professor Mitchel, proposing the organization of a Federal University Board, composed of representatives of the various Faculties in the State which should hold annual sessions in Cincinnati for the purpose of examining candidates and conferring degrees; and contemplating further, the establishment of a high grade of scientific schools in connection with the Cincinnati College and under its control. The Board approved the plan and instructed the Committee to prepare a circular setting forth the proposition and send it to the President and boards of the other colleges of the State soliciting their cooperation. Three weeks later the Committee reported through Professor Mitchel that they had sent out the circular to the different colleges in Ohio and had received replies from several of them, some expressing approval of the scheme and a willingness to cooperate, while others doubted its practicability. The Committee was instructed to continue its work, but nothing came of their efforts to revive collegiate instruction in the Cincinnati College.

On his death in 1852, Ethan Stone, one of the founders of Cincinnati College (he was one of the commissioners appointed to raise money by means of a lottery for its establishment), bequeathed to the institution a reversionary legacy to be held in trust for the education of indigent students preparing for the ministry of the Episcopal Church. This was the first endowment to the Academic Department of the Cincinnati College. By 1869, on the eve of the establishment of the University of Cincinnati, this fund yielded $500 per annum.

The Law Department of the Cincinnati College, 1840–1860

As a consequence of the drop in enrollment after the withdrawal of President McGuffey, all the professors of the Law Department of the Cincinnati College tendered their resignations. In pursuance of a mutual understanding, however, the resignation of Professor Walker was not accepted; and he remained in sole charge of the school which he carried on until the close of the session of 1843–1844, with the exception of one year, 1841–1842, when, owing to his ill-health, there was no session.

A new College building, three stories high, was erected on the same site as the former one which had been burned down. The trustees sought and obtained from the General Assembly the power to issue bonds to the amount of $25,000. To secure the payment of these bonds the College building was deeded in trust to Griffin Taylor, John Kilgour, and James Baker who held it until 1867, when, the bonds having been paid, the property was reconveyed to the trustees of the Cincinnati College. The Young Men's Mercantile Library, a library organized in 1822, which had moved into the College building in 1840, contributed $10,000 to the construction of the new building, and in consideration for the advancement of this lump sum was given a leasehold on the entire front rooms on the second floor of the building free of rent, "for ten thousand years and renewable forever." This linked the affairs of the Library and the College together for sixty-eight years.

Under the direction of Professor Walker the number of students enrolled in the institution increased. He succeeded in inspiring his students with some of his zeal and devotion to the legal profession. For his classes in the school Judge Walker (Judge of the Court of Common Pleas of Hamilton County), wrote his *Introduction to American Law* which for many years was considered as the best first book for American students and as indispensable as the "Commentaries" of Kent and Blackstone. Justice Oliver Wendell Holmes years later told William Howard Taft, when the latter was Chief Justice of the United States Supreme Court, "It was Walker's *American Law* that first gave him an adequate conception of what law was and what was the profession upon which he was entering." Walker was also the founder and editor for many years of *The Western Law Journal*. To him belongs pre-eminently the merit of starting and firmly establishing the Cincinnati Law School.

In the spring of 1844, Walker resigned, and William S. Groesbeck and Charles L. Telford, formerly of the Academic Department of the College but a graduate of the Law School, were appointed professors and took charge of the School in the following fall. Groesbeck and Telford were partners in the practice of law. Due to the sudden death of Telford in 1849, and with the pressure of business, Groesbeck was compelled to resign his position on the staff of the Law School. It was during the administration of Groesbeck and Telford that the mode of instruction by lectures originally adopted was given up and that of examination based upon a select number of textbooks was inaugurated.

In the fall of 1849 the School opened with an entire new Faculty consisting of William Greene, Joseph P. Holcombe, and Judge Charles P. James. During the year, however, Holcombe resigned, and his professorship was filled by Judge Myron H. Tilden. The following year M. E. Curwen took Greene's professorship, a position he held for seventeen years and in addition acted as Dean. Besides these arduous duties Dean Curwen edited the *Revised Statutes of Ohio* in continuation of the series begun by S. P. Chase. In the same year (1850) Curwen was appointed

professor; Judge R. B. Warren was announced as a professor; and Judge
J. B. Stallo as a lecturer. Neither of them, however, delivered any lectures. In 1855, Judge James moved to Washington and resigned from the
Faculty. Judge Bellamy Storer of the Superior Court of Cincinnati was
appointed to fill the vacancy. For nineteen years he was a member of the
Faculty, and upon his retirement in 1874 he was appointed professor
emeritus with a salary of $800 a year. During the Civil War, when he
was nearly seventy years of age, Judge Storer shouldered his rifle and did
duty in the fortifications back of Covington at the time of General Kirby
Smith's threatened raid against Cincinnati.

No further changes were made in the Faculty of the Law School after
the appointment of Judge Storer until 1864, when Judge Tilden left the
City and Judge George Hoadly of the Superior Court of Cincinnati was
appointed to fill the vacancy; a position he held for twenty-three years,
even while he was Governor of Ohio. For many years Hoadly was a
trustee of the Cincinnati College. He was regarded "as one of the greatest corporation lawyers in the United States." In 1866–1867, Alphonso
Taft was a member of the Faculty. On the death of Professor Curwen in
1868, Jacob D. Cox was appointed to fill the vacancy. The next year,
however, Professor Cox became Secretary of the Interior in the cabinet
of President Grant, and Hiram A. Morrill was appointed to fill the
vacancy. Later Cox returned to the Faculty as Dean of the Law School
and for several years was also President of the University of Cincinnati.

In 1869 another fire seriously damaged the College building. The following year a third building was erected on the same premises on Walnut
Street between Fourth and Fifth Streets.

THE MEDICAL COLLEGE OF OHIO, 1840–1860

The collapse of the Medical Department of the Cincinnati College
marked the opening of a new era in the history of the Medical College
of Ohio. The establishment of the Medical Department of the Cincinnati
College caused a reorganization of the Faculty of the Medical College
of Ohio. In 1838, Reuben Diamond Mussey, John Locke, and Marmaduke
Burr Wright were appointed to the staff.

Reuben Diamond Mussey became professor of surgery, a chair he held
for fourteen years. In 1852 he left the College disgusted by the internal
dissension and was one of the founders of the Miami Medical College.
Mussey was the first President of the Academy of Medicine of Cincinnati
and the fourth President of the American Medical Association. He had
an international reputation as a surgeon. As Gross says: "Some of his
surgical exploits were of a brilliant and fearless character." Yet Mussey
"had no love for operative surgery itself and regarded it as a final recourse
when all other means had failed." He was a vegetarian, a total abstainer

from the use of both tobacco and alcohol, and an ardent temperance lecturer.

In the operating room Mussey was slow and cautious which must have been very trying on the patient before the days of anesthetics. In the pre-anesthetic period no operation was performed "without a long course of preparation; spare diet, purging, and frequent bloodletting were the means resorted to to prepare the patient for the ordeal. Laudanum or morphia (was given) the night before, and large doses of brandy during the operation." Mussey began "very early to use chloroform and ether as anesthetics." It was also reported that often before an important operation, Mussey "prayed for his patient, the better to secure his confidence, and to inspire him with hopes of safety."

John Locke was for fourteen years professor of chemistry in the Medical College of Ohio. He was a great medical teacher, scientist, and inventor. He was the first Cincinnati scientist to win national honors and international recognition and the only Cincinnatian ever to receive a Congressional grant for scientific invention. His crowning achievement was the invention of the "Electro-Chronograph" or "Magnetic Clock."

In 1838, Marmaduke Burr Wright was appointed professor of materia medica in the College. Two years later he became professor of obstetrics. He held this chair for ten years when he was removed by the Board of Trustees as a result of his active participation in the political strife in the institution. In 1860 he was reappointed to the chair of obstetrics in the Medical College, a position he held for eight years when he became professor emeritus at his own request. He was an able teacher and a popular lecturer. Wright was a skilled obstetrician. He originated the process of accomplishing cephalic version by combined external and internal manipulation.

These three men added considerably to the prestige of the Medical College, but due to internal dissension and the fact that the Board of Trustees, elected by the State Legislature every three years, were political appointees, there were frequent changes in the Faculty. As a result of the reorganization in 1849–1850, Drake accepted the chair of The Theory and Practice of Medicine in the College. Shortly after the close of the term, Drake, in disgust, resigned. Two weeks after he had resigned the trustees dismissed the entire Faculty, and another attempt at reorganization was made.

In 1852 the news of the death of Daniel Drake evoked universal expressions of profound sorrow in the medical profession of Cincinnati and in the nation at large. It was generally conceded that the science of medicine had lost an "indomitable pioneer in the medical education." As Sir William Osler said later, Daniel Drake was "the most unique figure in the history of American medicine." In the course of his career this "indefatigable man" had "occupied eleven different chairs in six different schools, several of which he had himself founded"; and had besides "traversed the whole country, as it then was from Canada and the Great Lakes to the Gulf, and as far westward as Iowa, collecting material for his great work, historically a classic, *The Diseases of the Interior Valley of North America.*" Throughout the history of the Medical College of Ohio the hand of Drake was to be felt, who was, as John S. Billings said, "the great organizer and the great disorganizer, the great founder and the great flounderer."

In the same year that Drake died a new medical college, the Miami Medical College, was founded. Mussey who had resigned from the Faculty of the Medical College of Ohio became the center of a small group of able men who persuaded him that the time was opportune to start a new medical college. A charter was granted by the Commissioners of Hamilton County and on July 22, 1852, the first meeting of the Faculty of the Miami Medical College was held in the office of Dr. John F. White at the northwest corner of Race and Fourth Streets. Dr. Jesse P. Judkins was elected Dean and a Faculty was organized; among whom were such outstanding leaders as R. D. Mussey, professor of surgery; George Mendenhall, later the twenty-second President of the American Medical Association, professor of obstetrics and diseases of women and children; John A. Murphy, professor of materia medica, therapeutics, and medical jurisprudence; and Cornelius G. Comegys, professor of the institutes of medicine (physiology). In 1856, Elkanah Williams, the father of ophthalmology, was appointed to the newly created chair of ophthalmology, the first of its kind in the West. The Miami Medical College prospered until 1857 when the friends of medical education, believing that greater good would be accomplished by one institution, brought about the unification of the two medical colleges, a portion of each Faculty entering the new organization. In 1865, however, they were again separated.

The organization of the Miami Medical College spurred the Medical College of Ohio to erect a new College edifice and to strengthen its Faculty. A bond issue of $20,000 was authorized by the State Legislature for the construction of the new building and to help pay the interest on these bonds. Each of the professors annually was taxed $300, which caused much friction. The new College building at Sixth Street between Vine and Race Streets was completed in 1856 at a cost of over $50,000. It contained two large lecture halls, each capable of accommodating between 500 and 600 students. The entire building was lighted with gas, was well ventilated, and was thoroughly warmed during the winter by means of hot-air furnaces. It was considered one of the finest Gothic structures in the country and the most conveniently and well-arranged building of its kind at that time.

The College was strengthened by the appointment of the staff of George C. Blackman, a great scholar and surgeon, and James Graham, a "remarkable" teacher. Graham was clear, forcible, and logical as a lecturer. This made him popular with his classes. They understood him and what he said they quickly grasped.

Blackman caused much trouble. He was contentious, dictatorial, and overbearing toward his colleagues and frequently failed to meet his class in surgery. As this course was urgently needed by the students, the Faculty passed an inoffensive resolution requesting Blackman to perform his duties. This enraged him and during his clinical lectures he bitterly attacked his colleagues by name and declared they were persecuting him, especially Comegys, whom he particularly disliked. Blackman demanded that the Faculty apologize to him. They refused to withdraw their resolution or to apologize for it. In a tantrum Blackman submitted his resignation. The Faculty quickly requested the Board of Trustees to accept it when Blackman suddenly withdrew his resignation. The Board declined to interfere and when the Faculty threatened to resign as a body unless Blackman's resignation was accepted, all of the trustees resigned their office. The College was left without a Board; whereupon the Governor appointed a new Board of which three were members of the former one. The new Board confirmed a Faculty nominated chiefly by M. B. Wright with Blackman triumphantly in the chair of clinical surgery.

With the outbreak of the Civil War the attention and energies of the Faculty were diverted from their petty jealousies to more serious matters and as a result there was more harmony in the College. The disturbed economic conditions in the country naturally affected the institution. Enrollment declined from 123 matriculants in 1859 to 83 in 1860. The Board of Trustees found it very difficult to pay off the debt for the new building; and when they tried to assess the Faculty 40 per cent on the gross receipts arising from the sale of individual professor's tickets to their lectures; the Faculty strongly protested and declined to pay it. But after 1863 everywhere the medical schools of the country began to grow prosperous. The demand for army surgeons resulted in the inauguration of summer sessions and a moderate increase in tuition fees. Enrollment rose to 159 in 1863 and to 179 the next year. In 1866–1867 sixty-seven students were graduated, the largest graduating class so far in the history of the College.

Many of the Faculty were drawn into war activities. Blackman served on the Medical Board that passed on the appointment of surgeons and assistant surgeons for the Ohio regiments. After his retirement from this Board he was appointed a Brigadier Surgeon of Volunteers. He was present at the bloody battle of Pittsburgh Landing where he performed many operations on board a hospital ship. Subsequently, Blackman served on the staff of General McClellan and was present in many of the battles of the Wilderness. Comegys took an active part in the work of the Cincinnati branch of the United States Sanitary Commission. A portion of the Faculty and almost the entire student body of the College were among those who went down to Pittsburgh Landing to assist in the care of the wounded; the students being assigned positions as nurses. Comegys was in charge of the medical department of a hospital relief steamboat which brought back to Cincinnati the wounded from the battlefield. After the war many of the promising younger physicians who had been on active duty during the conflict joined the staff of the College and laid the foundation of the subsequent strong Faculty of the institution.

THE CINCINNATI COLLEGE AND THE MEDICAL COLLEGE OF OHIO IN RETROSPECT

By the end of the Civil War more than forty years had elapsed since the Cincinnati College and the Medical College had been founded. During these decades conditions in both institutions had been chaotic. Twice the home of the Cincinnati College had been destroyed by fire, and in 1869 for a third time it was burned down. Twice the Cincinnati College had attempted to give collegiate instruction and each time because of a lack of funds had been compelled to give it up. The citizens of Cincinnati were always talking about wanting a seat of learning in the City; and although they had contributed at times, their subscriptions were never large enough to provide an adequate endowment for a real university.

During this period the Cincinnati College had had four Presidents—Elijah Slack, Philander Chase, Thomas Biggs, and William H. McGuffey—but only the last named had given any prestige to the institution. He alone could lay any claim to being an educator. McGuffey, however, was primarily a writer of elementary texts; and although his writings had a tremendous influence upon future generations, there is no indication that he was interested in the problems of higher education. None of these Presidents had shown any real administrative ability. The only department of the Cincinnati College that had functioned continuously since its establishment was the Law School. Yet in spite of these handicaps, the Cincinnati College had inaugurated the first course in music and one of the first courses in civil engineering given in any institution of higher education in this country; and the first chair of pathology in the United States had been created in the Miami Medical College which for a time, during these years, united with the Medical College of Ohio.

On the Board of Trustees of each college there had been no outstanding figures or anyone who had any conception of how to manage a college. The different colleges had really been governed by their respective Faculties. As a consequence, there had been constant discord, confusion, and disorganization. This had been particularly true in the case of the Medical College which had had especially weak trustees and too many academic politicians. The Medical College had had during these years many distinguished men on the Faculty, such as Daniel Drake, Samuel Gross, John Locke, and Reuben D. Mussey; but the internal dissension in the Faculty had militated against its real growth.

As one reviews in retrospect the history of these two colleges, it is evident that it was due to the zeal and energy of strong personalities such as Daniel Drake, Timothy Walker, and O. M. Mitchel that the Medical College of Ohio, the Law School, and the Academic Department of the Cincinnati College developed. Of all of these men only Daniel Drake had had the vision of founding a real university in Cincinnati. Walker and Mitchel were mainly interested in the development of their particular branches of learning. But the existence of "cliques" in the Medical College of Ohio had hampered in making Cincinnati a great medical center, except for the brief period when the Medical Department of the Cincinnati College functioned. As the *Lancet Observer* said:

For years the voice of the departed Drake was potent for mischief in certain circles and with certain minds; and if a proposition was made by certain parties, no matter what, but concerning the interests of medicine or teaching—there was at once raised the warning cry "beware" that is one of "Drake's schemes"; and if a certain man made an effort for personal or professional improvement, he heard the same admonition, "look out for him, he is a Drake man."

But Drake was dead, and the whole medical profession now did him reverence.

As yet Cincinnati did not have a real seat of learning in the City. In the succeeding years a new start was to be made as a result of a munificent bequest to the City of Cincinnati and a growing willingness of the citizens of Cincinnati to support an institution of higher learning in their midst.

6   *The Great Breakthrough*

What the name of John Harvard is to Harvard University, and Elihu Yale is to Yale University, the name of Charles McMicken is to the University of Cincinnati. It was the munificent bequest of Charles McMicken to the City of Cincinnati which finally laid the foundation for the University of Cincinnati.

Charles McMicken, the son of Charles and Mary (Fusil) McMicken, was born on November 23, 1782, in the township of Warren, Bucks County, Pennsylvania. His mother's family were of French origin. His father's family were Scottish people who came from Paisley, Scotland. They were strict Presbyterians. About 1700 they found the burden of support for the Church of England too heavy for their consciences and their purses and migrated to the United States. Being possessed of means, they purchased large holdings of land in Bucks County, Pennsylvania, erected a stone building, and operated a mill.

Little is known about the early education of Charles McMicken. Evidently it was limited, but on the farm he learned habits of industry and economy. As a youth he learned, like all pioneers, a little about surveying; and before he reached manhood, he taught in a country school.

It is related that one day while he was plowing he turned up a bumblebees' nest. He was severely stung, and his team of horses ran away. Both horses were injured by the plow. He was sharply reprimanded by his father for allowing them to escape. His elder brother, Andrew, also blamed him for the accident which, according to Charles, was unavoidable. Feeling that he was unjustly blamed by his father and brother, young Charles decided to leave home. His father said if he did leave he could have a horse, saddle, and bridle, or $100 in cash, as was the custom in those days. Charles chose the former, and hardly before he had attained the age of twenty-one, set out to seek his fortune with the tide of emigrants then migrating westward.

Accounts differ as to how he came West. Some say he sold the horse in the neighborhood and came across the mountains by stage. Others say he rode the horse throughout the journey westward. At any rate he seems to have reached Chillicothe, Ohio, where for several months he worked as a surveyor. In the spring of 1803 he arrived at the pioneer village of Cincinnati with a horse, bridle, and saddle. He sold the outfit and found employment as a clerk for John Smith, who with Thomas Worthington, was United States Senator from Ohio. (Smith became involved in the Burr conspiracy. In the meantime McMicken had moved to Louisiana and gone into business. Smith came there, and McMicken reciprocated by employing him as his clerk.) McMicken remained with Smith in the general merchandise business for a short time when he decided to trade with New Orleans on his own account. He loaded two flatboats with flour and floated down the river. This was before the United States had acquired Louisiana. The boat was tied up above the City to save wharf- age while McMicken went into New Orleans to sell produce and purchase necessary supplies. On his return he found his boat had sunk, and only his horse was saved. After paying off his helpers McMicken had only three eleven-penny bits left.

Neither poverty nor misfortune discouraged his spirit. There were eleven stores in New Orleans. He was refused employment at nine of them, but at the tenth he was engaged until the nephew of one of the firms arrived from Baltimore. He had only a suit of clothes, and no price was set for his services. Six months later his employers paid him at the rate of $80.00 per month and gave him an additional suit of clothes. They also helped him obtain a new position at increased wages. By close at- tention to his work and rigid economy McMicken began to prosper. He left New Orleans and went up the river to Bayou Sara near the town later called St. Francisville, then called Valencia, situated in rich cotton lands. McMicken located there in the latter part of 1807 and engaged in shipping cotton and the business of general merchandise.

It is worthy of note that McMicken's first investment in cotton, like his first investment in flour, was a failure. His first shipment of cotton was to James Clay, a brother of Henry Clay, who shortly thereafter failed. McMicken lost all he had and became a commission merchant. In 1837 he left Bayou Sara and returned to New Orleans. After that year he did not engage in any business enterprises, devoting his attention to the purchase of real estate and managing his estate.

His first purchase of real estate in Cincinnati was in 1835 at the north- east corner of Third and Main Streets. He continued to add to his estate and finally owned $500,000 worth of land in Cincinnati and the vicinity. He also purchased land in Louisiana, Texas, Missouri, Kentucky, Illinois, and elsewhere.

In 1835, McMicken came to Cincinnati to board; after that he ultimately left New Orleans in March, coming to Cincinnati where he remained until June. The months of July and August were spent at the eastern summer resorts. In September he would return to Cincinnati, staying until November when he went to New Orleans for the winter.

In 1840, McMicken purchased from the administrator of Lyman Watson what became the McMicken homestead on McMicken Avenue (formerly Hamilton Road) east of the Bellevue incline. The house was originally built by John F. Keyes in 1819. McMicken made this his residence during the latter part of his life. His nephew, Andrew, and his wife lived with him, as McMicken never married.

CHARLES McMICKEN: THE MAN

McMicken was a man of commanding presence, six feet in height, of massive build, weighing 250 pounds. He had a firm, square jaw; large nose and ears; penetrating eyes; and a face that revealed a man of inflexible will. He was blessed with a good constitution, a strong and vigorous frame, and he rarely ever was sick. He was strictly temperate in his habits, never using intoxicating liquors or tobacco. The vigor of his body and mind remained undiminished up to the time of his last illness.

Six years before his death McMicken had two busts made of himself in Brussels, Belgium. One of these was given to the University in 1926 by Judge Alfred K. Nippert. In 1932, Judge Nippert also gave the University a portrait of Mr. McMicken.

Charles McMicken was quiet and reserved in manner and expression, and very few knew him intimately. It is doubtful whether anyone knew anything about the details of his business or the cherished dream of his life. He was entirely self-reliant, rarely, if ever, consulting an attorney, making his own bargains, examining the titles of his lands himself, and never speaking of his estate or its extent even to his most intimate friends. He was just as reserved in speaking about his numerous donations to charity.

In the year 1848 the American Colonization Society made an appeal in behalf of what was known as the Free Labor Tropical Cultivation for the purchase of a large tract of land on the coast of Africa. In April of that year it was suggested in the Cincinnati press that an effectual blow might be struck at the slave trade by a liberal provision being made for the settlement of a colony of free colored people in the Republic of Liberia.

The idea aroused the sympathies of Mr. McMicken. He proposed a plan and offered sufficient funds to pay for the necessary amount of land for such a colony. President Roberts of Liberia, on visiting the United States shortly after the plan of McMicken had been announced, heartily endorsed the scheme. Mr. McMicken promptly pledged and remitted $5,000 to the Secretary of the American Colonization Society. Ohio in Africa was purchased with these funds and was expressly designed for the use and benefit of the colored people of Ohio, Indiana, and Illinois.

From time to time Mr. McMicken made generous donations to other causes. A few years before his death, he gave $10,000 to Farmer's College on College Hill, Cincinnati, for a chair of agricultural chemistry in that institution.

Mr. McMicken was a very religious man, but not a bigot. He was broadminded and tolerant of the views of others, yet tenacious and decided in his own convictions. Some say that he was at one time a member of the Methodist Episcopal Church. At the time of his death, however, he owned a pew in the Ninth Street Baptist Church.

About ten days previous to his death, while returning from New Orleans, Mr. McMicken contracted a violent chill. It soon assumed a malignant form and resulted in pneumonia. He early became conscious of the fact that it would be fatal. His mind remained unclouded to the last moment, and he bore his sufferings without a murmur. He made no mention of his worldly affairs during his illness. He died on March 30, 1858, in his seventy-sixth year and was buried in Spring Grove Cemetery from his residence. The *Cincinnati Enquirer* and the *Cincinnati Daily Commercial* carried announcements of his death and mentioned that he probably had left an estate worth at least $1 million. This statement was also carried in the *New Orleans Daily Picayune*. It seems strange that the death of Mr. McMicken attracted little attention either in Cincinnati or in New Orleans.

On October 18, 1866, the Board of Directors of McMicken University resolved, provided the City Council approved, to appropriate the sum of $5,000 for the erection of a monument to Charles McMicken; the work to be done under the direction of the Board. In May 1868 the Clerk of the Board was directed to advertise in the *Cincinnati Gazette, Enquirer,* and *Commercial* for proposals for a design to build a monument. The McMicken family protested the placing of the monument over the remains of Mr. McMicken. They were willing that it should be placed "at the head or side or center of the lot" or anywhere else upon the lot provided "it was not placed over the remains of any persons interred and the remains were left undisturbed and unmoved." In consideration for the feelings of the family the Board decided it was best "to procure another lot on which to erect the monument to Charles McMicken."

THE McMICKEN WILL

The last will and testament of Charles McMicken was dated September 22, 1855, and was admitted to record by the Probate Court of Hamilton

County, Ohio, on April 10, 1858, by Judge George H. Hilton. McMicken appointed as executors of his estate: William Crossman, Freeman G. Cary, John C. Chenoweth, William M. F. Henson, William Woodruff, and Andrew McMicken, his nephew.

The will contained thirty-nine sections. In the first thirty sections Mr. McMicken generously remembered by annual legacies and annuities all his relations, nephews, nieces, and their children. The bequests were not in large sums, because he believed "that everyone should be self-reliant and that fortunes, without labor, often (proved) a source of evil." In item 31 he came "to the wish of his heart, the central thought of his will." He said he had "long cherished the desire to found an institution where white boys and girls might be taught not only a knowledge of their duties to the Creator and their fellowmen, but also to receive the benefit of a sound, thorough, and practical English education, and such as might fit them for the active duties of life as well as instruction in the higher branches of knowledge, except denominational theology, to the extent that the same are now or may hereafter be taught in any of the secular colleges or universities of the highest grade in the country."

Having expressed his wish Mr. McMicken then proceeded to explain how it could be put into execution. He devised and bequeathed all his property, real and personal, to the City of Cincinnati and to its successors, in trust forever. The property devised was principally located in the City of Cincinnati; but in addition to this there were about 1,200 acres of land in the vicinity of Baton Rouge, Louisiana, and other real property in the City of New Orleans, as well as some in the town and parish of Jefferson in the State of Missouri. There was also bequeathed to the City of Cincinnati about 124 acres in Delhi Township, in Hamilton County, Ohio. In addition to these bequests Mr. McMicken bequeathed to the City of Cincinnati all his railroad bonds and railroad insurance and other stocks, his notes, and personal property. A large amount of property was devised to his various relations, including certain tracts of land located in Kentucky, Missouri, and Texas to his nephew, Andrew McMicken.

There is no record when Mr. McMicken first conceived the idea of his educational scheme except that in discussing it the first time with his intimate friend, Freeman G. Cary, he said that "he had labored since early manhood for its accomplishment." It is well to recall in this connection that Mr. McMicken came to Cincinnati at the time there was much discussion of founding Cincinnati University by means of a lottery. Mr. McMicken had witnessed the futility of that attempt, yet the idea of establishing an institution of higher learning in Cincinnati perhaps intrigued him. It is known that Mr. McMicken visited Girard College in Philadelphia, founded by Stephen Girard; and there is a marked similarity between the wills of these men.

The probable influence Mr. Girard had upon Mr. McMicken is most clearly reflected in item 36 of the latter's will which provided for the education of orphans "if there should be sufficient funds left" after the establishment of a college for boys and one for girls. Each of these two wealthy men left the bulk of his estate to the City authorities. Each of them provided for the education of poor white orphans; McMicken for both male and female; Girard only for male orphans. Both men forbade the admission of orphans in the institution "until their parents or guardians had relinquished all control over them." Each directed that these orphans between the ages of fourteen and eighteen should be bound out "to some proper art, trade, occupation, or employment." Both of these men were opposed to any sectarian instruction in the colleges they established. Mr. McMicken definitely prohibited the teaching of "denominational theology" but definitely specified in section 34 of his will that "the Holy Bible of the Protestant version, as contained in the Old and New Testament," should "be used as a book of instruction in the said colleges."

There are other interesting features of the McMicken will. Why did Mr. McMicken prefer to give the control and management of his estate to the corporate authorities of the City rather than to a private agency? Why did he not bequeath at least some of his wealth to charities or to endow hospitals rather than leaving the bulk of it for the erection of institutions of higher learning? He had had few opportunities to obtain an education, yet this want of opportunities had not made him jealous of those who had been fortunate to have had them; nor had it closed his mind to the importance of education. No less significant is his provision for two colleges, one for young men and one for young women. Although he was a bachelor he did not want to discriminate against the female sex in his bounty. Young women as well as young men should have an equal chance to obtain the highest culture. Yet he evidently had his doubts that it was practical and safe to educate the two sexes together, notwithstanding the fact that boys and girls were being educated together in the high schools.

Mr. McMicken in his will laid great stress upon the importance of moral instruction in a collegiate education. He believed that the result of higher education should be not only useful citizens but good citizens as well. "It is my desire," said Mr. McMicken in his will, that they be "deeply impressed with a knowledge of their duties to their God and to their fellow men, but with a love for their country and its republican institutions, the blessed and peaceful enjoyment of which it is my fervent prayer they and their descendants may continue to live."

Years later at the dedication of the new University building in Burnet Woods Park, Samuel F. Hunt, twice Chairman of the Board of Directors of the University, in commenting on this part of the will said: "There never was taught a better morality; there never was taught a better theology; there never was taught a more sublime patriotism than that declared by the founder of the University . . . they should be inscribed in imperishable letters . . . on the very portals of the University of Cincinnati."

The McMicken will prohibited the sale of any property situated within the City of Cincinnati or the lease of any property for more than fifteen years. The will directed that the College buildings should be "plain but neat and substantial" and so constructed that, in conformity with their architectural design they might from time to time "be enlarged" as the rents of the estate might permit and the purposes of the institutions might require.

The College buildings were to be erected on the site of the McMicken homestead; the boys' college on a plot of ground from five to six acres, north of the road lately cut through the ground; the girls' college on a plot of ground of three acres, south of this road. Should additional grounds be required for the girls' college, the lot adjoining the premises on the west should be purchased for the erection of boardinghouses for the female students and for the female orphans when required.

The will also directed that any slaves owned by Mr. McMicken at the time of his death should be given their freedom; and if they desired to go and live in Liberia, the executors were to give each of them $100 to defray their expenses for removal to that country. When Mr. McMicken died he had a slave boy, Henry, and a slave woman, Rose. It is recorded that the slave woman disappeared.

When Mr. McMicken died it was estimated that the total valuation of his estate was more than $1 million, of which he bequeathed $800,000 to $900,000 to the City of Cincinnati. The taxable valuation of his estate in Hamilton County, Ohio, was $271,650 of which $850 was personal property. The value of the real estate assessed in his name was $270,800. An inventory of the value of the McMicken property in New Orleans was $33,317.45. The West Feliciana property was valued at $5,475.11. There was $8,755 deposited in his name in the Bank of Louisiana at New Orleans.

When the will was entered in the Probate Court, the *Cincinnati Daily Times* referred to the munificent gift of Mr. McMicken to the City of Cincinnati and said if the fund were "wisely and competently managed" it would reflect "permanent honor on the benefactor" and the "great good of the City." The paper pointed out, however, that a City Council was subject "to periodic fluctuations and susceptible to influences" which were "not calculated to promote the cause of science and learning"; it was the imperative duty of all intelligent citizens "to see that the City Council was fully cognizant" of the great responsibility "thrust upon it" by the trust. The *Cincinnati Enquirer* expressed grave misgivings that the estate would "be dissipated" by "the noble array of lawyers" which already "hovered around the will and the estate." The *Cincinnati Commercial* also expressed the fear that "this splendid estate" would be "frittered away in litigation."

These apprehensions of the local press soon appeared justified. On June 15, 1858, an application to set aside the bequest of Mr. McMicken to the City of Cincinnati was filed in the United States Circuit Court of Ohio by Charles McMicken Perin, a nephew of the testator, and certain other heirs of Mr. McMicken on the ground that the City of Cincinnati had no right to accept such a trust. Suit was also brought in the Second District Court of New Orleans by certain heirs of Mr. McMicken to prevent the carrying out of his will; insofar as it applied to property situated in that State. Thus did many of the nephews and nieces of Mr. McMicken attempt to defeat the "cherished desire" of their uncle. Many years were to elapse before all the legal difficulties regarding the estate were finally settled. In the meantime that portion of the property of Mr. McMicken located in the State of Louisiana was lost entirely to the City of Cincinnati by a decision of the Supreme Court of that State. These Court decisions are of the greatest importance in tracing the history of the University.

The Decision of the Supreme Court of Louisiana

The validity of the McMicken will, insofar as it pertained to property situated in the State of Louisiana, came before the Second District Court of New Orleans. The plaintiff (Franklin Perin) was the surviving husband of a niece of Mr. McMicken and brought suit in behalf of his three minor children who were collectively heirs-in-law for a ninth of the estate.

In his petition before the Second District Court of New Orleans the plaintiff alleged that the will of Mr. McMicken was null, insofar as it disposed of his property in the State of Louisiana on the following grounds: (1) that the bequest to the City of Cincinnati was contrary to the law of Louisiana prohibiting substitutions and *fidei commissum* (an invalid trust by the Louisiana Civil Code); (2) that the City of Cincinnati was a foreign corporation and without capacity to take property situated in that State; (3) that the City of Cincinnati was without the constitutional and legal capacity to take or hold property in trust for any purposes whatever; (4) that the bequest involved a perpetuity of ownership, putting the property forever out of commerce; (5) that the colleges mentioned in the will for whose use the bequest was intended, were not in existence at the testator's death; and the boys and girls for whose benefit the said colleges were designed to be created and maintained were not described with sufficient certainty to show for whom the donation was intended; the bequest was, therefore, void for a want of a devisee; and (6) that the will was not clothed with the formalities prescribed by the laws of Louisiana to devise the immovable property situated in that

State. The defendants, the City of Cincinnati, and the executors of the estate asserted the validity of the will and the bequests made to the City of Cincinnati. Andrew McMicken, a nephew of Mr. McMicken, joined the executors of the estate in maintaining the legality of the will, specifically asserting that bequest to him in trust for the benefit of his wife and children in Section 4 of the will was legal.

The District Judge decided that the will, insofar as it related to the movable property (personal property) in the State of Louisiana, left to the City of Cincinnati and the bequest of Andrew McMicken was valid; but insofar as it related to bequests of immovable (real estate) in Louisiana to the City of Cincinnati was declared null and void. From this judgment, the plaintiff, the City of Cincinnati, and the executors of the estate appealed. The case came before the Supreme Court of Louisiana on appeal from the Second District Court of New Orleans and was reported under the title of *Franklin Perin et al.* vs. *Charles McMicken heirs* (15 La. Ann. 154).

In the case before the Supreme Court of Louisiana the plaintiff denied that there was any error in the judgment of the Second District Court of New Orleans, as claimed by the City of Cincinnati and the executors of the estate, but that there was an error to the prejudice of the plaintiff in that the District Court did not declare null and void the personal as well as the real estate located in Louisiana in the bequest to the City of Cincinnati; and that there was further error in the judgment of the District court in that it did not order a partition of the said property among the legal heirs of Mr. McMicken. Wherefore the plaintiff joined in the appeal that the judgment of the District Court be awarded in these particulars, but affirmed in all other respects the judgment of the Court, except as to the claims of Andrew McMicken.

On March 11, 1860, Associate Justice A. M. Buchanan rendered the decision of the Supreme Court of Louisiana. Judah P. Benjamin, afterwards Secretary of State for the Confederate States of America, was the counsel for the City of Cincinnati in the litigation. Mr. Benjamin was known at that time as the "commercial lawyer of New Orleans," because he specialized in such cases in the Louisiana courts and before the United States Supreme Court. The City of Cincinnati was thus represented by one of the most distinguished lawyers in the country in defending its claims to the bequest of Mr. McMicken. Unfortunately, the argument presented by the defendants' lawyers in this case before the Supreme Court were not recorded.

The Supreme Court of Louisiana held that a disposition in a testament having for its object the foundation of a municipal corporation as trustee forever was prohibited *fidei commissum* and substitution contrary to the Louisiana Civil Code. The Court did not pass upon the point that the

City of Cincinnati was a foreign corporation and, therefore, without capacity to take the property situated in Louisiana; as it was unnecessary to pass on that question. For a similar reason the Court held that the bequest to Andrew McMicken in Section 4 of the will for the benefit of his wife and children was also null and void. As to the personal estate situated in the State of Louisiana the Court made no decision, leaving that to be determined in the event of the suit then pending in the Supreme Court of the United States should it be adverse to the City of Cincinnati. The costs in both cases (inclusive of the appeal) were ordered paid by the City of Cincinnati and the executors of the estate, with the exception of the costs of the intervention of Andrew McMicken which were to be paid by him. This decision was never reviewed in the United States Supreme Court.

DECISION OF THE UNITED STATES SUPREME COURT

On June 15, 1858, some of the New Orleans relations of Mr. McMicken brought suit in the United States Circuit Court for the Southern District of Ohio, sitting in equity against the executors of the estate and the City of Cincinnati to prevent the bequests of Mr. McMicken; insofar as they concerned the Cincinnati property as they had also done with regard to the property in the State of Louisiana to the City of Cincinnati in trust for the purpose of establishing and maintaining two colleges.

The plaintiffs claimed that the bequest of Mr. McMicken to the City of Cincinnati was void, urging in their argument that the City was not capable of taking the property and executing the trust for want of corporate power. The defendants claimed that the City had power adequate to take and execute the trust; and secondly, that if the City lacked the corporate power, the trust was a good and valid one, and a "Court of Equity would not let it fail for want of a trustee."

In their argument the defendants maintained that Cincinnati was a corporation authorized by law with power "to acquire and hold and possess real and personal property" and "to exercise such other powers, and to have such other privileges, as were incident to municipal corporations of like character or degree, not inconsistent with this act or the general laws" of the State of Ohio. The defendants claimed, therefore, that "Cincinnati had full power to take property by will" and "that to promote education was among the powers universally incident to such corporations."

If Cincinnati had no power "to accept a trust to promote the interests of the City by advancing its educational interests," argued the defendants, "it was the only City so limited in power for the good of its citizens in England or America." The statute expressly gave to the City all "the

powers and privileges incident to municipal corporations of her character and grade, not inconsistent with the act, or the general laws" of the
State.

The suit was finally appealed to the United States Supreme Court.
Judge Nicholas Headington and Thomas Ewing represented the appellants, the heirs-at-law; Alphonso Taft, George E. Pugh, and Aaron Perry
argued the case in behalf of the City of Cincinnati. The case was entitled
Perin et al. vs. *Cary et al.* and is reported in 24 Howard, 463.

The appellants claimed in their argument that the devise and bequest
to the City in trust should be held void on the grounds that the trustee,
the City of Cincinnati, was incapable of taking and executing the trust
and that the *"cestuis que trust"* (the beneficiaries) (were) dependent
on the selection and designation of the trustee; consequently, that there
(was) not, nor (could) there ever be, either trustee or *"cestuis que
trust."* It was further claimed that the will withdrew the colleges from
the power of the legislature in violation of the Constitution of Ohio and
made them immortal and created a perpetuity in the lands with which
they were endowed, "making them inalienable forever," which was
against "the letter and policy of the law."

The points stressed by Mr. Taft and Mr. Perry were: (1) that the bequest of Mr. McMicken to the City of Cincinnati created a "meritorious
and well-defined charitable trust"; (2) that the City of Cincinnati had
the "legal capacity to take the title of property given to her by deed or
will in trust for a valid charity"; and (3) that in the laws in Ohio, and
by the law of 1785 and the Ordinance of 1787, "education was to be
promoted" and charters were to be protected.

On February 25, 1861, Justice James M. Wayne of the United States
Supreme Court rendered a decision in favor of the City of Cincinnati.
The Court held that the will should stand and established as a proposition of law that "the doctrines founded upon the Statute of 43 Elizabeth,
c. 4 in relation to charitable trusts to corporations, either municipal or
private, (had) been adopted by the Courts of Equity in Ohio but not by
express legislation; nor was that necessary to give to Courts of Equity in
Ohio that jurisdiction." It further established the proposition "that the
English statutes of mortmain were never in force in the English colonies";
and "if they were ever considered to be so in the State of Ohio, it must
have been from that resolution by the governor and the judges in her
territorial condition; and, if so, they were repealed by the Act of 1806."
The Court thus held "in express terms, that the City of Cincinnati as a
corporation (was) capable of taking in trust devises and bequests in the
will of Charles McMicken." The Court further held that "Mr. McMicken's
direction in Section 32 of his will that the real estate devised should not
be alienated, (makes) no perpetuity in the sense forbidden by the law,

but only a perpetuity allowed by law and equity in the case of charitable trusts."

In his opinion Justice Wayne complimented both sides on "the learning and ability" they had shown in arguing the case. In many respects the case involved the same points of law as those in the famous Girard case in which Daniel Webster had appeared. The learning and ability displayed by Mr. Taft in the preparation of his brief and his arguments before the Court "which involved a laborious examination of the subject of religious and eleemosynary trusts under the Statute of 43 Elizabeth called forth from the bench expressions of high appreciation."

7   *A Durable University at Last*

On April 21, 1858, two weeks after the McMicken will was probated, the City of Cincinnati began the necessary legal steps to accept the McMicken bequest and to carry out the provisions of the will. The Common Council of the City appointed a committee, consisting of Theophilus Gaines and Henry Pearce, to confer with a committee of the Board of Trustees of the Common Schools, consisting of Rufus King and William P. Stratton, in reference to the McMicken bequest. A week later this Committee of Conference reported to the City Council that the City Solicitor said all that was necessary at that time was for the City Council and the School Board to concur in the adoption of a suitable resolution. This would request the Mayor of the City to notify the executors of the McMicken estate that the City of Cincinnati accepted the devise made by Mr. McMicken to the City in trust for the purpose of establishing two colleges, and that the City authorities were ready to receive the donation and enter upon the discharge of the trust. Subsequent litigation over the will, however, delayed action for a time.

Finally, on December 12, 1859, the Common Council passed a City Ordinance which provided for the establishment on the site of the McMicken homestead of a university for the free education, in separate departments or colleges, of the young men and young women of the City. It was to be known as The McMicken University. The government of the University as well as the management and control of the McMicken estate was vested in a Board of seven directors, six of whom were to be elected by the Common Council, each for a term of six years (except as was provided for the Board first elected). These directors must be residents and qualified voters of the City and "men of such learning and skill as were well fitted for the office." The seventh director should be the Mayor of the City. The ordinance provided that within thirty days after election of the first Board, the Mayor was to convene it at the City

Council Chamber and "there in his presence and under his direction determine by agreement or lot the time for which each of the directors so first elected should hold office"; so that "the term of one of the said directors shall expire each year."

In accordance with the City Ordinance the Council elected as members of the first Board of Directors of the McMicken University: Rufus King, James Wilson, Miles Greenwood, Cornelius G. Comegys, Henry F. Handy, and G. B. Hollister. Pursuant to a call of R. M. Bishop, Mayor of Cincinnati, the first meeting of this Board was held on December 30, 1859, in the City Council Chamber for the purpose of organizing. Mayor Bishop was elected Chairman pro tempore, and G. B. Hollister, Secretary.

Then, in accordance with the provisions of the City Ordinance, the Directors, under the direction of the Mayor, proceeded to draw lots fixing the term for which each director should serve. James Wilson drew the terms for six years; C. G. Comegys for five years; Miles Greenwood for four years; Rufus King for three years; Henry F. Handy for two years; and G. B. Hollister for one year. Rufus King was elected President of the Board; C. G. Comegys, Corresponding Secretary; and T. B. Disney was chosen Clerk of the Board at a salary of $800 a year. A set of by-laws, rules, and regulations of the Board were adopted. Rooms were obtained in one of the McMicken buildings over the bookstore of Rickey Mallory and Company at 1211 Main Street in which to hold the Board meetings.

DELAY IN ESTABLISHMENT OF THE UNIVERSITY

For a number of years the Board made no progress in carrying out the terms of the McMicken will in regard to the establishment of a university. The Board hesitated to set up such an institution and begin instruction for a number of reasons. In the first place, shortly after the McMicken will was probated, it will be recalled that Franklin Perin brought suit against the City of Cincinnati in the Circuit Court of the United States for the Southern District of Ohio to set aside the entire devise of Mr. McMicken to the City. Until this case was settled favorably to the City by the decision of the United States Supreme Court, the Board was reluctant to take any steps toward the fulfillment of Mr. Mc-Micken's plans, especially for two colleges. Furthermore, when the Mc-Micken estate was turned over to the City by the executors, many of the buildings were in a dilapidated condition. A large proportion of the McMicken estate was on Main Street and in parts of the City where property had not advanced in price in the same proportion as the property in the City generally. Moreover, Mr. McMicken's method of leasing was chiefly by the month and in consequence of the poor condition in which the buildings were left, the Board was compelled to concede to the tenants not only the usual reduction of rents allowed by all landlords but almost any reduction which the tenants chose to demand. Hence, the gross receipts from rents dropped from $20,049.68 in 1861 to $10,814.84 the next year.

The Board decided it was their duty and the safest policy to pursue for them to repair and rebuild all the City property worthwhile in their possession and to continue this course until the whole estate was put in a condition as required by the City Ordinance "to yield the most income." Then, as a consequence of the decision of the Supreme Court of Louisiana, all the McMicken property in the State of Louisiana was lost to the City of Cincinnati which greatly impaired the resources of the Board and made it still more difficult for them to carry out the terms of the McMicken will. In the meantime the outbreak of the Civil War enhanced the cost of living and brought on the currency inflation which caused even more financial troubles for the Board.

Proposals to Establish a Night High School

The Board did not feel warranted in trying to establish a university giving collegiate instruction because of the inadequacy of the McMicken fund to maintain the institution permanently; nevertheless, they thought they ought to investigate to see if any steps could be taken towards commencing the University. In the fall of 1863 a special committee of the Board was appointed to study the matter. This Committee reported that the state of the McMicken funds did not justify the organization of an institution to give a thorough course of collegiate instruction; but they did think that much good might be done by opening a night high school during the ensuing winter at no great outlay of money in which mathematics, natural science, language, and drawing could be taught. Seven years earlier the trustees of the Common Schools had started such a school, and it had been most successful. The Committee said that they felt warranted in predicting "most valuable results" from the opening at that time of an evening school with an advanced course of study and an able corps of instructors. The Committee, therefore, recommended the establishment by the Board of a free night high school of the McMicken University for both sexes to commence on the evening of the first Monday of November and terminate on the evening of the first Monday of the following March.

The Committee recommended that the course of study should include in mathematics—algebra, geometry, and trigonometry; in natural science —chemistry, natural philosophy, and mechanics; in languages—English, German, and French; and mechanics; and landscape drawing. Instructors in these fields should be employed at a salary not to exceed $60.00 per month. No students should be admitted to this school until they had been examined in mathematics and demonstrated their ability to study algebra.

The school should hold sessions five evenings each week, and each session should be for three hours. The Board approved this project and instructed the committee to proceed to organize such a school.

A month later the committee reported that they had advertised in three daily papers that such a school would be opened on the evening of the first Monday in November if 150 students made application, but only 47 applied for admission. The Board, therefore, resolved that the whole matter be dropped.

THE McMICKEN SCHOOL OF DRAWING AND DESIGN

A year later, however, in 1864 a donation to the Board made it possible for them to think about starting a different kind of school. In 1854 a group of women in Cincinnati had organized a school of design which they called "The Ladies Academy of Fine Arts." They had obtained from Europe some statues and some fine oil paintings of the old masters. Charles McMicken had given them $1,000 which helped them greatly in obtaining these works of art. The moving spirit in this organization had been the mother of Rufus King, Mrs. Sarah Peters, who had remarried after the death of her husband, Edward King. She had made several journeys to Europe to select specimens of art and models for the benefit of the Ladies Academy. In time, however, the women grew discouraged about adding to their collection and decided to bequeath to the Mc-Micken University the pictures and statuary bought by Mr. McMicken.

On January 16, 1864, Dr. Comegys announced this offer to the Board. The Board accepted the donation with thanks to the donors, and spent more than $500 in fitting up a room in one of the McMicken buildings on the corner of Third and Main Streets for the reception of this gift.

As a consequence of the repairs and improvements of the McMicken property, the Board began to obtain better rents. Since the estate had been exempted from taxation by the State Legislature, as it was primarily for educational purposes, by 1867 the Board through careful management of the funds had built up a reserve of $35,000. As the Board was being publicly criticized for its lack of activity in establishing a university, it began to think about what plan of instruction should be pursued in McMicken University when it was established. They agreed unanimously to provide for various branches of study instead of requiring all the students to take a prescribed uniform course. This was in accordance with the general trend toward the elective system in higher education which in the sixties was sweeping the country like wildfire. This was the method of instruction being pursued at Harvard under President Charles Eliot, although it was strongly denounced by President James McCosh at Princeton. The elective system apparently had many advantages: It allowed a student to have some voice in the selection of the courses he took, which permitted him to escape taking subjects he was not interested in or had no aptitude for. Furthermore, it made it possible for an institution to expand indefinitely the curriculum and thus include some courses that were frankly "bread and butter" courses which hitherto had not been regarded within the pale of educational respectability in institutions of higher learning. The Board, therefore, decided to set up distinct departments, each with its own corps of professors to the extent the resources of the estate could permanently support.

The adoption of such a plan would not alone be in accordance with general educational trends, but it would also permit them to carry out some of the educational objectives of Mr. McMicken who had prescribed in his will that the young men and the young women in the two colleges he desired to establish should be educated "to fit them for the active duties of life" as well as "in all the higher branches of knowledge." Since the Board had received the Ladies Gallery of Art they determined to establish a school of drawing and design as a beginning of the McMicken University.

On the first Monday of January 1869, the McMicken School of Drawing and Design was opened in the two upper stories of one of the McMicken buildings at the northeast corner of Third and Main Streets under the direction of Thomas Noble as the headmaster whose systematic training in European schools of this character well qualified him for the position. A circular was issued announcing that the special aim of this school was the application of drawing and design to the industrial arts. In other words, the school was not merely for the study of painting and sculpture, but for the improvement of the industrial arts by spreading among the working classes of the City a more thorough technical and scientific education in art and design as applied to manufacturers "so as to aid them in obtaining that taste and skill in the fashion and finish of their work." The first term was from January 4 to June 15. The regular term was from the third Monday in September to the middle of June. The sessions were for five days a week from nine o'clock in the morning to half-past two in the afternoon. The number of students was limited to sixty, and the school was open to both sexes. The instruction was free to residents of the City. The pupils were required to furnish all necessary materials. Punctuality and good order was required. The Principal could exclude a pupil from the school for absence of one month without an excuse. Loud talking and noise of any kind and the use of tobacco in the school were strictly forbidden. On June 5, 1869, the Board decided to open the School of Drawing and Design as a day school on Mondays, Wednesdays, and Fridays, and as a night school on Tuesdays and Thursdays; two days later it was opened as a part of McMicken University.

The School of Drawing and Design was an immediate success and within a short time the applications for entrance were as large as the

Author: McGrane, Reginald C.

Title: The University of Cincinnati

Publisher: Harper & Row

Place: N.Y.

Date: 1963

LC #   63-16550

rooms could accommodate, and there was a demand for more commodious quarters. The establishment of the School of Drawing and Design was the most important practical work accomplished by the Board of Directors of the McMicken University.

ATTEMPT TO CONSOLIDATE VARIOUS EDUCATIONAL TRUSTS

By 1868 it was plain to the Board of Directors of the McMicken University that the income from the estate of Charles McMicken alone would never produce a revenue sufficient to maintain a university as was contemplated in his will. In that year, however, suggestions began to come from various quarters of a possible way to set up a university.

When the newly elected Board of Education was organized in July 1868, a motion was passed instructing the delegates to the Union Board of High Schools—a body consisting of representatives of the Board of Education and representatives of the Hughes High School Fund and the Woodward High School Foundation to use their efforts to secure the consolidation of that "Board with the Board of Education proper, on some equitable basis, with a view of establishing a university as part of our educational system."

This action evidently aroused the interest of the Board of Directors of the McMicken University, for on November 23, 1868, Dr. Comegys was authorized "to confer with the directors of the Cincinnati College in reference to unifying their funds with the McMicken University to establish a school of higher learning in the City."

In the following month of December, Superintendent John Hancock of the Public Schools in his annual report gave added impetus to this movement. He pointed out that the City of Cincinnati would soon be possessed of funds that, if united, would be sufficient "to afford free instruction to every young man and woman in Cincinnati" who might desire "to go through a complete college course." He stated that the McMicken University endowment, "under careful management of its trustees" already "produced more than $25,000 net annual income" and within five years "ought to produce a net annual income of $30,000." The Cincinnati College property was freed from debt and "produced more than $10,000 net annual income." These two funds "should be united to support one great free college for the City instead of building up two comparatively feeble ones." It might be found "desirable, too, to increase this united sum by adding to it the Woodward and Hughes funds, which were left by their donors for a precisely similar purpose." Such a city university as might be built up from such resources, wrote Superintendent Hancock, "would prove the crowning glory of our public school system. Our parents would then have the opportunity of giving their children a collegiate education under their own eyes . . . the reflex

influence of such an institution on the schools below could not but be of
the most beneficial character. Renan has well said: 'The university makes
the school'; and another 'that the higher culture gives strength to the
lower'."

"As lovers of our fair city and her prosperity, we ought never to rest
satisfied until we have made her the educational center of the Mississippi
Valley. We have a right to expect from her age and position that she
should become such. This university when established, if conducted in
the spirit of the people and the age, will be a powerful means of bringing about this desirable consummation." Superintendent Hancock, therefore, recommended that the "McMicken, Cincinnati College, Woodward,
and Hughes Funds," be consolidated with a view towards establishing
a university.

As a consequence of this agitation, the Board of Education, at the
instigation of Dr. Max Lilienthal, on December 28, 1869, appointed a
special committee to report upon the feasibility of consolidating the
various educational funds in the City for the establishment of a university.

The Special Committee on the University Project, consisting of Abner
L. Frazer, J. B. Powell, James F. Irwin, Dr. Max Lilienthal, A. D. Mayo,
and Francis Ferry submitted a report. It was dated June 30, 1869, but
was issued and printed the following December. It gave the history and
status of the following educational trusts: Cincinnati Astronomical Society, Ohio Mechanics' Institute, Farmers' College, the Hughes and
Woodward Funds, Cincinnati College, and the McMicken Fund. It
recommended the union of as many as possible of these trust funds for
the establishment and maintenance of a university to be known as "The
University of Cincinnati." This University was to be free "to all citizens
of Cincinnati" and open to non-residents upon the "payment of a small
tuition fee." The management of this University should be vested in a
"University Board" consisting of the Mayor of the City, the President of
the University, the President of the City Council, and the President of
the Board of Education ex officio, and twenty-four others elected for
six-year terms (four expiring each year), elected by the Board of Education or by the City Council. The committee recommended the establishment of collegiate, law, medical, dental, astronomical, normal, music,
fine arts, and polytechnical departments; and other departments should
be added from time to time whenever demanded and deemed practical,
including departments of agriculture, military science and tactics, natural
history, science, language, and theology.

Some of the fruits of such a University [stated the Committee] would be to
draw together a group of *literati* whose influence would permeate our whole
community. It would open the door of higher education to hundreds in our
midst who are now hopelessly excluded from the same. Its retroactive effect

would infuse new life into our whole school system. And let us hope that it would rekindle that "sacred flame" which has often burned lowly in the socket —the ardor of the public-spirited citizen. It would reach the pulpit, the press, the bar, the home of the rich and poor alike. It would grow up in our midst an aristocracy of intellect and cultivation.

As the common schools of Cincinnati by general consent stand second only to those of Boston, so should our University stand second only to Harvard; and as Boston's educational system stands to all others on the Atlantic slope, so should the contemplated educational system of Cincinnati stand to all others in the Mississippi Valley; thus making our fair city, in educational matters, what she was designated to be—the Queen City of the West.

In the meantime, on March 22, 1869, a bill was introduced in the Ohio Senate by Henry Kessler of Hamilton County for the Common Council of Cincinnati entitled: "To aid cities of the first class in the promotion of education." This bill is supposed to have been drawn by Rufus King. The bill authorized the City Council of any city of the first class having a population of 100,000 inhabitants or more to which funds or property were given to found a university or colleges for the promotion of learning; to set aside or appropriate grounds for such an institution; and "for the further endowment or maintenance of such university or colleges" to accept as trustee any funds or property transferred to it by any person or corporation for educational purpose. The City Council was to choose a Board of Directors for the management of the University. The Board of Directors was to have the power to confer all the usual degrees. The bill was referred to the Judiciary Committee, but was not acted upon by the legislature for want of time.

Upon the publication of the Report of the Special Committee on the University Project in December 1869, the City Council appointed a committee to send out invitations to prominent citizens of the City to meet and confer with them on the University proposal. Judge Alphonso Taft, C. R. Taft, Charles Reemelin, Dr. Max Lilienthal, and a number of others accepted the invitation. At the meeting in the City Solicitor's office on January 27, 1870, speeches were made by Judge Taft, Charles Reemelin, and others all in favor of the scheme. They were all of the opinion that the time was "very opportune for carrying out the project of uniting the colleges of Cincinnati, and that a university should be established at once." Among other things the fact was alluded to that Cincinnati College (had) a law school at present which must be kept up in order to hold the charter, and the McMicken University already (had) an art school. The general feeling was that there was no need for "an immense building for the proposed university." Such was not the "case in Germany or in Europe." Nor was there any need for the "expenditure of a large sum of money." It was thought that the united funds "could at once be brought to yield an annual income of from $65,000 to $100,000." All present agreed that some legislation was necessary.

Since the university project met with the approval of the Common Council and had the support of leading citizens, the aid of the General Assembly of Ohio was invoked for the cause of higher education. On February 23, 1870, a bill was introduced in the Senate by Samuel F. Hunt of Hamilton County entitled: "A bill to enable cities of the first class to aid and promote education." A few days later on March 1, 1870, Mr. Hunt introduced a resolution of the City Council of Cincinnati petitioning the Legislature to pass this bill; and on the same day it was referred to the Standing Committee on Universities and Colleges. This Committee on March 21, 1870, recommended the passage of the bill with certain amendments. One amendment increased the number of directors from thirteen to nineteen and instead of vesting in the City Council the power of appointment without limitation, it provided that six of the Board of Directors should be appointed from a list of names nominated to the Common Council by the Board of Education. Another amendment provided that the Board of Education might in its discretion, upon application of the Board of Directors, assess and levy a tax on the taxable property of the City, not exceeding one-tenth of one mill on the valuation, to be applied by the Board of Directors to the support of the University. The bill, as amended, passed the Senate, March 22, 1870, with only four dissenting votes and the House of Representatives on April 11, 1870, by unanimous vote. The bill became a law on April 16, 1870. Rufus King, Dr. Comegys, Samuel F. Hunt, and Dr. Max Lilienthal played a prominent part in the movement for and the passage of this act.

THE ACT OF APRIL 16, 1870

The University of Cincinnati was chartered under the provisions of the law passed by the General Assembly of Ohio on April 16, 1870, entitled: "An act to enable cities of the first class to aid and promote education." The law provided that "the Common Council of any city of the first class now having a population of 150,000 inhabitants or more" was authorized and empowered to accept in the name and behalf of the city "any property or funds already given or hereafter given to the city" for the purpose of founding, maintaining, or aiding a university, college, or institution for promoting free education. For the "further indowment (sic), maintenance and aid of any university, college, or institution promoting free education . . . so founded in any such city" any person or persons or corporations holding property in trust for the promotion of education might transfer it to the city.

Any college or university so founded was to be managed by a Board of Directors, consisting of the mayor of the city ex officio and eighteen others appointed by the Common Council, six of whom were to be appointed from persons nominated by the Board of Education. They were to hold office for a term of six years, the terms of one of them expiring each year. Tuition was to be free to residents of the city. The Board of Directors upon the recommendation of the Faculty, were given the power "to confer such degrees and honors as are customary in universities and colleges in the United States and such others as with reference to the course of studies and attainments of the graduates in special departments, they may deem proper." The Common Council was given the power to set aside public grounds for such an institution; and the Board of Education might "in their discretion, upon the application of the Board of Directors assess and levy on the taxable property, not exceeding one-tenth of one mill per dollar of assessed valuation for the support of such university, college, or institution of learning."

ORGANIZATION OF THE UNIVERSITY OF CINCINNATI

Pursuant to this law the Common Council met in December 1870 and elected the Board of Directors of the University of Cincinnati. Nominations were submitted by the Board of Education, by a special committee of the Common Council, and from the floor. The entire list of candidates was balloted upon as a whole. The following men were elected for a one-year term: J. B. Stallo, W. S. Groesbeck, A. H. McGuffey; for a two-year term: A. F. Frazer, Gustav Bruehl, Jacob D. Cox; for a three-year term: Rufus King, George Hoadly, H. Pearce; for a four-year term: L. Ballauf, George B. Hollister, William Hooper; for a five-year term: Francis Ferry, Alphonso Taft, Larz Anderson; for a six-year term: William B. Davis and Lewis Seasongood. There was a large scattered vote for a number of other men. The Chair announced that the entire regular ticket nominated by the Board of Education and the Common Council had been elected except J. P. Carberry. By a voice vote, on the fifth ballot, Lewis E. Mills was elected as the third man for a six-year term.

The *Cincinnati Enquirer*, commenting on the election, stated that the selections "made were very good ones"; but it called attention to the fact that of the six men nominated by the Board of Education all had been elected save J. P. Carberry. "This gentleman" stated the paper, "represented the element opposed to the use of the Bible in the public schools, and it is understood that his defeat was brought about for this reason."

In 1869 an injunction had been issued against the Board of Education to restrain their striking out the clause providing for the reading of the Bible in the opening exercises of the schools. This so-called Bible case had aroused much discussion. The case came before the Superior Court of Cincinnati, and Judges Storer and Hagans, a majority of the Court, granted the injunction. Judge Taft dissented from this decision on the

68 THE UNIVERSITY OF CINCINNATI

ground that the School Board had the power to strike out this clause, and further because "the King James version of the Bible was not acceptable by the Roman Catholic population as the true Bible; and because the New Testament taught doctrines not believed by the Jewish population." The decision of the lower court was reversed by the Supreme Court of Ohio where the stand of Judge Taft was sustained.

This religious issue evidently entered into the selection of the first Board of Directors of the University of Cincinnati. At the first meeting of the Board on January 2, 1871, the name of the University was changed from the McMicken University to the University of Cincinnati; a set of by-laws governing the Board was drafted; and Rufus King was elected Chairman of the Board.

Rufus King, the first Chairman of the Board of Directors of the University of Cincinnati, was a distinguished man. He came of excellent American stock. His grandfather, Rufus King, was the distinguished Federalist Senator from New York who was three times the candidate of the Federalist Party for President of the United States. His father, Edward King, with Timothy Walker was one of the founders of the Law School of the Cincinnati College. His mother was the daughter of Governor Thomas Worthington of Ohio; and later, as Mrs. Sarah Peters, following her marriage after the death of Edward King, was one of the most prominent women in Cincinnati. Rufus King was one of the first trustees of the McMicken bequest and "for many years nursed it into the foundation of the University of Cincinnati." He was for many years a member of the Board of Education; one of the prime movers in the creation of the Cincinnati Public Library; for five years Dean of the Law School of the University; and, after resigning this position, was a distinguished member of its Faculty lecturing on constitutional law and the law of real property. He wrote for the American Commonwealth series a historical volume entitled *Ohio, the First Fruits of the Ordinance of 1787* which is one of the best accounts of the early history of Ohio." Rufus King was a refined, able lawyer, and an outstanding public citizen of Cincinnati.

At subsequent meetings of the Board in 1871 it was decided to continue meeting in rooms over the second floor of one of the McMicken buildings at the corner of Third and Main Streets. The Clerk of the Board, T. B. Disney, was authorized and directed "to place cocoa matting or rag carpet upon the floor," to have the walls painted a light color, and to have "such gas fixtures introduced as will give a proper light." One of the Board members objected to a rag carpet, and so this instruction was dropped. The Board requested the Board of Education to levy a tax of one-tenth of a mill on the dollar valuation of taxable property for the support of the University as provided in the Act of April 16, 1870. A committee of the Board was appointed to examine the orphan asylum, the high schools, and the Mechanics' Institute as possible temporary quarters for the University; and at the request of the Board the Common Council on March 14, 1871, passed an "ordinance to provide for the University of Cincinnati." By this ordinance the Directors of the Mc-Micken University were directed to turn over to the new Board all the property, books, and papers in their possession.

The general public expected when the new Board was created, elected, and organized that a university would be established at once. There was great disappointment, therefore, when a number of years elapsed before any tangible progress was made. Superintendent Hancock of the Public Schools kept reiterating that Cincinnati needed a university more than she needed the Southern Railroad which the City was then contemplating to build and which was subsequently completed in 1879. The idea of the orphan asylum as a temporary quarters was abandoned when the Common Council refused to supply funds needed to fit up the building. The Board of Directors did not think they had sufficient funds at their disposal to justify them opening any other school than the School of Design which continued to flourish.

On April 27, 1872, due largely to the efforts of Judge Taft, the State Legislature passed an act authorizing the Common Council of any city of the first class to issue bonds not exceeding $150,000 to provide the buildings and apparatus for a university. Meanwhile, Dr. Comegys strove unceasingly for the establishment of the University of Cincinnati. He visited the high schools and induced the pupils to sign a petition urging the City Council to grant aid. In order to have this matter brought before the Council he sought election to that body and was elected to the Council to represent the fifteenth ward. When he was ready to present the subject of the University to the City Council he had several high school boys present at the meeting. He got the attention of the Council and made an address. Since the City Council had "a political reputation and a name for making money," the absence of politics in this subject and the indifference to all matters pertaining to education caused them to give "little attention and respect" to the speaker. But Dr. Comegys demanded their attention, "saying among other things that he had sought election to the Council for the purpose of securing aid for the University of Cincinnati; that he had not bothered them before with ordinances nor with speeches"; and, therefore, "he claimed he had a right to demand their attention." His speech was effective and under the authority granted by the act passed by the Legislature, the City Council enacted an ordinance on December 6, 1872, authorizing and issuing $150,000 of bonds, bearing 7 per cent interest, "for the erection of buildings on the Mc-Micken estate and the purchase of apparatus for the University."

THE OPENING OF THE ACADEMIC DEPARTMENT

At length, in 1873, the first steps were taken towards establishing the Academic Department of the University. On August 2 an advertisement appeared in the *Cincinnati Commercial* announcing that by the courtesy of the Board of High Schools, the University of Cincinnati would begin to hold classes the next month at the Woodward High School under the management of the principal, Mr. George Harper. For the present, however, only classes for freshmen would be organized. For admission to the general course in Latin, philosophy, and science a certificate of graduation from a high school or an examination was required. For admission to the special scientific and professional courses students were required to take an examination in all the mathematics, physics, and chemistry taught in the high schools and in addition they had to show proficiency in English. About 150 persons, most of them girls, applied to Principal Harper for admission, but very few of them were found able to meet the requirements. The number admitted was 50, and of these 40 were girls.

In October 1873 the first classes in the Academic Department were held. Recitations were from two to five o'clock in the afternoons at the Woodward High School building. There were fifteen pupils in the mathematics class under Mr. George W. Smith; thirteen in the chemistry and natural philosophy class under Mr. Charles W. Stuntz; and six in the Latin and Greek class under Mr. W. H. Pabodie. All these teachers were of the regular staff of Woodward High School. Besides these classes there was an elementary and advanced class in French under Mr. Jules Laquiens, and similar classes in German under Mr. Thomas Vickers. Some of these classes grew smaller. It is claimed that only three of those admitted, and they were men, entered with any intention of pursuing a full four-year course. At the close of the year the students were told there would be a new Faculty in the fall, and that they would determine who would be permitted to go to higher classes. Principal Harper of Woodward High School was the executive head during the first year of the University.

In that year the School of Drawing and Design moved to more commodious rooms in the upper floor of the Cincinnati College on Walnut Street. There were 328 pupils in the School of Drawing and Design who were instructed in separate sections, three days and three evenings each week. In addition a class in wood-carving was organized upon the suggestion of Mr. Ben Pitman who agreed to teach the class without compensation until the experiment would be fairly tested. About 50 pupils enrolled in this class.

The work of the class in wood-carving which was exhibited in the Centennial Exposition in Philadelphia in 1876 received a high compli-

ment from the jury in household art. Classes were subsequently organized in modeling under Mr. Louis T. Rebisso.

The New Observatory Building

Besides beginning classes in the Academic Department and expanding
the work in the School of Drawing and Design, the cornerstone of a new
Observatory building connected with the University was laid in 1873.
The Board of Directors of the Astronomical Society was the only one of
the various boards of the educational trusts who had agreed to consolidate with the University; provided the latter in turn agreed to maintain
the Observatory as a part of its work. The Board of the University accepted these terms, and in 1872 the consolidation was effected. But new
difficulties then confronted the Board. The Mount Adams site was no
longer suited to astronomical observations. The smoke and heated air
arising from below the Observatory rendered it almost impossible to carry
on observations until a late hour at night. A resolution was brought forward in a meeting of the Astronomical Society to sell the ground and
with the proceeds purchase other land and erect a new building. But
this could not be done for the reason that the four acres of ground had
been donated by Nicholas Longworth for an observatory, and if this
purpose was not fulfilled the land reverted to the Longworth heirs. They
were consulted and agreed to join with the Astronomical Society in con-
veying the ground to the City; provided the property was sold and the
proceeds applied to an endowment for the School of Drawing and Design. The City agreed to accept the gift and maintain the Observatory
which should be connected with the University. The Mount Adams
property was sold to the Society of Jesus for $50,000.

The City now had a large telescope but no place to put it where it
would do the most good. At this opportune moment in order to help the
City carry out the terms of its agreement, Mr. John Kilgour came forward
and offered the City four acres of ground at Mount Lookout as a building site besides donating $10,000 for a building and equipping the edifice.

On August 28, 1873, the cornerstone of the new Observatory was laid
with impressive ceremonies in the presence of a large assemblage. The
site was admirably adapted to the purposes of such an institution. It was
one of the highest points in Hamilton County and commanded a beautiful
and extended view of the surrounding country. The cornerstone was laid
by Rufus King and was the same stone dedicated November 9, 1843, by
John Quincy Adams as the cornerstone of the old Cincinnati Observatory.
In the audience were many who had been spectators of that dedication.
In his speech Mr. King paid a glowing tribute to Ormsby M. Mitchel,
the founder of the Observatory, and to Professor Abbe. Speeches were
also made by the Mayor, George W. C. Johnston, and by George Hoadly.

72

It was known that Samuel F. Hunt was on the grounds, and the assemblage insisted that he make a few remarks. In his address Mr. Hunt dwelt on the disinterestedness and energy of the early movers of the enterprise and paid respect to the memory of Mitchel and Longworth and to the work of Mr. Kilgour.

In 1875, Ormond Stone, formerly of the National Observatory at Washington, D.C., was appointed Director of the Observatory. He began carrying on observations of double stars and making arrangements, under the control of the City Council, for giving exact time to the City by means of daily signals from the Observatory.

Selecting the First Faculty of the Academic Department

Meanwhile the Board began to appoint a Faculty. They were very careful in selecting the members of the first Faculty of the University and endeavored to obtain the best men they could. They wanted professors who were "not only able to teach but were thoroughly acquainted with their subject and creators of intelligence in their departments." For the first year of the operation of the University the Board decided to appoint three professors to fill the chairs of mathematics, astronomy, civil engineering, chemistry, physics, the ancient languages, and comparative philology. Instructors in German and French were also sought. A committee of the Board sent out a circular to Faculties in the smaller colleges, as well as to some of the leading professors in well-known institutions. The circular contained information as to the minimum salaries offered ($3,000 for a professor; $2,000 for an assistant professor) and solicited applications accompanied with letters of recommendation. As a result of their efforts the committee received applications and letters of recommendations from forty-five candidates for the chair of ancient languages and comparative philology; from thirty-three candidates for the professorship of mathematics and astronomy and civil engineering; and from thirty candidates for the professorship of chemistry and physics. The committee reported that all the candidates were comparatively young men, as the older professors with established reputations were unwilling to apply. Of the young men who had applied the committee stated, a considerable number were recommended as "teachers of brilliant promise." From this long list of applicants the committee submitted the names of three persons for each chair to the Board. The Board voted by secret ballot on the names submitted to them, and the candidate receiving a majority of the votes was appointed to the chair for which he had been recommended.

As a result of the balloting, the Board appointed H. T. Eddy of Princeton University, professor of mathematics, astronomy, and civil engineering; F. W. Clarke of Howard University, Washington, D.C., professor of chemistry and physics; and F. D. Allen of Harvard University, professor of ancient languages and comparative philology. E. A. Guetin was appointed instructor in French; and F. Van Rossum, instructor in German; each at a salary of $800 per year.

At the request of the Board, the Messrs. Eddy, Clarke, and Allen held a preliminary meeting of the Faculty on August 4, 1874, at Princeton, New Jersey. This was the first meeting of the Academic Department Faculty. They decided that it was advisable to admit students upon examination to all the regular courses. A regular course was one that met for fifteen recitation periods per week for four years. The hours of recitation were to be from 9:30 in the morning until noon, but there were to be no classes on Saturdays or Sundays. After the Faculty was formally organized in the fall H. T. Eddy was elected Dean, and the academic year was divided into three terms.

In September 1874 the University was opened with a class of nine under Professor Eddy; a class of eighteen under Professor Clarke; classes of eight in Latin and five in Greek under Professor Allen; and an elementary and an advanced class in French, together numbering thirty-six under Mr. Guetin; and two similar classes, together numbering fifty-eight in German under Mr. Van Rossum. The large number in the German and French classes was due to free tuition to residents and the fact that no examinations were required for admission to these classes. By the courtesy of the Board of Education these classes were held for the time being in the Third Intermediate School Building on Liberty Street near Sycamore.

The future proved that the Board had selected good men as members of the first Faculty. They elected Professor Eddy as their first Dean. When President Jacob Cox resigned the Board, the Board appointed Professor Eddy as Acting President and then elected him President of the University and increased his salary to $4,000 a year. But he declined the position and resigned to accept the Presidency of Rose Polytechnic Institute, Terre Haute, Indiana. In the course of time Professor Allen acquired a wide reputation as a classical scholar and was called to Harvard University to fill the chair of classical philology. Subsequently, Professor Clarke also resigned to accept a position as chemist for the Geological Survey.

In October 1875 the Academic Department, so long desired, was fully established and opened. Classes were held in the north wing of the new University building located on the McMicken estate; the site designated for it in the will of Charles McMicken. The building was on the slope of Vine Street hill, between Clifton Avenue and Hamilton Road (now McMicken Street), "in a commanding position, yet one of easy access by

street cars." Three courses of study were opened to students: the classical
course, leading to the degree of Bachelor of Arts; the scientific course,
leading to the degree of Bachelor of Science; and the course in civil
engineering, leading to the degree of Civil Engineer. Besides these
regular courses provision was made for special students who desired to
pursue particular branches exclusively. Any student who was a candidate
for any of these degrees was required to take at least fifteen hours of
classroom work per week during four years. The work during the first
year was rigidly prescribed but after that a large amount of option was
allowed except in the civil engineering course which "being professional
in its nature was mainly arranged by the professor." Instruction was free
"to youth of either sex" who were "bona fide residents of Cincinnati."
Non-resident students were required to pay "at the rate of thirty dollars
per annum for instruction in a single study and sixty dollars per annum
for any full course."

The distinguishing feature of the early days of the University was the
close relationship of the students and Faculty. Because of the small size
of the classes the students were in close personal contact with their professors. They appreciated this and at later reunions many of the early
graduates mentioned the benefits they derived from their close association with their professors and the private instruction they received.

The only thing approaching college life in the early seventies was the
formation of a male quartet. In 1875, however, twenty-two of the Academic Department students requested the Board of Directors to furnish
an unoccupied room on the fourth floor of the University building with
necessary apparatus for a gymnasium. This was referred to a committee
of the Board, but nothing was done.

In that year (1875) the Faculty was enlarged by the appointment of
E. W. Hyde as assistant professor of mathematics and civil engineering
and R. B. Warden as assistant professor of physics and chemistry. The
next year J. M. Hart, who already had a reputation because of his publications, was appointed professor of modern languages and literature;
and W. R. Benedict was appointed professor of philosophy and history.
In the same year Ormond Stone was appointed professor of astronomy
and Director of the Observatory.

In the early days of the University the professors were often called
upon to teach any number of subjects. For example, Professor Benedict
not only taught courses in philosophy and history; but at times courses in
logic, psychology, ethics, political economy, the Bible, and the history
of education. "Whew! What a schedule! Our professors are all over-
worked!" commented a student paper in the early eighties on the "chairs"
filled by Professor Benedict. Then it called attention to the resignation
of Professor Allen and offered this sage advice: "The loss to the University will be great and the Directors will not find it an easy matter

to fill (the vacancy); but they have themselves to blame and the sooner they open their eyes to the fact that a first-class professor cannot be retained indefinitely on a small salary, the better for the University."

But the Board at that time was having its own troubles with finances. The country was in the aftermath of the devastating Panic of 1873; and during the year 1878, "the University suffered from a general depression in the business and commercial circles." To make the financial problems of the Board even more difficult, the Board of Education in 1876 and 1877 had failed to levy the one-tenth of a mill on the taxable property of the City for the support of the University which was authorized by the statute under which the University was organized. The Board of Directors of the University were financially embarrassed by this action, because obligations had been incurred upon the faith of the passage of this levy. The General Assembly, however, in 1878 made it mandatory on the Board of Education to levy the one-tenth of a mill on the taxable property of the City for the support of the University as long as University bonds should be outstanding. As a consequence of the hard times the income derived from rents of the McMicken property decreased in the year 1878 by $1,200.

During the depression years the salaries of the professors were cut about $500 a year. In April 1877, T. B. Disney, who had been the clerk of the Board of the McMicken University as well as that of the University of Cincinnati from its establishment, "surprised the Board by the very unusual step of asking, without suggestion from any source except his own sympathy with the needs of the institution, for a reduction of his salary (then around $2,500) by the annual sum of $500." The Board acceded to his request "with no little regret."

During the year 1877 the University conferred the first degree—that of Bachelor of Arts on Frank G. McFarlan and of Master of Arts upon Herbert A. Howe and Winslow Upton. Both had pursued a postgraduate course of study at the Observatory.

The First Commencement of the University of Cincinnati

The first annual Commencement exercises of the University of Cincinnati were held on the evening of June 20, 1878, at Pike's Opera House. They attracted a much larger attendance than had been expected by the most sanguine friends of the institution. "The hall was filled, upstairs and down" with a "large and cultured audience." The interest manifested on this occasion indicated that the citizens of Cincinnati were not unconscious of the advantages to be derived in developing their educational system. The stage was decorated with plants and flowers and was occupied by the distinguished friends of the University, the Faculty, and the graduating class.

The Invocation and Benediction were given by Rabbi Dr. Max Lilienthal. He was well known both in the Old World and the New. He was a native of Munich, Germany, and received his education at the university there. Dr. Lilienthal became widely known in literary circles throughout Europe shortly after his graduation by his discovery of a large number of valuable manuscripts that had been deposited in the Royal Library of Munich which hitherto had been unknown to scholars. These manuscripts were in the Oriental dialects and of vast importance in Hebrew literature. He received a call to St. Petersburg where he was appointed to an important position in the Department of Public Instruction of the Russian government. After a brief but brilliant career Dr. Lilienthal left Russia for political reasons and came to America. He soon assumed a leading position in the educational circles of New York City and of the Jewish ministry there. In 1885 he came to Cincinnati which he made his permanent home during the remainder of his life. He became a member of the Board of Education and a professor in the Hebrew Union College. His action in helping to found the University has already been recounted; and as soon as the University was organized he was elected to the Board of Directors, a position he held for nine years. Dr. Lilienthal never neglected an opportunity to strengthen the University and to elevate its standards. The acquisition by the University of the Benjamin Lilienthal Geological Collection and the Fechheimer Geological Collection were both obtained through his efforts.

The Baccalaureate address was delivered by the Honorable George H. Pendleton, United States Senator from Ohio, who was nationally known as the originator of the "Ohio Idea," a plan to pay off the Civil War bond issues, whenever the letter of the law permitted it, in greenbacks instead of gold. In his address Senator Pendleton made an eloquent appeal for the democratization of higher education as it had been in the public schools and was warmly applauded.

After the address by Senator Pendleton, essays were read by members of the graduating class. Five of them received the degree of Bachelor of Arts; one the degree of Bachelor of Science; and one the degree of Civil Engineer. Two of them were sons of members of the Board of Directors; one was a native Brazilian; and one was a lady graduate of the class. The *Cincinnati Enquirer* stated that "the merits of the class essays were very high" and modestly claimed that they were "very much better than that of classes in most western colleges." "The general tone of the essays," said the *Cincinnati Enquirer* indicates that the tendency of the "young mind at Cincinnati University is to grapple with social problems."

The names, degrees, and essays read by the first graduating class of the University of Cincinnati are as follows:

BACHELOR OF ARTS

ALFRED BARNUM BENEDICT of Cincinnati. He chose "Popular Fallacies" for the theme of his essay. The local press claimed the essay was "one of genuine merit and evinced much research and careful study."

CHARLES BOYNTON HANCOCK of Cincinnati. He read a carefully prepared paper on "One-Sided Legislation" in which "he advanced many thoughts worthy of attention and study."

CHARLES GEORGE COMEGYS of Cincinnati. He read a paper entitled "The Duty of the State to Maintain Higher Institutions of Learning." It was "replete with sense, and was well received."

JOHN LINDSAY DAVIS of Cincinnati. He dwelt upon "Some Political Faults of Our People." He spoke principally of political corruption.

WINONA LEE HAWTHORNE of Newport, Kentucky. She was the only lady graduate of the class. She presented an interesting and really able "Plea for the Classics." The local press said she was "a talented and highly cultured young lady, and the reading of her very eloquent and masterly production was frequently interrupted with bursts of applause."

BACHELOR OF SCIENCE

PERCIVAL WERNER of Cincinnati. He chose for his subject "The Roots of Communism." There was much interest in the United States in the sixties and seventies in Karl Marx's conception of the aims of the labor movement, especially among the German immigrants of this country. Karl Marx and Friedrich Engels had issued in 1848 the *Communist Manifesto;* and Karl Marx had published in 1867 the first volume of his bulky treatise, *Capital.* In his essay Mr. Werner regarded the abuse of the American labor system as the "root of communism" and entered a plea for a higher rate of wages.

CIVIL ENGINEER

THOMAS D'AQUINO E CASTRO of Rio de Janeiro, Brazil. He read an essay entitled "A Good Foundation." It was devoted to engineering, and the press reported "it displayed a pretty thorough knowledge of that science."

Samuel F. Hunt, Chairman of the Board of Directors, awarded the diplomas to the graduates and awarded the following prizes to pupils of the School of Design for meritorious work:

IN DRAWING AND DESIGN

Day Class

For the most meritorious crayon drawing of original design, a gold medal, to HENRY ERRETT.

For the second best crayon drawing of original design, a silver medal, to GEORGE S. VREELAND.

For the most meritorious crayon drawing from the antique, a silver medal, to ELIZABETH NOURSE.

Night Class

For the most meritorious drawing from the antique, a diploma, to H. VOTH.

IN SCULPTURE

Day Class

For the most meritorious piece of work, design, and workmanship, both considered, a silver medal, to JOSEPH SIBBELL.

Night Class

For the second best piece of work, design, and workmanship, both considered, a diploma, to VALENTINE BONHAJO.

IN WOOD-CARVING

For the most meritorious piece of work, design, and workmanship, both considered, a silver medal, to ANNIE EMPSON.

For the second best piece of work, design, and workmanship, both considered, a diploma, to CAROLINE P. DIXON.

In his address to the graduates Mr. Hunt began by stating that: "The exercises of this evening mark an important event in the history of the University. This is the first Commencement and the graduates are the first to go out into active life after having completed the course of study prescribed in the Academic Department. The work of the University will have been in vain if it has not imbued them with a broad and liberal culture, and elevated them to a better and livelier sense of their responsibility to the commonwealth of man." He then recounted the early history of the University and discussed the bequest of Charles McMicken.

Mr. Hunt then called attention to the fact that the original endowment had been increased by the following donations: From the Astronomical Society, donations of its books and instruments which were valued at $8,000 to the City on condition that an Observatory should be maintained; from Joseph Longworth during his lifetime, at different times, the sum of $59,700 to the City for the support of the School of Drawing and Design; from John Kilgour, four acres of ground on Mount Lookout to the City for an Observatory site and an additional sum of $10,000 for a building; from Julius Dexter, $1,000 as an endowment for the Observatory; and from the Reverend Samuel J. Brown, a fund amounting to approximately $20,000.

Then the speaker addressed himself to the graduating class and said:

The just reputation of this University and all universities will depend upon the conduct and character of those who from time to time are subjects of its care. The graduate will be its sign, its name, its title to respect among the people. . . . We [the Board of Directors and the Faculty] will follow with an affectionate interest as you leave the college walls for the active duties of life. You cannot be faithless to the great obligations which these advantages and opportunities have imposed upon you without awakening a sincere regret in the officers and Faculty of the University.

In his annual report as Chairman of the Board of Directors, Mr. Hunt dwelt at some length on the graduation exercises "because," as he said, "the first Commencement marks an era in our institution." It did indeed, for the graduates were the initial results of a long struggle to create an institution of higher learning as a proper and necessary part of the City's legitimate activities. The first graduation exercises signified that a real beginning had been made towards fulfilling the cherished dream of its founder, Charles McMicken.

8 The Liberal Arts Gain Strength

For nearly six decades such continuity as there was in the evolution of the University was found predominantly in a succession of professional schools, chiefly law and medicine. The demand for training in those two professions was greater, and support from the profession in Cincinnati was more vigorous and informed. Towards 1880, however, there was growing interest in the liberal arts with the strong emphasis on classical languages that was characteristic of American education in the nineteenth century. Haltingly, with some civic storms over religious instruction and some abortive attempts to consolidate with rival schools, the still new University of Cincinnati began to take on the complexion and structure of a modern university.

Rector Thomas Vickers

Four years after the Academic Department was opened to students, Mr. King from the Committee on the University recommended to the Board of Directors that they proceed to procure an executive officer for the University. Up to that time the Dean of the Academic Faculty had been the chief administrative officer.

Accordingly, on November 28, 1877, a resolution was introduced at the Board meeting which declared that "whereas it is necessary to have an executive officer for the University the Board nominate one of its members with the title of Rector to act for the time being as President of the University; provided no salary be paid or allowed until further action to serve for such time and perform such duties as shall be prescribed by the rules and regulations of the Board." Upon the motion of Mr. Hunt the resolution was amended to strike out "one of the members of the Board" and insert the words "some suitable person"; and Mr. King moved to amend the resolution by inserting after the words "to nominate" the words "by ballot." With these amendments the resolution was passed.

The Board then proceeded to the election of a Rector. Three persons were nominated: Thomas Vickers, Julius Dexter, and William S. Groesbeck. At that time Mr. Vickers was a member of the Board of Directors and Librarian of the Cincinnati Public Library, and had been a lecturer in German in the first organization of the University. Julius Dexter and William S. Groesbeck were former members of the Board of Directors. Dr. Comegys undertook to secure the election of Mr. Dexter when he found out that Mr. Vickers had already, in person, solicited and obtained the promise of some of the members of the Board to support him for the position. When the vote was taken Mr. Vickers received nine votes; Mr. Julius Dexter, three votes; and Mr. Groesbeck, one vote. Mr. Vickers was declared elected, and the office of Dean of the Faculty of the Academic Department was abolished.

In his report to the Mayor, Chairman Hoadly of the Board announced the election of Mr. Vickers to this important trust in December 1877. "It is believed," said Mr. Hoadly, "that his services, which he gratuitously renders, will be of great assistance in securing harmony in instruction and discipline, and more efficient work."

The new Rector of the University had had an interesting, turbulent career. He was born on October 12, 1835, the son of Joseph and Grace (Chaffer) Vickers, at Otley, Yorkshire, England. Vickers was of Danish descent. In 1849 the family came to the United States. After attending public schools in Boston, he was graduated in 1863 with the degree of Bachelor of Divinity from the Unitarian Theological Seminary at Meadville, Pennsylvania, and then went abroad to study. He spent four years at the University of Heidelberg, Germany, and half a year at the University of Zurich, Switzerland. While in Germany he married Carolina, daughter of Martin Seeberger, by whom he later had four children. In Europe he studied languages, philosophy, history, and educational theory and practice. He became proficient in languages. Besides mastering Greek, Latin, and Hebrew he acquired a speaking and reading knowledge of the principal modern languages with the exception of the Slavonic tongues.

On his return to this country Mr. Vickers was chosen on January 6, 1867, pastor of the First Congregational (Unitarian) Church, located at the northeast corner of Eighth and Plum Streets. Judge Taft was a member of this Church. Reverend Mr. Vickers was a liberal in his views. When he went to Europe to study he took with him a circular letter from William Lloyd Garrison introducing him to the leading anti-slavery men and women in England, Ireland, and Scotland. Later, as pastor of the First Congregational Church, he became involved in the dispute over the reading of religious books in the Cincinnati public schools. Like Judge Taft and the Board of Education, the Reverend Vickers was opposed to the reading of the Bible in the public schools. In the discussion of this question, Reverend Mr. Vickers showed that he was a "brilliant and effective" disputant. His arguments were "witty, learned, and thorough."

During the first year of his ministry the Reverend Mr. Vickers engaged in a notable controversy with Archbishop John B. Purcell. In the course of an address at the laying the cornerstone of St. John's German Protestant Church, Reverend Mr. Vickers spoke of the "place of the early Christian church as a sanctuary and refuge of the common people from the violence of rulers and as a nursery of the classical scholarship of the ancient world." For centuries the early church was the only representative of science and culture. "But," continued the Reverend Mr. Vickers, "it was never possible for the mind to develop itself under her dominion; freedom of thought and investigation then as always, since have been treated by organized Christianity, especially in the Church of Rome, as heresies to be crushed. And for her hostility to the free activity of enlightened reason that church today is forsaken by all thinkers. It is, therefore, the mission of a living church to become the sanctuary of free thought and to reconcile to religion, from which they have been long divorced, modern science and modern intelligence." This discourse was published in the local press and was considered by the Roman Catholic Archbishop Purcell to be an attack upon his faith. He made a violent retort to the Reverend Mr. Vickers on the occasion of a dedication of one of his churches. This resulted in a lengthy correspondence, which was published in the *Cincinnati Commercial, Cincinnati Gazette,* and the *Catholic Telegraph.* The controversy attracted a great deal of attention in this country and abroad and almost wrecked the congregation of the First Congregational Church. At this opportune moment Reverend Mr. Vickers received a call to become the librarian of the Cincinnati Public Library, and so on April 5, 1874, he resigned his pastorate.

When the Board of Managers of the Cincinnati Public Library met to fill the vacancy created by the resignation of William F. Poole, the distinguished librarian who had accepted a similar position in the Public Library of Chicago, there was much discussion concerning the fitness of Mr. Vickers for the librarianship. Some of the members of the Board did not think that Mr. Vickers had the necessary experience for such a position; others thought that Mr. Vickers had made himself too unpopular as a result of his controversy with Archbishop Purcell. One of Mr. Vickers' strongest supporters was Mr. Carberry, who held that Mr. Vickers had popularized the idea of the secularization of the public schools. It will be recalled that Mr. Carberry later was not elected to the Board of Directors of the University owing to his stand on the reading of the Bible in the public schools. Despite this opposition Mr. Vickers was elected librarian of the Cincinnati Public Library by a margin of four votes; and at the end of his first year it was conceded by all that Mr. Vickers had all the qualifications necessary for the office, "a broad and liberal culture, administrative ability of the highest order, excellent business capacity, and a comprehensive knowledge of books in general." After his election as librarian it was confidentially asserted by the Board that "the most sanguine expectations of his friends were being realized."

But within a short time there was criticism of Mr. Vickers as librarian. He determined to reclassify the Library and referred sarcastically to the Poole catalogue as a very "injudicious" undertaking and a "complete failure." In fact Mr. Vickers approved of little that Mr. Poole had done for the Library. He changed the arrangement of the rooms, the system of delivery, and the classification of the cataloguing; yet, after Mr. Vickers became Rector of the University, the Library returned to the "methods originally proposed by Mr. Poole." Mr. Vickers was the first to suggest the establishment of branch libraries, but it was not until 1899 that the Board of Managers of the Library actually established delivery stations in the outlying districts of the City.

In September 1878, Mr. Vickers was appointed Rector of the University and professor of history at a salary of $3,500 a year, "with the understanding that he give further instruction in the Academic Department as the Board may from time to time require." He made a temporary arrangement with the University Board whereby he was to be permitted to devote certain hours of each day to the Public Library in consideration of which his salary was to be $1,000 instead of $3,500 a year. In this way he hoped to finish some of the work he had begun at the Library. It was not long, however, before Mr. Vickers realized that the double work was too great a strain upon him. As a consequence he resigned as librarian and devoted himself entirely to his duties as Rector and professor at the University. On his resignation the Board of Managers of the Public Library, who were also dissatisfied with this kind of arrangement, passed a resolution that "hereafter whoever is appointed librarian shall give his whole time to the duties of the office."

The Administration of Rector Vickers

During the administration of Rector Vickers a number of important changes were made in the University. The courses in the Academic Department were systematized and integrated; new degree courses were set up to meet specific demands; a Normal School was established; an attempt was made to affiliate the Cincinnati College of Pharmacy with the University; the School of Design was transferred to the Art Museum; the University began to give instruction in the Bible; and there were the first indications of the development of student activities on the campus. This was a period of experimentation. The Rector instigated some of these changes; others he approved.

REORGANIZATION AND NEW DEGREES IN THE ACADEMIC DEPARTMENT

The appointment of the Rector led to a thorough organization of every department in the University, and the whole course of instruction was systematized. The Rector took upon himself the function of professor of history; thus relieving the chair of philosophy of this work. A separate department of history was not yet established. In addition to his teaching courses in history and serving as Rector, Mr. Vickers, in accordance with the provisions of his appointment, was called upon at various times to teach courses in German, Spanish, Italian, pedagogy, rhetoric, and political science. In 1879, Professor Frederick D. Allen, of the chair of ancient languages and comparative philology, resigned, and Professor William O. Sproull was appointed to the chair of the Latin languages and literature and Arabic The chair of chemistry and physics was created; and on the resignation of Professor F. W. Clarke, Thomas Herbert Norton was appointed professor of chemistry. Instructors in botany, elocution, and metallurgy, and an assistant professor of modern languages, were added to the Faculty. The Faculty staff, however, was not greatly increased; there being eleven professors and instructors in the Academic Department when Mr. Vickers became Rector, and there were thirteen when he resigned. The number of students enrolled in the Academic Department during these years dropped from 128 to 111, probably due in part to student friction with the Rector.

Mr. Vickers was much concerned about the transient character of many of the students in the University. Many of the special students enrolled in the Academic Department were not adequately prepared for college work. Too many of these students came to the University with no definite purpose. They often took some course leading to a degree, found it too severe or the standard too high for them, dropped out of the University, and entered the Law School or one of the medical colleges in the City. In order to deal with this situation Mr. Vickers suggested that the high school curriculum be reorganized so that the work required be completed in three instead of four years. This would make it possible for the better students to enter the University earlier. In addition he suggested that the University combine the academic and professional courses so that at the end of five years a student could obtain both a Bachelor of Arts and a law degree or a medical degree. But neither of these proposals was adopted. The Board of Directors of the University held several conferences with teachers of the Hughes and Woodward High Schools about the reorganization of their curricula, but nothing came of it. The Board took no action concerning the Rector's suggestion as to the advisability of combining academic and professional study at the University, as they were hoping to bring about a combination of the various educational trusts in the City and make the University the center of all such instruction. Mr. Vickers' ideas on these topics were too advanced for the time, although in the future the University was to adopt some of them.

In spite of the heavy teaching schedules, some of the Faculty found time to write for publications. There was much interest during these years in the organization, internal workings, and administration of American colleges. Numerous articles on these educational topics written by President Eliot of Harvard and the Presidents of other colleges appeared in the popular magazines. One such article, by Professor F. W. Clarke, which appeared in the June issue of the *Popular Science Monthly* in 1882, attracted attention. Writing on "The Appointment of College Officers," he tried to analyze how college presidents and professors were chosen and how they ought to be selected. Evidently with Mr. Vickers in mind, Professor Clarke analyzed what qualities a college president ought to have for such a position. As Professor Clarke said, "he should be tactful; show that he had executive capacity and force; command the confidence and respect of the trustees, teachers, students, and alumni, and of the community in which he lived; be a good judge of men; and possess the knowledge, training, and experience of a teacher in order to fill properly vacancies in the Faculty." Professor Clarke acknowledged that it might be difficult to find all these qualifications in one individual; but as he said, "if the president failed in any one of these qualifications, he was liable to fail altogether, for the strength of the whole chain (was) but that of its weakest link."

The courses in the Academic Department were expanded. The course leading to the degree of Bachelor of Arts was modified by reducing the number of elective studies which a student might take. Three full years of prescribed study of Latin and Greek were required of all those seeking this degree. The Faculty, however, realized that there were many persons who wanted to take a more literary course and did not want to spend so much time studying the classical languages. To meet the demands of this class of students a new course in 1879 leading to the degree of Bachelor of Letters was established. This was a four-year course, in three of which years the student emphasized the study of English literature, history, and philosophy with electives in the modern languages, Latin, geology, and such other subjects as the Faculty deemed advisable. Four years later a philosophical course was added to the curriculum leading to the degree of Bachelor of Philosophy.

Rector Vickers also thought that the history of pedagogy and the theory and methods of training teachers should be regarded as coming within the scope of University work. Since the University was intimately connected with the public school system he proposed to the Board of Directors that they appoint a special committee for the purpose of conferring with the Board of Education as to the practicability and propriety

of uniting the Normal School, then under the control of the Board of
Education, with the University. This joint committee approved the idea
and recommended that the Normal School be united with the University
under the title of the Normal College of the University. All the theoretical instruction in this College was to be given by a professor of pedagogy who was paid by the University while the practical training was
to be given under the direction of the Board of Education. The normal
course was discontinued in the academic year 1885–1886 and the philosophical course in 1889–1890.

ATTEMPT TO AFFILIATE THE CINCINNATI COLLEGE OF PHARMACY

An attempt was also made to expand the University by affiliating the
Cincinnati College of Pharmacy with it. This College was one of the
older educational institutions in the City. It was chartered on March 23,
1850, by an act of the General Assembly which incorporated the Cincinnati Pharmaceutical Association and gave it the legal power for thirty
years to operate a College of Pharmacy for the purpose of "the cultivation, improvement, and diffusion of the science and art of pharmacy."
The Cincinnati College of Pharmacy was the first educational institution
of its kind west of the Alleghenies.

Those who were prominent in the establishment of this College were:
William B. Chapman, Adolphus Fennel, William J. M. Gordon, Charles
Augustus Smith, and Edward S. Wayne. Chapman was a graduate of the
Philadelphia College of Pharmacy and the Medical College of Ohio. He
had a drug store at the northwest corner of Sixth and Vine Streets which
was regarded as one of the show places of the City, especially its modern
soda fountain. In 1852 the American Pharmaceutical Association was organized, and two years later Chapman was elected President of the
Association. He was the inventor of Chapman's suppository mould, the
first of its kind on the American market. Fennel was an eminent analytical chemist. William J. M. Gordon was a prominent pharmacist.
Charles Augustus Smith was the first Vice-President of the American
Pharmaceutical Association. Wayne was a man of recognized scientific
attainments who at different times was a member of the Faculty of the
Medical College of Ohio and the Cincinnati College of Medicine and
Surgery. He was the chief chemist of the drug establishment of Suire and
Eckstein and drew a salary of $7,000 a year which was the largest salary
paid to any chemist in the country. He was known as the "Beau Brum-
mell" of the profession in Cincinnati because of his faultless attire and
courtly manners.

The first home of the Cincinnati College of Pharmacy was in Gordon
Hall, above Gordon's drug store at Eight and Western Row (now Central
Avenue). The College vegetated here for a number of years and subse-

quently in a room in the Cincinnati College, but with the outbreak of the Civil War both the Cincinnati Pharmaceutical Association and the College ceased to exist.

Early in the 1870's efforts were made to revive the College. The too-frequent occurrences of mistakes in compounding prescriptions, either from carelessness or ignorance, created an increasing demand upon the part of both physicians and druggists for more competent and educated pharmacists. A call was issued to the druggists of Cincinnati to attend a meeting at the Dental College on College Street on October 20, 1871, "for the purpose of organizing a society and considering the expediency of having a college of pharmacy." On that evening fifty druggists met; E. S. Wayne was elected President of the Cincinnati Pharmaceutical Association. When it was learned that all the records had been destroyed by fire, it was decided to start a new institution under the old name; and a new constitution and set of by-laws were adopted.

The Cincinnati College of Pharmacy has been in continuous existence from its reorganization in 1871. On December 4, 1871, the first class of thirty-eight students met in a room in the Cincinnati College building on Walnut Street. The first Faculty consisted of: Edward S. Wayne, professor of materia medica and pharmacy; J. F. Judge, professor of chemistry; F. H. Renz, professor of botany; and Adolphus Fennel, professor of analytical chemistry. The next year W. B. Chapman was appointed professor of pharmacy.

The first classes met in the evenings, and the method of instruction was known as the "Round Table Discussion." The professor and the class sat together about a round table and discussed informally the theoretical and practical problems connected with the evening's subject. Nearby was a raised bench on which to carry out the experiments and display the specimens.

Among the early matriculates in these informal discussions was John Uri Lloyd, one of America's greatest and most versatile pharmacists. He later became professor of pharmacy in the Cincinnati College of Pharmacy and President of the American Pharmaceutical Association. During his long and distinguished career of scientist, pharmaceutical manufacturer, teacher, and author of numerous scientific and popular books, he received six honorary degrees, three gold medals, and founded the Lloyd Library which today contains more than 150,000 volumes and about 90,000 pamphlets written in more than sixty languages covering the fields of pharmacy, botany, eclectic medicine, natural history, and allied subjects. Lloyd never failed to express his deep admiration for the men who composed the first Faculty of the College and the inspiration he derived from their Socratic method of instruction.

In 1880 a special committee of the Board of Directors of the University was appointed at the suggestion of the Rector to confer with the Cincinnati College of Pharmacy, looking toward the affiliation of the latter institution with the University. The College of Pharmacy was to retain its own Faculty; have control of its courses; and become a department of the University. A group of pharmacists in the City notified the University Board that they were opposed to the idea, so also did the Board of Trustees of the College of Pharmacy. In the face of this opposition Mr. Vickers suggested that the matter be dropped. Instead of this the Board of Directors of the University resubmitted the proposal to the Committee with instructions to confer at a later date with the trustees of the Cincinnati College of Pharmacy. Three years later the University again proposed the affiliation of the Pharmacy College with the University, but it was promptly rejected by the trustees of the College. The Pharmacy College was too prosperous at this time to consider the proposal; thus failed these early efforts for the affiliation of the Cincinnati College of Pharmacy with the University.

TRANSFER OF SCHOOL OF DESIGN TO THE ART MUSEUM

The most important event that occurred during these years was the formal transfer of the School of Design of the University to the Cincinnati Art Museum. In every respect the School of Design had fulfilled all the just expectations of its friends. From a small beginning it had developed into an institution with a corps of experienced instructors and at least four hundred students. The course of instruction had been expanded to include not only drawing and design but work in wood-carving, sculpture, plastic anatomy, oil painting, and drawing from still life. Principal Thomas S. Noble after a trip to Europe reported that the School of Design compared favorably with the best of such institutions in England. One of the pupils of the School had won the highest honor—the silver medal—at the Academy of Fine Arts in Munich, Germany, and his work had been placed in a special niche for display. It was the aim of the School to make its instruction useful as well as beautiful. The influence of the School of Design had been felt in all the industries in the City in which artistic design was employed to enhance the value of the manufactured article. It became, indeed, the parent of other schools of design and drawing. The citizens of Cincinnati were proud of it. Mr. Joseph Longworth had presented the Art Department of the University with $59,500 upon condition that the University add $10,000 which it promptly did. He intimated that if the School were successful he would increase his support of it.

In the meantime a group of prominent Cincinnatians organized and incorporated under the name of the Cincinnati Art Museum Association. The purpose of the Association was to stimulate the development of the fine arts in the City. They obtained a contribution of $150,000 from

Charles W. West for a building on the condition that others would subscribe as much to establish on a large scale an art school and an art
museum. These additional subscriptions were obtained, and the Art
Museum was built. But it was very soon seen that unless the School of
Design of the University surrendered all its belongings, classes, and
teachers to the Art Museum the new organization would not function
effectively.

At the time of the incorporation of the Cincinnati Art Museum Association, Mr. Joseph Longworth, alarmed at the appearance of politics in the
management of the University, announced that he was unwilling to give
further support to the School of Design. He let it be known that if the
control and management of the Art School of the University and the
property held in trust for its maintenance passed from the Board of Directors of the University to the trustees of the Art Museum Association,
he would give the latter Association a large contribution to establish a
thoroughly equipped art school. He wanted to make the Art Museum the
center and controlling force in the field of art in the City. Unfortunately
he died before he was able to accomplish his purpose. His son, Judge
Nicholas Longworth, determined to carry out, if possible, the wishes of
his father.

Accordingly on January 19, 1884, Judge Nicholas Longworth addressed
a communication to the City of Cincinnati and the Board of Directors of
the University offering to purchase the entire trust property held by the
City and in turn convey to the City certain property he held; provided
an arrangement was made with the Board of Directors of the University
to transfer the control and management of the School of Design to the
trustees of the Cincinnati Art Museum.

The Board of Directors of the University referred this proposition to a
special committee for consideration. The great objection to the transfer
of the School of Design was the want of authority to sell and invest certain property held in trust for the maintenance of an art school. This legal
obstacle was removed by the passage of an act by the General Assembly
of Ohio on January 30, 1884, which authorized and empowered the City
of Cincinnati and the Board of Directors of the University of Cincinnati
"to sell and invest certain property held in trust for the maintenance of
the Art School of Cincinnati and to transfer the control and management
of the said Art School and the property held in trust for the same to the
trustees of the Cincinnati Art Museum."

At a special meeting of the Board of the University the special committee reported that they "deemed it for the best interest of the Art
School of Cincinnati to accept the proposition of Mr. Nicholas Longworth." This report was unanimously adopted by the Board; and on
February 1, 1884, the control and management of the School of Design
was transferred to the trustees of the Art Museum.

In view of the fact that the University had been unable to get other educational trust funds to consolidate with the University, the Board apparently deemed it advisable publicly to justify their action. The Board maintained that it was "animated by no other purpose" in the action than "the public good." They said they realized that "the trust for the purpose of higher education did not necessarily comprehend a School of Design" and they felt "no selfish ambition should stand in the way of a concentration of all funds in the City devoted to art purposes." The Board said that they had "no other motive than that art education should be promoted, and that the generous spirit of Judge Nicholas Longworth should be met by a like public spirit in affording the best advantages which could come from munificent private donations in the further development of an Art School." It was certainly an act of great unselfishness on the part of the Directors of the University to yield the control of the Art School to the trustees of the Art Museum Association in order to assure the future welfare of art in the City.

PROBLEM OF READING THE BIBLE IN THE UNIVERSITY

Another problem that caused considerable trouble to the Board and later to the Rector, was the specific provision in the McMicken will which directed that "the Holy Protestant version as contained in the Old and New Testament should be used in the said colleges" to be created by his bequest. Early in April of 1876 the Board directed the Committee on the University to investigate this matter and report to them the best mode of carrying out this directive. The Committee referred the question to the Academic Committee which sought the views of the Faculty on the subject. The Academic Committee reported that in their opinion the University should give regular instruction in the Bible; but that it should be limited to the reading and exposition of the scriptures; should be given on a voluntary basis and at such times as would permit all who desired to attend. They explicitly declared that such reading and exposition and such Biblical instruction should be for the purpose of informing the student concerning the fundamental religious and moral duties which the Bible taught, but should "not enter into a discussion of the questions of the authority or inspiration or doctrines theologically so-called." The purpose of this religious instruction should be confined to satisfy the letter and spirit of the McMicken will which called for the use of the Protestant version as a book of instruction in the universal principles of morality and religion.

It will be recalled that at this time there was much discussion concerning religious exercises in the Cincinnati public schools. The courts had decided that this was unconstitutional as infringing upon the rights of a large class of citizens, and so the reading of the Bible was excluded from the Cincinnati public schools.

Mr. Vickers offered a resolution in the Committee that it was inexpedient for the University to take any action on the matter. His views were accepted by the majority of the Committee. On June 19, 1876, therefore, the committee reported to the Board of Directors that it was not expedient to take any action on this subject at that time. After this report was sent, Mr. McGuffey and Dr. Comegys from the same Committee presented a minority report. After referring at length to the provisions in the McMicken will that directed that there should be instruction in the Bible, and after pointing out that the University had been in operation for nearly three years without having taken any steps to fulfill this injunction of the will, they recommended that for the coming academic year (1876–1877) there should be given regular instruction in the Bible at least three times every week in the reading and exposition of the scriptures by a member of the Faculty, non-denominational in character, on a purely voluntary basis, and at such times as all who desired to attend could do so. In other words their recommendations specified the precise terms that the Faculty had previously submitted to the Committee. As soon as the majority and minority reports were read Mr. Vickers moved to postpone consideration of the matter until the regular meeting of the Board in October. The consequence was that the whole question was referred by the Board to its Committee on Law.

This temporarily quieted the discussion of the matter until in April 1877, on motion of Mr. McGuffey, the Committee on Law was instructed to report on the subject at the next meeting of the Board. It was not, however, until February 25, 1878, that the Committee on Law reported that "instruction in the Bible, not of a sectarian character, be given in the University at least once a month by one of the professors on a voluntary basis to all students who desired to attend." After much discussion this report was laid on the table. In December 1879, nearly two years after the matter had been referred to the Committee on Law, on motion of Mr. King, the resolution was taken from the table and referred to the Committee on the University in order to arrange with the Faculty for systematic instruction in the Bible. At the January 1880 meeting of the Board a plan was submitted by the Faculty to the effect that instruction in the Bible should be assigned to Professors Hart and Benedict. This was referred to the Academic Committee who in turn referred it back to the Board where it was filed. In November 1880, Mr. Vickers reported to the Board that the Faculty had set aside half an hour on Thursday of each week for Bible instruction. By resolution of the Board the clergymen of various denominations were requested in turn to give this instruction.

The arrangement of Bible instruction was not very successful, as the clergymen did not respond regularly. On May 13, 1881, the Academic Faculty proposed that Professor Benedict be assigned the duty of teaching the Bible. This was submitted to the Board and was approved by them.

Accordingly, the Rector and the Faculty proceeded to carry out this plan. It proved very successful. Professor Benedict gave expository lectures on the scriptures which were well attended by the students of all religious faiths in the University. Later Mr. Vickers was blamed for the long delay in carrying out the directive of the McMicken will. It was later claimed by his opponents that the Rector in fact had blocked for four or five years the fulfillment of Mr. McMicken's last testament. On the other hand it is quite evident that the Board was reluctant to deal at all with this question.

THE OBSERVATORY

The principal work of the Observatory continued to be the observation and measurement of the southern double stars and the preparation of a catalogue of these stars. The reason the Observatory selected this field for investigation was the small number of southern observations. The system of supplying standard time under the control of the City Council was perfected and found to be of great convenience to the general public. In 1880, Mr. John Kilgour brought suit against the University alleging that the Board of Directors was using a portion of the funds received by them from taxation for the establishment and maintenance of the Observatory to pay a portion of the salaries of the Rector and Professor Eddy. The case came before Judge Jacob Burnet of the Common Pleas Court. The Court refused to issue an injunction on the ground that the Observatory, the Academic Department, and the School of Design were all parts of a single institution and, therefore, there was no division of the funds. The following year Professor Ormond Stone resigned his position as astronomer to accept a similar position at the University of Virginia. Mr. H. C. Wilson was appointed temporary astronomer, and for a time the entire force of the Observatory consisted of him and the janitor. In June 1844, Mr. Jermain G. Porter, who had been an assistant in the United States Coast Survey, was appointed astronomer in charge of the Observatory at a salary of $2,500 a year, and Mr. H. C. Wilson, as his assistant, at a salary of $1,000 a year. The new astronomer offered his services to the Board of Directors for a course of lectures on descriptive astronomy in order to make the Observatory a real educational force in the community. This offer was accepted.

STUDENT ACTIVITIES

So far in the history of the University there had been no evidence of any student activities or college spirit. Within the space of two years (1880 and 1881), however, there appeared on the campus a literary and an art society, the publication of a student paper, and the formation of the first college fraternity. There were also rumors during these years of the need for the University to have a football team, a boat club, glee club, college songs and cheers, and a gymnasium. The classes of 1879 and 1880 revealed more enterprise and college spirit than had any of the previous classes. In fact, some of the students grew alarmed at "the remarkable growth" of student organizations. They thought their class-mates should aim "at higher literary efforts in their societies, at better articles, and a larger subscription list for the college paper" than to try to do so many things at once. They felt that the University should work its way up "slowly, patiently, and securely," and not immediately try to emulate all the first-rank colleges in all their activities.

During the first two or three years of the existence of the Academic Department of the University attempts were made to establish a literary society, but owing to the small number of students likely to take an active part in such an organization, the project was soon abandoned. With the rapid growth of the institution, however, during the succeeding years there was an increasing demand for the organization of a literary society. At the beginning of the year 1880 active steps were taken towards the practical realization of this proposal. The support came mainly from the students in the Academic Department, but great interest was also shown among the students in the School of Design. Accordingly, in February 1880, the McMicken Literary Society was formed with F. O. March as its first President. Students in all departments of the University were eligible for membership in this Society. The McMicken Literary Society had a successful career for some seven or eight years when it peacefully "went out of existence." In its day some of the ablest students in the University were members of this organization.

In the same month that the McMicken Literary Society was organized, an art society, the McMicken Art Association, was formed with C. L. Sargent as its first President. This organization drew its members mainly from the School of Design, although students of all departments of the University were eligible for membership.

On February 10, 1880, the first issue of a student journal, *The Bela-trasco*, appeared. It was published by Peter G. Thomson, measured nine by twelve inches, and contained ten pages of reading material. There were nine members on the editorial board; five chosen from the Academic Department; three from the School of Design; and one from the Observa-tory. It was intended to represent the work accomplished in the various departments of the University; the illustrations were supplied by the students of the School of Design. The first editor-in-chief was Edward N. Clingman of the Academic Department. After the Board had published five numbers the management of the paper was transferred to Max Senior of the Academic Department. *The Belatrasco* was a monthly publication and sold for $1.50 per year or fifteen cents a single copy. It contained articles of a literary, scientific, and artistic nature with one page devoted to local campus news items and exchanges from other college papers.

The last issue of *The Belatrasco*, in January 1881, quoted the sentiment of the following extract from an article on "College Journalism" which appeared originally in a current number in *Scribner's Monthly*. As they said it supported admirably the position which *The Belatrasco* had taken:

The purposes which the college paper accomplishes in American college life are numerous and important. It is, in the first place, *a mirror of undergraduate sentiment,* and is either scholarly or vulgar, frivolous or dignified, as are the students who edit and publish it. A father, therefore, debating where to educate his son, would get a clearer idea of the type of moral and intellectual character which a college forms in her students *from a year's file of their fortnightly paper, than from her annual catalogue or the private letters of her professors.* To the college officers, also, it is an indication of the pulse of college opinion. The discussion of all questions regarding the varied interests of the college—the dissatisfaction with Professor A——'s method of conducting recitations, or with the librarian's new code, or with the advance in the annual price of college rooms—is sure to voice itself in the college paper. Indeed, the spirit of rebellion among college men often flows out in ink when, if they had no paper in which to relate their grievances, it would—as it now too often does—manifest itself in boyish mobs and "gunpowder plots!" The college journal is, indeed, as a distinguished professor recently said of the paper of his college *"the outstanding member of the college faculty."*

In the columns of *The Belatrasco* can be found what the students were thinking about during these years. The editors of the paper criticized severely the lecture system then in vogue at the University and in other colleges. In their estimation the lecture system was "a mistake in conception, faulty in its execution, and pernicious in its results"; and furthermore they held that what its adherents claimed "as its chief advantages" were "in reality its most objectional features." Those who advocated the lecture system asserted it was possible to cover more material speedily. "There is no royal road to knowledge," asserted the editors. "Time and deep earnest application" were necessary in order for anyone to become "master of any subject." The editors held that the recitation method was far superior to the lecture system.

One student wrote to the editors that he did not think the University needed the establishment of a gymnasium. A petition of the students, supported by several members of the Faculty, had brought this matter before the Board of Directors who had referred it to the building committee where it lay dormant. The writer declared the Board had acted properly. The University had no dormitories; all the students lived at some distance from the school; and only came to the University to attend recitations and lectures.

We think [wrote the correspondent] it would be inadvisable to provide something which will induce the students to linger around the building longer than is necessary. Again, there are no baseball clubs, no football clubs, no boating clubs, and no athletic associations of any sort to use the gymnasium as a training ground. If the gymnasium should be established, at first, no doubt, many or nearly all would use it; but in a short time, nearly all would cease using it. Exercising upon the crossbars, raising weights, and other gymnastic devices, may have some novelty at first, but they soon become very dull and tedious, and the gymnasium would only become a place to congregate and while away the time stolen from recitations and study hours; a smoking room, perhaps, or a place that will be a disgrace to the students and all concerned. In addition there is the fact that no matter where located, the undertaking will be expensive. We think the Board will be acting unwisely and spending its money foolishly in establishing a gymnasium.

Why was it that so many students left Cincinnati and went to other colleges, asked another writer? Was it because the Faculty paid so little attention to the students, and the Board showed even greater indifference? The Board was and had always been composed "of men of intelligence, influence, and wealth." Yet, "during my attendance at the University" stated the writer, "I have seen but two Directors during recitation hours; although, as they are all Cincinnati gentlemen, it would be easy for them to drop in occasionally" to see how the University was progressing.

But except when they are reminded that it is their disagreeable duty to attend a Board meeting, it is probable that none of them bestow a thought upon the University or its affairs. Only to get a quorum of the Board is often a matter of extreme difficulty. These gentlemen are not doing their duty. Let them wake up. There are a number of men in the City who could be induced to donate one or two thousand dollars to the University for the founding of scholarships. There are many kindly disposed gentlemen who would advance money to aid poor and deserving students in their struggles for education, if someone would only interest them about it. And we are convinced that with a little extra exertion, money could be raised to complete the University buildings which, as they now stand, are quite inadequate to the needs of even the few students.

Although some of this carping criticism was unjustifiable, it does show that the student body was becoming more vocal and that the editors of *The Belatrasco* kept the columns of the paper open to a full expression of student opinion. *The Belatrasco* was published from February 1880 until January 1881. Then a rival student journal, *The University*, appeared. In March 1881 a new incorporated stock company, The University Press Company, announced the publication of a new monthly to sell for $1.00 a year subscription or single copies at ten cents. The new journal claimed that it would be a "permanent, impartial medium of information and opinion concerning the University of Cincinnati." The new journal hoped "to awaken the sympathy and command the support, not merely of all persons immediately connected with the Unversity of Cincinnati, in its several departments, but also many who are interested in other institutions of learning, both academical and professional, in our City and State, and of some lovers of good literature who have no official relation to any college or school." Only a few issues of this publication are still extant. It is not known by whom it was issued, and it soon ceased to exist.

Three months after the discontinuation of *The Belatrasco,* in April 1881, the McMicken Literary Society started a new journal, *The Academica,* with an editorial board consisting of D. S. Oliver (managing editor), John M. Nichols, Hattie L. Howard, Howard A. Johnston, Joseph Krauskopf, and Nathan Cohn. This was a monthly journal of nine by twelve inches and contained eleven pages of material. The subscription price was $1.50 per year; single copies, fifteen cents. In the second issue of the paper the editor announced: "The college paper is a mirror of the undergraduate sentiment and is a truer index to the true condition of a college than its catalogue or other publications. It is, in brief, *the outstanding member of the college faculty.*" As can be seen, this was a restatement of a quotation from *The Belatrasco* which appeared originally in *Scribner's Monthly.* But in implementing this motto, *The Academica,* created, as disclosed later, a furor in the College.

Another evidence of the growth of college spirit was the establishment of the first college fraternity on the campus. On January 23, 1882, several members of Sigma Chi, which had been founded in 1855 at Miami University, assembled in the parlors of the Gibson House and established the Zeta Psi chapter of Sigma Chi. This is the oldest college fraternity on the campus of the University of Cincinnati.

The Rector's Case

In the July 1881 number of *The Academica* there appeared a long editorial entitled "The Rector's Case." In this article the editors raised the question why it was that the University of Cincinnati was not more prosperous. It was pointed out that the curriculum was "the equal to the best in the country." There was a corps of able and efficient professors. The instruction was free to residents of Cincinnati. The high schools and other preparatory institutions in the City should serve as feeders to the University in the way of furnishing students. Yet the total enrollment during the last term of the past year was about ninety. Fully half of these were "specials," students taking two or more subjects but not working for a regular degree. There were only thirty regular candidates for degrees. The expenditures for the Academic Department the past year had amounted to about $30,000. In other words, it cost about "one thousand dollars per year to educate each student in the University—a rather costly enterprise." Now what was the cause of this state of affairs? The editors answered that it could be traced directly to the head of the institution. They stated that Mr. Vickers, the Rector, was the person "at whose door all blame must be laid." To prove their assertion the editors brought nineteen charges of incompetency against the Rector. In view of the furor created by this protest of the students it is necessary to examine in detail the phraseology of these charges.

1. They charged that Mr. Vickers had procured his election as Rector by indirect and unfair means. In 1876 he had himself elected to the Board while at the time he was librarian of the Public Library. Then he "magnanimously" offered to serve as Rector of the University *without pay.* The Directors readily agreed to this. In 1878 he had himself elected Rector of the University, and, in addition, professor of history, at a salary of $3,500 per year. He still retained his position of librarian "which paid him an equal amount." Because he encountered great opposition in holding both offices, he resigned as librarian and since then had devoted his services exclusively to the University.

2. Having firmly established himself as Rector, his next move was to procure a "henchman" who should be to him "an assistant and helpmate." He found this person in Mr. Emil Kuhn, then a teacher of German in the high school who was "on the verge of dishonorable discharge from his position." Through Mr. Vickers' influence, Mr. Kuhn was appointed professor of Greek. Mr. Kuhn while he remained was "a disgrace and burning shame" to the University. "He lacked all the essentials of a gentleman. Rude and uncouth in manners, his very presence was repulsive and forbidding." His person was "bloated by excessive drinking and frequently in the classroom he experienced great difficulty in maintaining his equilibrium on account of too great indulgence in potations." His treatment of ladies was "simply outrageous, and his remarks often brought the scarlet blush of shame and outraged modesty" to their cheeks. His teaching was a "farce." His recitations were "scenes of hilarity and boisterousness on the part of the students." In addition, every so often he would start on a "grand spree and be absent from his place for days." Mr. Vickers was fully cognizant of these facts, "but never reported them to the Board of Directors" as was his duty. Last March Mr. Kuhn was arrested "for disorderly conduct and was roughly treated by the police." Even then Mr. Vickers did not report him, and the first the Board of Directors heard of it was that "some of the students reported

the matter to the *Cincinnati Gazette* and sent marked copies of the account to the Board." Yet Mr. Vickers' influence was "so great" that the Board instead of dismissing Mr. Kuhn accepted his resignation "with censure."

3. Mr. Vickers' reputation "as a German infidel and as a scoffer at things religious" in the community was such that parents did not want to send their children to the University. The editors declared they knew several students last year who went to eastern colleges "on this account alone."

4. Mr. Vickers was "unpopular" with the teachers in the high schools; consequently, they discouraged "graduates of these schools" from attending the University.

5. Mr. Vickers was a "politician and degraded the College in the eyes of the citizens." He was often seen in the company of ward politicians "in a saloon" setting them up for the boys. He spent his time in the manner which should have been devoted to preparation for the classroom.

6. He was "universally disliked among the students." The students once took a vote as to whether Mr. Vickers should be retained. The result was an overwhelming "No." The editors then gave a few reasons for this unpopularity.

7. The way Mr. Vickers handled the students' former paper, *The Belatrasco:* Mr. Vickers helped start the paper, but then he got Mr. Peter G. Thomson who published it to submit the proof of all articles to the Rector before publication. Although the editors said they could not definitely prove this assertion, it was probably true "from the fact that when two articles, somewhat caustic in their remarks about the College and Mr. Vickers, were handed to the printer for publication, Mr. Thomson informed the managing editor that they could not appear in the paper."

8. Mr. Vickers' conduct with regard to *The Academica* was somewhat similar. To the great surprise of the students Mr. Thomson suddenly announced in the last number of *The Belatrasco* the publication of a new student paper, *The University,* which he said would be the official organ of the student body. The students indignantly denied this and began to publish *The Academica.* Thus the College now issued two college papers: *The Academica,* published, controlled, and edited by the students; and *The University,* which (although it was unknown by whom it was issued) the editors of *The Academica* claimed was "edited principally, and certainly controlled, by Mr. Vickers." *The University,* "the official source of information about the College," contained "never a word about Mr. Kuhn's case." Affairs in the College had come to a "pretty pass" when the head of a college felt it "incumbent upon himself to issue a paper in opposition to that of the students."

9. Having started a paper under "inauspicious circumstances," Mr.

Vickers resorted to devious means to procure subscribers for his paper, *The University*. For example Mr. Vickers and Mr. Kuhn took the father of a student to a wine house, and after they had paid for the drinks, the father was induced to become a subscriber to the paper.

10. Another event in connection with the paper occurred just before the last Commencement. The students wanted invitations printed and distributed in order to get a good-sized audience present. For some "mysterious" reason Mr. Vickers opposed an appropriation until it leaked out "that he wanted the program of the Commencement published in *The University*." It is rumored "with how much truth we are not prepared to state" that two members of the committee on the Commencement who voted for the bid "were under the impression that the advertisement was to be in *The Academica*."

11. During the year 1879–1880 an effort was made to establish a Greek letter fraternity at the University. But the petition of the students was rejected by the national convention of the fraternity because of their unwillingness to found "a chapter in a college presided over by such a man as Mr. Vickers."

12. Mr. Vickers has carried on "a system of espionage" among the students and "in this manner he has been able to thwart many of their plans."

13. Mr. Vickers' dealings with the Faculty are unique in their way. He insisted that the rules of the Faculty be observed "except in his own case." For instance he prohibited Professor Benedict to give an examination in his class except at the specified hour; yet he gave an examination in his own class "before the regular time."

14. His treatment of professors who had incurred his displeasure or enmity was "very pronounced." Professor Benedict was a special object of his hatred. "The indignities—nay, open insults—to which Professor Benedict has been subjected are topics of current remark among the students. Professor Benedict is probably the most popular professor among the students." It may be that this fact "only increases Mr. Vickers' dislike." Certain it is that he is always casting "aspersions" upon Professor Benedict, either directly or indirectly, and endeavors in every way to undermine "his popularity among the students." In the formation of his newspaper enterprise Mr. Vickers "did not consult the entire Faculty or ask their cooperation."

15. Mr. Vickers did not regularly meet his classes. The editors listed a schedule of his absences from his class and declared that in one class he was away or excused the class "more than one-third of the time."

16. They cited instances where Mr. Vickers "had passed and graduated students, favorites of his, who had failed to take their examinations."

17. Mr. Vickers was also "very unpopular among the alumni." In fact at the Alumni Banquet this year an effort to condemn his action in regard

to advertising the Commencement in *The University* only failed because the majority thought "the occasion was not a proper one for such action, and not because they were not in favor of condemning him."

18. It was because of Mr. Vickers' character and reputation that the University "had not received a single gift worthy of mention during his Rectorship."

19. In their last point they reverted to Mr. Vickers' alleged hostility toward Professor Benedict. They recounted an involved story in which they said Professor Benedict who was granted a leave of absence at the end of the second term last year on account of sickness, notified his classes that he would examine them next September but promised Mr. Vickers to return in June and examine all his classes. Had Professor Benedict prevaricated to the students? They, subsequently, learned that the Academic Faculty had notified Professor Benedict that his arrangement would be difficult in regard to examining the graduates next year. Professor Benedict had then written to Mr. Vickers and asked if the difficulty would be obviated if he returned in June and examined the *graduating* class then. But he was *"never informed of the action taken by the Committee."* After he left the City, however, he was informed by the Academic Committee that he was expected to forward questions for *all* his classes at the regular time, and that Mr. Vickers would send him instructions when they would be held. But Mr. Vickers mailed him these instructions so as to reach him on June 1, and the examinations began on June 6. As a result Professor Benedict had to rush his questions to the students. "Mr. Vickers later excused himself to the students by saying that he had written to Professor Benedict in ample time; thus casting all the blame on him." In other words Mr. Vickers had "shrewdly" handled the whole affair in a manner calculated to cast odium on Professor Benedict, "especially as in his absence he would be unable to defend his seemingly strange conduct."

Conclusion. Therefore, the editors appealed to the Board of Directors. "What they had said was true." They were not motivated by "any spirit of malice or spite." They had done this "purely and disinterestedly for the sake of the College." Therefore, they "solemnly protested against the retention of Mr. Vickers as head of their Faculty." In the name of the students, alumni, and of all the citizens who had the welfare of the Institution at heart, they requested the Board to remove Mr. Vickers; and in his stead select a man fit to be head of the University.

This article was reprinted in the *Cincinnati Gazette* and the *Cincinnati Commercial.* The day following the publication of the article, Mr. Vickers summoned Mr. Howard A. Johnston, the Literary Editor of the paper to his office. The Rector informed Mr. Johnston that he had sent for him on the supposition that he (Johnston) had had nothing to do with the publication of the article. When Mr. Johnston informed him that his supposition was incorrect, Mr. Vickers altered his manner. He said the article was libelous and that he intended to discipline the editors. In other words the Rector threatened to expel the editors from the University.

As soon as the fall session began Mr. Vickers called a meeting of the Faculty. He directed their attention to the article published in the student paper attacking him and reflecting on the Faculty in order that some action might be taken in the case. Mr. Vickers stated that the board of editors appeared to take upon themselves the full responsibility for the publication and refused to divulge the name of the author of the article in question. In defense of their position the editors had submitted a written statement to the Faculty in which they declared: (1) They knew of no rules governing the actions of the students, or covering any point of discipline; (2) since the University had no dormitories or student quarters, the Faculty had no control over their actions outside of the college buildings; The Academica was edited outside of college hours, and was published, maintained, and controlled by the McMicken Literary Society which was not under the jurisdiction of the Faculty; therefore, they could not see how the Faculty could take any action against them; and (3) the article was published during the summer vacation when the Faculty had no control whatever over their actions; finally (4), they had been informed that they had violated a technicality in presenting their plea directly to the Board of Directors. Technically it seemed all communications to the Board of Directors from the Academic Department should be presented through the Faculty. Since the charges were directed "against a member of the Faculty, even against its presiding officer, they had adopted this method of procedure as the only rational one open to them."

The Faculty adjourned without taking any action, but met the following day to discuss the matter. At this meeting Professor Hart moved that "for the present and until further notice, the Faculty considered it inexpedient to publish a student paper"; and Professor Clarke moved that the Faculty reserve the "right to suspend or expel any student who was adjudged guilty of improper or immoral conduct, of disrespect towards any professor, or of any behavior tending to injure the discipline of the University." Both of these motions, however, were tabled. At the suggestion of Mr. Vickers the Faculty decided to notify the McMicken Literary Society that if it wished to continue to meet in the University building it must obtain permission from the Faculty. In addition the Faculty passed two resolutions which were transmitted to the students. In these resolutions: (1) The Board of Editors of The Academica would be restored to their classes pending action elsewhere only upon condition of apologizing for the publication of the article "as a breach of discipline against the Faculty of the University" and publishing this apology in "at least three daily American papers of the City"; and (2) that this apology be submitted to the Faculty for approval before publication.

After long deliberation there appeared on the editorial page of the October number of *The Academica* a statement signed by all the editors to the effect that they were now "persuaded" that the publication of the article was "improper" and "a grave breach of college discipline." They, therefore, apologized "sincerely" to the authorities of the University for its publication. This apology was accepted by the Faculty; and, in consequence, the editors were restored to their classes. This should have ended the whole affair. The Faculty had compelled the students to acknowledge that they had erred in publishing the article, but in their apology the students had not admitted that their charges were untrue.

The whole question was reopened by the publication in the *Cincinnati Gazette*, six days after the students had apologized, of an article entitled "Vickers and the University at Odds." The next day the Faculty held a meeting at which one of their members called attention to the many inaccurate statements in it. A committee of three was appointed to draw up a statement in behalf of the Faculty with regard to the article in the *Cincinnati Gazette*. This committee submitted a majority and a minority report. The majority report signed by Professors Hart and Eddy said the article was "absurd." It assumed a state of affairs which did not exist. The committee pointed out that the article stated it was Mr. Vickers who had forced the students to apologize; claimed he and the Faculty had no control over the students during vacation periods; held the Rector responsible for the expulsion of the students without a hearing; said the Rector had asked the Faculty not to investigate the truth or falsity of the charges; and that he had said the student apology was inadequate. The committee corrected these misstatements. As a matter of fact it was the Faculty not Mr. Vickers who had demanded the students apologize; both the Faculty and the Rector claimed they had the right to discipline any student during the summer as well as any other time; the Faculty, not Mr. Vickers, had suspended the students without a hearing; the Faculty, not Mr. Vickers, had decided not to investigate the truth or falsity of the charges; and both the Faculty and Mr. Vickers considered the apology inadequate. Professor Benedict for the minority agreed with the majority that many of the statements in the article were incorrect but objected to the strong language of the majority report. The minority resolution was adopted by the Faculty. The Faculty took the blame for many of these actions. The Rector was exonerated of many of the charges. The literary editor of *The Academica* later confessed that he had given the *Cincinnati Gazette* an interview, but that paper had misquoted much of his information.

Mr. Vickers brought the entire issue to a crisis. In a public letter on October 17, 1881, addressed to the editor of the *Cincinnati Commercial*, Mr. Vickers said that a conspiracy had been formed to ruin himself and the University; that he now appealed from accusation to the proof; and that at the meeting of the Board of Directors that evening he intended to ask for the appointment of a committee to investigate all charges that had been made, or that anybody was desirous of making, affecting his position as Rector of the University. He suggested the names of certain parties in the Board of Directors, in the Faculty, in the alumni, in the undergraduate courses, and outside individuals to be questioned regarding the charges brought against him.

Mr. Vickers carried out his promise. At the meeting of the Board of Directors Mr. Vickers read a paper in which he asked that a Committee of Investigation be appointed and suggested a list of persons to be questioned. At the same meeting the Board received a communication from the alumni requesting a thorough investigation. The Board proceeded by ballot to select a committee of five consisting of Alphonso Taft, Samuel F. Hunt, Patrick Mallory, Dr. C. G. Comegys, and Dr. John A. Murphy. Hunt resigned, and Hiram D. Peck was substituted in his place. Taft was chosen Chairman of the Committee on Investigation.

The Committee on Investigation met at the office of the University, northeast corner of Third and Main Streets, and decided to hold meetings secretly, to swear all witnesses to secrecy, and to report the testimony to the Board of Directors through an official stenographer. Then they summoned three of the editors of the college paper and two alumni to appear before them.

On October 21, 1881, the editors and the alumni appeared before the Committee. They declined to testify unless they could first make a preliminary statement to the Committee. They then submitted a paper in which they set forth their terms: (1) The issue before the Committee was whether the retention of Thomas Vickers, as Rector of the University, was beneficial that institution; (2) all meetings of the Committee should be public; (3) they insisted upon having the opening and closing of the case and the right to examine and cross-examine all witnesses; (4) the right to argue the whole case after all the testimony had been closed; (5) they insisted upon the right to employ counsel; and (6) they asked that time be given to them to prepare their case. The Committee refused to accept these terms. They did not think the students should "prescribe the rules of proceeding in the investigation"; nor did they think the Board of Directors had authorized the Committee "to give the control of the investigation into the hands of the editors." The students were, therefore, put in another room and called in separately. At subsequent meetings of the Committee different members of the Faculty were also called in to testify.

While the Committee was carrying on their investigation the students started more trouble. In the December 1881 issue of *The Academica* there appeared two communications to the editors, one signed by "Cave" which criticized some of the professors' methods of asking examination questions; and the other signed "Junior" calling for the organization of the junior class. As a consequence the Faculty notified all the editors of the student paper that they were suspended until September 1882. No editor would be relieved from this suspension unless he could satisfy the Faculty that he was in no way responsible "for the aspersions cast upon the Faculty and its management of the University" in the December issue of the paper. In addition the editors were forbidden "to make any communication or to furnish the cause or occasion for public comment upon this or other measures of the Faculty." If any of the editors wanted to offer any extenuating statements they must appear before the next regular Faculty meeting which would be held on December 16, 1881.

Furthermore, shortly after the editors were suspended, the McMicken Literary Society was notified that the Faculty would *only* consent to the publication of a student paper; provided it contained "no personal reflection and no criticisms upon the government of the University, its courses or methods of instruction" and restricted its contents "to purely literary and scientific topics and items of college news." The editors were also instructed to remove from the paper the statement on the editorial page "referring to the college paper as the outstanding member of the college Faculty."

In accordance with the permission given them the editors appeared before the Faculty on December 16. They had drawn up a written statement setting forth the circumstances which in their judgment exonerated them of responsibility for the article. The Faculty refused to allow the editors to submit the statement and adjourned *sine die* "without giving them any hearing whatever." The editors promptly notified the Board of Directors of their suspension, and at the same time the alumni and the senior class requested the Board to remove the suspension. The day after the editor's appeal to the Board a copy of all the petitions was given to the *Cincinnati Gazette,* and they were reprinted accompanied by some disparaging remarks concerning the Rector.

The three communications from the ex-editors, alumni, and seniors were laid before the Board of Directors in an executive session; and after some consideration, a special meeting was called for January 3, 1882, at which the Faculty were requested to be present. Because of the lack of a quorum of the Board three times, the Faculty did not meet with the Board until January 16. As the matter was discussed in executive session there are no records of what was said; but on the following day, the ex-editors were notified that the matter of their suspension was referred to the Faculty.

In accordance with the order of the Board the Faculty held a meeting, and the following day notified the ex-editors of the action they had taken. The ex-editors were informed they would be given an opportunity to satisfy the Faculty at their January 23 meeting that they were in no way responsible for the aspersion cast upon the Faculty and its management of the University in the December number of *The Academica*. They had been suspended not because of their protest against their former suspension, or for remarks they had made concerning the *University* paper, as these were matters under consideration by the Directors in their investigation; but for "their improper criticism of the Faculty and the University, especially the articles signed "Cave" and "Junior." Furthermore, they should explain "their apparent disobedience for the publication of articles appearing in the *Cincinnati Gazette* and the January *Academica* referring to their suspension," and for neglecting to remove the statement on the editorial page describing the paper 'as the outstanding member of the college faculty.'" Their remarks must be confined strictly to their suspension, and they must appear before the Faculty "separately" and not together. No written statements were permitted.

The ex-editors appeared before the Faculty. They declared they were not responsible for sentiments expressed in communications such as those by "Cave" and "Junior"; but *the articles were true as far as known.* In regard to the publications in the *Gazette,* the editors said "they had been suspended so long," they deemed themselves entirely beyond Faculty control. As to their neglect to remove the objectionable item from the head of the editorial column, their statement was they had received no *official* notice from the McMicken Literary Society that such action was required. After an examination which lasted three hours the Faculty notified the editors, in view of their extenuating statements, their suspension was withdrawn and they were restored to their classes; provided they retired immediately from the editorship of *The Academica*. All the editors complied with these conditions, and the McMicken Literary Society proceeded to elect a new board of editors under the management of Max Senior.

After eight months of careful deliberation the Committee on Investigation finally presented two reports to the University Board. The majority report, signed by Alphonso Taft, Patrick Mallon, and Hiram Peck, exonerated the Rector "of any and all the charges preferred against him." The report declared the charges were "wholly unfounded"; and that the Rector was entitled "to the confidence and support of the Board." There was no evidence that the Rector had been "intoxicated or drank in excess." The majority of the Committee refused to discuss his fitness for the position, as the Commitee had been instructed to investigate only charges of "misconduct or improprieties." "To permit a handful of unreasonable and unreasoning malcontents to drive away a professor or Rector would be a suicidal policy." The minority report, signed by Dr. C. G. Comegys and Dr. John A. Murphy, sharply disagreed with the majority report. It contended that the Committee should have heard the testimony of the students; that Mr. Vickers had electioneered among the Directors to obtain his position; and had sustained Professor Kuhn long after he knew of his delinquencies; that his reputation in the community had kept students from the University; and that he was responsible for a long time in blocking the reading of the Bible in the institution. Mr. Vickers' appointment of such men as Professor Kuhn, and his dealings with the students showed his lack of executive ability. Therefore, the minority recommended that "the office of Rector be abolished and that the Board elect a member of the Faculty to act as Dean of the Academic Department; and that a chair of German Language and Literature be established in connection with the chair of history and that Mr. Vickers be transferred to that post."

The Board, apparently unwilling to take any definite action, referred these reports to a Conference Committee, consisting of John S. Woods (Chairman), Dr. W. W. Dawson, J. B. Peaslee, Louis Ballauf, and William Meirs, to work out a compromise plan. Wishing to further the interests of the University and promote harmony "this committee proposed to vacate the office of Rector and all the professors in the Academic Department and the Board reorganize the Faculty anew." Furthermore, that the Board direct that "all the evidence in the majority and minority reports be destroyed."

On the evening of June 19, 1882, the Board met to consider this report. As it was an executive session all the newspaper reporters, four in number from the *Cincinnati Gazette, Cincinnati Enquirer, Cincinnati Commercial,* and a German paper were excluded. Nevertheless, they heard a good part of the discussion. The *Cincinnati Gazette* reporter later told a wild story of returning to his office and listening to the "lively secret session" over a kind of microphone which he had adroitly placed earlier in the Boardroom. He confessed that some of his account was incorrect. Others said he learned what took place from "two leaky Board members." The reporters of the *Cincinnati Enquirer* and *Cincinnati Commercial* said they climbed a telegraph pole opposite the room in which the Board met and got as much of the discussion as they could over the transom of a window which the Board forgot to close. All the papers agreed in their general account of what occurred; and the *Cincinnati Gazette* acknowledged that the *Cincinnati Enquirer* was more accurate in reporting what different individuals said.

"The meeting got so exciting," reported the *Enquirer,* "that it was difficult to tell for a few minutes whether it was a session of a dignified Board of Directors or a dog fight." After some routine business the Board took up the conference report. Then the discussion became heated. Dr. Dawson was in favor of adopting it. He did not think that by firing the Faculty they would disorganize the University. Such action had been done in the medical colleges which went on all the same. Dr. Murphy who was a rugged, intensely aggressive individual, wanted to know "if Rector Vickers was such a precious piece of humanity that he could not be discussed freely." He turned to Dr. Dawson and "referred him to some antics that some of the medical students had set up" and told how Dr. Dawson "bounced them." Then Dr. Murphy asserted that Mr. Peck had reported a state of affairs at the University that "he knew did not exist." Here Mr. Peck "excitedly jumped up and called Dr. Murphy a d——d liar." Mr. Peck shouted: "Let me at him, and I'll settle him in a minute." He started for Dr. Murphy who cried out: "You keep away from me now." Everything was in confusion. The chair called Mr. Peck to order, and after things had quieted down a little Mr. Peck "got up and apologized to the Board for his conduct."

The Board finally voted on the Conference Report and rejected it by a vote of eight to five. Dr. Comegys then called for a vote on the minority report which also was rejected by a vote of nine to five. A vote was then taken on the majority report which was adopted by a vote of seven to six. The *Cincinnati Gazette* maliciously reported "Vickers Is Not Bounced"; and the next day gave a lurid account of how Mr. Vickers and his friends had celebrated the victory with beer at a saloon "over the Rhine."

The long, bitter contest was over. The Rector's Case had given the University an unenviable notoriety. The reputation of the institution and of all the parties involved had been seriously injured. In their zeal to show that the University was imbued with college spirit, the editors of *The Academica* had misinterpreted "freedom of speech" as "license of speech." Many of their statements against the Rector were based on malice or vague rumors which could not be substantiated, and their arrogant attitude toward the Board and the Faculty did not help their case. The Rector had shown that he lacked tact and executive ability, and whatever usefulness he might have had for his position was impaired by the systematic attacks upon him by his enemies. The Faculty had been too impetuous in exercising their authority. They had suspended the editors twice, then rescinded their actions; but in the end they had compelled the students to submit to their control. The Board of Directors had at times shirked their responsibility or exercised it too late while their rash statements in the midst of heated debate were unbecoming the dignity of their position. The scurrilous comments of the daily press kept igniting the flames of passion.

One significant outcome of the Rector's Case was a change in the method of selecting the Board of Directors of the University. It will be recalled that the original charter of the University had provided that twelve members of the Board were to be chosen by the City; the other six by the Board of Education, with the Mayor ex officio as a member. The Rector's Case had clearly revealed the influence of politics in the appointment of the members by the City Council. Accordingly, in 1881 an amendment to the charter was passed by the General Assembly which provided that twelve members of the Board should be chosen by the Superior Court of Cincinnati, or if no such court existed, by the Common Pleas Court of Hamilton County. Evidently it was thought that appointment by the judiciary might eliminate the political factor. It was not, however, until 1888 that the Superior Court of Cincinnati made their first appointment of members of the Board of Directors.

Two years after the close of the Rector's Case, on April 21, 1884, Mr. Vickers tendered his resignation as Rector of the University and professor of history to the Board of Directors. They accepted it to take effect at the close of the academic year. The executive duties of the office were assigned to Professor H. T. Eddy, the senior member of the Faculty who was appointed Dean of the Faculty and Rector pro tempore.

SUBSEQUENT CAREER OF THOMAS VICKERS

Before his resignation as Rector, Mr. Vickers brought suit in the Common Pleas Court for a divorce against his wife whom he had married in Germany. The hearing was held, but while it was apparent that the union was not a happy one the judge declined to grant the divorce on the ground that there was no evidence upon which a decree could be founded. The Court, however, fixed certain alimony which was to be paid monthly to the wife who had gone with two of her children to Germany to live with her parents.

Soon after this Mr. Vickers left the City and went to Dakota Territory. There he became the editor of a newspaper. He instituted a new suit for a divorce and was granted it. He then returned to Cincinnati where he married Miss Lenora Oppenheimer who had been an assistant in the Cincinnati Public Library and later his private secretary while he was Rector of the University. In 1888 he was elected superintendent of schools at Portsmouth, Ohio, but was dismissed because of a quarrel with a high school class. In 1901 he was elected superintendent of schools in Mansfield, Ohio, but left at the close of the year and joined a firm of cotton exporters at Montgomery, Alabama, where he died on June 7, 1917. After World War II a magazine writer found the two aged daughters of Mr. Vickers living in a German internment camp in the Netherlands.

9   *A Versatile President*

A "university atmosphere" was not easy to come by in the lusty Queen City of the 1880's. Cincinnati had more than 250,000 people as the decade opened and was still growing rapidly. It was not a model of order and dignity in those years. Contemporary accounts confirm that it was a "wide-open town" of gambling and fancy women, of heavy drinking, and flourishing crime. Nine murders in nine days set a new record at one stage in 1883. And of fifty murderers apprehended in a longer period, only four were convicted and sentenced to death. The citizens were outraged and doubly so when, as occasionally happened, the murderers had the gall to sell the bodies of their victims to the Medical College of Ohio at the going rate of $15.00 a body.

An Ohio River flood early in 1884 was a further unsettling influence. It damaged thousands of Cincinnati homes and destroyed hundreds of business houses. Public anger over the crime rate and the ineffectual work of the police and courts continued to mount, leading finally to the courthouse riots of February 28–30—three days of terror and violence as mobs attacked the courthouse and militiamen from various Ohio counties fired on the crowds. The toll exceeded 50 dead and 300 wounded.

In the wake of such grisly events and in a community so stamped by disorder, it was perhaps appropriate that the next executive officer of the University should be a general and former governor.

At its meeting on March 16, 1885, the Board of Directors formally considered the matter of the election of a new President of the University. They unanimously agreed that a President of the University should be elected at the earliest possible date at a salary of $3,000 a year. The Board Committee of the Academic Department was directed to make nominations. A month later, on April 13, the Committee submitted the name of ex-Governor Jacob D. Cox for the position. Governor Cox had already previously signified his willingness to accept the office. The Board unanimously approved the recommendation of the Committee. The selection of Governor Cox as President of the University received the cordial approval of the entire Faculty. The Dean of the Academic Faculty, Professor Eddy, continued as the executive head of the institution until Governor Cox assumed his office on April 15 with the understanding that Cox should continue his connection with the Law School of the Cincinnati College as Dean and professor.

THE NEW PRESIDENT

Jacob Dolson Cox was born on October 21, 1828, in Montreal, Canada, where his father, a well-known New York building contractor, was engaged in the construction of the roof of the Church of Notre Dame. He was the son of Jacob Dolson Cox and Thedia (Thedia Redelia Kenyon) Cox. His father was born in New York City of Hanoverian descent. His mother was a lineal descendant of Elder William Brewster of Plymouth, Massachusetts. The family returned to New York City shortly after the boy's birth. The family suffered financial reverses during the Panic of 1837 which somewhat impaired his early education. Young Cox attended a private school for a few terms and, as he aspired to a lawyer's career, at the age of fourteen he became a clerk in a law office. Then he entered the office of a Wall Street broker as a bookkeeper and accountant in order to become versed in business forms and methods.

For a time Cox thought of going to sea, but his plans were changed in the winter of 1842 by the arrival of the Reverend Samuel D. Cochran, a graduate of Oberlin College and Theological Seminary, who came to New York City and arranged a series of revival meetings at Niblo's Gardens in which he was assisted by the Reverend Charles G. Finney, at that time professor of theology at Oberlin College. Cox, his mother, and oldest sister were converted and joined the church. Under the influence of Reverend Mr. Cochran and Mrs. Cox, young Cox resolved to study for the ministry, and for two years he spent all his leisure time in preparing for college. The Reverend Mr. Cochran guided him in his studies, and he was tutored in part by a Columbia University student. In the spring of 1846, Cox started for Oberlin, Ohio, to enter college.

As his preparation was incomplete, Cox studied a year with the senior preparatory class, entering Oberlin College in the fall of 1847 and graduating in 1851. He earned part of his college expenses by baking bread at the college boardinghouse, and during one year taught algebra at eighteen cents per hour.

While still an undergraduate Cox married Helen C. Finney, the eldest daughter of Reverend Mr. Finney, who was then President of the College. At nineteen, a widow with a small son, she had returned to her father's house. Cox married Helen on Thanksgiving Day (1849) and moved into his father-in-law's house while President Finney made a preaching tour of England. Cox began the study of theology, but when President Finney returned from his tour he and Cox differed on certain theological doctrines. Cox decided to leave Oberlin but always remained loyal to the College. From 1876 to 1900 he was a trustee of the institution. After leaving Oberlin, Cox served for two years as superintendent of schools in Warren, Ohio; resumed his study of law; and in 1853 was admitted to the bar.

His Oberlin experience, his marriage, and other influences combined to make him anti-slavery in his sentiments. In 1855 he was a delegate to the convention at Columbus which organized the Republican Party in Ohio, and four years later he reluctantly accepted the nomination of the party and was elected to the Ohio Senate. There Cox joined James Monroe, an Oberlin friend, and James A. Garfield to form the "Radical Triumvirate," a potent force which, together with his friend William Dennison, later Governor of the State, helped shape legislation on the eve of the Civil War. In 1860, Cox was appointed brigadier general of the Ohio militia, and with Garfield made an intensive study of military science.

When War broke out in 1861, Cox actively entered the Union forces, although he was in poor health, heavily in debt, and the father of six children (he later had two more). He was made brigadier general of the Ohio Volunteers. He was one of the most brilliant of the volunteer officers, serving in the Kanawha Valley campaign, at South Mountain, and later in the Atlanta, Franklin, and Nashville campaigns. In 1864 he was commissioned major general. In later years General Cox became widely known for his military writings, and from 1874 to his death he was the military book critic for *The Nation*. It is held by present-day historians that when Herndon's *Lincoln* was published, "the most controversial Lincoln biography ever written," Jacob D. Cox wrote the "most penetrating review of the book in *The Nation*." In addition to contributions to this and other journals, General Cox wrote several books, including two in the *Campaigns of the Civil War* series.

In 1866, General Cox was elected Governor of Ohio. He served from 1866 to 1868, and then was appointed Secretary of the Interior by President Grant. He broke with the President over Civil Service and served only one year. In 1872 he joined the Liberal Republican Party, and in 1876 was elected to Congress from the Sixth Ohio District by an unprecedented majority. After one term in Congress he abandoned politics. Cox became a member of the Faculty of the Cincinnati Law School in 1868, but shortly thereafter he was called to the cabinet of President Grant. For seventeen years (1880–1897) he was Dean of the Cincinnati Law School and from 1885 to 1889 he was also President of the University.

112   THE UNIVERSITY OF CINCINNATI

Cox was a tall, graceful, well-proportioned man, with erect military poise, a man of great integrity, recognized as an elegant and forcible speaker and writer, a skilled and effective administrator as President of the University and Dean of the Cincinnati Law School, an able field general, and one of the foremost military historians of the country.

In his letter accepting the Presidency, Governor Cox set forth his reasons why he had taken the position and what he hoped to accomplish He said he hoped to be of some real use to the cause of liberal education in Cincinnati. For the University to be of real service to the community three conditions must be fulfilled:

It must have the complete confidence of all intelligent friends of higher education as to the thoroughness of its instruction, the wisdom of the selection of its several courses of study, and their adaptation to the discipline and developmental power in different directions. Next, there must be no room for question as to the high moral tone of the whole institution and the elevating character of all its influences upon its students, as well in the personal characteristics of the Faculty as in the high aims and methods of the instruction given. Lastly, it must add to this confidence the warm affection and pride of all of our citizens.

In his inaugural address delivered at his first Commencement, President Cox elaborated on some of these ideas and showed his breadth of view. He chose as his subject: "A Liberal Education; its object, scope, and value." In his remarks he stressed the importance of a university education and the value of a liberal education. "The treasures of wisdom and of art," he said, "are wealth of which no financial panic bankrupts us, which does not clog in the using, nor waste in sharing with others. For this intrinsic value and imperishable delight they are really worth our search, and are the most precious boon we can confer on our children. For itself, therefore, and not merely as a means to an end, I would urge the desirability and worth of a truly liberal education."

On November 7, 1885, a fire was discovered in one of the chemical laboratories of the newly completed University building on the Mc-Micken homestead. Only the most strenuous exertions of the fire department prevented the destruction of the whole building. The damage to the University made it necessary to provide for some temporary rooms in which the class recitations and lectures could be held. The Reverend Dr. Isaac M. Wise, President of the Hebrew Union College and a Director of the University, graciously offered the services of the Hebrew Union College building as temporary quarters for the University. This generous hospitality was gratefully accepted, and instruction in every department in the University proceeded without interruption. By the following February the repairs had so far progressed that the University was again occupied. The Hebrew Union College declined to accept any compensation for the occupancy of their building. The fire made it pos-

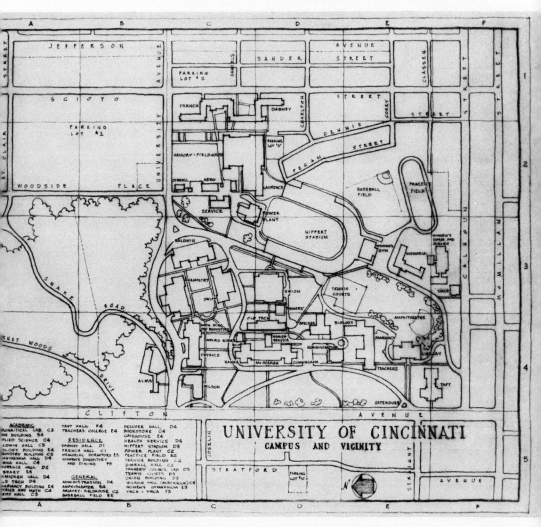

Map of Buildings of the University of Cincinnati, 1962

The University Buildings
1900

Original University of
Cincinnati Building

The Evening Co
in Operation

The second home of the University of Cincinnati College of Law, on approximate site of present Mercantile Library Building. This building was erected sometime after 1845 and was destroyed by fire in 1869.

Cincinnati College Building—erected 1816, destroyed by fire, 1844

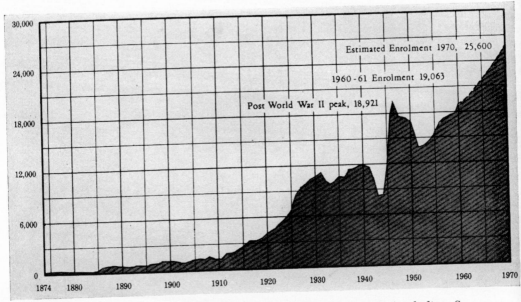

Annual Enrollment at the University of Cincinnati since 1874 (excluding Summer School)

Charles McMicken, 1782–1858

Daniel Drake, Dean of the College of Medicine,
1819–1822

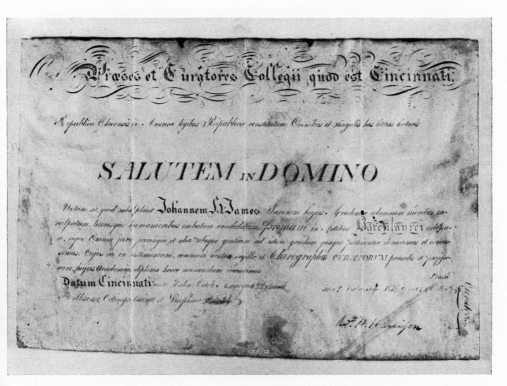

First Diploma Issued by Cincinnati College to John H. James

Medical College of Ohio, 1827

Timothy Walker, Dean of the College of Law, 1839–1844

Ormsby MacKnight Mitchel, Director of the Observatory, 1843–1859

Professor O. M. Mitchel. Cincinnati, Ohio.

Quincy, Mass 3. Oct 1843.

My dear Sir

I had made some arrangements for the distribution of my time, with a view to reach Cincinnati between the 10th and 15th of next month; but on receiving your letter and that of judge Burnet of the 6th ult. I have been and am endeavouring to accommodate my days and hours to your convenience.

I propose to leave my home on the 25th of this month — allowing myself 13 days to arrive at Cincinnati by the way of Buffalo, Ashtabula and Cleveland. If some unforeseen accident should detain me beyond the 6th you will ascribe it to any cause other than my will. If a spark of your enthusiasm for the cause of Science, and the honour of our Country, burns in my bosom, it shall live until the corner stone of your observatory shall have been laid, nor shall it be delayed an hour by any neglect, indolence or indifference of mine.

I am with great respect, Dear Sir

your friend and servt

John Quincy Adams.

Letter from John Quincy Adams to Dr. Mitchel, October 3, 1843

Rufus King, First Chairman
of the Board of Directors,
1872–1876

William Howard Taft,
Dean of the College of Law,
1897–1900

sible to make some improvements in the arrangements of the building and also raised the question of the suitability of the McMicken homestead as the permanent home of the University. Rector Vickers in his last report had called attention to this subject and had recommended it to the careful consideration of the Board.

ATTEMPT TO CONSOLIDATE EDUCATIONAL ENTERPRISES

One of the first moves made by President Cox at the beginning of his administration was to attempt to bring about a consolidation of the various trusts of the City with the University. The prior attempt to consolidate the various educational trusts in the early seventies had not been very successful. Probably the reason for the renewal of these efforts of the University for a co-operative affiliation with other schools was in part the growing conviction of the inadequacy of the building and the grounds of the McMicken homestead as the permanent site of the University.

The Board of Directors at their meeting on April 26, 1886, directed the President of the University to inquire into the possibility of forming an alliance of certain educational institutions under the aegis of the University of Cincinnati. Many of the most earnest friends of liberal education in Cincinnati had long felt that under the University charter might properly be collected several other endowed institutions of similar aims. Enough of these existed in Cincinnati to make one strong single organization, each with separate ownership of its trust funds and separate business management.

In accordance with this directive President Cox on May 4, 1886, sent out a circular letter to the constituted authorities of educational institutions in Cincinnati having authority to confer degrees, the question of the feasibility of co-operative union. The practical questions which President Cox submitted to these constituted authorities were: (1) Was such a co-operative union feasible? and (2) if it was, in what form and upon what terms, assuring their separate endowments, property, administration, and responsibility of their trusts would the Trustees and Faculties of these several institutions agree to unite in one University organization? The departments which it was thought could consistently unite in one grand institution of learning were: (1) the Academic Department of the University, (2) the Cincinnati Observatory, (3) the Law School of the Cincinnati College as the Law Department, (4) the Medical College of Ohio, the Miami Medical College, and the Clinical and Pathological School of the Cincinnati Hospital as the Medical Department, (5) the Dental College, (6) the Cincinnati College of Pharmacy, (7) the Public Library, (8) the College of Music, (9) the Art School of the Museum of Art, (10) St. Xavier College, (11) and the classes of the high schools in which courses were adjusted for entrance to the University, to be known as the Preparatory Department.

The progress of the alliance of the other educational trusts with the University was much more successful this time. In 1886 the Clinical and Pathological School of the Cincinnati Hospital formally united with the University. The following year (1887) the Miami Medical College, the Medical College of Ohio, the Cincinnati College of Pharmacy, and the Cincinnati College of Medicine and Surgery became a part of the institution under the terms of the union; and the following year the Ohio College of Dental Surgery, established on January 24, 1845, the second school of its kind in the world, entered the alliance.

The development of the University during the administration of President Cox attested to the increased confidence the general public had in the instruction. He won public confidence in the solid value of the curriculum and the moral and mental tone governing the institution in all its work. He cultivated the relationships of the University with the high schools and the private schools of the City with the result that there existed a more cordial and sympathetic attitude and more confidence in the University among the authorities of these institutions toward the College. This was confirmed in the report of the Superintendent of Schools in Cincinnati in 1888 who thus spoke of the University:

The University has unceasingly gained the confidence not only of the general public, but of that class of our citizens upon whose interest and good will the institution must depend for students. The parents who send their sons and daughters to college are, as a class, wisely solicitous respecting the influences which will surround and permeate their children's college life, and an institution that does not respect their solicitude in this direction will not long hold their confidence nor secure their patronage. The fact that the University is now matriculating from fifty to sixty students each year, largely the graduates of our City high schools, is gratifying evidence of largely increased confidence. A continuance of the present able leadership and wise policy will in the near future reach and win the confidence of college patrons in the entire region of which Cincinnati is the natural educational as well as business center.

CURRICULUM AND FACULTY

The University made steady progress during the administration of President Cox. The decline in enrollment was gradually changed to an increase. During the first year of President Cox's administration the attendance in the Academic Department was 116 as against 86 for the previous year, and by the end of his administration the whole number of students enrolled for degrees was 130.

The curriculum was also improved. On January 16, 1888, the Academic Committee of the Board recommended that different members of the Faculty be assigned the duty of reading the Psalms of the Old Testament on four mornings of each week. Since the Academic Faculty unanimously were of the opinion that religious instruction was impractical, the discussion was postponed for a month when the Board definitely agreed that such religious instruction should be given by different members of the Faculty. On September 21, 1889, the Academic Committee of the Board recommended that history, political economy, English composition and elocution be introduced in all courses and that philosophic studies be introduced into the degree for Bachelor of Science and especially into the civil engineering course. As for the civil engineering course in particular the Committee recommended that the technical studies be eliminated from it as far as possible and philosophic studies be prescribed. The liberalizing of the course in civil engineering was strongly endorsed by the Academic Faculty and adopted. The Academic Department requested the Board to permit certain members of the Faculty to give a six weeks' summer session to teachers and advanced students, but apparently the Board did nothing about this. In order to give the Board more definite information concerning the conduct and regularity of instruction, beginning with the year 1888 all professors submitted as part of the President's report to the Board sub-reports showing the progress of each department in teaching and the work at the Observatory.

New Faculty members were appointed, and the liberal arts courses were considerably expanded. At the beginning of his administration President Cox gave a course of lectures to seniors and juniors on the outline of history and political economy. The Board realized the necessity for a course of lectures in history and political economy and in 1889, when President Cox resigned, Professor Philip Van Ness Myers, President of Belmont College, College Hill, was appointed lecturer in history and political economy and instructor in rhetoric. The next year Professor Myers discontinued his instruction in rhetoric, and thereafter devoted himself to the chair of history and political economy. Professor Myers was widely known for his history textbooks, which had a large circulation in their day. He was a tower of strength to the University of Cincinnati in this era when it was still a small institution.

In 1890, James Morgan Hart, professor of modern languages and literature, tendered his resignation and was elected to the chair of English and rhetoric at Cornell University. The Board filled the chair left vacant by electing Edward Miles Brown, lately acting professor of English literature in Cornell University. The following year (1891) the chair of modern languages and literature was divided, and a chair of English language and literature was created with Professor E. M. Brown in charge and a chair of French and German was created under the direction of Professor Charles F. Seybold. In 1892 the name of the chair of natural sciences was changed to the chair of biology.

STUDENT ACTIVITIES

There was a revival of student activities during this period. A new college paper was established, and the old McMicken Literary Society was rejuvenated. In October 1886 about seventy students organized the McMicken Publishing Company for the purpose of publishing a college paper. They elected a board of editors and a board of directors. When the newly elected managerial board took hold of the late *Academica* they found it had run badly into debt. The board considered various means to erase this debt and continue the publication of the paper. At last they decided that if $200 could be raised within three weeks, the paper would be published. If this was not done, it was to be discontinued. As the requisite amount was not raised, the managers and editors resigned.

Some of the more energetic students who thought the University ought to have an official organ, decided to organize a stock company. The capital stock was to be $500, divided into shares of $5.00 each. All the shares were soon taken, and a meeting was called to adopt a constitution and elect officers. It was at this meeting that the name *McMicken Review,* the successor of *The Academica,* was adopted. The credit for establishing the *Review* was due to Max B. May, who was elected President and manager of the McMicken Publishing Company.

In January 1887 the first number of the *McMicken Review* appeared with an editorial board composed of Martin Wright Sampson, Anna von Kienbusch, Evelyn M. Pritchard, Henry W. Bettmann, Charles Levi, and Louis William Hoffman. The *McMicken Review* was a great improvement over previous student papers. In their first issue the editors stated they would try to make the paper "of interest to the students and an expression of college sentiment." The *McMicken Review* was only reprimanded once by the Faculty. In June 1889 the Faculty disapproved of the articles published in the paper as reflecting upon a department of the University. The editors were reminded of the resolution passed December 6, 1881, whereby the Faculty had only consented to the publication of a student paper provided its contents were restricted "to purely literary and scientific topics and items of college news."

In a communication to the editors of the *Review* the students frequently criticized the local press for neglecting to boost the University to the citizens of the community. The *Commercial Gazette* was criticized for casting reflections upon the caliber of the Faculty and the *Times-Star* for implying that the City was spending too much money on the Institution. The students declared the motto of the City press seemed to be "disparage everything we have at home." As a consequence people of the City only knew there was a University somewhere in the City but knew nothing about the professors or the curriculum. This was one reason for the "humiliating spectacle" of so many Cincinnati young men going to eastern colleges instead of attending the University.

In January 21, 1887, the McMicken Literary Society was revived; and in February 1888 a glee club was organized. In 1885 the first annual of the University, *Al-Munir*, was published. *Al-Munir* was an Arabic word meaning "The Illuminator" and was suggested by Professor William O. Sproull, professor of the Latin languages and literature and of Arabic. It was published by the Zeta Psi chapter of Sigma Chi, the only college fraternity at that time on the campus. It was a small thirty-two page, paperbound annual and summarized the history of the student organizations that existed or had existed up to that time. A second volume never appeared.

Other college fraternities began to be organized as well as the first sororities. On October 22, 1889, Sigma Alpha Epsilon—founded at the University of Alabama, March 5, 1856—organized a local chapter at the University. The first Panhellenic banquet was held on January 2, 1890, at the Gibson Hotel chiefly to welcome Sigma Alpha Epsilon into the Greek world. In the same year (1890) Beta Nu chapter of Beta Theta Pi, which had had a former chapter at the Cincinnati College in 1841, was chartered. In the spring of 1891, V. C. P., the first sorority (a local) founded at the University, was organized; and the next year, on May 23, 1892, the first national sorority, Delta Delta Delta, founded at the University of Boston (1888) organized a chapter on the campus.

In January 1891 the first convocation of the students and Faculty was held. These assemblies met regularly on Friday morning of each week. Essays were read by members of the senior and junior classes at these assemblies. Citizens of the City were invited to attend these meetings, and many of the members of the Board of Directors were present at these exercises and sometimes addressed the students. Dean W. R. Benedict of the University for that year claimed that the innovation was "of great benefit to the University. It has aided to develop a college spirit and has materially helped the members of the senior and junior classes in the matter of public address."

At that time the students fought hard to oust Professor John Moore Leonard, who had occupied the chair of Greek since 1881. The Board of Directors referred to the Academic Committee charges brought against him. They held an investigation but reported that they did not think "they should sit in judgment on a colleague"; and so referred the whole matter back to the Board. The Faculty did say they thought the whole matter could be relieved "only by the voluntary retirement of Professor Leonard or by his vindication after careful investigation." The local press characterized Professor Leonard as "a harmless man who had outlived his usefulness in the task of controlling unruly sophomores." "His strange and pedantic way of talking was not appreciated by the harum-scarum undergraduates." The students and the alumni between them pestered the professor until in June 1890 he resigned because of illness.

The date of the first flag rush is uncertain. There are records, however, of two flag raisings in the month of June 1887. In that month the freshmen (class of 1890) astonished everybody by quickly putting the flag out one morning and without much difficulty keeping it there. A week later the sophomores put theirs out. The freshmen tried all sorts of plans to get it down but without success. On November 16 of the same year the new freshmen (class of 1891) made an unsuccessful attempt to flaunt their flag in the face of the upperclassmen. But the secret was found out, and their flag was burned.

The system of the flag rush did not really begin until three years later, in 1891, in the fight between the class of 1893 and 1894. On Saturday, April 11, 1891, the freshmen of the class of 1894 took advantage of the University buildings being open and the absence of the sophomores to run their class flag up on the University flagpole on the top of the building. All the doors leading from the chemical laboratory to the roof were carefully locked and guarded; and the freshmen dispersed, certain that their flag would be safe until Monday at least. But the flag was spied by some wandering sophomores, and one of them climbed out a narrow window looking out from the laboratory and hauled down the freshman flag.

The sophomores soaked the freshman flag with alcohol and were about to burn it with appropriate ceremonies when, suddenly, during the second hour on Monday morning, the freshmen burst from their recitation rooms, leaving the professors alone in their glory, not knowing what was the cause of the uproar. The freshmen bore down on the sophomores, seized their flag, and rushed madly down the hall to Moerlein's Brewery before they were overtaken. Here the battle was renewed in the presence of a large number of spectators attracted to the scene, but the flag was never recovered by the sophomores. The students held "the freshman flag was good advertisement for the University."

The flag rush was to see its greatest development in the succeeding years. The class of 1894 not only won their flag rush as freshmen but also the following year as sophomores. Among the members of the class of 1894 were such leaders of the University as Frank Sanford Brown, Alfred K. Nippert, and Daniel Laurence.

ATHLETICS

The spring of 1885 witnessed a sudden outburst of enthusiasm for athletics. The clamor for a gymnasium became louder but remained unheeded. A pair of boxing gloves and fencing foils made their appearance in the basement. The Dean put a stop to boxing and fencing. His ruling was arbitrary and unpopular, but it was obeyed.

It is hard to realize all the difficulties that confronted those interested in developing college sports. The classes were so small it was hard to organize teams. The class of 1888 that entered as freshmen in 1884 numbered ten members, and one of these was a girl. The total attendance at the University was less than sixty. Some of the students were indifferent to athletics; a few were hostile. The same was true of the Faculty, some indifferent, some hostile. The players had to supply their own uniforms and prepare the grounds for the games. Yet within four years the University had a baseball and football team, a field day for sports, and had begun the organization of an athletic association.

The first sport was baseball. In May 1884 a University baseball team played Hughes High School and was defeated by a score of 7 to 4. No two members of the University team were dressed alike. A second game played in October against Woodward High School resulted in a score of 14 to 3 in favor of the University. In May of the following year (1885) the freshmen and sophomores played a baseball game. This was probably the first intramural contest of the University. After the third inning, with the score tied 5 to 5, both teams lost interest, and the match was called off.

In March of that year, a Student's League of Baseball Clubs was organized composed at first of teams from the University, Hughes High School, and Covington and Newport High Schools of Kentucky; later the "Riversides," a crack, well-known team was admitted. It was due to the enthusiasm of H. W. Singer that this League was organized; and with money that was never repaid, the University team played in regular uniforms, white and blue. Each club in the League was "to play four games with every other club." The title "Champion" was to be given the club which should win the greatest number of games, and a pennant costing $10.00 was to be the trophy. The expenses of the League were paid by an appropriation of $5.00 by each club. Each club was required to furnish suitable grounds for its "home games" and had exclusive jurisdiction over admission fees and other details on its home grounds. The games were to be of only seven innings, owing to the distance to be traveled by the visiting team. During April 1885 the University played four games, won 3 and lost 1. During May the team went to pieces. Five of the nine members were laid up with injuries. As a result the University lost four games. This ended the existence of the Varsity team for the spring of 1885.

In 1886 the University played three games. On May 1 the University challenged Miami College, went to Oxford at their own expense, and came home victorious, winning by a score of 14 to 5. To accomplish this feat the University had to borrow a battery from a local club, and the victory was partly due to them. A return game played by Miami in Cincinnati was also won by the University by a score of 16 to 12. The University was defeated by the Riversides by a score of 4 to 2.

In 1887 the University played one game on April 15. The University, without an error, on a windy, rainy day, beat Woodward High School by a score of 19 to 4. In 1888 little was done. The team went to Hamilton and was beaten by a score of 19 to 18. Two scrub games were played with the Medical College of Ohio, the University winning the first, losing the second. On May 5 the University was beaten by the Carriage Manufacturers' Club by a score of 23 to 1.

In five years the University played eighteen games. Nine were won, and nine were lost. The football record of the University was much better. In the four years (1885–1888) the University played seven games. The record was five victories, two draws, and no defeats.

The first University football team was organized through the efforts of David Graham Philipps, one of the most popular political novelists of the first decade of the twentieth century engaged in exposing the system of corruption and special privileges, who aroused interest in football in Cincinnati. Since the Cincinnati sporting goods stores did not handle football equipment, Philipps in 1885 sent to New York for a football. The next year when the University was ready to play its first game they found the bladder in the football was no good. A new football had to be secured from New York before the game could be played.

The University played its first football game on October 23, 1885, with a Mount Auburn team. There were just two spectators present, an uncle and a sister of Arch Carson, Captain of the first Cincinnati team. Another member of this team was Henry Wald Bettman. The score of this game was 0 to 0. On November 14, 1885, a cold and rather windy day, a return match was played at the Union Ball Park and was won by the University, 26 to 6. Such was the beginning of the history of football at the University.

In 1886 the University met Mount Auburn again for two games and was victorious in both, the first by a score of 8 to 6; the second 16 to 6. The students paid for the grounds out of their own pockets, whitewashed the fields, and dug holes for the goal posts. In 1887 one game was played. It was against Woodward High School, and the University won by a score of 8 to 4.

In 1888 the University played two games. On Thanksgiving Day it beat the Walnut Hills Gymnasium 8 to 6. On December 8, 1888, the University played its first game against Miami at Oxford. It was also the first collegiate game the University had played. Although Carson had graduated in 1887, he captained the team. The game was played in a drenching rain, and neither team scored. There were "no officials" and the team wore "no uniforms." The boys played in track suits and gym shoes. The timekeeper was a University of Cincinnati student.

The following year (1889) a Varsity team, composed of graduates and outside talent, defeated an Avondale team 12 to 0; but was defeated by Miami, 34 to 0. This was the first defeat the University had known so far in its football history.

According to football star Bettman ('88), Field Day did more to arouse class spirit and to attract the attention of the public than any other single factor had ever done. The project was first broached in 1886, but it failed at first to arouse much interest. In 1887, however, Field Day became an assured fact. A committee of twelve students was placed in charge of making the arrangements. Everyone was urged to subscribe; one dollar the highest contribution, twenty-five cents the lowest. One hundred and ten dollars were collected. The committee secured the grounds, bought hurdles and other implements, and laid out the tennis courts. The Faculty refused to recognize Field Day officially and denied a student request that a holiday be granted. The first Field Day was held on June 3, 1887. There were at least three thousand people in the audience. There were running and jumping contests, tennis (single and doubles), throwing the baseball, a potato race, and a "tug of war." The first Field Day was highly successful; a surplus of $550 was reported by the treasurer of the committee. Two medals were bought and bestowed upon a champion jumper and a champion runner.

In 1889 the Board of Directors broke all precedent by appropriating $50.00 toward the expenses. The Cincinnati Ball Park was secured. Music was supplied by the Cincinnati Orchestra. A large crowd filled the grand stand and the boxes. When college athletics finally began to catch on, it soon gathered momentum. The Field Days gave a decided impetus to athletic sports and class spirit. They united the student body; led to physical training at the University; increased the interest of the Faculty in athletics; attracted students from the high schools; helped boom the University and advertised the institution better than it had ever been before.

Administrative Changes

There were a number of important administrative changes in the personnel of the University at the end of the eighties. In June 1889, Jacob D. Cox retired as President of the University, although he continued as Dean and professor in the Cincinnati Law School. It was known to the Board and the Academic Faculty that Cox accepted the Presidency only as a temporary arrangement. Notwithstanding the fact that the Board and Academic Faculty earnestly requested Cox to withdraw his resignation, he refused to do so by reason of his duties in connection with the Cincinnati Law School. The Board reluctantly was compelled to accept it after paying high tribute to his scholarship and efficiency as an administrator. The Board declared that he had given "character to every department of instruction in the institution"; had elevated "the tone of scholarship and education"; and had won "public confidence" as was witnessed by "the increased number of matriculants" as well as by the increased size of the graduating classes "which were now the largest in the history of the University." This praise was justified, for President Cox had improved the relations of the University with the high schools and private schools of the community and had won the public support of the citizens of the City for the University.

During the two years following the retirement of President Cox there were a number of resignations of Board and Faculty members. On March 17, 1890, Alphonso Taft resigned as a member of the Board of Directors after many years of faithful and valuable service. Three months later Samuel F. Hunt, who had been Chairman of the Board for the past ten years, submitted his resignation due to his election as Judge of the Superior Court of Cincinnati. The Board urged Mr. Hunt to withdraw his resignation "for at least a time" in view of the present "critical period in the history of the University" as "his advice and counsel were greatly needed." The Board tried to convince Mr. Hunt that "several eminent lawyers" had assured them his holding of the office as Judge of the Superior Court of Cincinnati was "in no wise a contravention of the law." But Mr. Hunt was inflexible; he could not be persuaded from his determination to retire from the Board. He, therefore, insisted upon the acceptance of his resignation. The Board reluctantly accepted it after expressing "their high appreciation of his singular fidelity and devotion to the interests of the University and the cause of higher education in the City." At the June Commencement, Mr. Hunt was awarded the honorary degree of Doctor of Laws.

Upon the retirement of President Cox, Professor Henry T. Eddy became executive head of the institution as Dean of the Academic Faculty. On May 26, 1890, he was elected Acting President while continuing as professor of mathematics, engineering, and astronomy. In September of that year Eddy was elected President of Rose Polytechnic Institute, Terra Haute, Indiana, at a salary of $4,500. The Board tried to retain Eddy by electing him President of the University and increasing his salary to $4,000. They were unable to keep him, however, and his resignation was accepted with regret.

At a meeting of the Board upon the retirement of President Eddy it was voted that the senior professor of the Academic Faculty be requested to serve as Dean for one year only to be succeeded by the next senior professor. President Cox had suggested this method of filling the vacancy of the Presidency before his retirement. At that time Dr. James C. Culbertson, editor of the Lancet-Clinic, had said he did not believe any group of professorial minds were ever created or built on a plan for that purpose. The future history of the University was to prove the accuracy of this prophecy.

10

The Cincinnati
Law School

After the resignation of President McGuffey, it will be recalled, the only department of the Cincinnati College that continued to function was the Law School. Attempts were made after the Civil War to unite the Cincinnati College with the University of Cincinnati. On April 13, 1869, before the Act of 1870—providing for the establishment of the University of Cincinnati—was passed, Dr. Comegys on behalf of the trustees of McMicken University invited the Board of Trustees of the Cincinnati College to co-operate in building up "a great institution of learning in the City." The Board of Trustees of the Cincinnati College appointed a committee consisting of Rufus King, Stanley Matthews, John D. Thorpe, and Alexander H. McGuffey to consider and report their opinion on the proposition.

Two years elapsed with no action being taken. To bring the subject definitely before the Board of Trustees of the Cincinnati College, Stanley Matthews on May 18, 1872, introduced a resolution that the funds and property of the Cincinnati College be united with the endowment of the University of Cincinnati, provided that this could legally be effected; and that these funds should be used for the establishment and support of a Department of Law and to aid the Astronomical Observatory at the University. On motion of Mr. King it was ordered that this motion be laid on the table; that it be printed and circulars sent to all members of the Board of Trustees for their consideration; and that at the next meeting of the Board of Trustees the Committee appointed report their opinion upon the legality of the transaction. The subject continued to lie on the table as the Committee seemed unable "to report their opinion upon the questions of law involved."

One of the objections to uniting the two institutions was the fact that the Board of Directors of the University was appointed at that time by the City Council. Some feared that if the union were effected the Board of Trustees of the College in the future would most likely reflect the political character of those by whom "it was created and might not be as free of political influences as it then was." Even the chairs of the professors might be filled "through the influence of the police." This might appear "very far-fetched," but as has already been related previously there was much justification for such accusations during the administration of Rector Vickers. Opponents of unification had no objections to the College aiding the University. They were even willing for the College to pay "the salary of a professor or professors" in the University from year to year provided the College had control of its funds and could be sure that the "right kind of men" were appointed.

Even when President Cox proposed an alliance of various educational trusts, the Cincinnati College declined to affiliate with the University of Cincinnati. A committee of the College consisting of Alexander H. Mc-Guffey, William H. Neff, Howard Sargent, and Jacob Burnet reported that they apprehended any such alliance would be attended with many entangling results which would be disastrous to the institution. In the first place the graduates of the institution would not be graduates of the Cincinnati College but would be under the necessity of taking their degree from the University. Secondly, the independence of the Board of Trustees of the College in all matters relating to its affairs would be "greatly impaired, if not altogether lost." For sixty-seven years the institution had been kept out of "the arena of municipal politics" and had maintained its distinctly "Christian character," and, therefore, the committee respectfully declined the alliance between the University and the College.

Meanwhile the College had made certain changes in the Faculty and curriculum. In 1869, Henry A. Morrill was appointed to the Faculty. Three years later (1872) J. Bryant Walker was added to the staff, and in 1873–1874 served as Dean. The following year Manning F. Force and Clement Bates joined the Faculty.

By 1874 the College was free from "financial embarrassments," had a "good building," and a "steady income." The Board of Trustees, accordingly, decided to reorganize and enlarge the Faculty. Henceforth, one of the Faculty was to be given the definite title of Dean, whose salary should be $3,000 a year. He should devote his entire attention to the Law School "save that he might be allowed to give counsel but not practice in court." A Faculty of philosophy should be established consisting of two lectureships: one called the lectureship of Christian philosophy, and the other the lectureship of Christian jurisprudence. These lectureships should cover all those topics of philosophy, jurisprudence, legislation, and economy which were connected with the fundamental principles of civilized society. Each of the lectures should give a course of not less than twelve lectures, at least one of which should be free to the public; and should receive a salary of $1,000 a year in addition to any fees derived from admission fees as regulated by the trustees. The trustees quoted the statement of Alexis de Tocqueville who had said: "Philosophy has touched America but little." In their estimation, "even that strong common sense" which Bacon called "superior to science" had not saved "numbers of educated men" in America "from being confused by the genius of false philosophy and bewildered 'in wandering mazes lost'." American philosophy was "as much needed" now as once was that American government which had "startled the world" and had freed the American people "from the bondage of ages." For these purposes the trustees held that these lectureships should be created. Furthermore, to aid the Faculties of law and philosophy the trustees appropriated $5,000 annually for the maintenance and increase of a library which should include the best books on law, jurisprudence, legislation, and philosophy.

ADMINISTRATION OF DEAN KING, 1875–1880

In accordance with these actions Rufus King in 1875 was appointed Dean of the School. He succeeded J. Bryant Walker, who was Dean from 1873–1874. King, however, was the first real Dean of the Cincinnati Law School, as he had been the first Chairman of the Board of Directors of the University of Cincinnati.

When Professor King became Dean of the Law School it was still located on the east side of Walnut Street opposite the Gibson Hotel. The Faculty consisted of Professors King, Hoadly, Force, and Morrill. The student body was seated alphabetically according to the initial letter of each surname. Dean King was seated on a raised platform in the lecture room. He taught the law of real property and constitutional law. He was a man of medium height, wore thin gray whiskers, and "a long lock of gray hair which had grown mostly on one side of his head" and was then carried "over the dome of the right side and securely anchored on the other side." The students always called him "the Grand Old Man." After his resignation as Dean, King was retained as professor and remained on the Faculty until his death in 1891. George Hoadly was professor of pleading. As recounted elsewhere Professor Hoadly had a national reputation and was one of the counsels for Samuel J. Tilden in the Hayes-Tilden disputed Presidential election of 1876. Professor Manning F. Force was very precise and dignified and taught the subject of equity. Henry A. Morrill was a careful painstaking lecturer who taught the subject of contracts. At this time the tuition was $60.00 for the first term and $30.00 for the second term. It was estimated that the textbooks cost each student $40.00. Rooms could be obtained at from $2.00 to $4.00 per week;

board varied from $3.25 to $6.00 per week; and fuel and lighting from $10.00 to $20.00 per month. The total cost for each student, depending upon his habits and mode of life, was approximately:

Rent and care of room, $2.00 to $4.00 per week .	$52.00–$104.00
Board, $3.25 to $6.00 per week	$84.50–$156.00
Fuel and lights per month	$10.00–$ 20.00
	$146.50–$280.00

The College prospered during the administration of Dean King. The Faculty was enlarged. In 1875, President James McCosh, President of the College of New Jersey, was appointed lecturer on Christian philosophy, and Martin B. Adams, President of Rochester University, was appointed lecturer on Christian jurisprudence. The following year Noah Porter, President of Yale University, lectured on Christian philosophy, and James B. Angel, President of the University of Michigan, lectured on Christian jurisprudence. As conditions grew worse following the Panic of 1873, these lectureships were suspended in 1877. The following year with improved economic conditions, John W. Stevenson was added to the regular Faculty.

Under Dean King the curriculum was extended. No particular course of previous study, academic or legal, nor any examination, nor any license to practice law was required for admission to the School. Students were advised but not required before entering the College to read Walker's *Introduction to Law*, Blackstone's *Commentaries*, and Kent's *Commentaries*, under the supervision of some competent practicing lawyer. On the first three days of the term the professors gave an outline of the course of study. The classes were regularly and daily examined on the prescribed reading and on the lectures. The student was expected to take careful notes of the cases discussed by the lecturers and be ready at the next session to be able to apply his knowledge to any hypothetical case the examiner might put to him. The juniors had courses on the institutes of law and elementary law, contracts, mercantile law, and law of real property. The seniors had courses in pleading and civil procedure; evidence, equity jurisprudence, torts, law of real property; constitutional law, criminal law, and wills and administration. Moot courts were held weekly. Attendance at these courts was compulsory for seniors, optional for juniors. These courts were presided over by the professors in the term, and members of the senior class were appointed to act as counsel. At each of the moot courts students were required to prepare and read essays on topics previously assigned.

In 1877, Julius Dexter, one of the trustees of the College, established two prizes of $75.00 to those who passed the best oral examination, and a prize of $75.00 for the best essay on the "relations of law and equity and the province of each." An additional prize of $25.00 was given either for the best examination or the best essay as determined by the Committee of the Bar appointed by the District Court. In 1891, Frank F. Dinsmore, who later became one of the distinguished members of the Board of Directors of the University, passed the best examination and was awarded the first prize. The annual provision for these prizes was continued by Mr. Dexter until 1881, when the temporary arrangement by him was assumed by the Board of Trustees of the College.

In May 1878 an alumni association of the Law School was organized. Charles Drake was elected the first President.

Rufus King had a hereditary interest in the Law School, for his father, Edward King, was one of its founders. This interest Rufus King manifested, not only by his earnest and able work as professor and as Dean, but when he died in 1891 he left a bequest amounting to $25,000 in real estate and cash, the income of which was to be devoted to the professorship of constitutional law.

THE ADMINISTRATION OF DEAN JACOB D. COX, 1880–1897

It was reserved, however, to the period comprised by the seventeen years of the administration of Dean Jacob D. Cox for the Law School to attain its highst excellence in the nineteenth century and to make its greatest impression upon the public mind. Cox was not a graduate of any law school; but he had a national reputation as a Civil War veteran, as a military historian, and as an important figure in state and national affairs. Dean Cox enhanced the prestige of the Law School as he did that of the University of Cincinnati of which he was President also during a part of this period. During these years 1,254 young men and women received the degree of Bachelor of Laws. During this period the number of students who annually received the degree of Bachelor of Laws increased from 65 to 106, and the attendance of all classes increased from 120 to 174. The Faculty was enlarged by the addition of George R. Sage in 1886, Chauncey Richards in 1888, and Hiram D. Peck in 1891. The number of lectures was increased and the usefulness of the institution was promoted so that the Cincinnati Law School deservedly achieved "the reputation of being the most thorough and efficient school of law in the West as it already had been recognized as the first school of the kind west of the Alleghenies." Until 1885 there was no other law school in the State of Ohio.

ATTEMPT TO AFFILIATE CINCINNATI LAW SCHOOL AND THE UNIVERSITY OF
CINCINNATI

In November 1891, Judge M. B. Hagan, a member of both the Board
of Directors of the University and of the Trustees of the Cincinnati
College, submitted a request from the Board of Directors of the University for the affiliation of the two institutions. Committees appointed
by each institution held meetings and finally agreed to recommend that
the Law School be united with the University as the Law Department
of the University of Cincinnati. Meanwhile, on April 15, 1892, over the
strong protest of the Cincinnati College, the General Assembly of Ohio
passed an act which set forth that "as the endowment of the Cincinnati
College was then not sufficient to enable it to carry out the purposes of
the original charter in the opinion of the General Assembly," it would be
advantageous "to consolidate the Cincinnati College with the University
of Cincinnati." So Sections 3, 4, and 5 of the act of January 1819 were
amended; and by the terms of the act the affairs of the Cincinnati College were thereafter to be under the management of the Directors of the
University of Cincinnati who were to constitute the Board of Trustees
of the Cincinnati College and were authorized "to exercise all the powers
granted by the law to the Board of Trustees of the Cincinnati College."
Moreover, "the management of the funds and of matters belonging to
or connected with the said Cincinnati College were to be solely in the
hands of the Board of Trustees aforesaid" and the said funds "were to be
used to carry out the objects of the charter of the Cincinnati College."

After the passage of this act the Board of Directors of the University
demanded that the Board of Trustees of the Cincinnati College surrender
to them the books and property of the College. The trustees of the Cincinnati College, however, refused to do so, claiming that the act of the
General Assembly was unconstitutional and void. Thereupon, suit was
brought in the name of the State of Ohio on the relation of the Directors
of the University against the trustees of the Cincinnati College to oust
the latter from the position held by them; and on March 12, 1895, the
Supreme Court of the State of Ohio decided the case of *Ohio ex rel* vs.
Neff declaring the act of the Legislature of April 15, 1892, unconstitutional and void in the following language:

The property of a private eleemosynary corporation, although charged with
the maintenance of a college or other public property, is private property
within the meaning and protection of that clause of Section 19, Article 1 of
the Constitution of this State which declares that "private property shall ever
be held inviolate"; the result of the statute passed April 15, 1892, relating to
the Cincinnati College which in terms gives absolute control and management
of the affairs and property of the Cincinnati College to the Directors of the
University of Cincinnati is to take the property of the former and donate it

to the latter institution. The statute, therefore, conflicts with Section 19 of Article 1 of the Constitution of this State and is void.

Thwarted in its efforts by this court decision to bring the Cincinnati College and the University together, the Board of Directors of the University on May 18, 1896, adopted resolutions providing for the creation and organization of a Law Department within the University itself. It was due largely to the industry and enthusiasm of Alfred B. Benedict, a graduate of the University (1878) and of the Cincinnati Law School (1880) and at that time a member of the Board of Directors of the University and Chairman of the Law Committee of the Board, that the Law Department of the University was established. When his plans matured he found his fellow members of the Board of Directors eager and willing to take the steps essential to the formal organization of the school. By-laws were passed which vested in the Faculty of the Law School complete control of the internal affairs of the School. Since the University did not have the financial resources justifying the payment of adequate salaries to the members of the Law Faculty an agreement was made between the Board of Directors and the Law Faculty by which the Board should pay all the expenses of running the School except the compensation to the members of the Faculty for their work. In lieu of salaries, authority was given to the Faculty to charge an annual tuition fee to each student not exceeding $100, and the income thus secured was to be divided among them as they should agree.

The Law Department of the University of Cincinnati

On June 15, 1896, the Law Department of the University was created and began operations the following October on a self-sustaining basis. The Faculty consisted of six professors of law. It included such prominent leaders of the legal profession of the City as William Howard Taft, who was appointed Dean as well as professor, Judson Harmon, Lawrence Maxwell, Rufus B. Smith, Gustavus H. Wald, and J. D. Brannan. In the conduct of the School the Faculty decided that the wisest course would be to follow, as closely as circumstances would permit, the course and methods of study prevailing at the Harvard Law School. In nearly all the subjects the old methods of instruction by lectures and recitations were discarded and the instructors adopted the "case" system as it was pursued at Harvard. As Dean Taft said, this system of instruction would not only help the students to pass their bar examinations at Columbus, but would also give them "the foundation for a knowledge of the law which would fit them to meet readily the problems that come up in all phases of a legal career." The law course was extended from two to three years, and an arrangement was made with the Academic Faculty whereby a student in that branch was permitted to take five to six hours in the junior and senior years in the Law Department, and such courses were to be credited in the fulfillment for degrees in both of these departments.

Classes in the new school were conducted for a year above Herschede's Jewelry Store on the north side of Fourth Street, between Vine and Walnut Streets. At the same time the old Law School of the Cincinnati College continued to operate in its property on the east side of Walnut Street north of Fourth Street. The two schools were in competition. The new School was handicapped by the lack of prestige. The old School was handicapped by the lack of a university association.

The Union of the Cincinnati Law School and the Law Department of the University of Cincinnati

The establishment of the Law Department of the University speeded up the union of the Cincinnati Law School and the Law Department of the University of Cincinnati. In May 1897, on the initiative of the trustees of the Cincinnati College, a contract was drawn up by which the Cincinnati Law School was affiliated with the Law Department of the University. This contract of union was to continue for a term of ten years at least. By its terms the name of the new School was to be the "Cincinnati Law School." The Board of Directors of the University and the Board of Trustees of the Cincinnati College were to confer degrees jointly on the graduates of the School. The new School was to be financed from the net income derived from the trust property held by the trustees of the Cincinnati College, $1,000 contributed annually by the Board of Directors of the University, and such a sum as might be realized each year from the tuition fees paid by the students. The trustees of the Cincinnati College were to furnish the lecture rooms and the library rooms needed for the Law School, together with the law library they undertook to maintain. By the terms of the contract, the Faculty of the new school was to be made up of the Faculty of the Law Department of the University, together with two members of the Law School of the Cincinnati College, Governor Jacob D. Cox and Professor H. A. Morrill. Governor Cox declined to accept the professorship tendered him, and instead Judge John R. Sayler was elected. The next year (1898) A. B. Benedict and Harlan Cleveland were added to the Faculty as professors and Frank B. James and Charles M. Hepburn as instructors.

By this union the University of Cincinnati was able to offer a thorough legal education to those who desired it. The University also acquired a considerable endowment fund and a law library of good size and value for the use of its Law Department, together with the advantages of the good will and long distinguished history of the Law School of the Cincinnati College. The Law School of the Cincinnati College was enabled to continue its unbroken record of continuous legal instruction of more than half a century.

The union of the two schools was effected without much difficulty under the direction of Dean Taft. The reorganized Law School commenced in October 1897, with an enrollment of 149 students and an increased Faculty. The following June (1898) a class of 46 students was graduated, the first from the newly organized Law Department of the University of Cincinnati.

11

A Turbulent Time
in Medical Education

For two decades after the Civil War both the Medical College of Ohio and the Miami Medical College enjoyed concurrent prosperity. There was keen rivalry during these years between the two institutions; figuratively if not literally, the champions of one college were always ready to knife the others. The bitterness of their competition stimulated both institutions to put forth their best efforts, and in so doing advanced the medical life in the community, but it was also a bad factor in perpetuating factional strife within the medical profession. It ultimately resulted in the disruption of the Academy of Medicine of Cincinnati, the leading medical society in the City, and led to the establishment of a new medical society, the Cincinnati Medical Society.

In February 1865 a group of former members of the Faculty of the Miami Medical College decided to revive the old institution which had ceased to exist during the Civil War after a three-year merger with the Medical College of Ohio. A Faculty was organized in 1865 with three of the original professors—Judkins, Murphy, and Marshall as a nucleus. They were joined by William Clendenin, Elkanah Williams, Chandler B. Chapman, E. B. Stevens, William H. Taylor, B. F. Richardson, H. E. Foote, and William H. Mussey, the son of the distinguished Reuben Diamond Mussey. One hundred and fifty-six students matriculated for the first course to be given by the new Faculty of the Miami Medical College. The home of the new institution was the building of the Ohio Dental College on College Street which was obtained at a rental of $500 a year. Encouraged by the success of their new venture, the Faculty purchased a large lot on Twelfth Street near Plum and proceeded to erect a new building that was formally opened in 1866. The new School under the vigorous leadership of Dr. John A. Murphy grew in professional favor. In 1866 twenty-six graduates received their diplomas; in 1872, sixty-nine.

CINCINNATI, A GREAT MEDICAL CENTER

In the decade after the Civil War, Cincinnati was recognized as an important medical center. There were many advantages here for those who wanted to enter the medical schools. There was the Medical College of Ohio, the Miami Medical College, and the Cincinnati College of Medicine and Surgery, founded by A. H. Baker in 1851 for members of the "regular" profession. In addition, for members of the "irregulars" there was the Pulte Medical College (homeopathic), the Cincinnati Eclectic Institute, and the Physio-Medical College (botanic).

In 1869, Cincinnati erected a new hospital, the name of which by an act of the State Legislature was changed from The Commercial Hospital to "The Cincinnati Hospital." The new Hospital in its day was considered the most complete and well-equipped institution of its kind in the Western Hemisphere, and for many years was one of the greatest architectural attractions in this part of the country. Cincinnati could also boast of other hospitals, such as St. Mary's Hospital located at Betts and Linn Streets, the Good Samaritan Hospital at Sixth and Lock Streets, and the Jewish Hospital at Third and Baum Streets. Then there were two medical societies in Cincinnati, the Academy of Medicine founded in 1857, and the Cincinnati Medical Society organized in 1874 for members of the medical profession.

PERICLEAN AGE OF THE MEDICAL COLLEGE OF OHIO

The two decades after the Civil War formed the Periclean Age of the Medical College of Ohio. It was the Golden Age of both the Medical College of Ohio and the Miami Medical College. Between 1877 and 1886 the Medical College of Ohio had 2,569 students and 871 graduates; in the same period the Miami Medical College had 968 students and 376 graduates.

A number of new men entered the Faculty of the Medical College during the two decades after the Civil War. They were strong individualists who did not develop according to a prescribed pattern but advanced from conventional plans to develop a character of their own. It was this type of man that ushered in the halcyon days of the Medical College of Ohio.

One of those who became a member of the Faculty was James Graham. In 1851, at the age of thirty-two, Graham was appointed a member of the Faculty of the Cincinnati College of Medicine and Surgery. Whittaker told the story that the students in the other medical schools thought Graham's appointment was a joke, and so made up a crowd to give him a reception when he delivered his first lecture. "They went down," says Whittaker, "armed with paper wads and such missiles of juvenile aggression. They came pouring in at his door. Dr. Graham was just at his desk and was stopped by the noise. For a moment he was thoroughly confused; then straightening himself, he begged for a few moments' attention. Forthwith he commenced his subject and, as though stimulated by the opposition, he continued his lecture. He poured out such a stream of simple eloquence as won every heart. Cheer after cheer went up as he closed. The whole class was won."

Graham was a remarkable teacher. He was clear, forcible, logical, but essentially didactic. This made him popular with his classes. They understood him, and what he said they quickly acquired. But it was as a lecturer in clinical medicine that Dr. Graham was pre-eminent. It was at the bedside rather than at the desk that he excelled. "It was indeed a rare privilege," claimed Whittaker, "to hear Dr. Graham lecture on a case of heart disease, so systematically and succinctly could he make a diagnosis, and so clearly and convincingly establish the principles of its treatment." In 1855, Dr. Graham became professor of materia medica and therapeutics in the Medical College of Ohio. Four years later (1859) clinical medicine was added to his chair. In 1864 he became professor of the practice of medicine. He held this chair for ten years when he was appointed emeritus professor. In the opinion of Juettner, "Graham was without a doubt one of the greatest lecturers that has ever stood before a medical class in this country."

In 1874, Roberts Bartholow succeeded Graham as professor of medicine in the Medical College of Ohio. From 1857 to 1864, Bartholow had been in the service of the United States Army. At the close of the Civil War he was appointed to the chair of chemistry in the Medical College, and five years later was transferred to the chair of materia medica. He held this chair for five years; on the retirement of Graham, Bartholow was appointed to the chair of the practice of medicine. Five years later (1879), when he was forty-eight years old and had "the largest and most lucrative practice in Cincinnati," Bartholow was appointed to the chair of materia medica and therapeutics in the Jefferson Medical College of Philadelphia, a position he held for fourteen years.

Bartholow was a born teacher, a prolific author of the first rank, and a daring practitioner. His crowning work, *Materia Medica and Therapeutics,* was for many years the leading textbook on the subject; 60,000 copies were sold. Eight editions of his *Treatise on the Practice of Medicine* were printed, and the work was translated into Japanese. Bartholow was also the first to operate on the human brain, for which he was severely censured by medical journals in this country and in Europe.

Graham and Bartholow joined the Faculty of the Medical College in the sixties; in the next ten years a galaxy of medical leaders became members of the Faculty—William W. Dawson, James T. Whittaker, Chauncey D. Palmer, and Samuel Nickles.

In 1871, William Wirt Dawson succeeded the peerless Blackman as professor of the principles of surgery in the Medical College of Ohio, where he made an international reputation as a lucid and popular lecturer on surgery. Dawson held this chair until 1887 when he was succeeded by Phineas S. Conner, but he continued to lecture on clinical surgery.

Dawson's best work was done as a clinical teacher of surgery in the amphitheater of the Good Samaritan Hospital. An eye witness has described his method of operating in this Hospital:

He entered the operating pit with great gusto and noise, took off his detachable cuffs, rolled up his coat sleeves, took a great big knife and did an amputation of a thigh a little above the middle. During the operation a towel fell on the floor which he picked up and wiped off the raw stump. . . . After he had finished operating, he washed his hands, took a chew of tobacco of which he was very fond, and proceeded to tell the class all about amputations.

Dawson was a master in the art of surgery and an outstanding medical lecturer. He was a skillful operator and performed a number of brilliant operations. In order to stimulate interest in surgery, Dawson for many years held an annual contest for the students of the Medical College of Ohio "on bandaging, surgical dressings, drawings, and dissections for which he gave as prizes gold medals and surgical instruments."

Dawson took a great interest in the advancement of the medical profession. He was deeply concerned with the quality of medical training in the United States and with the quality of the young men who were to become medical students. He held a number of local and national offices in the medical profession. The crowning achievement of his career was his election in 1888 to the Presidency of the American Medical Association. In his Presidential address he said: "Give us liberally educated young gentlemen, and we will furnish graduates worthy of the degree. Medical colleges, however, do not make the physician. They merely furnish the foundation; the individual must do the balance. In no place is evolution so marked—the fittest will and should survive."

In 1870, James T. Whittaker was appointed the first professor of physiology in the Medical College of Ohio. The following year clinical medicine was added to his chair. When Roberts Bartholow left the City to go to Philadelphia in 1879, Whittaker became professor of the practice of medicine, which chair he held until his death in 1900. Whittaker was a "brilliant and most instructive teacher," whom Ransohoff, himself a born teacher, said "painted disease before our minds in such a way that it could never be forgotten." He made a scientific pilgrimage to Berlin with the purpose of coming in personal contact with Robert Koch and became the first demonstrator of the tubercle bacillus in this country. Whittaker conducted the first clinic west of the Alleghenies on the diseases of children; gave the first course in histology in the west; and

opened the first bacteriological laboratory in the United States. He published a large volume on the *Theory and Practice of Medicine,* and in
the classroom impressed upon his pupils the necessity for respecting
their profession.

In 1870, Chauncey D. Palmer was appointed to the chair of obstetrics
and diseases of women and children. Two years later he was appointed
to the chair of gynecology, which he held until 1906 when he resigned.
He was twice elected President of the Academy of Medicine of Cincinnati.

In 1874, Samuel Nickles succeeded Bartholow as professor of materia
medica in the Medical College of Ohio. Nickles, like Blackman, Graham,
and other giants of those days, was a great medical teacher who did his
best work in the lecture room.

In 1887, Phineas Sanborn Conner succeeded Dawson in the chair of
surgery, holding it for eighteen years. He did much to put the Medical
College of Ohio on a high scientific and professional plane. For more
than forty years Conner taught anatomy and surgery in the Medical College; for over thirty-five years he was on the staff of the Good Samaritan
Hospital; and for twenty-one years on the staff of the Cincinnati Hospital.
As a teacher, both didactically and clinically, Conner's lectures were
"masterpieces of a logical, clear, and thorough presentation of the subject in the purest English." He was one of the most distinguished surgeons America has produced, with few peers in the difficult operations
for head injuries, gunshot wounds, cancer of the upper jaw, and diseases
of blood vessels. For twenty-four years Dr. Conner delivered a course of
lectures on surgery every spring and summer at Dartmouth College. At
the close of the Spanish-American War, Dr. Conner was appointed one
of the Commissioners charged with the investigation into the food that
had been furnished to the American soldiers. His voluminous report on
this subject created a sensation at the time, and he was highly complimented for its thoroughness. Dr. Conner "was of medium height, slightly
stoop-shouldered, prominent nose, heavy drooping moustache, prominent
chin, and with a square lower jaw which reminded one somewhat of the
characteristics of a bulldog." His most striking features were his deep-
set piercing eyes. It was said when he died that the name of Phineas
Sanborn Conner was a "synonym for the Periclean age in the history of
the Medical College of Ohio." He was the last of the Old Guard. With
him vanished "the last remnants of an age that produced not only great
physicians but great men."

With such a galaxy of distinguished men on its Faculty, the Medical
College of Ohio enjoyed unprecedented prosperity. When on March 1,
1871, the Medical College held its semicentennial anniversary in the hall
of the Cincinnati College on Walnut Street, the room was crowded with
fifty members of the graduating class, representatives of the medical

profession of the City, and friends of the institution. Dr. M. B. Wright delivered the address on behalf of the trustees in which he gave many interesting reminiscences of half a century of the history of the College. Dr. James T. Whittaker gave an address in behalf of the alumni. The Honorable Flamen Ball, President of the Board of Trustees, delivered the diplomas, and Professor William H. Gobrecht delivered the valedictory.

In 1872 there were 224 matriculants in the Medical College; the graduating class numbered 90. In that year the institution ranked first in the West and third in the United States in enrollment. Many attributed the prestige of the College to the energy and enthusiasm of the younger members of the Faculty who had been added to the staff. They had disproved the direful predictions of those who had feared the transfusion of so much youthful blood would have disastrous results. By that year nearly 2,000 alumni had been sent out from the old halls of the College in her more than half a century's existence. It was claimed that no less than fifteen of those who were professors and lecturers in the hospitals held their diplomas from the Medical College of Ohio. In 1875 an alumni association was formed. Deafening cheers greeted the response to the remarks of the only member of the first class of 1821, the venerable James T. Grubbs.

Four years later (1879) the graduating class of the Medical College broke all records. The graduating class numbered 121, and the Commencement exercises had to be held in Music Hall. Many thought that the Faculty would make themselves the laughingstock of the City by holding the Commencement exercises in such a large edifice as Music Hall, but to their astonishment the Hall was full and overflowing. When in 1871 a colored student requested information as to the admission of such students in the College, the Faculty handled the difficult racial question as adroitly as possible. He was notified that there was no objection on the part of any member of the Faculty to his admission, yet as a question of policy they were compelled, at least at that time, to deny his request. On the other hand the Medical College placed itself on record as being positively opposed to the admission of women to the study of medicine. It was not until 1898 that women were admitted in the Medical College.

In their addresses to the graduating classes at these Commencement exercises the Faculty stressed the importance of the medical profession and what should be the ideal of the physician. The graduates were urged not to regard themselves as only vendors of pills, powders, or lotions to those who desired such stuff for real or imaginary ailments. The ideal of a physician should be one whose great aim was to be of service to his fellowmen. He should minister not only to the body diseased but to the mind diseased. He had to deal with passions, feelings, and emotions of human beings as well as their physical maladies. They must realize that the practice of medicine was an arduous profession. The public expected of their doctor what they never dream of exacting from any other human being: that his knowledge should be ready for application at any moment of the day or night.

In his address at the Commencement of 1895, Professor Whittaker gave sound advice both to the graduates and to the Board of Trustees. He pointed out the reasons why the College had such a high reputation and what the Faculty expected of their pupils. He listed the names of some of the great men who had taught in the College—Drake, Eberle, Locke, and Mussey in the old days—Blackman, Graham, Dawson, and Wright in his own day. And so, having such men, the College had been able to turn out *men.* "When the Athenians," declared Whittaker, "asked for more ships to repel the enemy," Demosthenes said to them: "It is not ships that you want but men." On the Faculty of the College had been a host of great men, and what they had strived to instill in their pupils was the acquisition of knowledge. "With all the getting, get understanding." In fact, if one got wisdom the rest followed—wealth, place, and fame. But wisdom can only be acquired with work. So the Faculty taught their pupils to work. They taught their men that "ease is a disease"; that "still waters stagnate"; that "drawn wells are the sweetest."

And then Professor Whittaker offered some advice to the Board of Trustees. He paid honor to the men who sacrificed their time in the service of the public. But when these trustees made appointments of unfit persons, they did more harm than good. They were like the man who

> With one hand put a penny in the urn of poverty
> And with the other took a shilling out.

In the hope of making the Commencement exercises more democratic in tone, the Faculty in 1890 prohibited the public from giving bouquets and floral designs to members of the graduating class. By so doing they hoped to avoid the jealousies and embarrassments of students not so highly favored as their fellow classmates.

INTERNAL AND EXTERNAL DISPUTES

The Faculty of the Medical College was more homogeneous during this period than ever before in the history of the institution. This does not mean, however, that Faculty meetings were not enlivened at times by protracted wrangles and internal friction. In the early years after the Civil War, Dr. Comegys and Dr. M. B. Wright, who had not lost his old-time belligerence, frequently clashed. Whenever a vacancy occurred on the staff there was always a lot of political maneuvering and hard feelings created before the final appointments were made, and even then amicable feelings were only temporary.

The appointments to the staff of the Cincinnati Hospital were a constant bone of contention between the Medical College of Ohio and the Miami Medical College. From 1870 to 1887 the Miami Medical College practically controlled the Cincinnati Hospital. About the year 1871 the Board of Trustees of the Hospital passed a rule excluding from the staff all professors in medical colleges. A year or two later this rule was rescinded and from that time in 1887 only one member of the Faculty of the Medical College was able to get an appointment upon the Hospital staff, although personal applications were repeatedly made by many of the Faculty of the Medical College when vacancies occurred. All such positions were filled by men from the Miami College for the year previous to examination in order to secure the influence of the representatives of the Hospital staff in the Miami College.

The Faculty of the Medical College of Ohio were told that they had control of the Good Samaritan Hospital and that should satisfy them. Adherents of the Medical College pointed out that the City of Cincinnati, as a corporation, had no interest in the Good Samaritan Hospital, the teaching part of which was private property, developed in self-defense, and supported exclusively by the Faculty of the Medical College of Ohio. Besides, contended the Faculty of the Medical College, their relationship with the Good Samaritan Hospital had nothing whatsoever to do with their rights in the Cincinnati Hospital.

The law establishing the Hospital had been the work of Daniel Drake, the founder of the Medical College, and for forty years the Faculty of the Medical College, in compliance with the provisions of the law, had been compelled and did render gratuitous service to the Hospital and had given the clinical instruction in the Hospital. But this control was lost after forty years of uninterrupted service by the law of 1871 expelling all teachers from the staff of the Hospital, and since that time the Hospital had been under the control of the Miami Medical College. The Faculty of the Medical College asserted that Dr. David Judkins, a member of the Board of Trustees of the Hospital and also a member of the Faculty of the Miami Medical College had "uniformly refused" to recognize their just claims; had displayed "persistent animosity to the College"; and for these reasons tried to prevent his reappointment to the Hospital Board of Trustees.

In 1887 a bill was passed by the State Legislature which compelled the trustees of the Cincinnati Hospital to give proper recognition to the Medical College of Ohio in the appointments to the staff of the Hospital. Shortly thereafter six members of the Faculty of the Medical College were appointed to the staff of the Hospital. After that time both Colleges controlled the Cincinnati Hospital, barring all other colleges and the rest of the profession. The long controversy between the two Colleges with the management of the City Hospital was over, but the healthy development of the scientific work and philanthropic purposes of the City Hospital continued to be handicapped by politicians and political doctors.

The most serious trouble the Medical College had during these years was that involving the institution in the desecration of the grave of John Scott Harrison. On May 29, 1878, the body of Harrison, the son of former U.S. President William Henry Harrison, was laid to rest in Congress Green Cemetery, North Bend, Ohio, alongside the tomb of his honored father. As there were rumors in North Bend of the presence of ghouls in the neighborhood because of the rifling of the grave of a young man, August Devins, who had been buried a few days earlier, every precaution was taken to safeguard the grave of Harrison.

The day after the burial of John Scott Harrison, his son, John Harrison, and nephew, George Eaton, came to Cincinnati to search for the body of their friend, August Devins, supposing that it had been brought to one of the medical colleges in the City. They read an account in the *Enquirer* of the mysterious smuggling into the Medical College of Ohio of the body of a deceased person. A search warrant was obtained, and Harrison and Eaton proceeded to the College. They made a careful examination of the rooms in the building without finding anything, and they were just about to abandon their search when the detective accompanying them called their attention to a taut rope that looked as though something was attached to it. This rope was connected to a windlass and was suspended in the chute or hoist through which the cadavers were brought up to the dissecting room. The detective seized the crank and began to turn the windlass. A naked body covered with a cloth was brought up. When the cloth was removed the spectators were shocked to recognize the features of John Scott Harrison.

The discovery of Harrison's body in the dissecting room of the College created quite a furor. During the excitement the Miami crowd did their "utmost to make it hot" for the Medical College. Of course, the Faculty of the College denied all knowledge of the affair and assured the Harrisons that they would "seek the guilty one" who had perpetrated such an act. All the time it was claimed that the medical Faculty of the Ohio College knew "that an active rural graveyard had in part been consumed in the Miami dissecting room and in part had been shipped through the College to Ann Arbor as the long list of receipts from the American Express Company showed." It was subsequently found that the body for which Harrison was searching (young Devins) "had been shipped through the Miami College to Ann Arbor." The Grand Jury after "struggling over the matter for ten days concluded to indict the janitor of the Medical College." The tragic John Scott Harrison affair gave the College much unfavorable notoriety and ultimately led to more stringent laws dealing with dissection in Ohio and a number of other states.

For many years the scheme to unite the Medical College and the University of Cincinnati was the source of discussion among the members of the Faculty of the College. In 1871, Bartholow suggested that an effort be made to buy the college building and present it to the University of Cincinnati as its medical department, the present Board of Trustees of the Medical College to be retained as the controlling power in the medical department. Professors Graham, Bartholow, and Dawson were appointed a committee to interest the citizens of Cincinnati in the plan. The scheme aroused no enthusiasm among the citizens and was dropped. Then a plan was proposed to incorporate the Medical College as the Medical Department of the University of Cincinnati and to have the staff of the Cincinnati Hospital adopted into the College as its clinical professors. This project was characterized by one of the Faculty of the Medical College as a plan conferring "honor upon everybody." Finally, in 1887, the Medical College of Ohio became nominally the Medical Department of the University of Cincinnati by affiliating with the University. In the same year the Miami Medical College, the College of Pharmacy, the Clinical and Pathological School of the Cincinnati Hospital, the Cincinnati College of Medicine and Surgery, and the Ohio Dental College of Surgery also became affiliated with the University of Cincinnati.

The Medical College Becomes the Medical Department of the University

The "affiliation" of the various medical colleges with the University of Cincinnati in reality meant nothing. It imposed no obligations and conferred no rights either as far as the Colleges or the University were concerned. The absurdity of the arrangement soon became evident, and in 1894 all the medical colleges formally severed their connection with the University of Cincinnati. The Ohio College of Dental Surgery alone continued its relationship with the University until 1906–1907.

In the meantime the University acquired permission to change its location from the old McMicken homestead to a site in Burnet Woods Park, and there was a desire on the part of the Board of Directors to create new departments and make the institution a real university. Accordingly, on May 31, 1895, the Board adopted a resolution authorizing a committee to proceed to formulate plans and to secure a Faculty for a medical department within the University. This committee promptly conferred with a committee of the Medical College of Ohio to see if an agreement could be worked out by which the Medical College would become the Medical Department of the University.

It was agreed by both the University authorities and those of the Medical College that the interests of both institutions would be promoted if they were organically united. But there were certain conditions the Medical College wanted clarified before it was willing to enter such an arrangement: (1) The name of the Medical College of Ohio should be permanently retained; (2) the present Faculty should be retained and all additions to the Faculty should be nominated by the Faculty of the College to the Board of Directors of the University; (3) the buildings on the McMicken estate should be transferred to the Medical Department; and (4) all the financial affairs of the department should be controlled by the Faculty of the College.

The Faculty of the Medical College also sent out letters to many of the medical colleges in other institutions to find out whether their Faculties received regular salaries or were paid out of the fees received from the students, and if the fees were in the hands of the medical Faculty. Yale replied that since 1877 the medical Faculty had been salaried, and the finances were in the hands of the medical school. In all other institutions it was found that the medical Faculties were paid from fees received from the students, and the finances were in the hands of the medical Faculty.

At this juncture of the negotiations Dr. Charles A. L. Reed, who was a member of the Board of Directors of the University as well as of the Faculty of the College, sent a communication to the Faculty of the Medical College in which he worked out a program which he said he would personally support. He suggested that the Medical College secure amendments to its organic law in order to make the Board of Directors of the University the successors in perpetuity to the Board of Trustees of the Medical College and should transfer all its property to the University; and that the title of the new school should be the Medical Department of the University, but the name of the Medical College of Ohio should be retained as an additional title. The McMicken homestead should be assigned as the building of the new department to the Medical College; the present Faculty should be retained and general, special, and clinical professorships created and all elections should be by the Faculty; and all the money derived from fees should be under the control of the Medical Department. This plan was accepted with minor changes by both the Medical College and the University. An act was passed by the General Assembly which permitted placing the Medical College under the control of the Directors of the University.

On April 27, 1896, the Directors of the University and the Faculty of the Medical College signed an agreement provisionally merging the College with the University. The College gave up its charter and agreed to operate under the charter of the University. The Board of Directors of the University became the governing body of the Medical Department, and the new home of the College was in the old McMicken building. The union of the Medical College with the University marked an epoch in the history of the University, but the future was to disclose whether the Medical Department was actually an organic part of the University.

In commenting on the final establishment of the Medical Department the Board of Directors expressed their deep appreciation of the conspicuous services rendered by Doctors T. A. Reamy and Charles A. L. Reed in this important matter. Both of these men were members of the Board of Directors of the University and were also members of the Faculty of the Medical College. Dr. Reamy was professor of clinical gynecology; his lectures were orations, but they held the attention of his students and fixed in their memories the essential principles of the subject. Dr. Reed was one of the most versatile and dynamic personalities in American medicine. He was one of the founders of the American Association of Obstetricians and Gynecologists and President of this organization in 1898. Two years later he was elected President of the American Medical Association. A gifted speaker with a vigorous and genial personality, Dr. Reed won for himself a national and international reputation.

On April 9, 1897, the seventy-eighth Commencement of the Medical College, now the Medical Department of the University, was held at Music Hall. The first class of Doctors of Medicine, 111 in number, received their diplomas bearing the seal and insignia of authority of the University from Frank J. Jones, Chairman of the Board of Directors. After the awarding of the prizes and the announcement of internes in the various hospitals, the surprise of the evening came when Professor Thad A. Reamy stepped to the front of the stage carrying in his hand a parcel which he placed upon the speaker's table. In his brief introductory remarks he covered the history of the College, then launched out in praise of one of the Faculty to whose energy he said much of its later success was due. Unwrapping the parcel he then displayed a beautiful loving cup of massive silver, and still leaving the audience in the dark as to the name of the prize winner, he gave a witty history of the origin of the cup in medieval times. Finally, he turned to Professor James G. Hyndman, professor of laryngology and for many years secretary of the Faculty, and presented it to him. Dr. Reamy said the cup was filled "not with wine but with the love and regard of his fellow professors." It was a fitting close to a memorable occasion.

12

In the Gaslight Era

The "gay nineties" were as gay in Cincinnati as anywhere. They marked a time of political corruption on a scale that later came to seem appalling, but that seemed less so at the time. Influenced greatly by the heavy German immigration of preceding decades, the Queen City had taken on a marked Teutonic influence. This showed itself in diverse ways—in the growth of savings and loan companies as the thrifty Germans set the pattern, in the abundance of elegant saloons and lavish beer gardens with music and entertainment, and in the emergence of Cincinnati as a center of music.

The theater prospered greatly towards the turn of the century. The Cincinnati Symphony Orchestra was founded in 1895, supplementing the May Festival that had been launched many years earlier. German singing societies were almost beyond counting. Two rival schools of music, Conservatory and College, were strengthening the cultural tradition of the community. They were to combine much later, finally in 1962 becoming an integral college of the University of Cincinnati.

In 1891 the Cincinnati Baseball Club, which had produced the first professional team in the country, rejoined the National League for keeps. Among many pastimes, cycling clubs became a mania in the nineties. The decade also saw the beginning of horseracing on a large scale and the building of the City's first golf club. There was much wealth in Cincinnati by this time. It was an age of elegant gentlemen in beautiful carriages, of spacious living, of *gemütlich* pleasure in the Over-the-Rhine section of the town, from the canal northward.

The University had retreated up the hill to Burnet Woods by now, but it was increasingly a part of the intellectual life of the City. In the last decade of the nineteenth century (1890–1900) the University made important strides forward. The University moved from its location at the McMicken homestead to a new permanent site in Burnet Woods Park.

The wisdom of making this change was soon demonstrated and proved. The beautiful and healthy surroundings did much to benefit and invigorate the students as well as the Faculty with enthusiasm and new energy. Furthermore, the citizens of Cincinnati began to discover that, despite the soot and smoke, somewhere on Clifton Avenue there was a building devoted to university purposes.

By the middle of the nineteenth century the University of Cincinnati had been in operation for two decades. A comparison of the catalogues of the University in 1875 and in 1895 gave some indication of the growth of the University during these twenty years. In 1875 the catalogue of the University was a small pamphlet of twenty-nine pages, of which nineteen were devoted to the School of Design. The Faculty of the Academic Department consisted of three professors and two instructors. The total enrollment numbered fifty-eight. In 1894–1895 the catalogue numbered eighty-seven pages. There were 892 matriculants, and the Faculty consisted of twelve professors and twelve instructors. In 1895 only one of the original members of the Faculty (E. W. Hyde), and only one of the first Board of Directors (Cornelius G. Comegys) were still connected with the University.

The name of the Academic Department was changed to that of the McMicken College of Liberal Arts which it was to retain for many years. The Board of Directors had long felt that the name of Charles McMicken should be given to the department which had been designated as the Academic Department in order to commemorate the name of the man who had given so much of his estate for the establishment of a free school of higher learning in his adopted City. When the City received his property it had been determined to give his name to the whole assemblage of schools that constituted a university, and it had been denominated the McMicken University. It soon became apparent, however, that the McMicken estate was not sufficient to sustain so large an institution; and when the charter of the University of Cincinnati was obtained, the term "Academic" was given to the department where the usual college courses were taught. But as other departments were organized the Board decided in 1892 to designate the Academic Department by the name of the McMicken College of the University. When the University moved to Burnet Woods Park the main building was called McMicken Hall. After 1904 the name of the College was changed to the College of Liberal Arts, and later (1906–1907) the name was changed again to the McMicken College of Liberal Arts. To give additional recognition to Charles McMicken the Board decided to select a day in each year to be observed as Founder's Day with appropriate exercises.

The Board also began to think about the need of preserving all the records and documents of the University with a view toward the preparation of a historical sketch of the University. A historical commission was created consisting first of Professors North, Sproull, and Hart. But the man most interested in pushing the project was Cornelius G. Comegys. On April 17, 1893, he gave a sketch of the history of the University from its organization to the Board. The Historical Commission was requested by the Board to commit to writing remarks and to proceed to write an official history of the University. The Commission gathered much biographical data collected from graduates of the University and from records of the Alumni Association concerning the Board of Directors and other persons officially connected with the University. The *Cincinnatian* (1896) prepared a historical account of the University based largely upon data supplied by Cornelius G. Comegys and Samuel F. Hunt.

But the first history of the University of Cincinnati was not published until 1907, when a history of the *University of Cincinnati: A Municipal University* was prepared by Henning W. Prentis, Jr., Secretary of the University, 1905–1907, later President and Chairman of the Board of Directors of the Armstrong Cork Company. It was published in the *Ohio Magazine*, January 1907.

The erection and dedication of McMicken Hall was soon followed by bequests from Henry Hanna, Briggs S. Cunningham, and Asa Van Wormer. This led to the construction of Hanna and Cunningham Halls and the Van Wormer Library.

The University began to expand as new departments were organized. In 1896, with a view toward the establishment of a College of Pharmacy as an organic unit of the University, the contract by which the Cincinnati College of Pharmacy was affiliated was cancelled. This was done with the consent of the latter institution, but it was to be many years before the University would have a College of Pharmacy as an integral part of the institution.

For many years the relation of the Ohio College of Dental Surgery to the University was merely an affiliation of the loosest character, and in 1906 it was definitely terminated. In the same year the affiliation with the College of Pharmacy was cancelled; the Medical College of Ohio became the Medical Department of the University; and the following year the Law School of the Cincinnati College and a newly established Law Department of the University were united. Meanwhile the curricula were enlarged; standards were raised; fellowships and prizes were created; and the influence of the University was extended in the community by the establishment of University extension courses.

Not only did the number of students and the Faculty increase during these years but also the number of student publications and organizations. A weekly college paper in addition to a monthly magazine was issued, and the first *Cincinnatian* (annual) made its appearance. An Alumni Association and an Athletic Association were formed, and both the Faculty and the students became more interested in sports.

By the turn of the century the University of Cincinnati was beginning to assume the aspects common to other institutions of higher learning throughout the country. But it was still a small college. In 1900 one office registered the students, advised them in the selection of courses, took care of admissions, did the printing of the catalogue, edited alumni records, and consulted with students on probation.

THE UNIVERSITY AND BURNET WOODS PARK

It will be recalled that even before the burning of the University building in 1885, Rector Vickers and the Board of Directors raised the question of the suitability of the McMicken homestead as the permanent home of the University. When Charles McMicken in his will specifically directed that the college buildings should be erected at his homestead, the neighborhood of the University was rural in character. As the years passed it became a distinctly manufacturing neighborhood, with the result that the University building was surrounded by factories of various kinds, whose tall chimney stacks were constantly belching forth clouds of black smoke, filling the building with soot, and damaging the apparatus in the laboratories. Besides, an inclined-plane railway ran within a few hundred feet of the college edifice. Moreover, the sliding of the declivity of the steep hill had made it necessary to place the building just beside the avenue to Clifton. The dust and noise arising from this still further embarrassed the operations of the College and to all this was added the difficulty of access, especially in wet and wintry weather.

In October 1888 the Board referred the question of changing the location of the University elsewhere to its Law Committee. The Committee visited possible sites in College Hill and in Washington Park but were most impressed by the beauty and healthfulness of Burnet Woods Park as the proper location for the main edifice of the institution. But in view of the provisions of the McMicken will, they believed it would be unwise to make a change without first obtaining a release from the McMicken heirs or else without a decree from a proper court authorizing such a move for fear of endangering the whole or part of the funds derived from the McMicken bequest. The Board had no resources for the purchase of a new location, but the law enacted for the establishment of the University had authorized the City Council to set apart and appropriate any public grounds of the City for a site of the building and grounds of the University.

The Board, therefore, appointed a committee of three members to request the City Council to set aside a part of Burnet Woods Park for University purposes. This the Council did on September 20, 1889, without a dissenting vote. A City ordinance was passed which gave to the University the use of more than forty-three acres (43.302) of land in the southern part of Burnet Woods Park (south of Molitor Street) for the purpose of erecting a University building and such other buildings as might incidently be connected with the University; provided that within three years the construction of a main building was begun, and that within five years at least $100,000 should be expended on such building. It was expressly understood and agreed that the remainder of the land not occupied by the University buildings was to remain open to the public as a part of Burnet Woods Park forever. In case the University failed to meet these conditions the City had the right to retake the land. The passage of this City ordinance was largely due to the efforts of Dr. J. C. Culbertson, editor of *The Lancet and Clinic*. Subsequently, as the question of the legality of the transfer of this land to the University arose, the State Legislature in 1892 passed an act affirming the power of the Council or Board of Education to convey public land to a municipal university.

The transfer of the University to the new location in Burnet Woods Park was delayed by a series of obstructive lawsuits. The Board of Directors could not avail themselves of the land donated by the City Council until they had obtained first an interpretation of the McMicken will permitting it. Therefore, the Board petitioned the Common Pleas Court of Hamilton County for the right to change the location of the University. The McMicken heirs contested this and appealed to the Circuit Court which decided unanimously in favor of the right of removal, and then to the Supreme Court of Ohio which on March 7, 1893, confirmed the decision. This put an end to this disagreeable and protracted legislation. The Board thanked Judge J. D. Peck, Max B. May, and its Committee on Law—William M. Ramsey, William Strunk, and Edmund K. Stall—for their "prolonged, successful, and gratuitous services in the courts in securing authority to change the site of the University building from its present location to the heights of the Burnet Woods Park."

In the course of the cross-examination of the testimony of C. G. Comegys, he was asked by the counsel of the defendants (McMicken heirs): "Do you know whether any colored pupils have ever been admitted to the University"? He replied, "Yes," and declared that "a very distinguished one graduated about five years ago (about 1886)," but he did not identify him by name. As there are no extant records of the University which classify the matriculants by race, this data is not as complete as desired; but it does disclose the fact that by the middle of the eighties, colored students were attending the University.

Furthermore, in Judge Peck's argument before the Supreme Court, he gave an interpretation of the phrase in the McMicken will which provided for "two colleges for the education of white boys and girls." Judge Peck pointed out that it had been repeatedly held by the Ohio courts that it was legal in Ohio to provide separate schools for white and colored children. But he declared that although the McMicken bequest was intended "primarily for the benefit of white boys and girls"; since the words of the will did not definitely exclude colored persons, they could be admitted to the University.

On April 20, 1893, the City Council by authority granted by an act of the State Legislature which empowered the Council or Board of Education to convey public land to a municipal university, passed an ordinance providing for the issuance of $100,000 of 4 per cent bonds for the erection of a main building and its equipment in Burnet Woods Park. On September 22, 1894, the cornerstone of the main building called Mc-Micken Hall was laid with imposing ceremonies. Mayor John A. Caldwell made the opening speech. He was followed by Henry W. Bettman, President of the Alumni Association. The cornerstone was planted by the Chairman of the Board of Directors, Dr. Cornelius G. Comegys. The ceremonies were brought to a close by an oration delivered by Judge Samuel F. Hunt, who had been for several years Chairman of the Board of Directors, on the history and progress of the University.

At the opening of the fall term in September 1895 the Board of Directors, Faculty, and students assembled in the building and led by Dr. Comegys marched in procession through the corridors, classrooms, and other rooms in order to stress the importance of the opening of the new building in the history of the institution.

On November 23, 1895, McMicken Hall was formally dedicated. The Invocation was given by Reverend David H. Moore, editor of the *Western Christian Advocate*. Short addresses were given by Mayor John A. Caldwell, Dr. C. G. Comegys, William Strunk, P. V. N. Myers, General Jacob D. Cox, General Peter Michie, Max B. May, Frank J. Jones, H. D. Peck, and Samuel F. Hunt. The Benediction was given by Rabbi Dr. I. M. Wise.

McMicken Hall was a three-story building with a basement. It contained lecture and recitation rooms, a library, an assembly hall, and a gymnasium. In the basement was the lunch room and the gymnasium. The alumni of the Academic Department secured the necessary equipment for the gymnasium and had installed four hot and cold shower baths. On the third floor of the building was located the general library. The Board of Directors decided in 1892, before the new building was obtained, that one of the members of the Faculty annually should be elected librarian. The first librarian of the University was W. E. Waters, professor of Greek and comparative philosophy. In 1895 the Board directed that the library should be catalogued.

One of the features of the new building which appealed strongly to the Faculty was the seminar rooms. They were considered as essential for the departments of language, literature, history, and mathematics as the laboratories were to the scientific departments. The seminar rooms were equipped, insofar as the funds permitted, with such apparatus as were required by the students in these departments to carry on their work.

The first Commencement in the new University building was held on the evening of June 16, 1896, in the auditorium of McMicken Hall. It was an important occasion in the history of the University. Thirty-seven graduates received their degrees; thirteen receiving the degree of Bachelor of Arts; sixteen receiving the degree of Bachelor of Letters; and eight receiving the degree of Bachelor of Science, and, in addition, one young man who had been graduated from the University in 1894 received the degree of Master of Arts.

The transfer of the Academic Department of the University from the old building (which was later occupied by the Medical Department) to the new McMicken Hall was a landmark in the history of the institution. The pleasant and commodious new home did much to stimulate college spirit and to foster college loyalty among the student body.

The Donations of Henry Hanna, Briggs S. Cunningham, and Asa Van Wormer

Within the three years after McMicken Hall was erected the generosity of benefactors of the University made possible the construction of additional buildings in Burnet Woods Park. Among the donors was Henry Hanna who in the year 1895 gave to the University the sum of $45,000 for the construction of a north wing of the new University building in Burnet Woods. The Board accepted the gift and at once resolved to name the building Hanna Hall.

When the bids for construction were received, however, it was found that the lowest cost amounted to $49,091.07. Mr. Hanna promptly raised his contribution to this figure and directed that the construction proceed on this basis. The following year (1896) Mr. Hanna donated an additional $20,000 for the fitting and equipment of the building, bringing his total contributions to the sum of $69,091.07. Hanna Hall was dedicated on May 13, 1897, exclusively to scientific instruction and was intended for the permanent home of the departments of chemistry and civil engineering.

The next year (1898) Briggs S. Cunningham, a member of the Board of Directors, notified his colleagues that he wished to give to the University the sum of $60,000 for the building and equipment of a south wing to the University building. This "magnanimous" offer was accepted, and the Board resolved to name the building Cunningham Hall. The building was not dedicated until June 20, 1903, along with those of the Van Wormer Library and the athletic field.

In the same year that Mr. Cunningham made his donation, Mr. Asa Van Wormer had transferred to the University 1,000 shares of stock in the Cincinnati Street Railway Company, par value $50,000, for the construction of a library building to be known as the "Van Wormer Library, with a stone tablet placed on the wall inside of the building" in which should be cut the words "erected with money given by Asa Van Wormer in memory of his wife, Julia Ann Van Wormer, and himself." The Board accepted this "generous gift" on these terms.

Hardly had the Board extended its gratitude to Messrs. Cunningham and Van Wormer for their gifts than the Board was informed in 1898 by Mr. William A. Procter that he was donating to the University his Robert Clarke Library as a nucleus for the building up of a University library. Mr. Procter had secured the library of Mr. Robert Clarke, a well-known collector of *Americana*, consisting of 6,574 volumes estimated at $50,000. The next year Mr. Procter gave the University the Enoch T. Carson Shakespearian Library, comprising 1,420 volumes; and in 1900 the chemical library of Professor T. H. Norton, containing 992 volumes. In 1898, Mr. Lewis Seasongood donated $500 to the Latin Department for the purpose of equipping an alcove in the Library with Latin and Semetic works, and Charles F. Windisch donated a "unique" and extensive collection of microphotographs of snow crystals. In 1899, David Sinton gave the University $100,000 to be used for the maintenance of the Academic Department.

In order to further the interests of the University in the community, a Citizen's University Committee was formed in 1894. This Committee was composed of prominent citizens of the City. It included: M. E. Ingalls, Alexander McDowell, J. G. Schmidlapp, Charles F. Fleischmann, Matthew Addy, W. P. Anderson, C. A. Holmes, F. W. Alms, W. O. Sproull, L. Marbreit, A. B. Voorheis, T. J. Emery, Max B. May, T. W. Graydon, and Lewis Seasongood.

To further broaden the influence of the University it was reported in the local press in 1895 that the Board of Directors considered the advisability of granting free tuition to students in Hamilton County as well as to those of the City. They recognized the fact that such a step would be illegal, but the members of the Board argued that "it would be for the betterment of the University and would never be called in question." It was claimed that each of the Board members could point to instances of young men and women who were deprived of opportunities of higher education "on account of the tuition of seventy dollars a year." But this proposal was soon dropped.

Dr. Cornelius George Comegys

On February 10, 1896, the University and the City sustained a great loss by the death of Cornelius G. Comegys. He, more than any other man, was the real creator of the University of Cincinnati. As a member of the City Council he had obtained the charter to establish a university to carry out the bequest of Charles McMicken. Dr. Comegys laid the cornerstone of McMicken Hall, and from 1873 to the time of his death he was a member of the Board of Directors of the University and during the last six years of his life, was President of the Board.

Dr. Comegys was an eminent and successful physician for almost half a century in this community. He assisted in organizing the Miami Medical College and the Cincinnati College of Medicine and Surgery, at one time was identified with the Medical College of Ohio as one of its trustees, and was also a member of its Faculty. He was one of the founders and twice President of the Cincinnati Academy of Medicine; and as chairman of a special committee of the American Medical Association initiated the movement which ultimately led to the establishment by President Dwight D. Eisenhower in 1953 of the Department of Health, Education, and Welfare. When James N. Gamble decided to found the Deaconness Home and Hospital he naturally consulted his friend, Dr. Comegys. These two men were also responsible for the founding of Christ Hospital. Dr. Comegys was the first President of the medical staff and was always regarded by the members of the staff as the "Father of Christ Hospital."

Dr. Comegys was also pre-eminent as a citizen. As a member of the School Board, the Board of Aldermen, and later the City Council he made significant contributions to the life of the City. He was instrumental in starting a night high school for the instruction of young businessmen. As Chairman of the Public Library Committee he secured the unification of the Public and Mechanics' Institute Libraries and the passage of tax measures for the support of the Cincinnati Public Library.

As a man, Dr. Comegys was a typical example of the old school physician. He was a man of positive convictions, courteous, dignified, and cultured, who believed that the medical profession should always adhere to high ethical standards. He believed that everything deserved most painstaking attention and care. Since frivolity had no place in his character he left the impression of being austere; but those who knew him best "realized that under the mask of austerity was a very sensitive, kindly, and lovable personality."

Faculty and Curriculum

It will be recalled that after the retirement of General Cox from the Presidency, and upon the solicitation of the Faculty itself, the Board of

Directors enacted a rule prescribing that each professor should hold the office of Dean of the University for only a year at a time; each one succeeding to it in the order of seniority. In conformity with this plan Professor W. R. Benedict assumed the duties of Dean, and the following year was succeeded by Professor Edmund W. Hyde who then was followed by Professor William O. Sproull.

This policy of rotating the office of the Dean among the members of the Faculty soon became the source of trouble. It caused jealousy and bickering among the members of the Faculty and also created friction between the Faculty and the Board. Many of the Faculty pointed out that it was the custom and usage of American colleges and universities that the Faculty formed a co-ordinate branch of the administration, and that the Board of Directors should make no appointments of professors or decisions regarding the presiding officer of the University without previously consulting the Faculty. While the Faculty recognized that the Board of Directors had the legal power and responsibility of making all such appointments, they claimed that the general welfare and harmony of the University would be advanced for the following reasons: (1) No one could possibly have a more vital interest in the success and prosperity of an institution of learning than its Faculty whose success and reputations were involved; (2) the position of the Faculty enabled them to understand more thoroughly and judge more wisely the needs of an institution than anyone who did not share in its life and work; (3) the well-being and fame of a college or university were absolutely dependent upon the composition of its Faculty; (4) there could never exist complete harmony and unity of action between the Board of Directors and the Faculty unless the latter had some voice in all matters relating to its organization; and (5) the lack of such co-ordinate action between the Faculty and the Board of Directors would lead to disharmony and have calamitous effects upon the prosperity of the institution.

The Faculty presented these views to the Board. At first the Board agreed to take no action regarding the appointment of professors or the election of a presiding officer of the Faculty without previous consultation with the Faculty. When, however, the Faculty later complained that they could not cooperate with Dean Sproull, as they claimed he did not consult them about measures he proposed, the Board added the words "when practicable" at the end of their former resolution.

It soon became evident that the rule of rotating the Deanship and consulting the Faculty was an "apple of discord." As just shown, the first effort to rescind it failed because of the opposition of some of the members of the Board who felt that it ought to have further trial. The continued trial, however, only revealed that as each professor succeeded to the Deanship "either he, or some friend of his, sought to make his appointment either permanent or a stepping-stone to the vacant Presidency while other members of the Faculty, equally ambitious, were equally active in preventing such a consummation." The friction thus developed in the Faculty became so pronounced and its disastrous results so evident that the Board of Directors rescinded its rule about consulting the Faculty with regard to the appointment of professors and selecting a Dean and passed a new rule stating that the Board of Directors had the power to select from the Faculty a Dean who should serve at the pleasure of the Board.

This action was made possible as a consequence of a change in the methods of selecting the members of the Board of Directors which wrought important changes in the personnel of the Board. In 1892 a law was passed by the General Assembly which provided that all vacancies in the Board should be filled by appointment by the Judge or Judges of the Superior Court of Cincinnati. The City Council no longer could appoint any members of the Board, thereby eliminating some of the political influences which had affected the character of the Board.

In 1895, Professor P. V. N. Myers was elected by the Board as Dean. His acceptance of the office was "cordially urged and approved by the Faculty"; and the Board declared that "under his direction and supervision the work in the various departments of the University was prosecuted with marked success and satisfaction." Two years later Professor Myers tendered his resignation as Dean of the Faculty, because he wanted "to devote all his time and strength to the chosen and congenial work of his department (history)." At his request the Board accepted his resignation with a statement expressing their "cordial appreciation of his fidelity and devotion to the interests of the University." The Academic Faculty elected Professor E. W. Hyde as Dean, and his election was approved and confirmed by the Board of Directors. Nevertheless, the demoralization which had been engendered by the plan of rotating the Deanship had destroyed anything like a wholesome *esprit de corps* in the Faculty, if it had ever existed.

Notwithstanding these internal stresses and strains, the general condition of the University improved. Enrollment in the Academic Department rose from 121 in 1890 to 537 by the turn of the century. The Faculty raised the required passing grade for students in the Academic Department from 50 to 60; and in order to stimulate scholarship, degrees were awarded with "distinction" to outstanding students.

The greatest incentive to the stimulation of scholarship, as well as national recognition of the position of the University among institutions of higher learning on the basis of equipment and thoroughness of work, was the founding in 1898 of the Delta chapter of Phi Beta Kappa. The first banquet of the Phi Beta Kappa chapter was held at the Sinton Hotel on May 26, 1899; and the next month on June 15 the first initiation was held.

Courses in the catalogue were numbered for the first time. This was of much convenience to the students as well as to the professors.

In 1892 the Faculty allowed one hour credit for Bible instruction. No examinations or grades were given in this course. Three years later the Faculty decided to invite two representative clergymen from each of the religious denominations to give non-doctrinal or non-denominational lectures. In 1896 the Reverend Charles S. Goss of Avondale was appointed lecturer on the Bible. He gave one lecture each week and was permitted to call in representative clergymen of the various denominations and any special students of the Bible to assist him.

In 1895 the students requested the Faculty to put them on their honor during examination periods. The Faculty agreed, provided the students signed a pledge that they had neither given nor received help during the examination. The honor system was used the following year in all examinations, although the students did not like to sign the pledge.

A delegation from the Labor Council, an organization of the laboring men of the City, requested the University to establish night classes in order to afford the laboring classes the advantages of higher education. The Board replied that they were in full sympathy with the idea, but the lack of necessary funds made it impossible. The initiative of the Labor Council foreshadowed the later establishment of an Evening College, which in mid-twentieth century would rival the day colleges in total enrollment.

In 1893, Major Frank J. Jones founded a prize which was to be awarded to the member of the senior class who wrote and delivered an English oration in the best manner. The subjects were to be chosen by the Dean of the Academic Faculty and the Chairman of the Board of Directors. Three citizens of Cincinnati were to be appointed by the Chairman of the Board of Directors to sit as judges and to award the prize of $40.00. The first Jones Oratorical contest was held in the Odeon, a hall in the City, on March 31, 1893; and the prize was awarded to Charles H. Williamson.

The Academic Faculty requested the Board to establish a fellowship in each department of the University in order to encourage scholarship. The Board approved the recommendation, and the first of these fellowships were awarded in 1896. They carried no stipend but exempted the holder from tuition, incidentals, and laboratory fees.

In the same year the Board converted the southeastern part of the basement in McMicken Hall into a lunch room. This served both the students and the Faculty.

One of the notable undertakings of the Faculty which met with great success was the establishment of University extension courses. In the summer of 1889, Mr. E. W. Weaver, Superintendent of Schools, Bellevue, Kentucky, attempted to organize teachers into classes to receive advanced instruction at the University. He sent out letters to the teachers, but as he only received two encouraging replies, the effort failed. Mr. Weaver attributed the failure of the project to the fact that he was a stranger to many of the teachers whom he hoped to interest. In May 1891 he proposed the idea to Mr. C. M. Flowers, Superintendent of Schools, Norwood, Ohio. Mr. Flowers threw his influence behind the movement which had long been established in England. With the help of Professor Sproull the University extension courses in 1891 were inaugurated. The purpose of the University extension courses was to carry university instruction to those who could not attend the University. The lectures were given by members of the Faculty of the University on Saturdays, and certificates were given to those who attended two-thirds of the lectures and classes and passed satisfactorily a voluntary examination. The fee for a course of six lectures was $75.00; for twelve lectures $140, when the course was given by an instructor or by a special lecturer, a young man who had graduated from the University. Fifty per cent was added to these fees when the courses were given by a professor. The University Extension Department served as a medium for the extensive advertisement of the University.

STUDENT ACTIVITIES

With the opening of the new McMicken Hall the students established a weekly as well as a monthly college paper. The *McMicken Review,* a monthly publication, still existed; but now the students maintained that a weekly paper was "essential to the welfare of every important college." Two members of the senior class began the publication in 1895 of such a paper under the title *The Cincinnati Student.* The burden of this paper became too great for two men to carry. An opportunity to sell the paper to a private corporation presented itself. The matter was referred to the Faculty; and instead of selling the paper to a private corporation, the managers of the paper surrendered its entire control to a provisional board of students chosen from the Department of English. Only one issue of *The Cincinnati Student* appeared. At the beginning of the second semester the new management changed the name of the paper to the *Burnet Woods Echo.* Bryant Venable was in charge of the first issue; but in March 1896, G. A. Ginter, Jr., became editor-in-chief. The *Burnet Woods Echo* was a four-page paper which sold at a subscription price of one dollar a year. Some of the lectures of the professors were published in this paper.

The senior class of the Academic Department published in 1894 the first annual, *The Cincinnatian.* It came very nearly being called the "Mick," but after much debate and a "few bloody noses" the name chosen was *The Cincinnatian.* The students declared that the publication of an annual was needed, because nearly every other college had one. Furthermore, it would be of incalculable advantage in advertising to the outside world the educational and social status of affairs in old McMicken. The publication of an annual would also be the means of chronicling every college event and be of the greatest service in recording the permanent records of the athletic teams and of individual athletes. The corps of editors of the first *Cincinnatian* were: Frank Sanford Brown and Alfred K. Nippert, managers; Raymond Ratliff, editor-in-chief; Frank Sanford Brown, Alfred K. Nippert, Henry W. Curth, Isaac Marcuson, Lulu M. Lambdin, Maude H. Squire, Jane S. O'Hara, Walter Fanfersiek, Edwin S. Smith, and Merril Hibbard, associate editors. It was largely due to the "industry and unabated work" of the Messrs. Brown and Nippert that the annual was published.

The first *Cincinnatian* was dedicated to the memory of Charles McMicken. It recorded histories of the various classes, fraternities, and other student organizations; data concerning the Faculty of the Academic Department and those of the affiliated colleges; a sketch of the University Extension work and of the alumni association of the Academic Department; comments on student life; and a picture of Joseph Frey, head janitor and private watchman.

"Old Joe" and Mother Kate Frey, with his sister Kate and "little Georgie," came to the University in 1884. They occupied the original McMicken homestead near the college building opposite Moerlein's Brewery on McMicken Avenue. When the University was moved to the new buildings in Burnet Woods Park they were given four comfortable rooms in the southwest basement of McMicken Hall where they were "at home" to all *"mine poys."*

"Old Joe" was, no doubt, janitor and famulus without peer, and beloved of all, *"stoodunts,"* and alumni alike. Dean Benedict called him the irrepressible "German Disturbance" who was a necessary evil in keeping the home fires burning in the fifteen lecture rooms.

Joe's greatest humiliation came when on a cold and snowy winter morning in 1894 a police patrol from the Fourth District backed up to the McMicken homestead and forcibly put "Old Joe" into the Black Maria and gave him a free ride to the City Hall jail; charged with failing to clear snow from eight hundred feet of sidewalks bordering the University on Clifton and McMicken Avenues. Ellis Gregg was the police judge. Daniel Laurence, Sanford Brown, and Alfred Nippert were Joe's distinguished advisers and counsel.

The comedy of Joe's trial and his personally conducted defense made history which none of the arresting officers ever forgot. He was acquitted amid the applause of the assembled police court habitués. His speech on the duties of a police officer as compared to the responsibilities of the head janitor (there was only one janitor at the time) was a classic which is recorded in the *Cincinnatian* (1895).

"Old Joe" was a jovial, industrious servant of the College. He knew every student and alumnus by first name; and great was his joy when the old boys returned to their Alma Mater and looked in on their old friend, Joe Frey. With the expansion of the University, Joseph Frey was authorized in 1896 to employ two helpers. He appointed his son, George Frey, one of them; and when Old Joe died on November 10, 1909, the Frey dynasty was carried on by "little Georgie."

There were some clashes between the Faculty and the student body concerning student publications and the conduct of senior classes at their night exercises during Commencement week. The trouble arose from the fact that the class of 1897 made certain pecularities of the professors the whetstone of their wit at the Class Night exercises. Some members of the Faculty took offense at some of their remarks and at some of the jokes in the class annual. The Faculty decided thenceforth to censor the annual and supervise Class Night exercises.

The class of 1898 knew about the trouble of their predecessors; so they decided to hold no Class Night exercises, but they were determined to have full control over the publication of their annual. At their class meeting in the fall of the year they decided to discontinue the practice of ridiculing members of the Faculty. In fact the students, themselves, had grown tired of this kind of joke. But when the Faculty declared that all manuscripts intended for publication in the *Cincinnatian* of 1898 should be submitted to them for examination; even though the class had decided not to publish such material, the staff of the annual declined to do so or to promise not to publish such articles. The controversy between the Faculty and the students reached a crisis when the editor-in-chief of the *Cincinnatian* rather than, as the students said, "sacrifice his honesty of purpose and personal convictions" resigned his office.

The editor of the *McMicken Review,* who was a fellow in the Department of English, took up the students' cause and wrote "some scurrilous editorials regarding the relations between the Faculty and the senior class." This infuriated the Faculty, and he was suspended as a student and also from all connection with the *McMicken Review.* The Board of Directors canceled his appointment as a fellow in English unless he should be able "to exculpate himself to the satisfaction of the Faculty." The editor appeared before the Faculty; after apologizing for his statements and asserting that he was ignorant of the existence of a Faculty rule which forbade a student paper to publish anything in the nature of personal reflections and criticism of the government or administration of the University, his suspension was removed and he was allowed to retain his fellowship. The whole unfortunate affair ended, but the Faculty sent a communication to the students that there was only one interpretation of their rule, viz.: "that no comment whatever should be in the student publication upon any Faculty action or policy."

The growth of student life was reflected not only in the establishment
of new publications but likewise in the organization of new fraternities,
societies, and other activities. Beta Theta Pi petitioned the Board of Directors in 1895 for permission to erect a chapter house in Burnet Woods
Park, but the Board replied they had no right to grant such permission
"unless the society was a society of the University itself." In 1894 the first
oratorical and debating society, the Neotrophian, was started. The Philo-
logical Society, composed of professors of languages in the University,
in the high schools and in private schools of Cincinnati, graduate and
undergraduate language students, was formed. The students began to
urge the necessity of formulating rules to govern flag rushes which had
become "akin to real warfare." At the request of Alfred K. Nippert, President of the University Glee and Mandolin Club, the Board appropriated
a sum of money toward defraying the traveling expenses of the Club to
go to the Chicago World's Fair where it gave a series of public concerts
which received much favorable press publicity.

On June 1, 1894, the class of 1894 inaugurated the practice of an annual
senior boat ride as a part of the Commencement week program. The
McMicken Review pronounced the boat ride "the most successful thing
ever attempted by any University class" and said "the name of '94 will
go down in history because of it." On June 12, 1896, the first recorded
Junior Prom was held. In 1897 the Board endorsed a movement started
by the students to organize an endowment fund association for the purpose of obtaining a reserve fund for the University.

ATHLETIC SPORTS

For the first twenty years of its athletic history the University of Cincinnati was hardly known as a real college. It was looked upon more
as a high school contestant. Occasionally a game of football or baseball
would be arranged with one of the local high schools or clubs of the
City. These purely local contests did little to instill into the minds of the
students at McMicken a true college spirit. The inauguration of an annual
field day in 1888 did something to awaken the dormant feeling, but this
event occurred but one day in each year, and its effect was limited.

In the 1890's a new spirit imbued the student body. In the class of
1894 were a number of energetic leaders; Frank Sanford Brown, Alfred
K. Nippert, and Daniel Laurence; due largely to their efforts the University began to make football history. The first thing to be done was to
have the football team trained by a capable coach, and to that end in
1894 the services of Walter Durant Berry were secured. He had played
on the celebrated Yale team with Alonzo Stagg, and for one season had
coached the brawny sons of Centre College, Kentucky. Before this, in

lieu of a coach, the Cincinnati players had obtained their instruction from magazine articles written by Walter Camp.

The effects of the appointment of a regular football coach were soon felt. From a small high school of development athletics at the University rose at once to the level of regular college contests. The football squad were now put through a systematic training course.

In the spring of 1896 football captain Lyman Eaton instituted the first spring practice in football at the University. Eaton had received special instruction in this kind of work from the new football coach, William Reynolds of Princeton. The players did not appreciate the real worth of this practice. In the fall of that year Coach Reynolds inaugurated the first training table for the team.

It is asserted that the game with the University of Chicago in 1893 was arranged through the "unaided, untiring efforts" of Alfred K. Nippert. The game was played on the last day of the World's Fair then in progress in Chicago. The Cincinnati team was defeated by a score of 20 to 0, but it is reported that "Coach Stagg complimented the Cincinnati players and commented the score might have been closer if the Cincinnati players had refrained from liquids." After the game the Cincinnati team and their followers had a hilarious time parading down the Midway led by Judge Samuel Hunt, a former member of the Board of Directors. It is claimed that Ralph Holterhoff was "touched for twenty dollars on the Midway"; Samuel Iglauer ate "too many bratwursts" and had to be rescued by his teammates; and some of the players became very excited on their ride on the Ferris wheel.

When the Cincinnati team went to Columbus that year (1893) after the Chicago game to play Ohio State University they had some strange experiences. It was reported that Dan Laurence by mistake got on a train going to Pittsburgh and "had to take a train back to Cincinnati and then one to Columbus to make the game." The team left Cincinnati with eleven men but somehow or other one was lost en route, and they arrived with only ten men. The Varsity team had to borrow one man from Ohio State before they could go on with the game. In those days headgear was unknown, and football players did not have their hair cut from the beginning to the close of the season. It is claimed that Samuel Iglauer who played halfback against Ohio State invented in this game the "forerunner of the modern helmet." He had broken his nose, and the nose guard had loosened several teeth. Fearing that his ears might start to cauliflower he "made a cotton helmet and covered it with a woolen cap."

In 1894 the University team went to Madison, Indiana, to play Hanover College. They took with them a famous center who had played on several college teams. The Hanover boys refused to allow him to play, as they said he had previously attended their College. They finally consented to let him referee the game. The Cincinnati boys soon had a comfortable lead. To meet this emergency the spectators surged on the field. Hanover began to make large gains with the crowd serving as "interferers." It looked as though Hanover and the spectators would win the game. In this crisis the referee called the game on account of darkness with the score 14 to 12 in favor of UC. When the Cincinnati team left the field in a bus they were showered with Indiana clay all the way to town. The Hanover team refused to pay the hotel bill of the visitors. As the Cincinnati boys started for the steamboat which was to take them home the hotel proprietor appeared with a shotgun. He collected all the money in the crowd, before he would permit them to leave.

The University team was highly successful during the 1897 season, winning 9 games, including a 34 to 0 victory over Ohio State and tying one game. The University lost only one game, 10 to 0, to the powerful Carlisle Indians.

It was shortly after the Thanksgiving game of that year that the University team journeyed to New Orleans to play a post-season game there with the Southern Athletic Club on New Year's Day. They were royally entertained in the Crescent City and won the game with comparative ease, the score being 16 to 0. At the football banquet given the team that night the Louisiana State University challenged the Cincinnati players to a game the next day at Baton Rouge. The challenge was accepted and in the ensuing game Louisiana State University was overwhelmingly defeated by a score of 28 to 0.

It will be recalled that the University played its first intercollegiate game of baseball in 1886. Several years went by before another intercollegiate game was played, although there was each year a team which played with the high schools. In 1893 the University played three intercollegiate games of baseball. The first game was played with the Cincinnati Redlegs. Of course, the University was defeated, the score being 32 to 7. However, the proceeds from this game furnished the team with new uniforms. This game became an annual event until 1896, when the Athletic Advisory Committee forbade all varsity teams to play games with professional teams. In the two remaining games of 1893 the University of Kentucky was the opponent. The first game resulted in a tie; in the second game the University of Kentucky won by a score of 6 to 4. The following spring (1897) was a prosperous one for the McMicken baseball players. This was the first time that the University team made an extended trip in Ohio, Kentucky, and Indiana. The University won five games on this tour and lost four.

The first game of basketball was played by the University in 1896. A University interclass basketball tournament proved to be a great success. Most important of all, basketball provided an activity for the women's athletic program. The following year the University Athletic Committee sponsored a class basketball championship.

In 1898 the basketball team of the Academic Department played but one game with a team representing the Medical School. The score was a tie, each team scoring two points; and by mutual consent it was allowed to remain that way. Basketball was not very popular with the men of the University. This lack of interest was probably due to the fact that the pillars in the small gymnasium made it hazardous to play the game. For two years it practically disappeared from the program of competition. In 1902 the sport was revived, and the University team played with great success. All the college teams encountered with the exception of that of Yale were defeated by the varsity boys. In 1902 and 1903 the tallest man on the team was about six feet tall; the average height of the team was about five feet eight inches. Few fouls were called since one had "to virtually slug or trip an opponent to have a foul called."

On the other hand the game was quite popular with the coeds. They enjoyed the game and played it according to the rules much more thoroughly than the boys. The girl varsity team played three games in 1898, winning two from Hughes High School and losing one to the basketball team of Glendale Seminary.

Interest in track was kept alive during these years. This was particularly so in the annual Field Day events.

CONTROL OF ATHLETICS

The growth of athletic sports created a need for the organization of an athletic association to manage the intercollegiate athletic program. According to the *McMicken Review* the causes which led to the establishment of such an association in the fall of 1890 were:

(1) the University basketball and football teams were unable to play with those of other colleges, as there were no funds to bear traveling expenses. Money had to be raised for each game by private subscription; (2) the majority of the students had absolutely nothing to do with the choice of players or the management of the teams; consequently, the games did not represent the University and failed to interest the student; and (3) the players being selected for occasional games were rarely in practice and did not act in unison with one another. There was no regular manager.

To remedy this situation the students in January 1891 drafted and adopted a constitution providing for a Student's Executive Committee. The constitution gave this Committee authority "to act as the representative of the students in the organization and support of student organizations, and as an official agent in behalf of the students in all affairs in which the latter were a part." The Committee was composed of four seniors, three juniors, two sophomores, and one freshman elected by their respective classes. The University now had a functioning organization which gave the students a limited control over the management of intercollegiate athletic sports.

Meanwhile as college sports developed, all the larger American universities set up Faculty committees on athletics which had general supervision and control of all the various lines of physical training and athletic programs. By 1894 the need for such a committee was apparent at the University of Cincinnati. After a careful examination of the schemes for the government of athletics then in vogue in the best American colleges, the Academic Faculty of the University decided to adopt the Harvard plan. "It was well-known that at no place in this country was there a better tone in athletic matters than at Harvard University." The Student Executive Committee voted favorably upon the establishment of an advisory committee system.

Accordingly, in the spring of 1895 the Faculty provided for the creation of a Committee on the Regulation of Athletics. It was to be composed of three representatives from the University Faculty, three from the Alumni Association, and three from the undergraduate students. The Committee was authorized to appoint the managers and trainers of the various college teams. The election of the managers and captains of the team was left with the student organizations. A Director of the Gymnasium was to be appointed who should give each student entering the gymnasium a thorough examination. From such data the Director was to prescribe the exercises appropriate in each case. The Committee was to encourage not only the present teams in football and baseball, but the organization of active clubs in tennis, cycling, rowing, lacrosse, rifle practice, and track athletics.

The members of the First Committee on the Regulation of Athletics were: Faculty representatives—Professors C. L. Edwards, F. L. Schoenle, W. O. Sproull; alumni representatives—Archibald I. Carson, '87, F. Sanford Brown, '94, A. K. Nippert, '94; student representatives—E. Starnuck Smith, '96, C. W. Andrews, '96, A. T. Smith, '96. The Faculty members stressed the importance of preventing the employment of any non-college men on any of the athletic teams. As the Chairman of the Committee, Professor Edwards said, while "it was very desirable to win games," they should "rather sacrifice victories than hire professionals to win the pennant" for the University. This attitude was in accord with a notable reform movement then being carried on in the college world which had for its aim the promotion of honesty and manliness in athletic contests.

In the fall of 1895 the Board of Directors appointed Walter Durant Berry, the new football coach, director of the gymnasium, and instructor in physical culture, at a salary of $500 a year. He was authorized to charge each student desiring to enter classes of physical culture a fee not to exceed $5.00 a year. The Academic Alumni Association procured equipment for the gymnasium and had installed hot and cold shower baths.

The next step in the control of intercollegiate athletics was the organization of an association among the colleges in Ohio. In May 1896 a conference of representatives of a group of Ohio colleges met at Columbus, and there formed the Ohio Intercollegiate Athletic Association. The constitution which was adopted contained very stringent rules, including severe eligibility rules for all contestants. The rules provided that no person should be permitted to represent any college at any intercollegiate event between members of the Association who was not a "student of that institution in full and regular standing." He should be attending "at least eight hours of lectures or recitations" and have attended the institution "two terms preceding the events." These lists must be certified by the President or three members of the Faculty. No person should be chosen as umpire or referee in any game who had any connection with either of the colleges contesting. No student should be allowed to receive "any form of compensation for participating in athletics." The smaller colleges instigated one rule which was objectionable to the larger institutions. The rule debarred anyone holding a Bachelor's degree from participating in any intercollegiate contest. The convention also fixed June 6 and Columbus as the place of the first field meet.

These were excellent eligibility rules, but the difficulty lay in enforcing them. In the fall of 1896, Dean Myers wrote a long letter to the Board of Directors in which he proved conclusively that the University of Cincinnati; nothwithstanding the fact it had been one of the prime instigators in organizing the Association and in the formulation of the rules, did not live up to them when they handicapped her in winning football games.

For instance, Dean Myers recounted the recent game with Miami University. Before the game Miami, in accordance with the rules, submitted a list of her players and certified that all were regular matriculated students. The manager of the Cincinnati team refused to submit such a list. When requested to do so on the day of the game, the University Committee on the Regulation of Athletics not only sustained its manager in his infraction but declared that Cincinnati was no longer a member of the Association. The game was played with four ineligible men on the Cincinnati team, but they were outclassed none the less, and Miami won the game by a score of 6 to 4. Dean Myers declared the University, for not living up to its contract to keep athletic sports wholesome, should be "ostracized"; and at a special meeting of the Faculty a resolution was passed "instructing its Committee on Athletics to take prompt and effective measures to restore the fair name of the Faculty in connection with the matter of intercollegiate sports."

Shortly after this occurrence, Dean Myers said the Faculty refused to allow a student to matriculate because they could not satisfy themselves that his primary object in wishing to be enrolled was not his desire to become eligible to play football. Unfortunately, a few days after this action was taken by the Faculty, the registering clerk, by mistake, "notified the student he was enrolled." When Dean Myers learned of this he notified the Athletic Committee that the student was not properly enrolled and sent a special messenger with a note to Professor Sproull, the Chairman of the University Athletic Committee, informing him of the recent action of the Faculty and directing Professor Sproull to see that "under no circumstances" should this student be allowed to play. But, said Dean Myers, when the Athletic Committee met, over the protest of Professor Sproull, the wording of the rules of the Athletic Committee was changed; and, as a consequence, the student was put on the team and played in the game against Centre College. Two days later the Faculty, said Dean Myers, had repealed the action creating the Athletic Committee because "contrary to the express instructions of the Faculty" men had been permitted to play on the football team who were not bona fide students of the University.

Dean Myers also informed the Board of Directors that he had learned from one of the medical Faculty that three men had been matriculated in the Medical Department "simply for the purpose of playing football." Dean Myers said he had also learned from the secretary of the medical Faculty that "his own son had matriculated" for this purpose and that his fee of $5.00 had been "paid by a member of the Athletic Committee."

The athletic troubles of 1896 convinced the Academic Faculty that it would be wise to withdraw from all connection with the management of intercollegiate athletics. They, consequently, abolished the Committee for the Regulation of Athletics.

The alumni and students then proceeded to organize an Athletic Council. A committee representing the alumni appeared before the Board of Directors and submitted a set of rules for the regulation of athletics at the University; but the Board decided, since the government of athletics was already vested in the Faculty, not to interfere with their authority.

Consequently, by action of the Board of 1897, a Faculty committee organized the Athletic Council. The Council consisted of the managers of the teams—football, baseball, track—and two members of the Academic Department, one from the Law School, one from the Medical College, five from the academic alumni, and three alumni selected at large. The Board charged the new Council with the responsibility of managing the men's athletic program. The Board decided the Faculty should be entrusted to formulate a set of eligibility rules for athletics. As Dean Hyde who had succeeded Professor Myers as Dean said: "In order, however, to insure the honesty and strictly amateur character of the contests, and to prevent the enrollment upon the University teams of such as were not *bonafide* students, or of such as were disposed to neglect their studies for the sake of athletics, a set of rules of eligibility was drawn up by the Deans of the Academic, Law, and Medical Departments, acting as a committee appointed and empowered by their respective Faculties for this purpose." The new rules set scholarship and residence at the University as the basis of eligibility. The Board decided that the captains of the teams should be held responsible for reporting correct tests of eligible players.

The new system for the regulation of intercollegiate athletics worked well and without friction. The Athletic Council and the officials of the football team showed "a genuine determination to act in accordance with the rules of eligibility." Furthermore, the football team of 1897 made an enviable record for itself. During the season it piled up 146 points as against 22 for its opponents; winning 5 games, tying 1, and losing only 1 game. But during the ensuing years the Athletic Council continued to be troubled with problems of organization, administration, and finances.

In April 1897 the first women's game of basketball was played; and in the same year a Women's Athletic Association was formed to have control of women's athletics. The Association consisted of a Student Executive Committee and two Faculty members.

THE UNIVERSITY IN THE SPANISH-AMERICAN WAR

Like other American colleges and universities, the University of Cincinnati was affected by the Spanish-American War. As the United States began to drift toward war with Spain, the Board of Directors in June 1897 made written application to the Secretary of War for the detail and assignment of an officer of the United States Army for service in the University as instructor in military science. The request received a respectful consideration but was declined on the ground that the full allotment of officers by law for such special service had already been made, and there were no vacancies in the list.

When war was declared by the United States in 1898, the student body quickly reacted to the war spirit sweeping the country. The students cut recitations to witness the departure of the Fort Thomas troops, and a few days later all classes were dismissed by action of the Dean in order to allow the students an opportunity to accompany the Ohio National Guard boys to the depot. The Faculty made provision for time in the curriculum for military drill. The students reflected public sentiment against the reported Spanish brutal methods of warfare by hanging "Butcher" Weyler, the Spanish Commander in Cuba, in effigy on the campus. A number of war songs were published by the students. The most popular of these songs was one called "Marching to Cuba" written by

Edwin E. Schneider, '97, which was sung to the tune of "Marching Through Georgia." It emphasized, as the following words show, the fact that the Spanish-American War began to mark the reconciliation at last of the North and the South.

Unfurl the starry banner, boys; we'll follow it once more,
The blue and grey together, when Old Glory goes before,
We'll follow it to victory as our fathers did of yore,
        While we are marching to Cuba.

Hurrah! Hurrah! We bring the jubilee,
Hurrah! Hurrah! The flag that makes us free,
The chorus now we sing from northern lakes to southern sea,
        While we are marching to Cuba.

We've suffered long enough the Spanish Don's insulting boast,
A patient nation roused to wrath we haste, a mighty host,
To sweep the brutal tyrant from our freedom loving coast,
        While we are marching to Cuba.

Hurrah! Hurrah! We bring the jubilee,
Hurrah! Hurrah! The flag that makes us free,
The chorus now we sing from northern lakes to southern sea,
        While we are marching to Cuba.

When war was declared a movement was inaugurated among the men students of the University to form a company of volunteers. How many enlisted is not known. There are records of eight of the graduates of the University in the Army. So far as is known none of them saw action. They were: Alexander Laist, '87; William Mayo Venable, '92; John B. Hayden, '93; William Ross Tenney, '96; John M. Thomas, '96; Charles E. Tenney, '98; Emerson Venable, '98; and George C. Green, '01.

The women students of the Academic Department took an active part in war work. For a month after the War began the girls held meetings twice a week making bandages and surgeons' sponges and attended clinics at the Laura Memorial College. When the girls learned that hungry soldiers were passing through the City they supplied five thousand soldiers with lunches at the trains. When the College closed for the summer they held meetings once a week at the Avondale Presbyterian Church, spending the afternoon in sewing for the soldiers.

In the belief that their efforts could be better utilized by their becoming a part of some other organization there was organized the Women's Auxiliary Corps of the Army and Navy League of Hamilton County. The League voted $50.00 to assist in paying for lunches provided for the soldiers, and from this time forward, the lunches were purchased at a restaurant instead of being supplied by friends.

When Fort Thomas became a hospital two girls each week were held responsible to make daily beef tea for the inmates. The demand for tea finally became so great that it was found difficult to meet it, and after some weeks a room was obtained at Fort Thomas where it was prepared by the University Auxiliary Corps. This small kitchen later developed into a diet kitchen which the girls claimed was "the first established in connection with a military hospital."

On August 10 and 11, 1898, the University Corps formed other branches of the Women's Auxiliary Corps of Hamilton County to serve lunches to businessmen for the benefit of the Army and Navy League. These lunches were served mainly by students or graduates of the University and netted a sum of $525.

A private contribution enabled the University Corps to supply the soldiers at Fort Thomas with ice cream and fruits during the end of the summer months. The invalid soldiers at Fort Thomas sent a note to the Corps expressing their deep appreciation for getting "the refreshing food" and explaining how the soldiers spoke with "affectionate praise of the ministering angels who provided it."

13   *Problems of Leadership*

The executive work of the University was mounting. The transfer of the University to Burnet Woods Park, the erection of Hanna and Cunningham Halls and the Van Wormer buildings, and the subsequent addition of the fully organized Medical and Law Departments caused the Board of Directors to recognize the imperative necessity of selecting a President for the University who should assume all the executive duties of the various departments and thus relieve the Deans of those departments from such administrative work. For two years (1890–1891) Professor Eddy had been Acting President but during the succeeding eight years (1891–1899) the Dean of the Academic Department, rotating among the members of the Faculty, had acted as Executive Head of the University. It will be recalled that this arrangement had proved most unsatisfactory.

Early in 1895 the alumni of the Academic Department offered to raise a fund by subscription to pay the salary of a President for five years. The University Board appointed a committee of three, consisting of Frank J. Jones, Edmund K. Stallo, and Dr. Charles A. L. Reed to work with the alumni committee on this matter. The Board was well aware of the necessity for an executive head of the University; but, unfortunately, the Board of Education in 1897 reduced the levy for the support of the University from three-tenths of a mill to two-tenths of a mill for one year. Consequently, the University lost about $18,000 of annual income. As a result the University Board was unable and unwilling to invite anyone to become President, and so the hope of securing a President had to be abandoned temporarily.

As business conditions improved after the election of William McKinley as President of the United States in 1896, the Board became more optimistic; on June 22, 1898, it decided to take the first action toward the appointment of a President of the University. A resolution introduced by Dr. Reed was adopted by which a select committee of three, in conjunction with the Deans of the three Faculties, was appointed to take the necessary steps to secure at the earliest practical moment a President of the University, and "after securing for him the indorsement of a majority of the joint Faculties" to report his selection to the Board for final action. Under this resolution Oscar W. Kuhn, Frank J. Jones, and Dr. Charles A. L. Reed were appointed; together with the Deans of the Academic, Law, and Medical Departments.

On February 20, 1899, Dr. Reed reported that the members of the Committee, while they had tried to carry out their assignment, had been unable to secure anyone; and so asked the Board to empower them to send a subcommittee of not less than two members "to visit several universities and cities for the purpose of more carefully investigating the qualifications of candidates for the Presidency." The Board did so, and the Committee appointed William Howard Taft and Oscar W. Kuhn to perform this duty. This committee made inquiries at Princeton, Harvard, Yale, Columbia University, the University of Pennsylvania, Ann Arbor, Chicago, and elsewhere concerning prospective candidates for the Presidency.

On May 15, 1899, Dr. Reed submitted the report of the Committee on the Presidency and recommended the appointment of Professor Howard Ayers of the University of Missouri at a salary of $5,000 a year with a written statement highly recommending him signed by William Howard Taft, Oscar W. Kuhn, Frank J. Jones, F. W. Hyde, and Dr. Reed.

This report and recommendation were faulty in that the resolution by authority of which the Committee was acting required that any selection made by the Committee should be approved by a majority of the joint Faculties before being reported to the Board for final action. Upon the contrary it was signed by three members of the select committee (Taft, Kuhn, and Jones), and only by the Deans of the Law (Taft) and Academic (Hyde) Faculties; the latter of whom signed under protest, and then only when assured by the Chairman of the Board (Kuhn) that "no professor could or would be removed except by the board, and then only upon charges and a full hearing." This report was never submitted to the joint Faculties "for their consideration and it never was so submitted or approved."

The Committee on the Presidency submitted with their report "after consultation with Dr. Ayers" another report recommending a series of additions to Article IX of the By-Laws of the Board defining the powers and duties of the President. These provided: (1) "the President shall be *ex officio* a member of each Faculty, and it shall be his right and duty to preside at any meeting"; (2) he shall have "the power of nominating the Dean of each Faculty subject to the approval of the Board of Directors"; (3) he shall have "the right to attend all meetings of the

Board and address them; and shall be an official member of all standing committees"; (4) he shall have "the exclusive right to transmit all communications from each Faculty and from each member thereof to the Board"; (5) he shall have "the right to recommend to the Board the vacation of professorships and other positions in the academic departments"; (6) he shall have "the exclusive right to nominate professors in all departments insofar as this be inconsistent with the contracts under which certain of the departments were then conducted"; (7) he shall have "the ultimate authority in all matters of discipline"; (8) he shall have the right to advise the Board in all matters of expenditures; and (9) he shall have the power to control all employees and be the chief custodian of the buildings.

The Committee suggested in their report that these statutes be submitted "to the Law and Medical Faculties for their consent and also to the trustees of the Cincinnati College" because no provision was made "for the President of the University and his powers and duties in the contracts by which the Law and Medical Departments were added to the University."

The Board adopted the report of the Committee on the Presidency with one amendment, the salary of the President was increased to the $6,000 requested by Dr. Ayers; and on June 12, 1899, Professor Ayers accepted the position of President of the University, effective July 1.

The Faculties of the Academic, Medicine, and Law Departments on June 12, 1899, ratified the appointment of Dr. Ayers as President of the University; but in each instance qualified their acceptance of the statutes defining his powers and duties. The Academic Committee "recommended to the Board the appointment of all instructors then employed in the Academic Department for one year at their present salaries." The Medical Faculty accepted the proposed statutes "except insofar as they were not in conflict with the conveyance and contract of April and May 1896" by which the Medical College became a part of the University. On the ground that some of the proposed amendments to the by-laws were inconsistent with the terms of their contract in uniting with the University, the Law Faculty objected to the proposal empowering the President to appoint the Dean of their Faculty and to recommend the vacation of professorships. Dean Taft notified the Board that while he was "in favor of enlarging the powers of the President insofar as the Academic Department was concerned" in regard to his own department he said: "It seems to the Faculty that it would be unwise to give to the President power to recommend vacations of or selections to the Law Faculty."

The way in which the Medical and Law Faculties agreed to the proposed statutes defining the powers and duties of the President clearly shows how jealous the members of their Faculties were of the privileges secured to them by their contracts, and how fearful they were lest the

President might seek to reduce them or destroy them. Unless the new President understood the circumstances by which these Colleges had united with the University and the terms of their contracts, there was a strong possibility of trouble, as the future soon revealed.

THE NEW PRESIDENT

In their report to the Board, the Committee on the Presidency traced the career and qualifications of Dr. Ayers for the position. Dr. Ayers was born in 1861 in Olympia, Washington Territory. While he was still an infant his father, a hardware merchant, moved from Olympia to Fort Smith, Arkansas, where young Ayers received his primary and secondary education in the common schools and high school of that City. His father sent him to the University of Michigan where he took a scientific course and became deeply interested in biology and kindred subjects. He left Ann Arbor after three years' stay and went to Harvard where he found better opportunities for biological study. He was graduated from Harvard in 1883 with the degree of Bachelor of Science and with the highest honors of his class. While at Harvard he won the first Walker Prize, offered by the Boston Society of Natural History and open to contestants from all parts of the world for the best scientific memoir.

After receiving his degree he went abroad and studied for two years at the Universities of Heidelberg, Strasbourg, and Freiburg. At Freiburg he obtained the degree of Doctor of Philosophy *magna cum laude*. Subsequently, he pursued his studies and work of original research at the Marine Zoological Station of Vienna University at Trieste, and at the Station Maritime of the University of Paris at Banyal-sur-Mer, France, and attended lectures at the College de France and at the Sorbonne.

On his return to the United States he became instructor in biology at the University of Michigan for one year. The next year he was called to Harvard where he taught for two years both in the University proper and in Radcliffe College. In 1889 he was appointed director of the Allis Lake Laboratory of Biology at Milwaukee. He remained for four years at the head of the Lake Laboratory engaged in original biological study. When this Laboratory was transferred to Menton, Dr. Ayers was invited to take charge of it. He declined the offer. In the fall of 1893, Dr. Ayers was called to take the chair of biology in the University of Missouri at Columbia, Missouri. Dr. Ayers became a member of the academic, the medical, and the agricultural Faculties. He reorganized the Department of Biology and made it one of the prominent, successful departments of the University. He published many articles on biological and kindred subjects in English, German, and French. Since 1889 he had been continuously in charge of biological research at the Marine Biological Laboratory at Wood's Hole, Massachusetts.

While in Europe he gave special attention to the methods of education in German gymnasia and universities. At the University of Missouri he strove to raise the standard of collegiate education and improve its methods. He spent much time representing the University in visiting the high schools and other preparatory schools of the State and was successful in securing more thorough secondary education. He was instrumental in bringing about progressive changes in the curricula and methods of study in the academic, medical, and agricultural departments of the University.

The Committee stated that it was "the unanimous verdict of his colleagues with whom he had been associated for the last six years that he possessed 'the executive and administrative faculty in a high degree'." He was a man "of fine physique, of tremendous energy, and unwavering fixity of purpose." He had high and broad "ideals of education" and was "ambitious to realize them." While at the University of Michigan and at Harvard he was a member of the University football teams, and he rowed on the class crew at the latter institution. The experience had given him "an open sympathy with the student body" and as a consequence he wielded "more influence with them than any other member of the Faculty." He was a "forcible, lucid, and direct speaker" and was "generally chosen to speak for the University at public meetings and elsewhere." Although Dr. Ayers was only thirty-eight years of age he held a position "in the very front rank of biologists in the country." The Committee acknowledged that "his power and capacity" as the executive head of a great University "was yet to be proven by the fact" but he had in him the elements which insured his becoming "a great educational leader and administrator." The Committee said they had had "personal interviews with Dr. Ayers" and had discussed "with great candor the situation" at the University. Dr. Ayers was inclined to think that the Board "should pay to one worthy of the Presidency, 'in order that he might be as useful as possible,' the annual salary of six thousand dollars." After consultation with the heads of several eastern universities, the Committee did not advise the Board at the outset to pay to a new President a larger salary than $5,000. But the Committee said that they felt assured, if he should "prove to be successful" and should "build up the University as they hoped" the Board would show themselves "not to be niggardly in recognizing his worth by increasing his compensation." As has been shown, the Board disregarded the Committee's recommendation concerning the salary and agreed to pay Dr. Ayers $6,000.

OTHER IMPORTANT EVENTS OF 1899

Besides the election of a new President in 1899 other important events occurred during the year. One was the magnanimous donation of David

Sinton of the sum of $100,000 to be used for the maintenance of the Academic Department which subsequently resulted in the establishment of the David Sinton Professorship of Economics. The other was an arrangement reached between the Board of Directors of the University and the Historical and Philosophical Society of Ohio by which the entire collection of books of the Society, consisting of 20,000 bound volumes and 40,000 pamphlets were to be transferred to the Van Wormer Library and housed there as soon as it was completed. The collection of the Society contained many rare and valuable books relating to the early history of Ohio and of the Miami Valley. It was finally deposited in the Van Wormer Library building in 1902 where it was made available for research purposes to students of the University.

FIRST RECOMMENDATIONS OF THE NEW PRESIDENT

One of the first recommendations of the newly elected President, and adopted by the Board, provided for the establishment of a summer school; thus placing within the reach of the teachers of the public schools of the City the opportunity of taking work at the University. It will be recalled that during the summer of 1877–1878 a limited number of lectures was given by members of the Faculty of the University, especially for teachers in mathematics and astronomy. By the end of the nineteenth century all the larger American universities and many colleges had established summer schools. There were many reasons for the popularity of these summer schools. By the establishment of summer schools an opportunity was afforded to many students to continue their educational study during the summer; thereby reducing the number of years necessary to complete their college courses. It enabled teachers in high schools and secondary schools to devote a portion of their vacation to systematic study; thus advancing themselves in their profession. It made it possible for students from high schools who lacked a sufficient number of credits for admission to a university or to a college to make up these deficiencies during the summertime. Furthermore, the University plant could be operated during the entire year instead of only three-fourths of the year; thereby reducing the cost of higher education to the student and the general public and likewise reducing the per capita cost of a college education.

In 1900 the University opened its first summer school. Courses of instruction, especially designed for teachers, were organized on Saturdays and in the afternoons of the other days of the week. The summer session was divided into two terms of six weeks each. The tuition was $15.00 for a course and $10.00 for each additional course. The summer school was highly successful at first, but the attendance later declined probably due to the disorganized state of affairs at the University. In 1904 it was discontinued.

Another recommendation of the President which was carried out by the Board was the physical improvement of the University buildings and grounds. During President Ayers' administration the University campus was surveyed and plotted. The Clifton Avenue frontage was graded. Two cement sidewalks were constructed on the Clifton Avenue frontage. Two flights of massive stone steps with four broad cement platforms and connecting sidewalks were built immediately in front of the entrance to McMicken Hall to provide easy access to the University halls from Clifton Avenue. A cinder track was constructed. The ground was graded and rolled for three tennis courts. The most important improvement in the interior of the University buildings was the installation of a new steam heating plant which replaced the old hot-air system. For the first time in the history of the University the buildings were kept warm in the cold weather. An adequate water supply system for the protection of the University plant and for the water supply of the laboratories was constructed.

CHANGES IN THE FACULTY AND ADMINISTRATIVE PERSONNEL

The most important event that occurred during the year 1899 was the reorganization by President Ayers of the Faculty in the Academic Department. There were two ways in which this could be effected. The changes could be made gradually or they could be made all at one time. While the first method was the easier and might have prevented complications, President Ayers resolved to use the second method. He did this he said in order to give the men notified of his impending changes more time to make other arrangements, and thus prevent unnecessary hardships. Besides there would be less disturbance of the work of the university by making all the changes at once than by extending them throughout the years.

Accordingly, early in January 1900, President Ayers explained to certain members of the Faculty that their resignations were requested and would go into effect by July 1. In case none of them tendered their resignations, he would recommend to the Board the vacation of their professorships.

The professors of civil engineering, chemistry, and physics tendered their resignations. Subsequently, the professor of civil engineering and the professor of physics withdrew their resignations and the professor of chemistry alone requested that his resignation be placed in the hands of the Board.

On January 19, 1900, the Board adopted the recommendation of President Ayers that vacancies be declared in the departments of mathematics, civil engineering, Latin, Greek, physics, and biology; that the lectureship in comparative literature be discontinued; and that the professorships of French and German be abolished; all to take effect from and after the close of the academic year in July 1900. The President was empowered to recommend suitable successors to the various incumbents of the several departments in which vacancies had been declared and to reorganize the departments of French and German, dividing them into the departments of Romance and German languages, respectively.

The specific changes made in the instructional force as a result of the reorganization of the academic and engineering departments were as follows:

Professor E. W. Hyde was retired; and Professor Harris Hancock, a graduate of Johns Hopkins University who had received his Doctor's degree at the University of Berlin and was teaching at the University of Chicago, was appointed professor of mathematics.

Professor W. O. Sproull was retired; and Dr. John Miller Burnam who, after receiving his Doctor's degree at Yale University had studied in Paris, Madrid, Berlin, and was teaching at the University of Missouri, was appointed professor of Latin.

Professor Thomas French was retired; and Dr. Louis Trenchard More who had received his Doctor's degree at Johns Hopkins University and was teaching at the University of Nebraska, was appointed professor of physics.

Professor T. H. Norton resigned the professorship of chemistry, and the instruction was given temporarily to younger members of the department.

Professor P. V. N. Myers was retired; the professorship of history and political economy was abolished; and two new chairs were established. Dr. Merrick Whitcomb who had received his Doctor's degree at the University of Pennsylvania and was teaching there, was appointed professor of history and, subsequently, Dean of the Academic Department.

Dr. Frederick Charles Hicks who had received his Doctor's degree at the University of Michigan and was teaching at the University of Missouri, was appointed professor (Sinton) of economics and civics.

Professor W. Baldwin was retired, and Professor Harry Thomas Cory was appointed professor of civil engineering.

The professorship of French and German was abolished, and two new chairs were created. Dr. Max Poll who had received his Doctor's degree at the University of Strasbourg, then taught at Harvard University, was appointed professor of German languages; and Dr. Joseph Arthur Davidson who had received his Doctor's degree at the University of Leipzig and had taught at Leland Stanford University, was appointed professor of Romance languages.

Dr. F. L. Schoenle was retired; and Dr. Joseph Edward Harry who had received his Doctor's degree at Johns Hopkins University and was teaching at Georgetown College, Kentucky, was appointed professor of Greek.

Dr. C. L. Edwards was retired; and Dr. Michael Frederick Guyer who had received his Doctor's degree at the University of Chicago and was then teaching as an instructor in biology at the University of Cincinnati, was subsequently promoted to professor of biology.

In addition to these changes made by President Ayers the University lost by death Dr. James T. Whittaker, professor of theory and practice in the College of Medicine, and Mr. Joseph F. Wright, for seventeen years Clerk of the Board of Directors. Subsequently, Dr. Frederick Forcheimer was appointed professor of practice of medicine and diseases of children to fill the vacancy created by the death of Dr. Whittaker; and Dr. P. S. Conner was elected Dean of the Medical College to fill the vacancy created by the resignation of Dr. W. W. Seeley. In 1902, Henry Davis, Jr., was elected Secretary of the Board; and the following year Daniel Laurence was appointed Clerk of the Board with Christie Wilkie as Assistant Clerk and Collector

In the Law Department, Judge William H. Taft resigned the Deanship to accept the Presidency of the Second Philippine Commission, and Dr. Gustavus H. Wald was elected Dean. Judge Rufus B. Smith resigned his professorship on account of the pressure of his duties as Judge of the Superior Court of Cincinnati. Mr. John W. Warrington was elected to the vacant professorship, and E. R. James and Robert C. Pugh were appointed instructors in law.

FIRST ATTACK ON PRESIDENT AYERS

At the first meeting of the Academic Faculty in the fall of 1899 the members of the Faculty looked forward to having the new President presenting to them his plans for the University. Instead of that, after routine business had been disposed of, the President announced that a motion to adjourn would be in order. Adjournment followed, and the President immediately left the room leaving the Faculty astonished and disappointed.

In January 1900 the Faculty and the student body were startled by the news that President Ayers had requested the resignation of certain members of the Academic family. Rumors spread that the President had asked for the dismissal of the entire Faculty; whereas out of a teaching corps of about 150 members the President had requested the resignation of only eight. A morning paper, the *Cincinnati Commercial*, immediately began a violent attack upon President Ayers and stirred up the alumni and citizens of the City in behalf of the professors. The Central Labor Council passed resolutions condemning the action of President Ayers.

The smoldering fire of rebellion assumed more portentous proportions when Professor P. V. N. Myers suddenly tendered his resignation to take effect as soon as possible. Professor Myers was one of the few members of the Faculty whom President Ayers had recommended should be retained. The President had recommended that Professor Myers be a lecturer on ancient and modern history instead of professor.

In his letter to the members of the Board, Professor Myers set forth his reasons for leaving the University. He said that he could not consent to work with President Ayers, because it would mean giving "approval to the professional assassination—I cannot use a less accusing word—" by a comparative stranger "of his colleagues of many years." He said that he preferred "exile and even death with them to association with him" who had shown himself by his recent action "to be of an almost tyrannical nature." Professor Myers furthermore stated that ever since the advent of President Ayers "the University had been disrupted" and had been dealt a blow from which it would be "slow in recovering." Professor Myers characterized President Ayers' course of procedure as "unreasonable, tyrannical, and unrighteous." The resignation of Professor Myers incensed many of the citizens of the City. He was regarded as one of the most prominent members of the Faculty and had "a great following among those interested in the University."

A public meeting was held and a Citizens' Committee was organized to investigate the methods and reasons of the recent discharges of professors by President Ayers. General A. Hickenlooper presided; and among those present were James A. Green, Dr. David Phillipson, Principal E. W. Coy of Hughes High School, John Uri Lloyd, the Reverend Charles F. Goss, and many other prominent citizens of the community. A request of the Citizens' Committee to meet with the Board was denied, but the Board agreed to appoint a special committee to meet with one of their committees. A joint conference of representatives of the Board and of a committee of the Citizens' Committee met in Dr. Reed's office at which it was agreed that the report of the Citizens' Committee should be brought to the attention of the Board.

When the Board met on February 19, 1900, there was a delegation of the Citizens' Committee present. In response to Chairman Kuhn of the Board, General Hickenlooper requested the Board to reconsider their vote disposing of certain members of the Academic Faculty and that, pending the result of that vote, the Board give the members of the Faculty "a full, a fair, an impartial, and deserving hearing."

A lively discussion ensued. Dr. Reed defended the action of the Board and moved that the entire matter be referred to the special committee of the Board, consisting of Oscar W. Kuhn, Dr. Charles A. L. Reed, John B. Peaslee, Max B. May, and Elliot H. Pendleton. Dr. Thaddeus Reamy objected on the ground that only a minority was represented on the special committee. Furthermore, that committee had already once reported unanimously in favor of sustaining President Ayers. Besides he thought that the Citizens' Committee should be given a full hearing. It was finally decided upon motion of Dr. Reed that the special committee should draft a report and present it at the next meeting of the Board.

Accordingly, at a special meeting of the Board on February 21, 1900, Dr. Reed presented the Report of the Special Committee on behalf of the Board. Dr. Reed recounted the previous history of rotating the Deanship among the members of the Faculty; the discord thus developed in the Faculty, and how the professors had accused each other of incompetence. As the report said: "if all the suggestions of removal by members of the Faculty against members of the Faculty had been acted upon, not a single member of the present teaching body would have been left in position. If the statements made by the professors against professors were true, the verdict should be upon that basis; if the statements were untrue, the moral perturbation thereby implies their authors unfit to be connected with an institution of learning; in either event the Faculty falls as a self-condemned body." These facts forced the necessity of action upon the Directors.

At the conclusion of the reading of the report by Dr. Reed sustaining the action of President Ayers, a vote was taken and of the fourteen members present, only one negative vote was cast, namely by Dr. Reamy, who was both a professor in the Medical College and a member of the Board of Directors, a coincidence of service which was regarded as a violation of correct principles of university government.

The battle so long and bitterly waged against President Ayers was apparently abandoned after he was vindicated of the charges of arbitrarily and unjustly reorganizing the Academic Faculty. The *Cincinnati Times-Star* temporarily ceased its denunciation of the President. The community at large recognized that an efficient and harmonious Faculty had been installed; that the attendance had been increased; that the standard of scholarship had been advanced; and that the student body had been loyally co-operative with the new regime. For two years after the reorganization of the Faculty there was greater tranquility in the Faculty of the Academic Department than there had been for many years.

UNIVERSITY PROGRESS DURING THE AYERS ADMINISTRATION

The Calm Before Another Storm

During the years of comparative placidity in the Academic Department the University progressed. The new professors, later always referred to as the "Old Guard," made a very favorable impression upon the City and the student body. Graduate work was encouraged by President Ayers, and the degree of Doctor of Philosophy was added to the list of graduate degrees conferred. In 1901 the Cincinnati chapter of the Daughters of the American Revolution established a graduate fellowship with a stipend of $100 for graduate work in American history. This was the first privately endowed fellowship in the University.

At the suggestion of President Ayers in March 1901, Miss Emilie Esselborn was appointed instructor in Romance languages and the first Dean of Women for the session 1901–1902 at a remuneration of $200.

The professors, alumni, and students of the University, assisted financially by private citizens, maintained in one of the most crowded districts of the City on Liberty and Plum Streets, a settlement house in which there were a free kindergarten, a gymnasium, circulating library, amusement clubs for boys, and classes in cooking, needlework, and such things for girls. In the University Settlement the students of the University were given an opportunity to study local social conditions and to learn how to help ameliorate them.

In 1900 the *University Bulletin* was issued. In it were published general announcements of the University and original contributions by members of the Faculty in their respective fields. The following year (1901) Mr. Charles P. Taft donated a completely equipped University Press.

In 1901, Mrs. Harriet Evans was appointed Librarian. The resources of the Library were enlarged during these years by a number of donations. The Library was enriched by the donation of Mr. William A. Procter of the Enoch T. Carson Shakespearian Collection and his library of books on the drama.

Student Activities

New student organizations were formed and new evidences of college spirit were displayed on the campus. In 1898 the campus YMCA and the campus YWCA were formed. In the same year (1898) two new fraternities, Phi Delta Theta and Sigma Sigma, were organized. Sigma Sigma was founded on the lower deck of the pleasure steamer, *Island Queen,* by Parke Johnson, Russell Wilson, Robert Humphreys, Walter Eberhard, Charles A. Adler, Smith Hickenlooper, and Adna Innes. Originally a sophomore society, by 1902 it had come to be regarded as an upperclass honor society. The purpose of Sigma Sigma was to bind in closer union the fraternity chapters then existing at the University and to promote college and class spirit in the University. By 1904 the society had become well known in the University annals as a result of two burlesque productions, *Hoop-La* and *Flip-Flap.*

With the growth of college spirit the first attempt was made to issue a song book. In 1901 the Stygian Society was organized. It was composed of kindred spirits who met once a month around the festive board to sing student songs and to make student speeches. Membership was limited to the upperclassmen of the different departments and to the alumni of the University and other universities and colleges. In that year the Stygian Society published a small volume of songs for the use of its members. The volume contained a number of original songs by graduates and undergraduates of the University. The book, however, was so small that only the words were printed, not the music.

One of the songs published in this volume was the varsity song which became the "Alma Mater" of the University of Cincinnati. The music and words of this song were by Otto Juettner. He received his Bachelor of Arts degree from Xavier University in 1885, and his Master of Arts from the same institution in 1887. The following year he received his Doctor of Medicine degree from the Medical College of Ohio. When the football teams of the University and Xavier University today battle in the field of Nippert Stadium, the loyal supporters of each of these Colleges sing their respective "Alma Mater's"; the words and music of each are by Otto Juettner. He was a pioneer X-ray specialist, a historian, musician, linguist, scholar, and connoisseur of the fine arts. He is best remembered for his monumental work entitled *Daniel Drake and His Followers,* which contains a wealth of information on the medical history of this area.

In 1902 a new weekly student paper, *The University News,* was founded. It was published originally by *The Forum,* a literary and debating society of the junior and senior classes. This weekly publication was the forerunner of the present *Cincinnati News Record,* as it marked the beginning of a permanent organization on the campus able to publish a weekly student paper.

The Technical School

At the suggestion of President Ayers an agreement was entered into between the Board of Trustees of the Cincinnati Technical School and the Board of Directors of the University by which the University agreed to maintain the manual training of the Technical School until such time as the Board of Education was able to establish a satisfactory normal training high school. The Technical School gave the University its entire equipment, valued at $6,000 and offered to erect a suitable building. The Technical School had been founded in 1886 by a number of public-spirited citizens for the purpose of remedying the lack of manual training and technical education in the City. As a result of this agreement a suitable building was erected at a cost of $25,000 raised by friends of the old school on the Burnet Woods campus. The south wing of the main floor of the Technical School was occupied as a manual training shop and machine shop; and the basement floor was occupied by a black smithy, forge shop, and a foundry. The north wing of the main floor was occupied with biological, chemical, physical laboratories, and a drawing room.

The Beginning of the Evening College

In 1902 the first attempt was made to organize an Evening College. In that year Christian W. Marx, professor of mechanical engineering who had come to Cincinnati from the University of Missouri at the invitation of President Ayers, requested the latter's permission to organize evening classes in engineering. Professor Marx may well be called "the Father of the Evening College." He conceived the idea of this kind of instruction by studying the work of the Cooper Institute of New York in adult education. President Ayers was impressed by the suggestion, but said there was no money available for such an undertaking. Dr. Marx offered to conduct his classes without compensation and said he believed that he could get other members of the Faculty to do so. After getting permission of the City Council, Dr. Ayers told Dr. Marx to proceed to organize a program.

The program was patterned somewhat after that of the Ohio Mechanics' Institute. It was not designed to be of college level, because the students were not adequately prepared in mathematics. The courses were given in Hanna Hall through the "round table" method. The City Council contributed a small amount of financial assistance for operating expenses but not for the salaries of those engaged in the instruction. There were no admission requirements for the program. Anyone was eligible who was employed during the day and who desired to continue his education at night.

The evening engineering program was not carried on the following year, because Professor Marx was unable to get other members of the Faculty to donate their time to the project. The attacks on President Ayres also militated against the progress of the plan. Although Professor Marx left the University in 1905, he continued to conduct the meetings in the evening and on Saturday afternoons at his downtown office.

Proposal for a College of Commerce

An effort was made by President Ayers to establish a College of Commerce and Finance. Prominent and influential members of commercial organizations of the City were invited to co-operate with the Board of Directors in creating such a department in the University; but the undertaking, although not abandoned, was for the time being unsuccessful.

The Law School

During these years many changes occurred in the Law Department of the University. In June 1902, Dr. Gustavus H. Wald, Dean of the Law Department, died suddenly. Later his brother and mother donated $25,-000 to the Law School in his memory for the establishment of the Gustavus H. Wald Professorship of Law. This sudden demise left the school near the close of its academic year without a Dean. The Faculty, however, took early action to safeguard the interests of the School by electing Harlan Cleveland to succeed Dr. Wald. Mr. Cleveland notified the Faculty that he would be unable to accept the appointment as a permanent one owing to his duties as United States Attorney for the Southern District of Ohio. After much correspondence and investigation on the part of the President and members of the Faculty, William P. Rogers, Dean of the Law School of the University of Indiana, was elected Dean.

During this year the Board of Trustees of the Cincinnati College leased the College building on Walnut Street for a long term, which enabled them by the income thus secured to build a new home for the Law Department. This building was located on Ninth Street between Vine and Race Streets.

On October 17, 1903, the new Law School building was formally dedicated with appropriate exercises. On this occasion E. W. Kitteridge, President of the Board of Trustees, delivered an excellent historical sketch of the school with a comprehensive statement of its funds and endowments. The principal address was delivered by Sir Frederick Pollock of England "who was considered the greatest jurist of the English law" on the subject of "The Common Law."

One of the events not on the program created some amusement. During the course of the first speech by President Ayers, Sir Frederick "began to nod his legal head in slumber from which he was aroused by the applause attending the close of the speech. He thereupon began to applaud, evidently having enjoyed the speech or its conclusion."

President Ayers, Dr. Reamy, and the Medical Department

In 1902, President Ayers was again in trouble, but this time the President clashed with the Medical Faculty rather than the Academic Faculty. The trouble between President Ayers and the Medical Faculty was one of long standing. It will be recalled that when the old Medical College of Ohio joined the University of Cincinnati and became the Medical Department of the University, it surrendered its charter and individuality; but by the terms of the agreement it retained for itself certain rights, and among these rights was that the Faculty should appoint its own professors. The Medical College was very jealous of its prerogatives.

On January 30, 1902, President Ayers recommended to the Board of Directors the establishment of a postgraduate course of medicine. Mr. Winslow of the Board moved that the President be requested to invite a committee from the Medical Faculty to consult with the Board Committee on the University regarding the establishment of the postgraduate course.

Three days later the Medical Faculty met in session with President Ayers presiding. President Ayers announced that he had called the Faculty together for the purpose of appointing a committee of its members to consult with the Board Committee on the University in regard to the postgraduate Medical School. Dr. Reamy called Dr. Ayers' attention to the fact that the Winslow Resolution merely requested him to invite the Medical Faculty to confer with the Board Committee, but that it did not authorize him to appoint the committee. President Ayers insisted that Dr. Reamy's memory was faulty, and that he was mistaken. Dr. Reamy "begged" President Ayers not to make an issue of this point as he (Dr. Reamy) was positive about the wording of the Winslow Resolution and that either President Ayers' memory was faulty or he was "deliberately misrepresenting the facts and was usurping authority that had not been conferred upon him." Dr. Reamy later claimed that the President "paid no further attention to what he said." Dr. Reamy thereupon made a motion that the Faculty select a committee of five, including the Dean. President Ayers ruled Dr. Reamy's motion "was out of order and adjourned the meeting," announcing he would appoint the committee; and he did.

At the next meeting of the Medical Faculty, when the secretary read the minutes for the previous meeting which recounted in detail what had taken place at the aforementioned meeting, President Ayers suggested that "it was not usual to enter in the minutes anything in the line of speeches or discussion but to confine the record to all the motions made and carried." The Faculty paid no attention to the President's requests; the minutes were approved as read "without a dissenting vote."

At the May 6 Commencement exercises of the Medical Department, the President attracted considerable attention by appearing in resplendent robes which it was said Dr. Ayers had brought back with him from a trip to Europe. The Commercial Tribune published a detailed description of the President's cap and gown and the Medical Faculty carefully kept a copy of it in their minutes. "He was attired," said the Commercial Tribune, "in an Oxford cap." But it was the gown of the President which attracted "special notice." It was made of black silk, purple-lined, with a vest of the same color. Across the sleeves were three strips representing the various degrees said to have been conferred upon President Ayers, B.S., Ph.D., LL.D., all in mighty contrast with a score or more men who sat around him attired in conventional black without any attempt at ostentation."

On June 9 another incident occurred in the clash between President Ayers and the Medical Faculty. The President again claimed that he had the right to appoint professors "not only under the provisions of the McMicken will but under the laws of Ohio." The Faculty voted him down. Dr. Reamy later claimed that as the President reached the top steps of the Medical Department at the close of the session he shook his fingers at the members remaining and said: "I propose to govern the Medical Department of the University if I have to go to hell to do it, and you gentlemen may as well understand it now as later."

Dr. Reamy later declared that he told this incident to Major Jones of the Board. Major Jones stated that he had confronted President Ayers with the charge, and that Dr. Ayers had "positively denied having used the language." Dr. Reamy replied "that President Ayers' denial raised a question of veracity between them and that he (Dr. Reamy) was ready to prove what he had said."

On June 17, Dr. Reamy exploded a bombshell in one of the hottest meetings of the Board on record. The trouble began when one of the Board members offered a motion to spend $5,000 in accordance with a recommendation of the President to build on the campus a building to contain the old telescope of the Observatory when a new one, which had been purchased, arrived. During the discussion it was pointed out that Professor Porter in charge of the Observatory objected to locating the new building on the campus instead of on the Observatory grounds. When the vote was taken the President was routed in his attempt to locate the Observatory on the campus. This was followed by another skirmish when President Ayers was again defeated in trying to keep Professor Porter off the committee to whom should be referred the location of the new refractory.

After these matters were disposed of, Chairman Kuhn was about to entertain a motion for adjournment when Dr. Reamy requested permission to speak. To the astonishment of the Board Dr. Reamy brought two charges verbally against the President and demanded that the Board investigate them. First he charged that Dr. Ayers in addressing some members of the Medical Faculty on June 9 had "used language grossly profane and unbecoming a gentleman"; and second, that President Ayers had "willfully, knowingly, specifically, and for a purpose misrepresented the substance and letter of the Winslow Resolution." When Dr. Reamy concluded his statement, Mr. Pendleton moved that the charges be reduced to writing. Dr. Reamy promptly did so; but before he could proffer them, Chairman Kuhn criticized Dr. Reamy for presenting the charges in public instead of at an executive session and quickly adjourned the meeting.

When reporters of the press later quizzed members of the Faculty as to what the President was alleged to have said, Dean Conner declined to comment. Dr. Hyndman, secretary of the Faculty, said he had been present and had distinctly heard the President utter them. Dr. Forchheimer said that the President's words could not be called "profanity"; and that he (Forchheimer) remembered "rightly" the President had said "that he would rather go to hell than not do his duty."

At first Dr. Ayers denied both charges brought against him. Later the President admitted that he had said he would govern the Medical Faculty if he had to "go to hell to do it" or words to that effect; but gave the excuse that he was "exasperated and that it was said in the heat of passion." He said he did not mean it "as the press had represented."

With regard to the charge of having falsified the record of the Winslow Resolution, Dr. Ayers declared that he had not appointed the committee simply because of his power as President, but that the records showed he had been authorized to do so. The President was wrong, for the records do not show this.

After a meeting of the Board held on October 17 for the purpose of hearing President Ayers reply to the charges brought against him, the Board issued a public statement. The Board said that they had "unanimously resolved that the charges of Dr. Reamy "be dismissed without record." They characterized the charges "inconsequential and immaterial"; and declined to order an investigation. But they had deemed it only fair that President Ayers be given an opportunity to make a reply if he desired. Since President Ayers had so desired, the Board had given him a hearing at which they said the President had "completely answered the statements of Dr. Reamy." Thus the incident "was closed." Furthermore, the Board said that they had been "fully cognizant at all times of the condition of affairs in the University" and at no time had it entertained Dr. Reamy's proposal for an investigation "of the frivolous charges brought forward." For a second time the Board had vindicated the President of charges brought against him.

THE DISMISSAL OF PRESIDENT AYERS

In the meantime, however, a significant change had been made in the method of selecting the Board of Directors of the University that was to have far reaching effects upon the career of President Ayers. In the early part of 1902 the Supreme Court of Ohio, in the case of State vs. Jones, rendered a decision which practically destroyed all of the then existing legislation relating to the government of municipalities in the State by declaring it to be special legislation, and, therefore, unconstitutional. As a result of this decision Governor Nash called the Legislature in extra session, which on October 22 passed a law known as the "Municipal Code of Ohio." One of the provisions of this law related to the control of municipal universities. In the new code the Legislature reduced the number of Directors of the University from 18 to 9, and their appointment was vested in the Mayor. Each member was to serve for six years, the terms of three expiring each second year. When the law was being drafted some of the friends of the University and the alumni sought to have the appointing power remain with the Superior Court of Cincinnati, or at least place the power in the hands of the Common Pleas Court. But, as was claimed later, through the influence of Ellis G. Kinkead, a prominent attorney of Cincinnati who brought pressure to bear on certain members of the Legislature, at the last minute the appointment was vested in the Mayor.

A new Board took office on the second Monday in May 1903, and a week later met and organized by electing Major Frank Jones as Chairman. The members of the new Board were: the Reverend Henry M. Curtis, who had been a member of the Citizens Committee that had opposed the removal of the old Faculty by President Ayers; Dr. Joseph Ransohoff, a member of the Medical Faculty, who supplanted Dr. Reamy on the Board; Samuel W. Trost, Major Jones, and Oscar Kuhn, the only two reappointments from the old Board; Alfred Benedict, John G. O'Connell, Ellis G. Kinkead, and Sanford Brown. Eight of the members appointed to the Board were Republicans and one was reported to be a Democrat.

At Commencement time of that year, June 20, 1903, Cunningham Hall, Van Wormer Library, and the Athletic Field were publicly dedicated by ceremonies that were the most successful in the history of the University. The Honorable James Wilson, Secretary of Agriculture, and the Honorable F. B. Loomis, the first Assistant Secretary of State, gave the principal addresses. The largest crowd that had ever gathered on the campus was present for the ceremonies, and the consensus was that the whole affair reflected great credit on Dr. Ayers.

Scarcely had the eloquence of Secretary Wilson and Secretary Loomis and the applause given to President Ayers over his achievements died into an echo when a concerted move was made to displace the chief executive of the University. The week following Commencement five members of the new Board, the Messrs. Curtis, Ransohoff, Benedict, Kinkead, and O'Connell held a caucus and resolved that the interests of the University demanded the immediate withdrawal of President Ayers. After the caucus a committee of these five waited upon some of the other members of the Board and informed them that they had a majority vote and pointed out to them the need for harmonious action in order to avoid the bickerings that the old Board had. Some of the alumni heard of this and immediately brought pressure upon some of the Board members with the result that the Messrs. Kuhn, Jones, Trost, and Brown refused to take any immediate action. On July 18, 1903, Dr. Curtis introduced a resolution at the Board meeting to the effect that, beginning on July 1, 1904, President Ayers' connection with the University should cease; and the consideration of this resolution was made a special order at the November 15 meeting of the Board.

As the public gradually became aware of what was going on at the University there was general surprise and consternation in view of the unmistakable evidence of the progress of the institution under the direction of Dr. Ayers. Major Jones was flooded with letters from loyal supporters of President Ayers. Dr. C. A. L. Reed who had declined reappointment by Major Fleischmann to the Board wrote to Major Jones reciting the hopeless state of demoralization existing in the Academic Department due largely to the policy of rotating the executive head of the University among the members of the Faculty before the appointment of President Ayers and the difficult task that had been imposed upon him when he assumed the Presidency. "What," wrote Dr. Reed, "were some of the objections to President Ayers"? He listed some of them and proceeded to answer them as follows:

There is, it is true, some talk about a "lack of tact"—but the tact of President Ayers seems to have given the University the best four years since its foundation by Charles McMicken; there are mutterings about "arbitrariness"—but the arbitrariness of President Ayers seems to be of the sort that has brought order out of chaos and established government instead of anarchy; and there are whisperings about "tone"—but the tone of President Ayers seems to be of the stuff that, imparted to Professors and students alike, has resulted in hard work in the classroom and fair play on the athletic field and that has infused high ideals into the lives of all who have been brought under his influence.

Mr. E. C. Goshorn, a leading manufacturer and businessman, wrote: "Today the University occupies a position of which we may all be proud, and it certainly would be a mistake to ask for the resignation of the man to whom this result is due in part if not wholly."

Mr. John W. Warrington, a leader of the Cincinnati Bar, wrote: "I had supposed that the last Commencement day of the University furnished satisfactory evidence to all, not only that good work was being done at the University, but that there was harmony among all concerned. I regard the present outbreak as highly injurious to the future of the institution."

Judge William Worthington, a former member of the Board and a patron of the Institution, wrote concerning President Ayers:

It is undoubtedly true that the University has prospered highly under his management, and that the teaching force has been strengthened, the morale of the Faculty improved, and the zeal and interest of the students stimulated since he took charge. What has been done is the more remarkable in view of the animosities aroused by the acts he was called upon to perform when he first took charge, and the constant criticisms, engineered in part by these animosities, to which he has been subjected. His entire and sincere devotion to the interests of the University cannot be denied and has brought good fruit which all may see.

On May 13, 1903, Max B. May, a former member of the Board, wrote to William Howard Taft, then Governor General of the Philippine Islands, soliciting his aid in behalf of President Ayers. It will be recalled that Mr. Taft had helped select Dr. Ayers for the Presidency, and as Dean of the Law School was well acquainted with University affairs. Mr. May recounted the clash between President Ayers and Dr. Reamy, his reorganization of the Academic Faculty, the change in the character of the Board as a result of the act of the Legislature in 1902, and the present charges against Dr. Ayers. "The only criticism," wrote Mr. May, "that has been directed against the President is that he is 'brusk' in manner and supposed to be irreligious (there were rumors that Dr. Ayers was an agnostic), though the gentlemen are very wary about giving instances substantiating this latter charge."

Governor Taft replied on September 22 as follows:

Dr. Ayers when he became head of the University, was charged with a very serious task, and that was of reorganizing the Faculty. Those who can recollect will remember that the Academic Department of the University had fallen into a condition which rendered it of little use in our community. It was not so much that the members of the Faculty lacked in individual ability and learning, but the lack of a head and of cohesion had led to a loss of discipline and a loss of *esprit de corps,* which had made the body a very useless one. Conditions were such that it was impossible to improve matters without wholesale removals. The members of the University Board knew this, selected Dr. Ayers with a view to his taking this method, and Dr. Ayers went about it in a direct, open, and courageous way. His course created enmities against him, which, evidently, have not subsided. He only did the work which he was employed to do, and he did it well. Today you have a fine Faculty and an excellent University, making for good in the community of Cincinnati. Why, after Dr. Ayers has accomplished that which he was employed to accomplish, and has brought about such an excellent condition of affairs, it should now be thought necessary or proper to dismiss him. I cannot, for the life of me see. It is true that Dr. Ayers came into conflict with the Medical Faculty and with the Law Faculty. The peculiar relations which existed between those two Faculties, growing out of the exceptional circumstances under which they were united to the University, he did not understand and was naturally impatient with, because the agreements of union reserved to the respective Faculties much of the power which is usually in the Board of Trustees of a university or in the President. His object was, as far as he could, to make the union of the two schools with the University closer. The members of the Faculties were jealous of their privileges, secured by contract, and were fearful lest the President was seeking to reduce them or destroy them. I was a member of one of the Faculties and know whereof I speak. I think it is a pity if the friction which arose from the circumstances I have described should now be allowed to play any part in the removal of Dr. Ayers from the University. It would be exceedingly difficult to secure a good President for the University should Dr. Ayers leave. His experience, the bitter personal attacks which he has encountered, and the ease with which prejudice can be aroused against the President of the University in our community, will make men worthy of the place very loathe to accept it. It would seem to be a time when those who have the interests of the University at heart should sink their personal likes and dislikes, and recognize that the man under whom the University has made such distinct progress should continue at the head of it a number of years longer.

The students of the University drew up resolutions which they presented to the Board requesting them to retain President Ayers. "We who know him best respect and esteem him most."

The Alumni Association also presented resolutions to the Board stating that they deemed it "inadvisable, inexpedient, and detrimental to the best interests of the University" for the Board to declare "the office of President vacant."

When the Board met on November 15, 1903, Dr. Ransohoff moved that the regular order of business be suspended and that it proceed to consider the resolution terminating the services of President Ayers on July 1, 1904; and that the Board's Academic Committee in consultation with the Deans of the Academic, Medical, and Law Faculties be authorized to institute measures looking towards the election of a President. The Board then went into executive session, but kept a record of the proceedings. In the executive session Mr. Kuhn moved that the discussion of the matter be postponed because Mr. Jones, the Chairman, was absent, but this resolution was defeated. The resolution to terminate the services of President Ayers was passed by a vote of 5 to 3, and the Clerk was instructed to inform President Ayers in writing of the adoption of this resolution. On motion of Mr. Benedict the Board then passed a resolution that "no members of the present Faculty should be considered for appointment to the Presidency." President Ayers let it be known that he would fight the move to dismiss him. He cited his record of achievements and determined to place the onus for his dismissal, if he had to be displaced, directly upon the Board.

Undisturbed by the attitude of President Ayers the Board, at a special meeting on January 12, 1904, elected Dr. Charles W. Dabney, President of the University; and the Law Committee in conjunction with the City Solicitor was instructed to draw up a contract after consultation with Dr. Dabney. A week later Professor Hicks resigned as Dean of the Academic Faculty, and Dr. Joseph E. Harry was appointed to the vacancy.

Since President Ayers refused to resign, the Board on April 18, 1904, held another stormy meeting. Mr. John G. O.'Connell introduced a resolution "that Dr. Howard Ayers is from this day relieved from all duties as President of the University; his salary to continue to July 1, 1904, and that Professor Harry be placed in charge of the University to that date." President Ayers, who was present, demanded to "know the reason for this as he had devoted five years to the best interests of the University."

Mr. Kuhn also demanded "the reason for this drastic move" and moved that the Board go into executive session. Mr. Kuhn's request was voted down. Chairman Jones relinquished the chair and addressed the members. He said he "feared the consequence might be serious and suggested that they defer action in order to talk the matter over." Mr. Kuhn also spoke in behalf of Dr. Ayers. He wanted the Board to give Dr. Ayers a hearing on any charges there might be against him. In his opinion the resolution was unfair to the President. Notwithstanding these protests, the resolution dismissing Dr. Ayers was passed. Hardly had the vote been announced when President Ayers sprang up and "in a towering rage denounced the action as an outrage." "You will regret this and so will your institution," he declared, and left the room.

The summary removal of Dr. Ayers from the Presidency of the University did not meet with the approval of many of the citizens of Cincinnati. This was shown in an emphatic way by the presentation to the Board a month later in a letter signed by more than one hundred prominent men of the City, many of whom had a national reputation. The signers of this communication endorsed the administration of Dr. Ayers and expressed their appreciation of "the valuable service he had rendered to the University." Among the subscribers were the names of William Howard Taft, Charles P. Taft, J. B. Foraker, Judson Harmon, M. E. Ingalls, William A. Procter, Henry Hanna, Briggs S. Cunningham, J. G. Schmidlapp, and many other business and professional men of the City. But it had no effect on the Board; and finally, on June 13, 1904, Dr. Ayers severed all his connections with the University by resigning his position as professor of anthropology and ethnology.

CONJECTURES ON THE DISMISSAL OF DR. AYERS

Thus came to an end another disturbing affair in the annals of the University. Many influences were undoubtedly responsible for this second upheaval in the office of the executive head of the University. The lack of security of tenure of the executive officer of the University was undoubtedly one of them. When President Ayers came to the University he asked the Board for a written contract and was informed that the Board could not make a contract for the payment of money "not in the City Treasury" and "upon the strong assurances given him by the Board and by other prominent citizens" he decided to accept the office of President "without exacting a legal document" which it was discovered, the Board was not in a position to execute. It is true that a five-year contract was signed by the Board with Dr. Dabney, "but this document had no value beyond the expression of a moral obligation in written form."

Furthermore, President Ayers accepted the position with the understanding that he was to reorganize the Academic Faculty which the

Board was fully cognizant needed reform because of the previous policy
of rotating the Deanship among the members of the Faculty. This inevitably created animosities which were increased by the way in which
President Ayers proceeded to reorganize the Academic Faculty. The fact
that the professors had to be removed through the executive head led to
the erroneous supposition that the changes were made upon the initiative
of President Ayers. Since some of the members of the Board were alumni
of the University and had been students of some of the deposed professors, they naturally took up the cause of their professors.

The presence on the Board also of members of the Faculty of some of
the Colleges which were very jealous of what they considered were their
prerogatives made the President's task even more difficult. The fact that
the governing Board was subject to the fluctuations of municipal politics
was likewise a contributing cause. For many years the control of the
University had been a bone of contention between opposing factions in
the City of Cincinnati, and the interplay of these political factors was
enhanced when the method of selecting the members of the Board was
changed. The extravagant statements made by the local papers of what
they claimed was going on at the University added to the flames of passion. The rumors concerning the religious views of Dr. Ayers also tended
to increase the tension. All the members of the Board, the alumni, and the
student body agreed that the University had made great progress under
the administration of President Ayers; but vague statements circulated
that he was not "fitted for the Presidency," that he lacked "tact" and was
"dictatorial," although never definitely pinpointed, were also used effectively against him by his opponents. All of these and many other intangi-
ble factors contributed to the second and last time that a President of
the University of Cincinnati was dismissed.

14

Sound Leadership, Solid Growth

Chastened by the distasteful experience of a civic uprising over President Howard Ayers, the Board of Directors moved carefully in selecting a successor. Years later Major Frank J. Jones told how the Board chose Dr. Dabney as President. As has already been told an attempt was made to conduct the affairs of the University without a President after the retirement of President Cox. The Board gave the Deans of the Academic Department the opportunity of sitting in rotation as the head of the University and of doing all the things that would be required of a President. But they soon found this plan was not a success.

Mr. Jones decided to go East and consult some of his friends with reference to a chief executive for the institution. He was not delegated by the Board to do this; he went on his own initiative and responsibility. Among those with whom he conferred was the Honorable David A. Wells, a prominent economist, who had been Special Commissioner of the Revenue. Mr. Jones told Mr. Wells something about the condition of affairs at the University. Mr. Wells asked him, "Who is your President?" Mr. Jones replied: "We have no President; we do not think we can afford a President." Mr. Wells said: "I do not think you can afford to live without a President; it is necessary that somebody should be at the head of the University to outline its plan of government and to make the citizens familiar with its conditions and the course of instruction."

Mr. Jones returned home and found that the Board too had decided that the wisest and best thing to do was to select a President. But as the administration of President Ayers aroused so much antagonism, the Board selected a committee consisting of Dr. Ransohoff, Dr. Curtis, and Judge Rufus B. Smith to make a pilgrimage to the South for the purpose of finding a new President. On this trip they met and interviewed Dr. Dabney, who had been highly recommended to them. At that time Dr. Dabney was President of the University of Tennessee. He had reorganized the University, elevated its standard of scholarship, and brought the institution into national recognition; but he was encountering difficulties because of his liberal views on the education of the colored people. Dr. Dabney was a staunch Presbyterian, and he asked Dr. Curtis whether his religion would affect his application; since one of the factors responsible for the dismissal of Dr. Ayers had been his religious views. Dr. Curtis said, "No."

Upon the invitation of the Committee, Dr. Dabney came to Cincinnati and stayed with Mr. Schmidlapp. After visiting the University and touring the City, Dr. Curtis asked Dr. Dabney what he thought about the place. Dr. Dabney said he was not greatly impressed, because he did not like the political situation in the City. At that time the local government was controlled by the notorious boss, George B. Cox, and his gang. Dr. Dabney said he wanted to meet "Boss" Cox. An interview was arranged; and in the course of the conversation "Boss" Cox assured Dr. Dabney that if he were selected and accepted the Presidency of the University, he (Cox) would guarantee there would be no political interference with his administration. It was this statement, apparently, that led Dr. Dabney to accept the Presidency; and George B. Cox carried out his pledge. In January 1904, Dr. Dabney was elected President of the University and signed a contract fixing his term of service to begin July 1, 1904, at an annual salary of $8,000, which was guaranteed for a period of not less than five years; and in addition to have the use, rent free, with heat, light, and water also free, of a home to be built upon University grounds and ready for occupancy by September 1, 1905.

No official residence, however, was ever erected for Dr. Dabney. The site for one was surveyed on the University grounds and officially designated. The matter was then taken into the courts which decided that the University Board had exclusive control of the forty-three acres of Burnet Woods Park set aside for University purposes and could erect any buildings it sought fit on the grounds. But then difficulty was encountered in securing the money—$20,000—to build the residence, as such use of University funds was not provided for under any law or City ordinance, and the Board was unable to raise such a fund. President Dabney and members of the Board also began to question the suitability of the University grounds for such a residence. Furthermore, Mrs. Dabney did not want a house, because she thought it would be too hard to keep up. The result was that Dr. Dabney obtained a private suite in one of the new apartments built in Clifton. In 1907 the contract with Dr. Dabney was modified. He released the Board of its obligation to build a residence, and the Board gave him an extra allowance of $1,900 to cover expenses for his apartment.

CAREER OF DR. DABNEY

Dr. Dabney was a prominent educator, who in 1904 already had had a distinguished career. He was a native of Virginia. His father, Robert L. Dabney, was at one time professor of theology at the Union Seminary in New York and later professor of philosophy at the University of Tennessee. During the Civil War he served as General Stonewall Jackson's Chief of Staff. His mother, Lavinia (Morrison) Dabney, was a daughter of the Reverend James Morrison of New Province Church, Rockbridge County, Virginia, and was a cousin of the wife of General Stonewall Jackson. Young Dabney was educated at Hampden-Sidney College and the University of Virginia. During the session of 1877–1878 he served as professor of chemistry at Emory and Henry College, Virginia. Then he went to Europe, studied at the Universities of Berlin and Göttingen; from the latter institution he received his Doctor's degree in 1880.

On his return home Dr. Dabney was appointed professor of chemistry at the University of North Carolina. He was the first to discover and make known the valuable deposits of phosphates in the eastern section and the tin ore in the western section of that State. In 1881 he married Mary Brent, the daughter of Major Thomas Y. Brent of Paris, Kentucky. From 1880–1887 he was Director of the Agricultural Experiment Station in North Carolina and represented that State upon the Board of Commissioners at several expositions. Dr. Dabney was Assistant Secretary of Agriculture in Washington during the second Cleveland administration. He put the Bureau of Agriculture under Civil Service. While in Washington he helped to organize the Washington Memorial Institution, which afterwards led to the establishment of the Carnegie Foundation. In 1887, Dr. Dabney was elected President of the University of Tennessee. He was a man of vision for the State and for the South. He wanted to develop the public schools of Tennessee and industrial education in the South. He helped found the Southern Educational Board and the General Education Board.

THE MAN

Dr. Dabney was a strong man, of brawn as well as brain, of muscular as well as mental force, who made an impression wherever he went. He was big-boned, rather heavy, deep-chested, and broad-shouldered. He was square-jawed with slightly protruding chin, and he was inclined to extend his lower lip. His face was ruddy, with dark eyes and a wiry mustache of black and gray, and black hair, both of which in time became snow white. When talking to a visitor in his office Dr. Dabney often assumed two attitudes; either he "leaned back in a revolving chair, hands clasped behind his head and now and then ran his hands through his heavy locks," or else he stood "at the window, looking over a five mile-stretch of hill and valley, rather grave in expression, and only occasionally turning to his listener."

THE INAUGURATION OF PRESIDENT DABNEY

On January 12, 1904, Dr. Dabney was unanimously elected President of the University, and the following July 1 entered upon the duties of the office. On November 16, 1904, he was inaugurated as President amid impressive public ceremonies. During the preceding evening a public reception was held in the McMicken Hall in honor of Dr. and Mrs. Dabney. At ten o'clock on the morning of the next day an imposing procession was organized and managed by Professor Louis T. More as grand marshal, assisted by several students selected from the various departments of the University. The procession marched into Music Hall, which had been handsomely decorated with flags and plants and filled to capacity with an enthusiastic audience. Among the marchers in the procession, most wearing academic gowns, were the Governor of Ohio, the Attorney General of Ohio, the Mayor of Cincinnati, the Judge of the United States District Court, the Presidents of Cornell University, Massachusetts Institute of Technology, the College of the City of New York, Ohio State University; Rufus B. King, Bishop Boyd Vincent, Rabbi David Phillipson, the Directors of the University, the trustees, Faculty, alumni, and students of its various departments, the Citizens Committee, and a large number of invited guests, representing other universities, colleges, and institutions of learning.

The Invocation was delivered by Rabbi Phillipson. An introductory address was given by Frank J. Jones, Chairman of the Board of Directors. The oath of office was administered to the President of the University by the Honorable Albert Clifton Thompson, Judge of the United States District Court. Short addresses were given by John Huston Finley, President of the College of the City of New York; Rufus B. Smith; Professor William Welch of Johns Hopkins University; Henry S. Pritchett, President of the Massachusetts Institute of Technology; and Jacob G. Schurman, President of Cornell University. The ceremonies closed with the Benediction by the Right Reverend Boyd Vincent, Bishop of Southern Ohio. In the evening after the inauguration ceremonies a banquet was given at the Phoenix Club, which was attended by more than 200. It was a fitting climax to the impressive events of this festal occasion.

DR. DABNEY'S EDUCATIONAL PHILOSOPHY

When Dr. Dabney became President there was much interest throughout the nation in the development of municipal universities. Leaders in the educational world heralded it as one of the most significant movements in the system of American education. Dr. Dabney became a staunch advocate of the municipal university idea. He believed that the municipal university was the logical outgrowth of the American idea of democracy in education which would make it possible for all the youth of both sexes, irrespective of the position and wealth of their parents, to obtain an opportunity to receive an education in tax-supported institutions from the kindergarten to the university in their own locality.

He held that the municipal university would make it possible for many who otherwise could not afford a college education to obtain one at home. It was, therefore, the duty of the municipal university to serve the needs of all the people in the community. It should become the directing force in the intellectual, political, industrial, social, and religious life of the community; and, therefore, should work in close relationship with the City government, the public schools, the manufacturers, professional groups, and working classes. It should make the citizens realize that the best investment of its funds was in developing scholars, teachers, scientific experts, laboratory technicians, business leaders, engineers, and doctors. These were the goals Dr. Dabney strove to achieve as President of the municipal University of Cincinnati, and for these reasons he expanded the activities of the University into many new fields in order to keep pace with the rapid growth of the urbanization and industrialization of modern America.

INNOVATIONS AND IMPROVEMENTS

A number of innovations and improvements were made as Dr. Dabney became President of the University. By a resolution passed by the Board of Directors on November 16, 1904, hereafter the third Monday in November of each year was to be known and celebrated as "University Day." On that occasion memorial exercises were to be held in honor of Charles McMicken, the founder, and other benefactors of the University. It was intended to establish a day similar to that known a decade previously as "Founders Day." The last of these celebrations had been held in 1892 in the old Pike Opera House.

It was not known until after Dr. Dabney became President that the University had no official seal. Two emblems had been used, one on the diplomas, and another on publications of the University; but neither of them had been officially authorized. Dr. Dabney recommended to the Board that the University should have a seal similar to the seals of other leading Universities, such as Harvard, Yale, and Johns Hopkins University. Acting upon his suggestion the Board adopted on September 26, 1904, as the design of the University seal "the insignia of the City of Cincinnati (the scales, sword, and Mercury's wand) upon a shield gules with the motto *Juncta Juvant* mounted on a pointed ellipse surrounded by a belt bearing the words University of Cincinnati and the date 1870. (*Juncta Juvant* means literally "Things joined are a help," or translated freely, "Strength in unity.") In the space between the shield and the belt was a wreath of oak leaves and below a scroll with the motto *Alta Petit* (translated freely, "She seeks the heights"). The seal was used for the first time on the invitations issued for the inauguration of President Dabney.

Dr. Dabney strongly urged the beautifying of the University grounds. He believed this would stimulate persons to make donations to the University. He held that people were not disposed to give money or buildings if the place looked neglected or even unattractive. At his suggestion a committee of prominent women of Cincinnati was formed to improve the University campus. Over one hundred trees were planted and an annual "Tree Day" was inaugurated. Flower beds were mapped out along the terraces leading to McMicken Hall, and shrubbery was planted.

Some idea of the pastoral nature of the campus and the surroundings as late as 1907 was picturesquely described in a series of letters written by President Dabney to Professor John T. Faig of the Engineering College in that year. "The Park Superintendent informs me," wrote President Dabney, "that under the law we are authorized to lock up any animals, like cows, that invade our grounds. You are, therefore, instructed to have any animals that appear on the grounds immediately driven to the basement of the Technical School, and locked up there until the owners pay the fine of three dollars apiece authorized by the law. If the owners see the animals being driven up and come for them, they must not be allowed to take them away until they have paid the fine. Please find out the names of animal dealers and owners who graze their cows in this neighborhood and send them to me."

In another letter to the City Board of Public Service, President Dabney called attention to the condition of the street and sidewalks at the corner of McMillan Street and Clifton Avenue. The street, not being paved, had become filled with holes and was "intolerably muddy." Since the street was usually full of freight and delivery wagons of various kinds it was a favorite place to water and feed the horses. "The horses slop the water over the pavement, which freezes in the winter, and makes it dangerous."

In 1904 the City Council voted to give to the University the statues of two lions which had once been a part of the collection of statuary belonging to Jacob Hoffner, whose estate was located at the corner of Hamilton Avenue and Blue Rock Street. His beautiful house and its gardens, including six acres of formal gardens, greenhouses, and lily ponds, were decorated with many statues which he had brought to this country from Italy, France, and other European countries. Since Mr. Hoffner had no heirs, he agreed to leave his estate to Cincinnati in the hope that it would become a City park, but because of some differences over taxes and litigation, his wish was not carried out. The City acquired title to the land in 1894 and leveled the grounds in order to make it a playground.

The objects of art were scattered, and the City donated the statues of the two lions to the University. A committee consisting of Frank J. Jones and Samuel W. Trost decided to place the lions on either side of the front steps of McMicken Hall. They were originally placed with their heads facing each other. Later it was noted that this position greatly hindered their duties as "sentinels" of the University. The statues, therefore, were reversed so that they would turn their heads away from the entrance in order to better perform their "guarding" duties. "Mick and Mack," as they are affectionately called, have become an integral part of the tradition of the University. They have become famous landmarks for class rallies and celebrations, and on frequent occasions they have been surreptitiously painted various colors by overexuberant students of rival colleges on the eve of athletic contests.

The organization of the University was improved in order to facilitate its administration, and steps were taken to interest some of the influential citizens of the City in the University. A University Senate was established to assist the President and the Board on matters of general policy. It was composed of the President of the University, the Deans of the Colleges, the Director of the Observatory, the Chairman of the Graduate Faculty, the Dean of Women, and one member elected at the close of each academic year by the Faculty of each of the Colleges. At the suggestion of Dr. Dabney the Board appointed twenty-five prominent citizens as members of a Board of Visitors. It was the duty of this Board to inspect and report on the work and needs of the several departments of the Institution. All their suggestions regarding the need for new buildings, apparatus, and increases in the instructional staff were not immediately carried out because of lack of funds; but the Board of Visitors familiarized the citizens of the City with the needs and work of the University. The Board of Visitors might be thought a precursor of the Deans' Advisory Committees of the mid-twentieth century.

Another innovation introduced by the Board was the expurgating of the minutes of Board meetings. At the suggestion of President Dabney the Board approved the policy of omitting from the records of Board meetings all communications of the President to the Board and all records of executive sessions of the Board.

EXPANSION OF THE UNIVERSITY

When Dr. Dabney assumed the Presidency, the University was composed of the following Colleges: the College of Liberal Arts, the College of Engineering, the College of Law (the Cincinnati Law School), the College of Medicine (the Medical College of Ohio), and the Technical School (a manual training high school). Affiliated with the University was the College of Dentistry (the Ohio College of Dental Surgery), but it was under the control of its own Board of Directors.

In the period between 1904 and 1913 the physical plant of the University was expanded; the scope of the work of the institution was broadened; and the standards in all the Colleges were raised. The growth and progress of the University during these years is revealed in the following statistics. By 1910 the value of the buildings and equipment in Burnet Woods exceeded $1,600,000, an increase since 1904 of $700,000. Since 1904 the productive endowments increased from $31,464.75 to $41,463.92, or 31.7 per cent. During the same period tuition, fees, and income from miscellaneous sources increased from $17,681.41 to $50,-365.34, or 184.8 per cent. Between 1904 and 1910 the annual income derived from the City increased from $75,145.46 to $147,196.39, or 95.8 per cent. The total income of the University increased from $123,991.62 to $267,543.65, or 115 per cent. The number of courses of study offered in the Burnet Woods Colleges increased from 241 to 366, or 64 per cent. The instructional staff in the Burnet Woods Colleges increased from 51 to 99, or 94 per cent. The attendance of regular students, excluding those in the Law and Medical Colleges, increased from a total of 547 to 1,150, or 110.2 per cent.

During these years a number of new Colleges were established while others discontinued. In 1905 a College for Teachers was erected. The following year a Graduate School was established and the co-operative system of education was inaugurated in the College of Engineering. In the same year (1906) external or extension courses, meeting in the late afternoons or on Saturday mornings, and offering regular university work, were inaugurated for the special benefit of teachers. Also in the same year the affiliation of the College of Dentistry with the University was dissolved. The next year (1907) the Technical School was closed, as the Board of Education announced it was going to give free instruction in manual training in the high schools. The building of the Technical School was turned over to the College of Engineering for the use of laboratories. Two years later (1909) the Medical College of Ohio and the Miami Medical College were merged and a new medical college was formed under the title of the Ohio-Miami Medical College of the University of Cincinnati. In 1912 evening classes in liberal arts were inaugurated and the College of Commerce, a Bureau of City Tests, and the Municipal Reference Bureau were established. In 1914 a home economics school which had been developed by the Cincinnati Kindergarten Association was taken over and became the School of Household Arts of the University.

The acquisition of additional funds obtained from the City aided materially in the growth of the University. One of the conditions which Dr. Dabney made when he was invited to come to Cincinnati was that $20,000 a year additional for five years should be raised for the purpose of developing the University. It was evident that the University must look to the City to obtain these additional resources.

Early in the year 1906 the Board of Directors appealed through the Hamilton County delegation to the General Assembly of Ohio for legislation authorizing the levying of a tax of five-tenths instead of three-tenths of a mill. It had previously been three-tenths of a mill since 1893 (with the exception of the year 1897 when the Board of Education had reduced the levy for that year from three-tenths to two-tenths) on all of the taxable property in Cincinnati for the support and maintenance of the University. Such legislation was passed, and under the provisions of this act the City Council authorized the levying of the increased tax. Two years later (1908) at the request of the Board of Directors the General Assembly passed unanimously an act authorizing "municipal corporations to issue bonds for constructing additional buildings for municipal universities." The Hamilton County delegation heartily supported this bill. By the provisions of this act any municipal corporation upon request of the Board of Directors was "authorized to issue bonds in any amount, at any time, for the erection of additional buildings or for the completion and equipment of buildings for a municipal university."

Under the authority of this act the City Council issued $26,000 in 1908 and in 1909 an additional $550,000 of bonds for the erection and equipment of new buildings for the University. In 1911 the University was threatened with as dire a disaster as could be contemplated. As mentioned above Section 7908 of the General Code which authorized the tax levy for municipal corporations authorized the City Council to assess and levy taxes on all property of the municipal corporation to the amount of five-tenths of a mill for the University and five one-hundredths of a mill for the Observatory. In 1910, however, the State Legislature passed the Smith One Per Cent Municipal Tax Law which reduced the rate of taxation to something over one per cent. The new law, as interpreted by the authorities, made the maximum that could be levied for the University "a rate which levied on the total valuation of all the property for the year 1911 would produce no greater amount of taxes than the former levy on the total valuation of the year 1910 would produce, plus six per cent for the year 1912, nine per cent for the year 1913, and twelve per cent thereof for any years thereafter."

The Smith law authorized the County Commission upon request of the City Council to levy an extra tax to meet the further necessities of the City; this second tax levy not to exceed ½ per cent. The proceeds of this levy the City Council could devote to the support "of any and all

City departments." The act further provided "that if in any year the taxing authorities of any taxing district shall desire to raise a less amount of taxes for a particular purpose than was levied for such purpose in the year 1910, the amount of taxes that may be levied for another or other purposes may be correspondingly increased." In other words, if the City had funds to spare within the limit of the first levy or the supplementary levy voted by the people, the Council could use them for any City district if found necessary.

The effect on the community, or at least on those who were in authority in City affairs, was to require a reduction in all City departmental expenses as to bring prospective income and expenses into agreement. As a result of this demand the Tax Commission reduced the allowance of the University "from $127,500 to $75,000," a sum which Chairman Robert W. Stewart of the Board of Directors said, "would have been totally inadequate to meet the needs of the University. To have been obliged to meet this reduction in income the University would have been compelled to cut off not only instructors and professors, but also to have cut off a number of departments." The result of this contingency, according to Chairman Stewart, was "to send members of the Board to all parts of the City and to all possible donors for help; to cause anxiety to the whole teaching force and almost throw the whole student body into a panic."

The University was saved from this threatened predicament by the citizens of the City, who in November 1911 voted an additional 2.34 mills for the City at large, and by the City Council and Mayor, who increased the allowance to the University to $98,860 for the current six months. That was somewhat in excess of what the University had been receiving.

The Board of Directors of the University and the Mayor and Council of Cincinnati then petitioned the State Legislature to pass a law restoring the special tax of one-half a mill for the University and placing it outside the ten mill limit. This the Legislature did, in an act approved by the Governor April 18, 1913, which reaffirmed the original Section 7908 authorizing "the City Council to assess and levy taxes on all the property of the municipal corporation to the amount of five-tenths of one mill for the University and five one-hundredths of one mill for the Observatory. It added the following paragraph: 'The above tax levies shall not be subject to any limitations of rates of taxation or maximum rates provided by law, except the limitations herein provided; and the further exception that the combined maximum rate for all taxes levied in any year in any city or other tax district shall not exceed fifteen mills.'" Thus in 1913 the University levy was removed from the 1 per cent limitation imposed by the Smith One Per Cent Tax Law.

Another factor which contributed to the progress of the University during these years was the changed attitude of the City towards the

University. In his annual report for 1913, Robert W. Stewart, Chairman of the Board of Directors, referred to the fact that for a number of years the hardest thing the Board of Directors and other officers of the University had to contend with was the "utter indifference of the influential people" of Cincinnati "towards the institution and everything connected with it." It had not been an uncommon thing to hear people say: "Cincinnati does not need a University and the tax payer—poor, downtrodden individual that he is—should not be called upon to support an institution of higher education." By 1913 this spirit had changed. By that date the disposition was to say: "Go ahead with the good work you are engaged in." The only criticism one heard from these same people was that the institution was growing so enormously that the question of support was becoming a more momentous one each year. Rufus B. Smith attributed the growth of the University to the fact that the Board of Directors was working more harmoniously, and that the President was working more harmoniously with both the Faculty and the student body.

THE COLLEGES, 1904–1913

The McMicken College of Liberal Arts

At the suggestion of Dr. Dabney the Board changed the name of the Academic Department in 1904 to that of the McMicken College of Liberal Arts. The academic year was divided into two semesters instead of three terms. Fifteen units were required for admission to the College, and a Director of the School of Affiliation (Admissions) was appointed to administer these standards. The elective system was revised. All freshmen and sophomores in the College were required to take certain fundamental subjects; juniors and seniors were allowed to select major fields for concentration.

There were numerous changes in the administrative officers of the College. From 1906 to 1910, Professor Merrick Whitcomb was Dean of the College. He was a scholar, the author of numerous books, a cultured gentleman, and one of the most popular lecturers on the campus. He was succeeded as Dean by Professor Louis Trenchard More, who held the office for three years. In 1913, Professor Frank W. Chandler was appointed Dean and held the office for thirteen years. For a few months in 1903–1904, Miss Margaret F. Washburn was Dean of Women. Then Miss Elizabeth Czarnomska was appointed Dean of Women and lecturer in English and Biblical literature. When she resigned in 1909 Miss Emilie Watts McVea was appointed Dean of Women.

The Faculty was strengthened by the addition of a number of new men. In 1904, Burtis Burr Breese of the University of Tennessee was appointed head of the Department of Psychology. The next year (1905)

Claude M. Lotspeich was appointed to the Department of German; and Edwin W. Glover, who had been for many years Director of the Cincinnati May Festival and Director of the Orpheus Club, was appointed Director of Vocal Music.

Two years later (1907) the College lost two able men by retirement, Wayland Richardson Benedict and Edward Miles Brown. Professor Benedict was the senior member of the Liberal Arts Faculty. He had held the chair of philosophy since 1875. He was a man of scholarly attainments with a large following among the students. Professor Brown was an able scholar and an inspiring teacher. He was recognized as an authority on the language and literature of certain epochs of Anglo-Saxon development. Under his directing influence the Department of English became the largest department of the College, notwithstanding the fact that for twelve years Dr. Brown was a martyr to an incurable affliction which rendered him physically helpless. Professor Guy Allen Tawney of the University of Illinois was appointed professor of philosophy to fill the vacancy created by the retirement of Professor Benedict. Professor George Philip Krapp succeeded Professor Brown.

Professor Krapp was not only professor of English but also the first Nathaniel Ropes professor of comparative literature. This new chair was established in 1907 by an endowment of approximately one hundred thousand dollars left the University in their identical wills by the Misses Mary Paul and Elizabeth O. Ropes of Salem, Massachusetts, as a memorial to their father, Nathaniel Ropes, who for many years was a prominent businessman of Cincinnati. In 1910, Professor Chandler, then at Polytechnic Institute, Brooklyn, New York, was invited to give a series of lectures on the Ropes Foundation. The night before Professor Chandler delivered one of his lectures the City was swept by a terrible blizzard which tied up the streetcar service and greatly diminished the size of the audience which had been attending his lectures. That night the audience was composed of one professor, two women, and a *Commercial Tribune* reporter. Undaunted by the size of his audience, Professor Chandler delivered his lecture. When Professor Krapp resigned that year Dr. Chandler was appointed professor of English and Nathaniel Ropes professor of comparative literature.

In 1907, Nevin Melanchthon Fenneman was appointed professor of geology and geography, and Charles A. Read, Librarian. The next year Robert Clarkson Brooks was appointed professor of political science. Two years later (1910) Philip Ogden was appointed professor of Romance languages; William Tunstall Semple was added to the Latin Department; Clyde William Park, to the Department of English; and Lucy Braun to the Department of Geology.

While Dr. Dabney was making these valuable additions to the Faculty, he did not hesitate to dismiss professors who brought discredit upon the

University. Professor John Willis Slaughter, a professor of psychology, was not re-employed in 1904 because of his advocacy of free love; and in 1908, Professor H. Heath Bawden of philosophy was dismissed because he also did not believe in the institution of marriage. "No man," said President Dabney, "either by word or his manner of life can teach things destructive of the very foundation of human society in any institution for which I am responsible."

On the other hand, Dr. Dabney wanted to retain and obtain more capable men. To do this he knew that something would have to be done about salary schedules. Bradstreet's tables showed that the cost of living had increased 50 per cent by 1908. Colleges were beginning to discuss with seriousness the need of strong teachers as distinguished from the need for the construction of more marble halls and ivory towers. "When a teacher, at the average age of thirty-four, has been elected to full professor in a college or university," said a Carnegie Report, "he has practically reached the limit of his earning power, at least in that institution. The successful professional man, on the other hand, is just beginning to reap the substantial rewards of his ability and his training." In 1908 the Carnegie Foundation reported a man who prepared himself for the teaching profession might hope to obtain "at the age of 28 a salary of $1,250; at 31 a salary of $1,750; at 33 a salary of $2,250; and at 35—at which age the able man will have gained his professorship—a salary of $2,500." No man was likely "to choose this life for the love of gain or for considerations of material advancement." What attracted able men to enter the teaching profession was their "love of teaching, of study, and of the scholar's life," for as President Lowell of Harvard observed, they lived "in the only recognized aristocracy in America."

It was to emeliorate the plight of the college teacher that Andrew Carnegie gave $10 million in 1905 to found the Carnegie Foundation for the Advancement of Teaching which made provision for retirement allowances to college professors teaching in a list of accredited schools.

Within a short time after the establishment of the Carnegie Foundation, Dr. Dabney made application to the Foundation for the admission of the University to its accredited list of institutions. After a short delay the Foundation informed Dr. Dabney that the executive committee had voted to admit the University of Cincinnati whenever the application of the Board of Directors was approved by the Mayor and the City Council. Mayor Leopold Markbreit and the City Council promptly gave this approval, and on June 8, 1908, the University of Cincinnati was formally admitted to full participation in the privileges of the Foundation. In that year three of the University professors were granted retiring allowances. Thus, thanks to the benefaction of Andrew Carnegie, there began early in the century an orderly program of old-age benefits that was to be broadened and improved from time to time until in the 1960's all University staff and employees were fully covered by Social Security, including major medical expenses. Three years later (1911) the Robert Patterson McKibben Memorial Prize, a gold medal of the value of $25.00 was established by the Reverend William McKibben, President of Lane Seminary, and family, in memory of their son, Robert Patterson McKibben, who had died in 1910 while a member of the junior class. He was one of the most popular students on the campus, President of his class, and editor of the varsity *Weekly News*. The prize was to be awarded to that young man of the senior class who in the judgment of the Faculty best exemplified the ideals of young manhood. The first McKibben medal was awarded in 1912 to Frank Stanton Burns Gavin, and the next year to Robert Heuck.

The College for Teachers

In the opinion of Dr. Dabney the organization of a College for Teachers was conceived "as the first concern" for a municipal university that should serve the city in every possible way. The movement for the education of the teachers in the local schools in Cincinnati had a long history. As early as 1829 two Cincinnati teachers formed an organization out of which grew two years later the "Western Literary Institute and College of Professional Teachers." This was probably the first teachers' association for professional training in the United States, and during the fifteen years of its existence, according to Henry Barnard, "it exerted a highly beneficial influence upon teachers, schools, legislative action, and public school systems in the West."

With the establishment in the early 1840's of high schools, responsibility was placed upon them for the improvement of teachers for appointment to positions in the public schools. In 1868 the Board of Education established a City Normal School to train better teachers. It operated until 1890, when it was closed because the Board of Education was embarrassed by the large number of these short-term Normal School graduates who clamored for appointment in the local schools.

Meanwhile the University of Cincinnati began to develop its literary and scientific courses in which teachers could be educated. At first only lectures in purely academic subjects were given by various University professors in response to the petition of the teachers themselves. The range of subjects was extended from year to year, and the number attending gradually increased. The popularity of these extension courses led to some of them being offered for university credit, including courses now and then of a quasi-professional character. Around the beginning of the new century Saturday classes for teachers were started at the University and during the years 1901 to 1904 there were summer schools for teachers. The University catalogue of 1902–1903 announced a "Teacher's

College," in which pedagogical courses were included, but there was no Faculty or other organization of a separate college.

The appointment in 1903 of a new Superintendent of Schools, Mr. Frank B. Dyer, and of a new University President in 1904, paved the way for a well-rounded curriculum for teachers. Both were men of vision. Both were convinced that in the interests of all its people all the educational institutions of the City should be brought into closer relations and organically united.

In order to elevate standards for the teachers, Superintendent Dyer first secured action by the Board of Education in 1903, whereby a preferred list of those who were "college graduates with pedagogical training" was established. This tended to improve the character of instruction and fostered a professional spirit among the teachers. The Board of Education also encouraged greater efficiency in the classroom through the establishment of a system of promotions based upon a fixed amount of pedagogical study. At the same time it adopted a schedule of higher salaries and made provision for pensioning teachers.

Finally, as a result of a series of conferences, an agreement was signed between the Board of Education of the City of Cincinnati and the Board of Directors of the University which formally organized in 1905 a College for Teachers. The College for Teachers was "under the joint management of the Board of Directors of the University and the Board of Education of the City." It was controlled jointly by the two bodies until 1930, when the College for Teachers was taken over by the University. Under the terms of the original agreement a Faculty was appointed consisting of a Dean, William Paxton Burris, and a professor of education, assistant professors, and instructors, aided by the supervisors of special subjects in the public schools of the City. Where desirable the services of cognate departments in the College of Liberal Arts, in the Kindergarten Training School, and the Art Academy of Cincinnati were used.

A "Committee in Charge" was created consisting of the President of the University, the Superintendent of Schools, and one representative from each of the Boards. Programs of professional study were adopted to fit persons for positions in kindergartens, elementary schools, secondary schools, teachers of German in elementary schools, and teachers of art in public schools, in addition to various advanced courses for graduate students. During the junior and senior years the student's time was divided about equally between elective courses in the College of Liberal Arts and study and training in the College for Teachers. All graduates, except those in training for teaching art, received the degree of Bachelor of Arts in Education conferred by the College for Teachers. If they preferred, however, they might by fulfilling the requirements of the College of Liberal Arts receive the corresponding degree from that College and a professional certificate from the College for Teachers. The graduates of the College for Teachers were placed upon a preferred list for appointment to positions in the local schools, the initial salary being $600 with an annual increase of $50.00 per year until the maximum of $1,000 in the elementary grades was reached.

On November 21, 1905, the founding of the new College was celebrated with appropriate ceremonies. The principal speaker of the occasion, Dr. James Earle Russel, Dean of Teachers College, Columbia University, spoke on "The Trend in American Education." It was a plea for "greater social efficiency." "Every man should be liberally educated as far as circumstances permit," but "in making a man make him good for something."

In 1910 there was a radical revision of the requirements for the professional training of teachers. The strictly technical courses in education were required to be taken during a single year. The number of credits in education was reduced from thirty to twenty-four. Seniors who completed this required amount of work might count the same toward the Bachelor of Arts degree in the McMicken College of Liberal Arts and receive a teacher's diploma from the College for Teachers. The diploma entitled the graduates to a place on the preferred list of those eligible to appointment in the Cincinnati schools (after two months of successful practice teaching in the local schools) without examination, except in the theory and practice of teaching, as then was required under the law of the State of Ohio.

The Graduate School

One of the most important public events of the year 1906 was that which marked the dedication of the Graduate School. Dr. Dabney firmly believed that good instruction in the arts and sciences could only be maintained where the teachers were encouraged to conduct higher studies and research. The best professors want to do this work; and if they cannot do it, they are apt to go to other universities, or else become mere dull, routine teachers. The experience of the academic world was that research and teaching must go together. He also knew that what marked a university as an institution of higher education was the work which came out of the laboratories and libraries of the Graduate School.

Graduate instruction in the University had been in the process of development for many years. As early as 1877 the Academic Department of the University announced that persons properly qualified would be recommended by the Faculty for the respective degrees of Master of Arts or of Science, or the degree of Doctor of Philosophy, provided they pursued a prescribed postgraduate course of liberal education and fulfilled the necessary requirements for those degrees. In that year the University conferred upon two candidates, Herbert A. Howe and Winslow Upton, the degree of Master of Arts. These were the first graduate degrees granted by the University. Before the Graduate School was founded, the University had granted 52 degrees of Master of Arts, 19 of Master of Science, 8 of Master of Letters, and 4 of Doctor of Philosophy; making a total of 83 higher degrees. In 1895 the Board of Directors on the recommendation of the Faculty established a fellowship in each department of instruction in the Academic Department of the University. Fellows at that time were exempt from the payment of tuition and laboratory fees, but received no stipend. For one year (1901–1902) a separate Graduate Department was maintained. The Graduate Faculty was then composed of the heads of departments in the Academic Department offering graduate courses.

On November 16, 1906, "University Day," the Graduate School of the University of Cincinnati was dedicated. The members of the Board of Directors, the Faculty, and guests of the University assembled in the afternoon of that day at the Cincinnati Law Building on Ninth Street and marched in cap and gown to the neighboring Ninth Street Baptist Church where exercises were held. Mr. Oscar W. Kuhn, Chairman of the Board of Directors, presided. President Dabney delivered a brief address and then installed Professor Joseph Edward Harry of the Department of Greek as Dean of the new division. President William T. Pierce of Kenyon College, who came as the representative of the colleges in the Ohio Valley, spoke of the importance of the University's new adventure in higher education in this section of the country and extended the best wishes of sister institutions upon its success.

The principal speech was made by Andrew F. West, Dean of the Graduate School of Princeton. He stressed the ideals and methods of teaching which were needed in American colleges and universities to advance scholarship in this country. Dean West stated that the best preparation for postgraduate study in any field was a broad liberal education. He thought that every scientific student in his undergraduate days should study not only mathematics, physics, and chemistry, but should also become acquainted with the best literature of the Old World and of this country and the classics. The opposite, said the speaker, was also true. Dean West deprecated the commercialism of the age which was attracting too much of the best brains of the country into business and the professions, and strongly urged that Graduate Schools maintain high standards of scholarship and encourage the study of the humanities.

In the fall of 1906, eighty-two students registered for advanced courses in the new College. The Graduate Faculty recruited from the Liberal Arts Faculty then consisted of twenty members, and the University Library contained about 50,000 volumes and 8,800 pamphlets. There were four fellowships in the Graduate School: the Hanna Fellowship in Physics established by Mrs. Mary J. Hanna in memory of her husband, Henry

Hanna, who had given Hanna Hall to the University, which carried a stipend of $500 a year; the Alliance Française Fellowship, which yielded an income of $300 a year and was awarded to a student in the Department of Romance Languages who was required to attend a summer course of instruction by the Alliance Française in Paris; a fellowship in American history established by the Daughters of the American Revolution with a stipend of $100 a year; and a fellowship in Ohio Valley history of the value of $500 a year, established by the Society of Colonial Dames.

A year after the Graduate School was founded, the Nathaniel Ropes Chair of Comparative Literature was established. In 1910 the Armstrong-Hunter Scholarship in English was founded in memory of Miss Sarah J. Armstrong and Miss Clara Hunter by eighty of their former pupils. The income on $1,000 in this fund was used to establish a scholarship in the Department of English to enable a woman graduate of the University to pursue advanced work in this field. In 1909 the Graduate School conferred its first degrees of Doctor of Philosophy on two candidates, one of whom was Robert Clyde Gowdy, who later became Dean of the College of Engineering in the University.

The College of Engineering

In 1906 the University began a significant new experiment in education. In that year the "co-operative system of technological education" was inaugurated by Dean Herman Schneider, its originator.

Herman Schneider was born on September 12, 1872, at Summit Hill, Pennsylvania, the fourth son of Anton and Sarah (Wintersteen) Schneider. His father was a descendant of a Bavarian family; his mother was of Dutch-English stock. As a boy he worked in his father's general store, attended the village public school, and at the age of fourteen went to work as a breaker-boy in a coal mine. He decided to study engineering, because an older brother planned to become a civil engineer. Young Schneider took a preparatory course at the Pennsylvania Military Academy at Chester, and in 1892 enrolled in the Civil Engineering Department at Lehigh University.

At Lehigh, Schneider came in contact with two men who greatly influenced his later career. One was Mansfield Merriman, professor of civil engineering, who taught his students how to analyze engineering problems. The other was William Lehan, architect and construction engineer, in whose office Schneider worked during his free hours. From the latter he acquired a practical approach to architecture and structural engineering.

For three years after graduation from Lehigh in 1894, Schneider engaged in structural ironwork at Cumberland, Maryland; and for two years he worked in the Northwest on the engineering staff of the Oregon Short Line Railroad. In 1899 he returned to Pennsylvania, and Professor Merriman offered him a position as instructor in civil engineering at Lehigh, which Schneider accepted.

Schneider taught four years at his Alma Mater. While there he be: gan to ponder the question: "How can theoretical knowledge and first-hand experience be combined?" His own experience had convinced him that his work in the mines and in an architect's office had enabled him to grasp more quickly than his fellow students the theory of engineering problems presented in the classroom. The belief was strengthened by an analysis he made of case records of Lehigh graduates. He found that most of those who had shown marked ability after their college courses either worked while attending college, worked during vacations, or stayed out of college a term in order to earn money to continue their studies. Why not train engineers concurrently in theory and practice by having students begin part-time employment during their college years and make this work a recognized part of the educational program?

In 1902, Schneider presented a statement of his plan to the director of several large industrial firms which were considering the establishment of a new technical school at Pittsburgh to give engineering training that would be better suited to industrial needs than that given in the engineering colleges. Schneider proposed that a school be established and have students "co-op" with industrial plants there. While some industrialists in the East encouraged him, they were apparently unconvinced that industry had enough to gain to bother with shop-training of engineers. This plan was abandoned when Mr. Carnegie founded the Carnegie Institute of Technology in the City of Pittsburgh.

Years later Mr. Carnegie told Dr. Dabney that Schneider's plan "would have saved him millions at Pittsburgh spent on shops." Since Lehigh also rejected Schneider's plan he decided to move to another part of the country. Upon the recommendation of Professor Merriman, Schneider was offered a position at the University of Wisconsin which he accepted. Then, late in 1903, another Lehigh graduate teaching at the University of Cincinnati who wanted to go to Wisconsin suggested to Schneider that they exchange positions. The idea appealed to Schneider, since Cincinnati was a large manufacturing center. Professor Christian Marx interviewed Schneider. As a consequence, in 1903, Herman Schneider was appointed assistant professor of civil engineering in the University.

At Cincinnati, Schneider, with the help of John M. Manley, Secretary of the Cincinnati Metal Trades Association, persuaded twelve metal trades firms to test the practical values his plan might have for them. Two men, Frederick A. Geier, President of the Cincinnati Milling Machine Company, and Ernest Du Brul, President of the Miller, Du Brul,

Peters Company, were particularly helpful in putting the plan into operation at the University because they were members of the Board of Directors. Dr. Dabney was also impressed by a paper Schneider sent him in 1904 entitled "A Communication on Technical Education" which contained his scheme of education. In 1906, Dr. Dabney recommended the young professor of civil engineering as Dean of the College of Engineering because, as Dr. Dabney later wrote Andrew Carnegie, "we think he is one of the most original thinkers in the educational world."

Dean Schneider later said he would never forget the resolution which was passed by the Board of Directors a few months after his meeting with Mr. Manley which gave Schneider the right to try out his plan. Five members of the Board, claimed Dean Schneider, voted for it, four were against it. Dean Schneider claimed that the resolution was worded as follows: "We hereby grant the right to Professor Schneider to try, for one year, this co-operative idea of education at the University of Cincinnati and for the failure of which we will not assume responsibility."

When Dr. Dabney was about to retire, Dean Schneider on February 16, 1920, wrote him as follows: "I want again to thank you most heartily for having given to me the finest thing one man can give another—opportunity. Your faith in the Co-operative Plan made my work there possible." On another occasion Dean Schneider told one of Dr. Dabney's daughters, "What I am today is due to you father."

The co-operative system of technological education was inaugurated by the University in 1906 with twenty-seven students and thirteen firms. In the first class there were six pairs of electrical engineers, six pairs of mechanical engineers, and one and one half pairs of chemical engineers. They were divided into two groups: one of which was assigned to work in industrial plants for one week while the other went to school that week. Later they alternated on a biweekly period. While the students worked in the shops they were paid first at the rate of ten cents an hour. After 1913 the rate began at fifteen cents an hour and increased one cent an hour every year. All catalogues of the College of Engineering carried then and even today the statement: "Co-operative students are required to obey all regulations of the company with which they work and are subject to all existing labor conditions and laws, including those pertaining to liability for accident." In the beginning the two men of each pair were required to meet on the job each Saturday morning in order to ease the break between the school and the shop.

Dean Schneider's great achievement lay "in the indomitable fortitude with which he correlated work with industry in an orderly way and convinced the world it would work." The Dean was the first "co-ordinator." Then the heads of the various departments made the job arrangements. Finally in 1911 the first professor of co-ordination was appointed, Professor Curtis Myers, with Max Robinson as his assistant.

Herman Schneider was a tall, loose-jointed, lean man, with a kindly face, deep-seamed, a lofty forehead, generous nose, sensitive mouth, and deep-set eyes. He was quiet, unassuming, a marvelous salesman who "sold ideas rather than gadgets," a "big gauge man" with no petty jealousies or resentments; an imaginative idealist, yet a realist with his feet on the ground.

The success of the "co-op" system was phenomenal. The first year there were 75 applications for admission, the second year, 800 inquiries. The plan proved stimulating to the students and revolutionary for the Faculty. For a while the Faculty held weekly meetings to discuss teaching problems. Within three years after its foundation, H. S. Pritchett, President of the Carnegie Foundation, and Frederick W. Taylor, the founder of scientific management, declared the plan was one of the most constructive steps in education and called attention to the spread of its nation-wide influence.

College of Medicine

There were many changes in the Faculty of the College of Medicine during these years. The Medical College in 1904 sustained a great loss in the death of Dr. James G. Hyndman, professor of laryngology. He had been on the staff twenty-seven years, and for twenty-three years faithfully filled the office of secretary of the Faculty. In the same year Dr. Christian R. Holmes was appointed to the chair of diseases of the nose, throat, and ear. The following year (1905) Dr. P. S. Conner retired from the office of Dean because of illness; Dr. Frederick Forchheimer, professor of the theory and practice of medicine, was elected Dean. Dr. Thaddeus A. Reamy also resigned and was made emeritus professor. The next year (1906) Dr. William H. Crane, professor of chemistry, died; and Professor Chauncey D. Palmer, after thirty-seven years of service to the College, resigned as professor of gynecology and became professor of surgery. He was one of the most distinguished and loyal supporters of the College. He was first elected professor of chemistry and served in that department from 1867 to 1868, when he was made professor of anatomy, in which chair he served for eighteen years. From 1887 to 1905 he was professor of surgery and also served for a number of years as Dean of the College.

The next year (1908) Dr. Samuel Nickles, emeritus professor of materia medica and therapeutics, died after having served the College for nearly thirty years. The same year Dr. Augustus Ravogli, professor of dermatology and syphilology resigned to become professor of surgery in the new Medical Department, with which he remained until his death. He had an enviable reputation as a teacher and an international reputation as an authority on skin diseases. Dr. Dabney acted as Dean of the

Medical College during the session 1909–1910, as the Faculty was re-organized with the establishment of a new College.

During the year 1910 more changes were made in the Faculty of the College. Dr. Paul Gerhardt Woolley, professor of pathology, was appointed Dean, an office he held for three years (1910–1913). Two emeriti professors, Dr. William H. Taylor and Dr. Nathaniel P. Dandridge, died. During the year, Drs. A. G. Drury, S. C. Ayers, and Philip Zenner became emeriti professors and Dr. Henry McElderry Knower was appointed professor of anatomy. Dr. Martin Henry Fischer was appointed to the Joseph Eichberg Chair of Physiology.

Important changes were also made during these years in the curriculum. At the beginning of the year 1910 an additional year in chemistry, physics, biology, and modern languages became a prerequisite for admission to the College. At first this premedical requirement tended to reduce the number of students. The following year (1911) two radical changes were made in the curriculum. One was the introduction of a co-operative course with the Board of Health, whereby a student in his junior year divided his time between active service in the Board of Health and the regular work of the College. The other change was that lectures on special subjects should precede clinical work and that a considerable amount of clinical work in medicine and surgery should be done by students in their junior year in preparation for the bedside work of their senior year.

The most important event in the year 1909 was the union of the Medical College of Ohio and the Miami Medical College and the creation of a new Medical Department of the University. Dr. Dabney always considered the unification of the two Medical Colleges and the establishment of a new Medical College in the University one of the most important contributions of his administration.

In 1905 the Board had requested the Faculty of the Medical College of Ohio to appoint a committee with one from the Board and one from the Miami Medical College for the purpose of making an alliance or merger of the Miami Medical College with the Medical Department of the University. The Alumni Association of the Medical College of Ohio vigorously objected to the taking of any steps looking toward the dropping of the name of the Medical College of Ohio. This was to be one of the stumbling blocks toward the union of the two Colleges; another was the fact that the Medical College of Ohio did not want to give up any of its privileges acquired in the contract made with the University in 1896, by which the Medical College of Ohio became connected with the University.

Nevertheless, on January 4, 1906, a joint committee composed of representatives from the Board and representatives of the Faculties of the

two Colleges met to consider a plan for the merger of the Miami Medical
College with the Medical Department of the University. The plan presented by the Miami Medical College proposed that: (1) the joint committee select a Faculty for the combined College; these selections to be
referred back to the respective Faculties for consideration; (2) in the
future all appointments and records for the individual Faculties be made
by the Board of Directors; (3) the professors in the chairs of anatomy,
physiology, chemistry, and pathology receive adequate salaries; (4) the
Miami Medical College give up its charter, disband its organization, and
turn over all its assets to the University; and (5) the diplomas issued by
the combined school have on them either the names of the Medical College of Ohio and the Miami Medical College or simply contain the name
of the Medical Department of the University. It was finally recommended
that the diplomas should be issued in the name of the Medical Department.

The Faculty of the Medical Department unanimously rejected the proposals submitted or any proposition involving the abandonment of the
name of the Medical College of Ohio, the abrogation of the contract existing between the Medical College of Ohio and the University, and any
scheme which implied a radical change of the government of this institution.

Since no progress was being made the Board suggested that the old
committee on conference with the Medical Department be reconstituted
and that it confer with the Faculty of the Miami Medical College. The
Medical College was asked to present a plan. The plan they submitted
proposed that the Miami Medical College close its institution and surrender its charter; that the students in the Miami Medical College be
admitted to the Medical College of Ohio, entering them in courses at the
point they had reached in the Miami Medical College.

After more negotiations, it was ultimately agreed on June 18, 1908, that
the Miami Medical College assign its charter and its property to the
University, and the Miami Medical College was to become a part of the
Medical Department. But during the year 1908–1909 the two Colleges
were to preserve their autonomy, and the Board was to create for the
schools the future Faculty of the combined school.

Finally on March 2, 1909, an agreement was made between the University of Cincinnati and the Miami Medical College by which the latter
institution became an integral part of the University and was united with
the Medical Department. A new Medical College was thus formed under
the title of the "Ohio-Miami Medical College of the University of Cincinnati." The agreement required that all positions on both Faculties
were to be vacated at the close of the session 1908–1909, and a new Faculty created for the new College. The new Faculty was announced in

June 1909, and the new College opened in the fall of the year in the old Medical College of Ohio building which had been repaired, refurnished, and equipped for it. There were 199 students in the new College.

With the merger of the two Colleges the long and bitter rivalry between these famous schools came to an end. Ninety years after the birth of the Medical College of Ohio, the new College began its career. During its career the Medical College of Ohio had graduated 7,000 students, and during its existence the Miami Medical College had graduated 3,000. Among the graduates of these two schools were some of the most prominent physicians in America.

The Law School

The Law School was prosperous during these years. Dean Rogers commented on the "high character and ability of the student body." In 1907 one-third of them were college graduates from Harvard, Yale, Princeton, Cornell, and other colleges. In that year the students unanimously voted to adopt the honor system in their examinations. At the end of the examination, each student certified that he had neither given nor received aid during his examination; and all pledged themselves to prevent cheating and to aid in its detection and punishment. The scheme worked well.

The only trouble Dean Rogers had with the students was about smoking. He believed that "law could be better assimilated in a clear atmosphere" than in a smoke-filled one. Smokers were confined to the clubrooms below the first floor. The only concession he granted to the nicotine slaves was a five-minute intermission between classes in which they might "draw strength or consolation from the fragrant weed."

While the attendance was good during these years some people wondered why the enrollment was not larger or was not as large as that of the earlier years of the school. Dean Rogers pointed out that the Cincinnati Law School until 1885 was the only law school in the State of Ohio. Since that time eight other schools had been established in the State. Indiana had 8 law schools; Illinois, 11; Kentucky, 4; Pennsylvania, 4; and Michigan, 2. All these 37 neighboring law schools with the exception of 6 had been established since 1885. In 1906 the Faculty established a six-week summer session, but the enrollment was so small it was discontinued within two years.

On June 5, 1908, the Cincinnati Law School celebrated the seventy-fifth anniversary of its founding. In the afternoon appropriate ceremonies were held in the Scottish Rite Cathedral. Dr. Dabney in his introductory remarks called attention to the fact that the School proposed a candidate that year for the governorship of Ohio (Judson Harmon) and one for the Presidency of the United States (William Howard Taft). Dean Rogers gave a comprehensive summary of the history of the School and called attention to the fact that Professor Henry A. Morrill, who had been on the Faculty for nearly forty years, retired that year. Other addresses were made by Dean James Barr Ames of the Harvard Law School and by Lawrence Maxwell, professor of law on "legal education." Dean Ames closed his address with this significant sentence: "The training of students must always be the chief object of the Law School, but this work should be supplemented by solid contributions of the professors to the improvement of the law."

In the evening a banquet was held at the Queen City Club at which Judge William Worthington presided and Judge Judson Harmon acted as toastmaster. A number of addresses were made. In the course of his remarks Dean George W. Kirchwey of the Columbia University Law School raised the important question, "What makes a university great?" "Oxford has been called with reproach," he said, "the home of lost causes. Is it a reproach for a great university to be the home of lost causes? Does it not depend on whether the causes deserve to be lost? Will you answer the success of a university with your commercial topic lines? What is it that makes a university great? Buildings? Endowments? Or is it the causes for which it stands? The ideals it represents? The standards of public service which it holds aloft?" The celebration of the seventy-fifth anniversary of the founding of the Cincinnati Law School was a gala day in the history of the University and the Cincinnati Law School.

College of Commerce

The College of Commerce began in a modest way. In 1901 at the instigation of Mr. Charles Dupuis, later President of the Central Trust Company, there was organized a group of young bank clerks as a chapter of the American Institute of Bank Clerks, later known as the American Institute of Banking. The initial aim of the organization was social, but Mr. Dupuis saw the need of these young men preparing themselves better for their careers in order to promote their advancement. He conceived the idea of their taking courses in banking subjects in the evening. With this in mind he approached Dr. Hicks who had recently come to the University and asked him if he would be willing to give some instruction. Dr. Hicks showed an interest in the project and agreed to give some lectures in the evening to the group in economics.

Some of the officials in the local banks, such as George Guckenberger, President of the National Atlas Bank, and Casper H. Rowe, Vice-President of the Market National Bank, lent their support to the project. They appeared before the group and discussed different phases of banking, economics, commercial law, and other subjects which they thought would broaden their knowledge of banking. There were others, however, who were opposed to the scheme. They were afraid the movement might lead to the organization by the bank clerks of a union. The good behavior of the young students soon dispelled this fear.

The first classes were held in the Lincoln Club at Eighth and Race Streets. Later some of the classes moved to the conference room of the Fifty-Third Bank, then called the Union Trust Company. The work of the various departments of a bank were discussed by members of the class; there were lectures on subjects of current interest; and some evenings were devoted to contests in money counting, mental additions, and adding-machine work with prizes to the winners of "umbrellas, cuff buttons, and stick pins." There were no tuition fees. Instructors were reimbursed by the students "passing the hat." Part of the time Dr. Hicks was paid five dollars a week; and this sum was raised by his students contributing fifty cents a week which sometimes was a real hardship for them. In time agitation developed for more college instruction and as a result in 1906 the Cincinnati College of Finance, Commerce, and Accounts was established. The American Institute of Banking gave a certificate to those who completed the program. In 1908 a degree program was inaugurated. Mr. Francis B. Jones, a lawyer, who had been instrumental in securing the incorporation of the College, was the first to receive a degree from the institution.

In 1910 at the request of the Board, Dr. Dabney prepared a special report on the subject of colleges of commerce and departments of commerce that had been established in this country. He pointed out that many American colleges and universities were giving instruction in finance, commerce, and administration. Harvard had established a graduate school for these studies, and other colleges were rapidly introducing them into their courses. This was in response to a general demand for vocational studies in colleges and also because there was a definite need for better trained men to conduct business enterprises which were rapidly becoming complicated and difficult to manage with the growth of large corporations. The number of those who were going to college for the purpose of obtaining a classical and literary training preparatory to entering one of the learned professions was growing steadily less, while a large number were going to college with the idea of entering business. Germany and Great Britain were rapidly developing evening schools of commerce to meet the needs of the highly competitive industrialization of their countries.

As a result of all of these forces the Board in 1912 took over by agreement with the College of Finance, Commerce, and Accounts and established a College of Commerce as an integral unit of the University. Dr. Hicks was appointed Dean and Supervisor of the night classes. During the period of World War I the regular courses were discontinued, only certain courses being offered in co-operation with the government in its educational program.

CRITICISMS OF THE DABNEY ADMINISTRATION

Dr. Dabney was a builder, fearless and courageous. He did not hesitate to voice his opinions on national subjects, even though he was the head of a tax-supported institution. Sometimes his actions caused considerable criticism.

One such occasion arose as a result of a speech Dr. Dabney made on May 6, 1906, in Toledo. He was the principal speaker at the Commencement exercises of the Toledo Medical College, which was under the auspices of the Board of Trustees of the University of Toledo. In his address Dr. Dabney extolled the advantages of a municipal university, and in the course of his remarks he declared that cities should own and operate public utilities. "The people are taking over more and more of the public utilities," said Dr. Dabney, "and indeed why should they not? The people are learning that they have the same interest and should work together."

As there was much discussion at that time of the monopolistic tendencies of large corporations, and especially of the Standard Oil Company, Dr. Dabney's remarks attracted considerable attention. The next day the *Cincinnati Times-Star*, owned by Charles P. Taft, published an editorial sharply criticizing Dr. Dabney. Said the paper:

With the individual views of Dr. Dabney upon any political subject there is no disposition to quarrel. In his individual capacity he has the right to hold and utter any views upon political matters that he may see fit. But when, as President of the University of Cincinnati speaking at the Commencement exercises of a kindred tax-supported institution, he takes it upon himself to deliver a political harangue, he makes a serious mistake. The tax-supported universities of the state are not maintained for the advancement of political doctrines, and their heads, when they speak in their official capacity, are violating every principle of justice and every tradition of their office if they advocate any political doctrine. The tax-supported schools of the state—and the University of Cincinnati comes under this heading—are supported by all the tax-payers, some of whom believe in municipal ownership and some of whom look upon it as a forerunner of socialism. It is an injustice to either of these elements that the funds taken from them by the State through the tax levy should be used in the advocacy and upbuilding of a political doctrine which they hold in abhorrence. When, as President of the University of Cincinnati, Dr. Dabney took the stump for municipal ownership he not only did himself an injustice, but he injured the institution of which he is the head. He ended his usefulness as an executive, and he aroused an antagonism to an institution that cannot have too many friends.

The editorial of the *Times-Star* provoked a storm. The *Cincinnati Post* took up the matter that afternoon and replied with a column article on the first page defending Dr. Dabney. The *Post* continued its defense of him in a two-column article the next day, giving the opinion of a number of citizens on the subject. Two days later another editorial in the *Times-*

Star appeared, provoked by an article in defense of Dr. Dabney which appeared in the *Citizens Bulletin*. The *Volksblat* also wrote a strong editorial defending Dr. Dabney; the *Enquirer* only printed one small article on the matter; and the *Commercial Tribune* did not discuss the matter at all.

Henning W. Prentis, Jr., the Secretary of the University, writing to Dr. Dabney about the furor created by the article, said it was the opinion of the University men and businessmen about the City that the causes for the *Times-Star* editorial were twofold. "First, it was well-known that Mr. Charles P. Taft considers any movement looking toward municipal ownership socialism pure and simple, against which he is 'exceedingly mad' owing to his large holdings of the stock of public service corporations in Cincinnati and other cities." Second, as one of the old political "machine (Republican), he is anxious to impede the City administration as much as possible and to pose as the people's friend in opposing any increase in the tax rate."

Friends of Dr. Dabney rallied to his support. Dean Harry declared "instructors should not be muzzled." Articles appeared declaring the citizens should not "let the Standard Oil Company have a monopoly of gagging professors," which was undoubtedly a reference to the rumored influence of John D. Rockefeller in the University of Chicago which he had heavily endowed. "A municipal university supported by taxation should be proud of a President that would devote his time to enlightening the public on such questions. We want more Dabneys; we want more municipal universities, free from the stifling influences of privileged interests," wrote one admirer of Dr. Dabney to the *Toledo Press*. Dr. Dabney wisely refrained from all comment on his speech. He neither defended his remarks nor retracted them.

Another controversial affair occurred just at the time when the Ohio and Miami Medical Colleges were to be merged and united with the University. It will be recalled that Dr. Dabney's original contract was for five years as President of the University. In 1909 the question came up of re-electing him for an indefinite period at his present salary of $9,900 or securing a new President. When the matter came up for discussion by the Board on May 3, 1909, the open session became "so strong that the reporters of the local press were excluded and an executive session was ordered." But Mr. Du Brul of the Board became so excited during the heated debate "that he could be heard above the noise made by the scrubwomen and the janitors who were cleaning the halls." Director James H. Hooker moved that Dr. Dabney be re-elected, so that he could help in the reorganization of the Medical Department which was made necessary by the merger of the Ohio and Miami Medical Colleges. Mr. Du Brul opposed this until the budget for the next year was taken up. He declared that the salary paid to Dr. Dabney was "exorbitant" and pointed out that no other Ohio College President received half as much. Other members of the Board argued that the salary was reasonable.

Chairman Geier declared that the welfare of the University demanded that the heated discussion cease and suggested an adjournment of the Board. Mr. Du Brul called for a vote on his motion to table Mr. Hooker's resolution, but his motion was defeated by a vote of 5 to 3. "The people of Cincinnati want to know who is to be the next President of the University," said Mr. Brown who moved that the matter be referred to the Committee of the Whole in executive session. When the Committee of the Whole reported on March 20, 1909, a minority report was submitted, signed by Messrs. Du Brul, George Guckenberger, and Fred A. Geier that Dr. Dabney be retained at a salary of $8,000. This report was rejected, and Dr. Dabney was re-elected President for an indefinite period by a vote of 5 to 3 at a salary of $9,900.

Two years later (1911) Dr. Dabney's position at the University was again jeopardized. Rumors spread that charges against Dr. Dabney had been filed against him with the Board. Dr. Dabney believed that such charges had been filed, but none of the Board would confirm or deny this. They united in referring the matter to Chairman Stewart of the Board. He said that no definite charges had been filed, but he did acknowledge that an unpleasant agitation had arisen over Dean Schneider's plans to expand the scope of the field of the co-operative system of technological education. Some members of the Board did not see how Dean Schneider's plans could be harmonized with the views and jurisdiction of Dr. Dabney who was said to be in favor of Dean Schneider's plans. It was claimed "that the three insurgents who had voted against Dr. Dabney's retention two years previously" were making "an effort to secure Dr. Dabney's resignation and have Dean Schneider succeed him." If there was any basis for these rumors nothing came of them; a Board meeting of June 7 was reported "amicable and serene." There appeared to be a tacit understanding that for the "best interests of the University" the opposition to Dr. Dabney would be allowed to subside or at least be stowed away in mothballs for the present.

STUDENT AND ALUMNI ACTIVITIES

In 1907 both students and the alumni began important projects. One was the establishment of a University Cooperative Bookstore. In the fall of 1904 the Misses Isabella and Ruby Sears and Sarah Bedinger, all of the class of 1905, requested authority of the Board to establish a book agency at the University. The request was granted, and they opened a small bookstore in the Van Wormer Library for the purpose of furnishing notebooks and supplies to the students. The business flourished, and within three months the enterprise outgrew its quarters and its modest aim. As a consequence in January 1905 the original proprietors organized the University of Cincinnati Cooperative Society. The capital stock of the company was $300 issued in 300 $1.00 shares. All these shares were quickly subscribed, and the store began to sell textbooks and stationery. The store was moved to a small room in McMicken Hall and in June 1905, paid its first dividend. The next year brought further success and growth and in April 1906, a specially designed and equipped store was fitted up by the University Board. The bookstore in its new and permanent quarters expanded more rapidly than ever so that at the annual meeting of the stockholders held in May 1906, the capital stock of the company was doubled. By its third year the Cooperative Society had become a fixture in the University life and a source of great convenience to all, both students and Faculty. But the number of shares was limited, and only the stockholders participated in the profits made in the store. This was too one-sided a scheme, and so at a meeting of the stockholders on July 26, 1913, it was decided to dissolve the Society, and the members received $2.65 for each share held. There was a reorganization of the Society, and henceforth all students shared in the profits of the store. For some years thereafter the store was operated by the students and was under the supervision of a Board of Control composed entirely of students of the University.

Another project begun was the organization in 1907 of an Alumni Association composed of alumni of all the Colleges. Up to this year there had been no general alumni association of all the Colleges. The Colleges of Liberal Arts, Engineering, and Medicine each had its own organization. In 1891 the academic graduates of the classes of 1879 and 1880 decided to give a reception to the graduates of the class of 1881 "So pleasantly was the evening passed," wrote an anonymous writer in the *Al-Muir,* "that it was the unanimous opinion of those present that an alumni association ought to be established." During the following winter the Alumni Association of the Academic Department was formed for the purpose of "promoting the welfare of the University and the welcoming of the graduating class." From the year 1884 the Alumni Association met annually and entertained the graduating class on Commencement night. In 1891 an Alumni Day was made a regular institution of the University. Through the efforts of Alfred K. Nippert the gymnasium was erected and given as a gift of the alumni to the University.

On University Day, November 21, 1907, the first reunion of the alumni of all the Colleges was held. The function was held in the University buildings in Burnet Woods and consisted of a joint meeting of the alumni of all the Colleges, and afterward, separate receptions of the law alumni, the medical alumni, and the alumni of the colleges of arts, engineering, and teachers were held. The joint meeting was presided over by Oscar W.

Kuhn of the class of '86, Chairman of the Board of Directors. The main address was given by Dr. Frank Thilly of the class of '87, Sage professor of philosophy at Cornell University. Dr. William H. Venable composed for the occasion a poem, "Cincinnati, A Civic Code," which was read by his son Emerson Venable of the class of '98.

Between 1877 and the time of the reunion (1907) the total number of graduates from the McMicken College of Liberal Arts and from the College of Engineering (which was not differentiated from the former until 1904) was 1,034. At this reunion a statement was issued of the accomplishments of those who had graduated from these two Colleges between 1877 and 1902, because it was held that those who had graduated since 1902 had hardly had a fair opportunity to establish themselves in life and so were not considered. Ninety-five of these graduates were ministers of religion or executive officers of religious societies; sixty were lawyers; and thirty were physicians. There were numerous civil, mechanical, and electrical engineers. Twenty were classified as manufacturers, merchants, bankers, and executive officials of large corporations. Sixteen were in state and city offices. Twenty-five were professors in institutions of higher learning. The great preponderance, it is obvious, were in the learned professions. The time was still to come when U.S. universities would feed a large stream of graduates into business life.

Within these same years the College of Law had graduated around 3,500 students. Among the distinguished alumni from the College of Law were: William H. Taft, elected President of the United States and later appointed Chief Justice of the United States Supreme Court; Joseph G. Cannon, Speaker of the House of Representatives; Oliver P. Morton, War Governor of Indiana; Charles D. Drake, Chief Justice of the U.S. Court of Claims; Judson Harmon, Attorney General and elected Governor of Ohio in 1908; Milton Sayler, Speaker of the Ohio House of Representatives; and Lawrence Maxwell, Jr., Solicitor General of the United States. Others included Benjamin Butterworth, Commissioner of Patents; Robert B. Bowler, Comptroller of the Treasury; Charles G. Dawes, Comptroller of the Currency and later Ambassador to England and Vice-President of the United States; John B. Stallo, Minister to Italy; Bellamy Storer, Minister to Austria; E. F. Noyes, Minister to Austria and to Russia; Major General William H. Lytle; and Lieutenant Governor James W. Bryan. There were many others who attained high judicial honors.

Within the same period more than 4,300 students had been graduated from the College of Medicine. Among the distinguished alumni of this College were to be found the names of Dr. John S. Billings, editor of the catalogue index of the Surgeon General's library; The Honorable Alonzo Garcelon, famous practitioner, Governor of Maine; Dr. William T. Whittaker; Dr. W. W. Seely; Dr. James Graham; Dr. Richard Eberle; and many other prominent physicians of the City.

In 1907 the Alumni Association issued the first real song book of the University. It will be recalled that the Stygian Society in 1901 published a little pocket volume of songs with only the words but not the music for the use of its members. Because of the popularity attained by these songs, a demand arose for their publication, providing both words and music. The Alumni Association decided that the work of editing such a book "required a person of remarkable gifts, a college man appreciative of college spirit, a musician who could select and arrange music, and above all a person of critical and executive ability." In the opinion of the Alumni Association "such a combination of gifts existed in one of the alumni, Dr. Otto Juettner, Medicine '88." Dr. Juettner consented to act as chairman of a committee on which were appointed George D. Harper, Academic '91, and Edwin W. Glover, musical director of the University. Of the forty-three songs published in the first edition, *Songs of the University of Cincinnati*, Dr. Juettner wrote the words and music of six, the words only of five, and the music only of seven; thus contributing in part or in entirety to eighteen of the total number.

Three years later (1910) the *Cincinnatian* gave a rendition of the way the average student sang Dr. Juettner's *A Varsity Song*, the Alma Mater of the University. Even today its sounds like this as sung by some of the students:

> UC, that is the magic name, a la l' la the world proclaim
> No sweeter word e'er charmed my ear
> Mum'm Um um um um um um
> O la l lala laa l'la al lan lla ah la l'la
> O Varsitee Deeeer Varsitee, thy loyal children we will be-eee
> Thy loyal, loyal tchilldren we-will be-eee
> Thy loyal tchiidren we-will-bee.

During these years women grew more prominent and influential upon the campus. In 1907, Elsie Loebman was elected the first woman editor-in-chief of the Varsity annual. In the same year Jean Heck received the highest scholastic record ever attained by any student in the University, but three years later this record was exceeded by Helen Stanley.

In 1913 three new national sororities, Chi Omega, Kappa Alpha Theta, and Kappa Delta, were organized on the campus. The same year a strictly local sorority composed of upperclasswomen, Mystic 13, was formed. The fundamental basis for selection in this sorority was "the spirit manifested toward the institutions and organizations of Varsity and the enthusiasm in working for her interests." In 1932, Mystic 13 became a chapter of a national honor sorority, Mortar Board. In 1914, Kappa Kappa Gamma was founded at the University. In the early days the sororities met in the homes of the members. Both Dean Czarmomiska and Dean McVea attested to the good influence of the sororities upon student life. The sororities were "active but did not control student affairs in any way, nor did they interfere to any appreciable extent with the solidarity of student life." Two new national men's fraternities were organized during these years, Delta Tau Delta (1909) and Pi Kappa Alpha (1910).

While these student activities won public approval there were occurrences that caused considerable criticism of the University. In 1906, 450 upperclassmen went on a rampage; and after marching up and down the corridors of McMicken Hall they went downtown and invaded Hughes High School. They marched into the halls of Hughes and threw the school into a bedlam of confusion. Then they marched downtown in a shirttail parade through the streets of the City. This rowdyism was denounced by Superintendent Dyer of the Public Schools and Principal Coy of Hughes High School. President Dabney dismissed four of the ringleaders.

As a consequence of the students' parade and raid on Hughes High School and the way the annual flag rushes were fought, Dr. Dabney referred to the Academic Faculty the question of devising ways and means to regulate these matters so as to mitigate the evils of the flag rush and to prevent a recurrence of rowdyism. The flag rush was not abolished, but the struggle was shortened to four hours instead of dragging the contest out for ten hours as in previous years. The students were also prohibited from smoking and loafing in front of the main building, and the Academic Faculty adopted stringent regulations to reduce cheating in examinations.

March 11, 1910, was a red letter day in the life of the students of the University. There was great excitement that day because Elsie Janis, the popular actress, appeared as a "fair coed" on the campus. Never was a convocation so well attended. Seats were at a premium when Jim Peaslee with "trembling hands pinned a couple of pennants on Elsie." Some of the Faculty were disgusted with the whole affair.

ATHLETICS

Football took a new lease on life during these years. More and better players were recruited; more attention was paid to training the teams; the character of the game changed; and loyal alumni and the student body took a greater interest in college athletics. But there were no scholarships or other financial inducements offered the players. It cost every player money to play in those days. It was the joy of playing, the friendships, and close associations formed, which held the men together.

Most of the players were drawn from the College of Engineering. In 1912, out of a squad of 28, only 8 were not in the Engineering College. Dean Schneider arranged to have those co-ops who wanted to try for the team put into the same section. In this way they would all be in school the same week and at the factory the next. (The co-ops at that time alternated every other week.) Under these conditions football practice was

held late in the afternoon in daylight one week and at night the next
week. In 1909 arc lights were placed on poles erected on the playfield,
and the football was painted white. This enabled the team to practice at
night every other week. These first arc lights of the University, which
cost $367 to install, were paid for by the Athletic Council, who were
later reimbursed by the Board.

Another historic event of these years was that the squad began to wear
numbers on their back. The numbers were stamped on squares of white
muslin and pinned with safety pins on the backs of the players. In 1910
when the University played Tulane University, not one of the squad had
his name spelled correctly on the printed program. The University was
improving its prowess in football, but appeared weak in orthography.

The flying wedge began to be discarded during these years as well as
the rule that permitted "the pushing or pulling of the ball carrier through
the line of scrimmage." The quarterback usually took the ball from the
center and gave it to the ball carrier. The forward pass was used a great
deal but was encumbered by the rules. The styles of the uniforms of the
players began to change. The old-time white, cotton, cross-stitched pants
began to be replaced with padded pants. The old laced canvas vest was
abandoned. The University provided the players with shoes, socks, pants,
sweaters, and a soft shoulder pad, but each player bought his own headgear.

Teams were better trained. They had a camp at the Island Canoe Club
near Lockland. In 1909 a group of loyal alumni—Ralph Holterhoff, Henry
Bentley, Victor Heinz, Walter Hyman, Dr. Henry Box, A. Morvill, and
others—combined their efforts and persuaded Alfred Brodbeck to leave
the Cincinnati gymnasium and accept the position of Director of Physical Education at the University.

The students and the alumni loyally supported the teams. Cheering at
the football games was organized and directed by cheerleaders. At the
suggestion of the Alumni Association, the Board formally named the
athletic field "Carson Field" in 1910 as an enduring tribute to Dr. Archibald I. Carson, an alumnus and Director, for his untiring services for
many years in the interest of providing athletic facilities for the students
at the University. In 1913 for the first time the UC rooters hired a military
band to accompany them in their songs.

On the 1908 team there were some promising players such as Robert
Marx, Ernest Du Bray, "Pat" Reese, "Russ" Easton, Hugh Krampe, and
Walter Montgomery. In the succeeding years a galaxy of outstanding
players appeared. It is impossible to name all those who added laurels to
UC football teams during these years, but in addition to those cited
above, mention should be made of such men as Walter and Robert Heuck,
J. E. T. ("Snake") Kennedy, Al ("Swede") Bismeyer, Burton Robinson,
Howard Goheen, John ("Ike") Stewart, Max Zange, Jerry Howard, Ralph

Flohr, Stan Perry, John Biedinger, Mac ("Snooks") McComas, "Fritz" Lotter, James Buchanan, "Dutch" Koening, "Butch" Haehnle, John ("Tubby") Allan, Charles Broeman, Victor W. Fishbach, Adolph Davis, and managers, Bill Cummings, Ellis McNelly and William Pottinger.

The halcyon days of Varsity football were the years the Heuck boys played. Walter Heuck was captain of the 1910 and 1911 teams, and Robert (Bob) Heuck was captain of the 1912 team. In 1911 the team under Walter Heuck won six games and one tie in a nine-game schedule. In both years when Walter Heuck was captain, UC defeated Miami by scores of 3 to 0 (1910) and 11 to 0 (1911); and tied Miami (21 to 21) in 1912 when Robert Heuck was captain. Bob Heuck played in every game the University played while he was in school (1909–1913), and missed only three days of practice in four years. He became a civic hero in the game with Miami on Thanksgiving Day, 1909, by recovering a fumble on his own five-yard line and running ninety-five yards for a touchdown with Charlie McCoy of Miami fruitlessly chasing him.

In 1907 there was no football, because the Athletic Council resigned in disgust. It claimed it was so hampered that it was unable to accomplish results. Football was resumed in 1908, and a new Athletic Council was organized. It consisted of nine members—four appointed yearly by the President from the Faculty, three appointed yearly by the alumni, and two student members elected yearly at a meeting of the Student Athletic Association. The qualifications for membership in this Association consisted of the payment of $5.00 subscription for the support of competitive athletics. In return for that consideration, members were supplied with season tickets to all athletic contests. This was the beginning of the establishment of a system of annual student subscriptions to make athletics self-supporting.

In 1912, Robert Heuck, W. T. Pottinger, and Ralph Holterhoff organized the first "C" Club. It was composed of all men who had won a letter in some athletic sport. The organization did not flourish at first, but later Coach Chambers induced Dr. Carson and Bob Heuck to try to revive it. Coach Chambers agreed to give each member of the "C" Club a free ticket to all football games and a special stand was erected for them on the field behind the players' bench. The Club began to thrive. In time this idea had to be abandoned because of the "ex-quarterbacking" remarks that the players heard. Thereafter a discount on season tickets was given instead of free tickets.

Other sports besides football were also encouraged. Between 1904 and 1909 baseball became an important sport in the intercollegiate program. Among the distinguished players of baseball graduated during these years was the "immortal" Miller Huggins. He played on the Cincinnati baseball team from 1904 to 1909 and the St. Louis team from 1910 to 1917. An effort was made to stimulate interest in field and track athletics.

On Thanksgiving Day 1906 a UC cross-country team defeated the Cincinnati YMCA in a race through Burnet Woods. In 1912 the University constructed a swimming pool, and a swimming team was organized. Interest in basketball increased and in 1910 C. Albert Schroetter, an old Varsity basketball player, was appointed coach.

15

The University in World War I

World War I proved to be an especially disrupting factor in a city as strongly Germanic as Cincinnati then was. It slowed educational progress at the University and forced many compromises. But before the entry of the United States into the conflict, some generous gifts and bequests had given great impetus to the development of both academic and professional colleges. Just before America took the fateful step, the University received the largest gift so far in its history, larger even than the foundation gift of Charles McMicken.

It was the bequest of Francis Howard Baldwin, who died on December 10, 1916. He was born of Puritan parentage in Bloomfield, New Jersey. His father was one of the earlier railroad builders of this country. In 1849, at the age of fifteen, young Baldwin came to Cincinnati and entered the employ of his uncle, William H. Howe, who was among the pioneer publishers of the West. He later joined the firm and engaged in the publishing business. Mr. Baldwin took an active part in the commercial and civic life of this community. He was a President of the Mercantile Library Association, a charter member of the Queen City Club, and at the time of his death the oldest member of the Cincinnati YMCA. He never married.

After providing for the members of his family, Mr. Baldwin left the residue of his estate, estimated at about seven hundred thousand dollars, to the City of Cincinnati in trust for the use and benefit of the University. The bequest to the University was unexpected and unsolicited. It was unencumbered by any limitations or restrictions, and no directions were given as to the purpose for which it was to be used. There was no request for any memorial, monument, or recognition of any kind whatever. Subsequently, however, the main building of the College of Engineering was named in his honor, Baldwin Hall. For some years Dr. Dabney had been bemoaning the fact that the College of Medicine had received no large endowments. But now the Medical College began to receive gifts, due

229

largely to the efforts of Dr. C. R. Holmes. In 1912, Mrs. Francis W. Gibson gave $31,500 and Mr. Henry Levy $50,000 to the College of Medicine. The next year Mrs. Mary M. Emery gave $125,000 for a chair of pathology, and Mrs. Henrietta Moos bequeathed $25,000. Later the public-spirited Mrs. Emery offered to give $250,000 for the erection of a new building for the Medical College, provided an equal amount was raised for the equipment and maintenance of the building. This amount was obtained, and in 1918 the new Medical College building was completed and dedicated. The College of Medicine received in 1916 from Mrs. Elizabeth Drake, the great granddaughter of Daniel Drake, a Daniel Drake memorial tablet which was placed in the entrance hall of the administration building of the General Hospital.

New colleges and new departments were created during these years. In 1908 the Cincinnati Kindergarten Training Association had founded a Department of Household Economics which developed into a school. In 1914 the Board of Directors passed a resolution whereby the School of Household Economics was taken over from the Cincinnati Kindergarten Training Association and was made an independent school, the School of Household Administration, in the University. In 1889 a group of Cincinnati women had established the Cincinnati Training School for Nurses. In 1896 this training school was taken over by the City and made an integral part of the Cincinnati General Hospital, under the title of the Cincinnati Hospital Training School for Nurses. In 1914 it was reorganized as the School of Nursing and Health in the Cincinnati General Hospital. Two years later (1916) the School of Nursing and Health became a department in the College of Medicine under the direction of Laura R. Logan.

In the same year (1916) that the Department of Nursing and Health was established, the Department of Hygiene and Physical Education also was created. Alfred Brodbeck resigned in 1916 as Director of Physical Education, since he and Dr. Dabney could not get along. Dr. Jesse Feiring Williams was elected professor of hygiene and physical education and head of the department. Also in 1916 the evening classes in the College of Liberal Arts were placed under the supervision of Dr. E. L. Talbert.

In 1916 important changes were made in some of the Deanships. Miss Emilie McVea, Dean of Women, resigned to accept the Presidency of Sweet Briar College in Virginia. Miss McVea had served the University as assistant professor of English for twelve years and as Dean of Women for eight years. She was an excellent teacher and as an executive officer she exerted "a fine influence, not only among the students, but throughout the City." She was of great assistance in securing funds for the erection of the Women's Building. Miss Loueen Pattee was appointed to fill the vacancy.

In 1916, Dean Harry of the Graduate School was granted sabbatical leave and, subsequently, left the University. Professor Louis Trenchard More, head of the department of physics, became Dean of the Graduate School. For twenty-four years Dean More charted the course of the Graduate School and by his breadth of vision and by his own example as a productive scholar gave a decided impetus to graduate work on the campus. At his suggestion the postgraduate work which in the past had been confined to the College of Liberal Arts and the College of Teachers was extended to include work in the Colleges of Engineering and Medicine and the personnel of the Graduate Faculty henceforth included the full-time professors in all these Colleges.

More stringent rules affecting the curriculum and student activities were instituted. The students in the College of Liberal Arts were subjected to more rigorous Faculty inspection and control, and the Faculty, itself, was stimulated to take a more direct and personal interest in the students. A new system of Faculty advisors was adopted. Every student at the beginning of his course was assigned to an instructor, who was expected to assist him in shaping his studies more intelligently so that he would derive the best advantages from his scholastic work. The courses taken by the student in his first two years were more strictly defined while those taken in the later years were largely under the direction of the professor in charge of the major subject chosen by the student. Another step improving the scholastic efficiency of the College was the adoption of a new rule whereby not more than six hours of work marked "D" or "poor" might be counted in any one semester toward a degree.

The Faculty endeavored in various other ways to stimulate the students' scholastic interests. In 1914 the Liberal Arts College inaugurated a prize day under the auspices of the Women's League at convocation exercises. The prizes consisted of gold-lettered ribbons; red for first prize, black for second prize. These prizes were given to students who had competed in the various branches of literature, art, and music. Faculty members acted as judges. Late in the spring of 1916 the students, under the direction of Professor Bertha K. Young of the English Department, put on an elaborate celebration for the Shakespeare Tercentenary. Expert English instructors in folk dancing were secured, and the performance given in Burnet Woods on June 9, 1916, engaged the interest of the students, many of the Faculty, and a large crowd of citizens. An appropriate conclusion to the festivities was the performance of *Much Ado About Nothing* by members of the senior class under the direction of Professor Benjamin C. Van Wye of the English Department. Under the direction of Dean Schneider the senior class of the Civil Engineering Department of 1916 gave to the College of Engineering a series of mural decorations for the library in the building. The paintings were by Mrs. Francis Wilet Faig.

Student activities were more carefully regulated by the Faculty. The sororities agreed to reduce their social functions and to limit their entertaining to Friday evenings and Saturdays. The most important innovation in student affairs was the creation by the Faculty in 1916 of a Board of Student Trustees to license all student activities and expenditures requiring an expenditure of money, supervise their business, and audit their accounts. The flag rush was not abolished, but it was more carefully regulated. During the Presidential election of 1916, President Wilson gave the students a thrill by visiting the University campus and making a short address standing up in his automobile parked in front of McMicken Hall.

CRITICISM OF DR. DABNEY

The outbreak of war in Europe in 1914 stunned and bewildered the American people. Despite the recurring international crises in Morocco and in the Balkans in the decade before 1914, few Americans perceived the gathering war clouds or were fully cognizant how critical the European situation was. When, therefore, the storm broke in Europe the first reaction of the American people to the War was one of revulsion and astonishment. To them the whole conflict was "senseless," "insane," and "utterly without cause." Why should the great powers of Europe have become involved in war even though the Archduke Francis Ferdinand, the heir apparent to the Hapsburg monarchy, and his wife had been assassinated in the little town of Serajevo in Bosnia?

No matter what might have been the spark which had set off the explosion, the American people in 1914 were determined that this country should not become involved in the conflict. The United States must remain a spectator and not become a participant, and in 1914 the American people were confident that the United States could remain aloof. Nevertheless, they got a thrill from reading the bulletins and following the War on their maps. Their interest was that of a "moving picture devotee." Yet notwithstanding the urgent appeal of President Wilson that the American people remain impartial "in thought as well as in action," on the whole they sympathized strongly with the Allies. On the other hand many German-Americans and other pro-German "hyphenated" Americans loudly expressed their sympathy for the Fatherland.

Dr. Dabney was strongly in favor of the Allies, and he did not hesitate to let his feelings be known. Many sensitive Cincinnati German-Americans were irritated by his statements concerning the War which they considered were attacks on the Fatherland. When they failed to curb his anti-German statements they made an effort to have him removed from the Presidency of the University.

In December 1914, Dr. Dabney made a speech in Columbus entitled "The Higher Patriotism, or Internationalism vs. Imperialism." In his address Dr. Dabney attacked imperialism, characterized the Germans as "robbers and murderers," and called for the right of all peoples to govern themselves. Mr. Colon Schott, a Cincinnati attorney, and the Cincinnati German Literary Club criticized him sharply for his speech which they said tended to create in the public mind a feeling hostile to Germany and Austria-Hungary.

Hardly had the uproar over this speech subsided when the *New York Times* published a private letter Dr. Dabney had written to an English friend abroad in which the German-American Alliance alleged Dr. Dabney gave an English interpretation of the War. A letter was sent by the Ohio branch of the German-American Alliance in the City to the Board of Directors of the University disapproving of the statements made by Dr. Dabney and calling upon the Board to dispense with his services. "The German-American Alliance," stated the communication, "believes in liberty of speech; but it disapproves of an official who, as head of one of our important institutions, makes false and misleading statements about a country whose descendants support the University of Cincinnati." The Board filed the communication but declined to take any action.

In the same year (1915) when the local University Socialist Club, which had twenty members, requested that Mrs. Rose Pastor Stokes, the wife of a New York millionaire Socialist, be permitted to give an address at the University, Dr. Dabney said she was a "very fine woman, but the Board of Directors considered that political speakers should not be allowed to use the auditorium." It was well known that Mrs. Stokes believed that the European War was brought about by issues growing out of capitalism. Mrs. Stokes spoke instead before the Cincinnati Woman's Club.

Letters of remonstrance did not cause Dr. Dabney to modify his views nor to refrain from expressing them. In 1916 he wrote a letter to Congressman J. Campbell Contrill of Kentucky, a kinsman of Mrs. Dabney, which was published, in which he urged the Congressman "to stand by the President" in a bill to warn Americans from traveling abroad on ships of belligerent nations. President Charles Schwab of the Cincinnati branch of the German-American Alliance said: "Dr. Dabney is entitled to his private views, entertained privately, but he has succeeded in getting his 'private letters' published, and they have been offensive to Americans of German origin." The Board of Directors of the University declined to take any action on the letter from the German-American Alliance charging that President Dabney "has seen fit to express repeatedly and in an uncalled-for manner his own views in pretended private letters in attempts to foist his dangerous opinions, personal fallacies, and national antipathies upon the community and turn the tide of opinion to his own liking." The letter demanded that "either Dr. Dabney desist in the future from all similar agitating acts, or that, in case of non-compliance, he be compelled to do so by proper authorities. The Board filed the letter after hearing Dr. Dabney's explanation.

In the fall of that year (1916) Dr. Dabney made a speech in New York in which he said some new citizens "seem neither to understand nor appreciate the free institutions of the United States." Some of his auditors of German descent interpreted these statements as an attack on their loyalty and Americanism. A notable exception to those in Cincinnati who felt offended by Dr. Dabney's remarks was Howard E. Wurlitzer of the City. "I cannot see anything in the speech to arouse the ire of German-Americans," he said. "Dr. Dabney did not mention any nationality by name." Dr. Dabney, himself, was surprised at the reactions to his speech. He said he had had no particular nation in mind. "What I said referred to foreigners of any nationality who were reared under a monarchial form of government." The *Volksblatt*, the Cincinnati German newspaper, however, severely criticized Dr. Dabney. In an editorial it said: "Dr. Dabney can be replaced very easily. The Germans of Cincinnati would have more interest in the University if there was a man at its head who would be more grateful for the sacrifices they make for the University instead of doing everything to belittle their loyalty and Americanism."

EFFECT OF WORLD WAR I ON THE UNIVERSITY

The entrance of the United States into World War I profoundly affected all phases of the life of the University. All the resources and all aspects of the life at the University were subordinated to rendering every possible assistance to the government in the prosecution of the War. Soon after the declaration of a state of war by the Congress and the President in April 1917, a census was taken of the Faculty, alumni, and students of the University in order to ascertain their abilities, training, and capacities for war service. The information thus obtained was analyzed, classified, and forwarded to the several departments of the government. All the facilities of the University similarly were placed at the disposal of the state and national governments. The Board of Directors adopted a resolution pledging to keep open the positions of the Faculty and all other employees of the University who entered any of the war services and to make up the difference between what they received for such services and the salary they formerly received at the University.

A Department of Military Science was established in the University in April 1917, and all regular students of the College of Liberal Arts and of the College of Engineering were given military drill. The military training of the students in the College of Liberal Arts was at first placed under the direction of Professor William Hammond Parker, before he entered the armed forces, and in the College of Engineering under the supervision of Major W. P. Stokey, Corps of Engineers, U.S.A. The tactical drill was under the direction of Professors C. W. Park, J. H. Kindle, and C. R. Wylie. In October 1917, Lieutenant John J. Long of the Engineers Corps, U.S.A., a former professor of civil engineering at the University, was appointed Commandant of the Department of Military Science.

President Dabney created much amusement during this period by making several trips to Washington in order to obtain, if possible, some wooden guns from the government to use in the military drill. The students' vaudeville show in 1918 alluded to this episode, and it is reported that "Mr. Haenhle brought down the house with his artistic rendition of the following song":

> Prexy Dabney went to Washington
> Sing a root-de-toot-de-toot
> Sing a root-de-toot-de-toot
> He went to get a wooden gatling gun
> Sing a root-de-toot-de-toot
> Sing a root-de-toot-de-toot.

War courses were organized in the several Colleges. Class instruction in military engineering was organized in the different departments of the College of Engineering. The Department of Civil Engineering gave instruction in military topography and map-making, in the construction of pontoon bridges, and in the erection of various structures with knots, splicings, and lashings. The Department of Electrical Engineering taught radio and buzzer work. The Department of Mechanical Engineering gave instruction in gas engineering as applied to motor transportation and airplanes; in the principles of mechanics involved in airplane construction and flight; in the design of special machine elements applicable in guns, gun carrying, and in machines for their production; in hydraulics, hydraulic machines used in the construction of ordnance and the analysis of hydraulic recoil; in buffer mechanics for guns; in the construction of charts; and in the principles applicable to the production of shrapnel and ordnance. For four months beginning with September 1918, the outside work of the co-operative course was discontinued in order that the students who remained might spend all their time in the work of the Students' Army Training Corps.

Many of the Engineering Faculty rendered war service. Early in November 1917, Dean Schneider was put in charge of the Industrial Service Section of the Ordnance Department. When the War Labor Policies Board was organized he became assistant to the Chief of Ordnance. When the Committee on Education and Special Training of the General Staff was formed, Dean Schneider was made a member of it. During his service for the government Dean Schneider returned to the University about once a month for consultation with reference to the work of the Engineering College. Other members of the Faculty who received commissions in the armed forces were J. J. Long, E. K. Ruth, E. K. Files, and G. W. Burns.

The College of Liberal Arts, through the Departments of Philosophy and Political Science, Economics, History, and Psychology, jointly gave a course of lectures dealing with the causes and issues of the War. A course in war gardening was given by the Department of Botany. The Department of Political Science offered a course in the problems of the War.

Members of the Faculty of the College of Liberal Arts did war work as follows: Professor F. C. Hicks was appointed an advisor in the Industrial Service Section of the Ordnance Department; Professor N. M. Fenneman was on the Commission of Inquiry of Colonel House collecting geographical information on Africa for the Peace Conference; Professor H. B. Shepherd was engaged in war work in the YMCA in France; Professors S. G. Lowrie, W. H. Parker, R. C. Gowdy, A. W. Davison, M. J. Hubert, Schnachne Isaacs, and A. L. Herold received commissions in the armed forces; and Louis Passarelli served with the 29th Division in France.

Many of the Faculty and students of the College of Medicine entered the armed forces. Dean Christian R. Holmes was commissioned a major and was in charge of the aviation section of the Signal Corps in Cincinnati. Dr. Roger S. Morris was in charge of the cardiovascular examinations at Camp Sherman with the rank of major. Dr. Paul G. Woolley was also a major as an epidemologist. Dr. William Gillespie was director of the Cincinnati Base Hospital unit. Dr. Albert H. Freiberg was a member of the Advisory Council on Orthopedics to the Surgeon General of the United States, assisted in compiling the Manual on Orthopedics for the Army and was later chief of the section on orthopedic surgery at the Walter Reed Hospital in Washington. Dr. Alfred Friedlander was a major stationed at Camp Sherman in Chillicothe. Dr. William B. Wherry, bacteriologist at the Cincinnati General Hospital, was on the Council of National Defense in Washington. Dr. A. C. Bachmeyer, Superintendent of the Cincinnati General Hospital, was a major in the Medical Corps and was in charge of the United States Army General Hospital at Carlisle, Pennsylvania. Dr. Joseph Ransohoff was commissioned a major in the Medical Corps.

The Cincinnati Base Hospital No. 25 was organized by the Medical Faculty and the staff of the Cincinnati General Hospital, and the sum of $25,000 was contributed by the people of Cincinnati for its equipment. The Hospital staff, nurses, and enlisted men of this unit were, with a few exceptions, from Cincinnati. The Cincinnati Base Hospital was sent abroad and was stationed at Allery-Sur-Saône, France, where there was a large hospital center. Upon their arrival they found the hospital buildings only partially constructed. The Château-Thierry drive was on, and when the first trainload of 350 wounded American soldiers arrived, the Hospital was totally unprepared for them. There were no ambulances. The wounded men had to be carried on stretchers from the train to the receiving ward of the Hospital. Medicines were at a premium, and surgical instruments were scarce. Requisitions for medicines and instruments were quickly rushed to the medical supply depots, and conditions gradually improved. The arrival of American nurses was of great assistance. On several occasions Base Hospital No. 25 was commended for its excellent services.

The School of Household Administration gave courses on food conservation and co-operated with the Food Administration of the Federal government. The University co-operated with the Red Cross and the Cincinnati Council of Social Agencies in conducting institutes for home service; the object of which was to train workers for service among the families of the men in the service. Miss Laura R. Logan, Director of the School of Nursing and Health, was Chief Nurse of the Base Hospital. She recruited the nursing personnel of the unit and served on many national and state boards.

The first service rendered by the University as an institution in the war effort after the United States entered the war was to give vocational training to draftees of the Army sent by the War Deparment. They were given instruction in automobile and electrical work by the Faculty of the College of Engineering. Three groups were sent for successive two-month periods for instruction in automobile mechanics. Later two additional groups were trained as electricians. The total number of men trained as auto mechanics and electricians at the University was 1,772.

The success attending the vocational training in the universities and colleges of the country caused the Committee on Education and Special Training of the War Department to request the universities and colleges of the country to make a more extensive utilization of their resources. The result of this request was the organization known as the Students' Army Training Corps, designated as the SATC. Under the plan devised for the SATC students were to become by voluntary induction uniformed soldiers in the United States Army subject to military discipline, and were to receive the pay of privates. To house and board this body of men the University utilized the old Medical College building and constructed thirteen temporary barracks on the campus at a cost of approximately three hundred thousand dollars which was later refunded by the national government. The SATC was established at the University and about six hundred other authorized colleges simultaneously on October 1, 1918. Later the Navy Department authorized the formation of a naval unit at the University. The total number of men in the SATC, including the naval unit, was 1,027. However, the influenza epidemic in Cincinnati was so serious that the Board of Health placed the University and all other schools under quarantine from October 5 to November 13. By taking precautionary measures and by the rigorous enforcement of the health regulations, the epidemic was confined to the student-soldiers in the barracks. And by that time, the War was over.

The SATC at the University was organized in three departments. The Board of Directors formed a special War Education Committee with the President as the chief executive officer for the SATC. Professor Edward S. Smith was the executive secretary of this committee. The SATC was divided in accordance with the general plan into two departments: Section A, the collegiate section; and Section B, the vocational section. Only high school students were admitted to the collegiate section, and the educational work was conducted under the direction of the Deans of the different Colleges; the instruction being given by the regular Faculties, aided by instructors temporarily hired. The vocational section was under the direction of Professor A. M. Wilson, acting chairman of the College of Engineering.

The courses of study given in the SATC were arranged in accordance with the curricula of the Committee on Education and Special Training of the War Department. The only course absolutely required of all students, except a few advanced classes, was one on war aims, offered by the Department of History under the direction of Professor Merrick Whitcomb, assisted by members of the Faculty from other departments. Dr. P. V. N. Myers, retired professor of history, was temporarily appointed lecturer in history to give a course of lectures on the issues of the War to the members of both the vocational and collegiate sections of the SATC. The operation of the SATC was never sufficiently settled to make possible a fair comparison between the interest shown by the students in the academic work under the SATC and peacetime conditions. The interest of the students in their academic work definitely waned after the signing of the Armistice.

The national government was determined, if possible, to safeguard the moral conditions of the men in the armed forces. The Army bill of 1917 prohibited the sale of any intoxicating liquor to any member of the military forces, and the Secretary of War was empowered to suppress any houses of ill-fame in the vicinity of the training camps. As a result of this law a "purity" zone having a radius of five miles was set up about the University. President Dabney felt it was his duty to see to it that these regulations were enforced. He corresponded at length with the War Department on ways to improve the methods of control of vice about the University, but conditions in Cincinnati with regard to drunkenness and immorality became much more serious after the signing of the Armistice. Dr. Dabney said there was a great deal of drunkenness in hotels, stations, and soldier clubs after demobilization began; since "many people seemed to think it was their duty to welcome and entertain the returning soldiers, giving them a drink."

The University was one of the first institutions in the country to offer scholarships to French students. Five young French women were brought to the University on scholarships provided by the University and the ladies of the French Students' Scholarship Fund Association. Later five French soldiers were sent to the University by the French government, their expenses paid by a Cincinnati committee.

The University was affected by war hysteria. Professor Martin Ludwich who taught German in the College of Engineering was dismissed, because he failed to become an American citizen. Professor Tawney of the Philosophy Department was accused of being a pro-German, because he had said in one of his lectures that Germany had "outwitted all her commercial rivals, even Great Britain." "Professor Tawney's patriotism is so well-known that no investigation is necessary," said President Dabney.

The first graduate of the University to die in the armed forces during World War I was Corporal Elmer Hoover Van Fleet. He was the only son of the Reverend John P. D. Van Fleet, rector of St. Stephen Church, Winton Place. He was graduated from the University in June 1917, and was awarded a Rhodes scholarship. He died in France of scarlet fever on January 17, 1918. Memorial services for the First Gold Star were held at the University under the auspices of the YMCA.

After the War memorial services were held on April 30, 1919, for the men of the University who had died in the service of their country. The names of the twenty-five men who made the supreme sacrifice were:

> Lieutenant David Hayward Ackerson, Lt. Leland Meyer Barnett, Lt. Robert E. Bentley, Corporal Cornelius J. Devereaux, Lt. Miles Gelwicks, Sgt. Herbert E. Green, Lt. John K. Grisard, Lt. William Worth Hays, Lt. John Henry Koenig, Justus Louis Kruckemeyer, Capt. Clement E. Laws, Clifford Grant McCormick, Judson McNanaway, Clifford J. Nelson, Sgt. Clifford D. Paddack, Lt. Edgar B. Ritchie, Harrison H. Rudolph, Lt. Eugene A. Scanlon, Sgt. Robert Schroder, Lt. Justus F. Sundermann, Lt. Hall A. Taylor, Corp. Elmer Hoover Van Fleet, Sgt. Major Ralph C. Waring, Capt. Charles H. Weintz, and Corp. Harry A. Wilson.

Corporal Michael Aaronsohn was blinded during the War. He returned to the University and was graduated both from that institution and the Hebrew Union College and subsequently became a distinguished rabbi in the City.

On the basis of very incomplete records published on March 14, 1918, the total number of men of the University in the Army and Navy was 620, exclusive of 162 men in the enlisted reserve corps at the University. According to these records the University was represented in the Army and Navy by the following:

Members of the Faculties and officers 65
Students in the year 1917 310
Alumni 187
Former students 58
                                         ———
TOTAL   620

By rank these men were distributed as follows:

Lieutenant Colonel 1
Major 17
Captain 36
First Lieutenant 154
Second Lieutenant 38
Non-commissioned officer 374
                                         ———
TOTAL   620

Student activities suffered as a result of the War. In athletics an attempt was made, in accordance with the policy of the government, to continue all sports; but football felt the loss of many of those best qualified to excel in the game, with the result the University showed an unbroken series of defeats at the end of the season of 1917. Coach Cortright resigned to enter the YMCA in France. Mr. Frank Marty was chosen to coach the football team; but Dr. Whitelaw Morrison, who was appointed director of hygiene and physical culture as a result of the resignation of Dr. Jesse F. Williams, assumed the directing of athletics. In 1918, Boyd Chambers was appointed coach, and the football record for that year was better. The University played only five games that year; winning three and tying two.

One sorority, Delta Zeta (1916); two fraternities, Lambda Chi Alpha (1916) and Sigma Alpha Mu (1917); and one honorary fraternity, Tau Beta Pi Engineering (1915) were organized during these years.

Social functions were reduced to a minimum in 1918. The girls gave tea dances on Friday afternoons with no refreshments served. The occasional large evening dances were characterized by extreme simplicity, and the proceeds for all functions were contributed to war funds.

OTHER ACTIVITIES OF THE UNIVERSITY

In spite of the many demands made upon the University by the War, peaceful pursuits were not entirely forgotten during these years. In 1916, at the request of the Faculty of the Cincinnati YMCA Night Law School, the University took over the institution and established the evening department of the Cincinnati Law School, but within a year this was discontinued.

At the election of November 1917, the people of Cincinnati voted a new charter for the City of Cincinnati that made important changes in the organization of the Board of Directors and the relations of the University to the Medical College and the Cincinnati General Hospital. Heretofore the mayor, elected for two years, soon after taking office appointed three directors of the University to serve for a period of six years, making a Board of nine members. Under the new charter, each mayor who served for four years, appointed every year one director to serve for a term of nine years. The mayor was authorized to inaugurate the new system on January 1, 1918. The charter further placed all the scientific, medical, and surgical work and the instruction in medicine and nursing in the General Hospital under the direction of the Board of Directors of the University. The Superintendent of the Hospital, however, was to be appointed by the Director of Public Safety. Furthermore, all teaching in the General Hospital was open to all students of any of the medical colleges in Cincinnati which were recognized by the State Medical Board. The new charter thus made the General Hospital a part of the College of Medicine for clinical purposes and for research and teaching.

The following year (1918) Mrs. Obed J. Wilson offered to finance the erection of a convocation hall to be located at the northwest corner of the campus at Clifton and University Avenues to be known as the "Obed J. and Amanda Landrum Wilson Memorial Hall." The Board accepted this magnificent gift with appropriate resolutions. The same year the University was designated as one of the institutions in Ohio to give training to teachers of industrial arts and home economics under the Smith-Hughes Act. The work of the College of Teachers was reorganized, and a new course extending over five years was offered as well as the regular four-year course. In both cases the students were to spend half the time of the last year in practice teaching in the public schools. The students taking the five-year course received the Bachelor of Arts degree at the end of the four years and a graduate diploma in education upon the completion of the work of five years. The students taking the four-year course spent two years in the College of Liberal Arts and the next two years in the College of Teachers and secured a Bachelor of Science degree from the College of Teachers.

In 1918 a closer union of the Cincinnati College of Law and the University took place. In 1897 the Law School of the Cincinnati College (the only department of the College still in operation) had affiliated with the University. The agreement signed was to last for at least ten years; actually it lasted until 1911 but then was discontinued by the Cincinnati College, because certain members of the Board of Trustees feared that the University was trying to extend its control over the College. Professor Alfred B. Benedict resigned from the Board of Directors and became the Dean of the Cincinnati College of Law.

For many years Professor Benedict had advocated and labored for a closer union between the Law School of the Cincinnati College and the

University because he believed that such a merger would promote the cause of legal education in the community. When Professor Benedict became Dean of the Cincinnati College of Law he deemed the situation ripe for such action. The status of the Cincinnati College of Law had declined. Dean Benedict set to work to persuade the principal stockholders and trustees of the College to surrender all their stock and the property of the School to the University. He first proposed to Rufus Smith, Chairman of the Board of Directors, to sound out the members of the Board informally to find out if they would be willing to contribute $13,000 to the support of the Cincinnati College of Law, and having secured this, he set to work to induce the Cincinnati College to transfer its school and property, amounting to at least $325,000, with an annual income of something over $13,000 to the University.

As a result of the efforts of both Professor Benedict and Judge Rufus Smith on May 7, 1918, the merger of the two Schools was consummated at a meeting of the trustees of the Cincinnati College and the Board of Directors of the University. The majority of the stockholders of the Cincinnati College voluntarily transferred their stock, the charter of the College, and its property and other assets to the Board of Directors of the University who elected themselves and three other persons of the Cincinnati College as trustees of the Cincinnati College. The University agreed to maintain the Cincinnati Law School as a high grade law school and to contribute $13,000 annually for its maintenance. The Faculty of the Cincinnati Law School was reorganized and consisted of twelve professors, three of whom gave their whole time to the School as required by the agreement. The instruction for the present continued in the building of the Cincinnati College on Ninth Street between Race and Vine. Thus the Cincinnati College became an integral unit of the University, and the President of the University of Cincinnati today also takes the oath of office as President of the Cincinnati College.

16
Progress in the Wake of War

On January 1, 1919, the war courses at the University were closed, and regular work recommenced. With the demobilization of the SATC the government established units of the Reserve Officers Training Corps (ROTC) to provide a limited amount of military training in selected colleges and universities throughout the country. The University was designated as one of these institutions, and the government authorized the establishment of five ROTC units there—engineering, ordnance, coast artillery, signal corps, and infantry. Army officers were placed in charge, and the equipment was furnished by the government. A professor of military science and tactics, Colonel Sidney H. Guthrie of the Coast Artillery Service, was detailed as commandant.

The College of Commerce and the College of Engineering were merged in 1919, and a five-year co-operative course in commerce and business administration was inaugurated with the opening of the fall session. The evening courses in commerce were continued under the supervision of Vincent H. Drufner as supervisor. The work of the Graduate School was expanded. The School of Home Economics was reorganized as a department of the College for Teachers. The year 1919 marked the one-hundredth anniversary of the College of Medicine and was commemorated with appropriate exercises. The attendance of students the first year after the War was the greatest in the history of the institution, with a net total of 3,346. The students in the University represented thirty-six states, the Philippines, and eight foreign countries.

After the War the colleges and universities of the country experienced a reaction from the War period. The first year after the War was a disappointing one to colleges in general with respect to scholarship. There was a letting down of serious effort, a tendency toward "frothy frivolity." The exaltation of the War which had carried the youth of America through the terrible ordeal was followed by disillusionment. Everyone had hoped that after the War there would be a better world. Owing to a lack of leadership throughout the world in the conduct of human affairs, however, the decade of the twenties was a period of social and intellectual unrest marked by a revolution in manners and moral standards. There was a revolt among young people, especially among the "flaming youth" on college and university campuses, against the rigorous rules of the Victorian era. There was a revolution in women's dress. Women began to wear fewer clothes. In 1913 it took about twenty yards of cloth to garb a woman; by 1928 the amount of cloth had declined to seven yards. Not only did women wear shorter skirts, but the bolder among them began to roll their stockings. Not content with abbreviating their skirts and exposing their knees, women began to bob their hair and to smoke and to drink openly in public.

While many of the older generation were shocked and alarmed by the breakdown of these barriers, there were no rumors of "escapades" and "scandals" on the University campus as there were at some other institutions. But in the fraternities here as elsewhere there was much criticism of profanity, drinking, and gambling in the chapter houses and of "general laxity of dress and manners." The situation became so serious that some of the national fraternities began to propose higher scholarship qualifications for initiation and to make the use and possession of intoxicating liquor in the chapter houses or its premises the grounds for the expulsion of their members. The inauguration of mothers' clubs by various fraternities and sororities after World War I helped some of these conditions.

The chief concern of the University administration during these years was to provide adequate salaries for the professors. The Board of Directors did everything possible to secure and to save funds for salary increases. But the restrictions on the taxing power of the City limited the amounts that could be derived from that source, and endowment income could not be utilized freely, as so much of it was earmarked for specific purposes by the donors. The position of the professor was a trying one in those days. The salaries of college professors everywhere were far below those of the other professions requiring corresponding preparation and experience. President Dabney showed that "city officials were paid better than University professors." The salaries of many clerks in commercial houses were higher than professors', and the heads of departments in these firms earned double the compensation of full professors. According to Dr. Dabney, "plumbers were paid more than associate professors and street car conductors more than assistant professors." The economic upheaval caused by the War left teachers "among other small-salaried men in a position inferior to that of the unskilled wage-earner."

The general public began gradually to awaken to the seriousness of the problem. As Professor Frank Thilly, a graduate of the University, then Dean of the College of Arts and Sciences at Cornell University, said in one of his reports:

The salary problem has more than local significance: the question is how we may induce men of brain to follow the academic calling at all. Persons of spirit and capacity who contemplate entering the profession are not tempted to it by the lure of gold, but they may be deterred from it by the certain prospect of a penurious existence. Those who have the welfare of higher education at heart and to whom the government of universities has been entrusted, must see to it that the profession may at least maintain the high standard of scholarship and character, which it has reached in this country; it is part of our duty to provide the coming generation with distinguished scholars and teachers.

To procure additional income the Board increased the tuition in the Colleges to equal that of other comparable institutions. Under the new schedules the tuition in the Liberal Arts College for non-residents was fixed at $150; in the Engineering College, for regular resident students at $100, for non-resident regular students at $150, for resident co-op students at $150, and for non-resident students, $200; while tuition in the Law School was set at $100; and in the Medical School at $250.

A New President

In 1920, Dr. Dabney reached the age of sixty-five, and under the by-laws of the Board of Directors was at that time retired. For sixteen years (1904–1920) Dr. Dabney had served as President of the University. When he came to Cincinnati the School could hardly be called a university. A small cluster of buildings overlooking a rocky ravine constituted the plant. The enrollment was about four hundred students, most of them in the College of Liberal Arts, a few in a rather ineffective technical school.

For a number of years the School had been controlled by politics. The University was dominated by the dictates of "Boss" George B. Cox and his "gang." Just as Dr. Dabney came to Cincinnati, a reform government under Mayor Julius Fleischmann had come into power. As already related (Chapter 14), "Boss" Cox assured Dr. Dabney that if he accepted the Presidency there would be no political interference with the internal affairs of the University. "Boss" Cox conscientiously lived up to his promise. A Board of Directors was appointed which had the interest of the University at heart. With their help and co-operation a new era for the University was made possible. The Board of Directors wanted to make the University the center of culture in the City. The establishment of the co-operative course gained for the University the support of the industrial and commercial leaders in the community; and as more and more students were graduated and began to win prominence in the political, intellectual, industrial, and social life of Cincinnati, the influence of the University grew.

At the end of his sixteen years as President, Dr. Dabney could look with pride at the wonderful growth of the University during his administration. During these years about eighteen acres of ground had been added to the College campus; eight new buildings had been constructed and the stadium partially completed. The productive endowments, including real estate, had increased from $575,920 to $2,788,991. The income from the City had increased from $75,000 to $357,000 annually, and the total income from $130,909 to $855,000. The number of professors and instructors had increased from 97 to 307, and the student body had grown more than 3,000. Departmental College developments during these years included: Engineering Department raised to a College (1904); a College for Teachers established (1905); a Graduate School organized (1906); a University College of Medicine established (1909); a College of Commerce created (1912); a Home Economics Department started (1914); a new City hospital and College of Medicine united by charter of the City (1916); a School of Nurses became a part of the College of Medicine (1916); a separate department of Physical Education was organized (1916); the College of Law made an integral part of the University (1918); and a Department of Vocational Education established in the College for Teachers (1918).

On May 26, 1920, the Board of Directors elected Dr. Frederick Charles Hicks to succeed Dr. Dabney. His selection was a surprise to a number of the citizens of Cincinnati. Several letters had been written to the Board asking that William Howard Taft be tendered the Presidency. At no time, however, had the Board considered Mr. Taft's name. Dean Schneider had refused to accept the position. For some unknown reason Dr. Hicks had resigned his professorship on May 6 and had to withdraw it after his election as President.

Dr. Hicks was born at Capac, Michigan, a village northwest of Detroit. His father, H. W. Hicks, was a Methodist minister. He received his elementary school education in the district school of Capac and his high school training at Corunna, Michigan. On finishing his high school work Hicks entered the University of Michigan. He was compelled to interrupt his college career for two years to earn money enough to pay his expenses. During that time he taught in a country school. In 1886 he was graduated with honors from the University of Michigan. After teaching two years as principal of the Laporte (Indiana) High School, he returned to the University of Michigan where he took his doctoral degree in economics. He taught in that institution for a year as instructor and was then appointed head of a newly created department of economics at the University of Missouri. Dr. Hicks remained at the University of Missouri for nearly nine years. In 1896 and 1897 he visited France, Germany, and Italy to study economic conditions in those countries.

In 1900, Dr. Hicks came to the University of Cincinnati as the first professor and head of the department of economics. In 1907 he was made Dean of the College of Liberal Arts and was also head of the College of Finance, Commerce, and Accounts. In 1912, Dr. Hicks became Dean of the College of Commerce and retained that position until 1917 when it was merged with the College of Engineering on a co-operative basis under the direction of Dean Schneider. From 1917 to 1920, Dr. Hicks resumed his duties as professor of economics.

Upon taking up his duties Dr. Hicks announced his creed: "Everything that I do will be to make the University of Cincinnati the best institution of higher learning in America. If that means that I shall have to break friendships, then I will do that. There will be nothing revolutionary during my term of office. I believe education should be a community affair. My method will be progressive conservatism."

Dr. Hicks was a quiet, unassuming gentleman. He was never a pusher or a self-seeker. As Dean Chandler said, he was a "conservative in the best sense." For more than half a century Dr. Hicks was a significant factor in the life of Cincinnati. He wrote an elementary text on economics, and his writings on gold and currency problems attracted wide attention during his career as a teacher and administrator. Dr. Hicks was an excellent didactic teacher of economics, who insisted that his students memorize verbatim his definitions of elementary economic terms. His philosophy was that a large enrollment was not a criterion in measuring the development of a great university. While he believed that student activities should have the loyal support of both the Faculty and the students, he was an ardent advocate of the theory that the University was primarily "for culture and technical instruction, not social enjoyment alone."

ADMINISTRATIVE CHANGES

There were numerous changes in the personnel of the administration during the administration of President Hicks. In 1921, Miss Loueen Pattie, Dean of Women, died. She had sought faithfully to fulfill her mission among the women students of the University as their guide. She was succeeded by Miss Josephine Price Simrall, a graduate of Wellesley College, who had taught at Sweet Briar College, Virginia, and had been Dean of Women at the University of Kentucky. In the same year Frank F. Dinsmore began his long, distinguished service on the Board of Directors with his appointment to fill the unexpired term of Otto J. Renner, who had died. Allison F. Stanley who had handled educational news on the *Enquirer* for several years and had done publicity work for the

University was appointed that year Director of Public Relations by the Board. After Mr. Stanley left the University in 1928 he became President of the United States Playing Card Company.

In 1923, Cincinnati and the University sustained a great loss in the death of Judge Rufus B. Smith. He was an alumnus of both Yale University and the Cincinnati Law School. His interest in the welfare of Cincinnati, his wide influence as a civic leader, and his ideals as a man enabled him to render invaluable services to the University. He was appointed to the Board of Directors in 1912; and two years later he became Chairman of the Board, a position he held until his death. Under his leadership and largely as a result of his personal efforts, an interest in the University was developed on the part of several of the large Eastern educational foundations, as well as on the part of local benefactors. This resulted in large and important gifts to the University. Due largely to his wise leadership, untiring industry, unfaltering loyalty, and sound judgment, the University was able to extend and develop its work. George H. Warrington was appointed to this vacancy. In the same year death came to another member of the Board, Robert W. Hilton, who had lent effective aid in the promotion of the co-operative course. Herbert G. French was appointed to fill this vacancy.

Four years later (1927) two other members of the Board, Major Frank J. Jones and Emil Pollak, died. Major Jones was first appointed to the Board in 1887. He was the seventh Chairman of the Board, from 1895 to 1896, and again from 1903–1908. He had founded the Jones Prize of Oratory, and through his life was a faithful and loyal supporter of the University. Emil Pollak had been a member of the Board for fifteen years. He was born in Vienna, Austria, and was a pioneer in the steel industry of the United States.

THE OHIO COLLEGE OF DENTAL SURGERY AND THE UNIVERSITY

It was during the administration of President Hicks that the Ohio College of Dental Surgery severed its relations with the University and then ceased to exist. It will be recalled that in 1887 the Ohio College of Dental Surgery became affiliated with the University. This relationship continued until its temporary discontinuance in 1906. In 1923 the College again affiliated with the University as the Dental Department of that institution. On July 15, 1926, the Ohio College of Dental Surgery finally closed its doors after eighty-one years of operation. As a private institution the College could no longer compete with state-supported schools of dentistry. Dean H. T. Smith, who personally owned the College building and all its equipment, offered to present all its property as a gift to the University, provided the University would name the institution in honor of his father, who had been its head for many years. The University de-

clined this offer on the ground that it did not have sufficient endowment
to maintain the institution properly as a college. Later Mr. B. H. Kroger
offered to give to the University one million dollars as an endowment
for such a college; but the University authorities felt that even such an
amount would not be sufficient.

Whether these decisions were wise, in the circumstances of the time,
is open to argument. It is beyond dispute, however, that the lack of a
dental college in Cincinnati had become an exceedingly serious matter
for the community and all of southwestern Ohio by the middle of the
twentieth century. Data gathered by public health authorities in 1960
showed that Cincinnati was well below the standard of neighboring large
cities in the number of dentists per 10,000 population, that most of its
dentists were in the higher age group, and that an astonishing percentage
of them had received their training in dentistry in Cincinnati.

THE COLLEGES IN THE HICKS ADMINISTRATION

The Graduate School

During World War I there was a drastic reduction in graduate attendance and graduate instruction. When the War was over, the enrollment
in the Graduate School rose from 157 in 1921 to nearly 300 in 1925, and
then dropped to a little over 200 by the end of President Hick's administration. The requirements for advanced degrees were made more
rigorous. Beginning with the fall of 1925 graduate students registered in
one department only, and that department became the advisor of the
student. Courses in other departments were agreed upon by the student
and his advisory department. This ruling was adopted by the Faculty
with the understanding that it would not lead to greater specialization,
but that the student might elect subjects which would broaden his education as well as to give him a thorough and exact knowledge in his
special field. Each candidate for the Doctor's degree was required to
show a reading knowledge of French and German in his field of study
at least one year before receiving his degree. A candidate might receive
his diploma before his thesis was printed, provided a typewritten copy ·
was deposited in the library and the sum of $50.00 deposited with the
registrar. The sum was returned upon the presentation to the library
of one hundred printed copies of the thesis, or ten printed copies if it had
been published in an approved journal.

After World War I the Board of Directors wisely decided, at the request of the Faculty, to encourage scholarly work by creating a separate
budget for the Graduate School. This was done by devoting a portion of
the income from the Francis Howard Baldwin Fund for the establishment
of fellowships, and by appropriating a fund for books and apparatus

for advanced instruction. In 1922 a donation of $3,000 a year was received from Mrs. Charles P. Taft to establish Taft Fellowships. In that year two members of the Faculty, Associate Professor Charles Napoleon Moore of the Department of Mathematics and Walter Bucher of the Department of Geology, were placed for one-half their time and salary on the Graduate School budget in recognition of their attainments in scholarship.

Two years later in order to promote scholarship, Dean More established the Society of Fellows which was divided into two classes. The first class was composed of fellows appointed annually who were usually preparing for the doctorate. This class included no members of the Faculty. The second class consisted of voting members of the Faculty of professorial rank on indefinite appointment whose formal teaching was presumably to be limited to advanced students. The primary service of these fellows to the University was assumed to be their productive scholarship.

The College of Liberal Arts

In the fall of 1919 the College of Liberal Arts resumed its normal work. Professor Chandler was Dean of the College, a position he held for fifteen of his thirty-three years on the campus. Under his guidance the College developed a high standing among similar institutions of higher learning in America. In his role as Dean he came into intimate contact with the entire student body of the University. His influence upon the University, and indirectly upon the literary culture of the City as a lecturer, can hardly be measured. To thousands of UC alumni he will always be remembered as "the genial Dean." They came to know and appreciate his remarkable talents as a teacher, his unassuming scholarship, his catholic tastes, and the famous wit which often shocked the more inhibited of his listeners but nevertheless delighted them. His innate kindliness, his sociability, and his human interests won for him the respect and admiration of his students, his colleagues, and a host of friends. They honored him for his many virtues and for his delectable vices.

Dean Chandler believed that the College of Liberal Arts had a definite function to perform. In one of his addresses he likened a university to a sandwich: "Its bottom layer is the College of Arts and Sciences which seeks to afford a general training of the mind and acquaintance with fundamental principles in the chief fields of knowledge. Its top layer is the Graduate School which undertakes the quest for fresh truths and the mastery of methods of research. Between the bottom and the top layers stand the professional schools which undertake to afford special training for particular occupations. All these members of a single organism are not rivals but coordinate and interdependent. It is their functioning together that constitute the University." The purpose of the College of Liberal Arts was twofold, "first, to provide thorough training in the arts and sciences for students who (wished) to complete the full course of four years; and second, to provide the general training necessary for those who, after a year or two in Liberal Arts (wished) to enter upon professional training." Dean Chandler held the aim of a College of Liberal Arts should be "education rather than instruction." Instruction meant "a building in of facts for a particular purpose." Education meant "a drawing out of Faculties for general uses." Both processes were essential, but "whereas the professional school emphasized instruction, the College of Arts emphasized education."

To achieve this concept of the aim of the College of Liberal Arts, the Faculty under the guidance of Dean Chandler in 1921 established an honors course to be pursued by those juniors and seniors who were deemed capable of more intensive study than the average and who, therefore, might be relieved of ordinary academic guidance and restrictions. A student who elected the course in honors was required to notify the Dean of the College not later than the beginning of the second semester of his junior year of his desire to work according to this plan. He had to obtain the approval of the head of the department in which he intended to take honors. He was eligible for graduation when the head of the department notified the Faculty that he had completed with distinction the course assigned; that he had passed a public examination; and that he had also completed creditable work in other fields, amounting to between eighteen and twenty-four hours.

The diplomas of students who were graduated from the honors course read "Extraordinary degree of Bachelor of Arts with Honors or High Honors." It was recommended that the Society of Phi Beta Kappa give preference in the choice of members to successful candidates for degrees with honors. In order to promote scholarship in other fields the Society of Colonial Dames established the Elizabeth Perry Groesbeck Scholarship of $200 to be awarded to a student specializing in American history, and Professor William T. Semple established a prize to be awarded to the freshman in the Department of Classics who attained the highest distinction in a special examination.

The scholarship of students in the College of Liberal Arts began to win national recognition. In 1924, Joseph Sagmaster, a senior who had specialized in English and philosophy, won a Rhodes Scholarship for three years at Oxford University, England, in a field of forty candidates from Ohio. Mr. Sagmaster was the second student of the University to receive this honor, the other having been Elmer Van Fleet, who was appointed in 1917 but who died while in the Army. The following year (1925) three members of the Faculty: Herbert Feis, J. Penrose Harland, and Robert Shafer were awarded Guggenheim Fellowships for study abroad. Only Harvard, with four fellowships, had a greater representation of Guggenheim awards that year and only one other, the University of Chicago, had an equal representation. In succeeding years numerous other members of the Faculty were to win these coveted Guggenheim Fellowships.

In 1922, Charles Albert Read resigned as librarian. He was succeeded by Julian S. Fowler, who immediately began to call attention to the need of increased library facilities at the University.

In 1928 the fiftieth anniversary of the first graduating class of the University of Cincinnati in 1878 was celebrated. Five of the original members of the graduating class of 1878 still survived; and two of them, C. G. Comegys and Percy Werner, were present.

College of Education

In 1922, William P. Burris resigned as Dean of the College for Teachers. Upon the recommendation of Superintendent Condon of the public schools, Louis Pechstein was appointed his successor. A psychologist, the new Dean had won recognition first by his novel research on the nature of learning in white rats and human beings, and second by his success in developing a department of psychology and education at the University of Rochester, and his organization of an extension division and summer session at that institution.

For a quarter century Dr. Pechstein was Dean of the College. Under his vigorous and capable leadership the College made marked progress. He was a competent and aggressive administrator and a leader in the spiritual and cultural life of the City. In a few years after his appointment the College was transformed. Upon Dean Pechstein's recommendation the Board in 1922 changed the name of the College for Teachers to College of Education. It bore this name during Dr. Hicks' Presidency, but became again the College for Teachers during the administration of President Schneider. In 1923 the College of Education was put on a cooperative basis, and in 1926 began to offer the strictly professional degrees of Master of Arts and Doctor of Philosophy.

During the administration of President Hicks the enrollment in the College of Education increased from 372 in 1922 to 2,489 in 1928. The number of graduates increased from 63 in 1922 to 197 in 1928, exclusive of students taking graduate degrees. During the same period the income from student fees was built up to the point where the College was self-supporting and was also able to contribute materially toward reducing the financial deficit. By 1928 there were more than 1,600 students enrolled in the summer session of the College of Education, thus providing not only for its own support but a surplus for use during the regular academic year.

College of Engineering and Commerce: Day and Evening

In 1919 the College of Commerce was merged with the College of Engineering; and, henceforth, for a number of years the College was known as the College of Engineering and Commerce. This merger resulted in the reorganization of the courses in both Colleges. A survey had revealed that business executives wanted men trained not only in the commercial phases of business organization but also with some knowledge of the engineering or productive side of industry. At the same time the experience of co-operative engineering students and alumni showed that engineering students lacked training in the commercial phases of industry. To meet these demands Faculty committees were set up in both Colleges to study these problems. As a result of their investigations it was decided in the Engineering Department to co-ordinate the work in the first two years in mathematics, chemistry, physics, and mechanics under the direction of a committee headed by Professor Louis Brand of the Department of Mathematics. The work in the later years was directed by committees under the chairmanship of Professor A. M. Wilson of the Electrical Department, and the instruction included courses in accounting, economics, finance, and history given by members of the Commerce Department.

At the same time a five-year day co-operative course in commerce was established, leading to the degree of commercial engineer. The first two years in the course for commercial students included instruction in the fundamental sciences on which engineering is based as well as instruction in some commercial subjects. In the later years more attention was given to the study of accounting, economics, finance, marketing, business law, world geography, and history. Both the Commerce and Engineering Departments required instruction in English under the direction of Professor C. W. Park and of history under the instruction of Professor R. C. McGrane. Dean Schneider was in charge of the work in both commerce and engineering. The commercial engineering students took over the management of the co-operative bookstore.

During the administration of President Hicks the scope of the College of Engineering and Commerce was extended. In 1920 women were admitted to the chemical and commercial engineering courses, and because of the small enrollment the regular engineering courses were abandoned. All the work in the Engineering Department was placed on a co-operative basis. Two years later (1924) a five-year co-operative course leading to the degree of geological engineer and a Department of Architecture were established. In 1924 an agreement was signed by the University with the Tanner's Council of the United States Association of Leather Manufacturers which provided for the erection of a research building on the campus estimated to cost $110,000. The work in the laboratory was to be confined to fundamental research of the process and materials of the tanning industry and was under the direction of the College of Engineering and Commerce. George D. McLaughlin was the first director of leather research, later succeeded by Fred O'Flaherty. The next year a department of lithographic research was established. With the expansion of the work of the College of Engineering and Commerce, Edward B. Luther was appointed Assistant Dean.

The most notable innovation of the College of Engineering and Commerce was the inauguration in 1922 of a series of lectures and discussions arranged exclusively for business executives and professional men known as the Business and Professional Men's Group. These annual meetings were held in the winter for many years and won for themselves a remarkable place among the men of affairs in Cincinnati. They were a real contribution to adult education in the City. Their popularity was due to the fact that the topics discussed were problems of a national and world significance; the speakers chosen were authorities in their respective fields and were the best available in this country; and the meetings allowed for answering questions in an informal atmosphere.

Vincent H. Drufner was appointed supervisor of evening courses in the College of Commerce. Under his dynamic, constructive guidance enrollment increased from 400 in 1920 to over 3,000 in 1928. New courses were offered yearly as the demand for them developed. The plan of instruction adopted by the evening College of Commerce included the study of certain fundamental and cultural subjects in the College of Liberal Arts, either in the day or evening; and the study of the co-ordinated commercial subjects in the College of Commerce in the evening. Businessmen in the City were appointed as lecturers in their special fields. A course leading to the degree of Bachelor of Science was offered as were also certificate courses in business administration, accounting, marketing, banking, credits and collections, and traffic management. In 1924 four evening courses in engineering were offered for the first time, and two years later (1926) evening courses in applied arts were inaugurated. Student activities were promoted. In 1912 the evening Commerce Club of the University of Cincinnati was organized; and in 1925, Delta Mu Delta, a national honorary scholarship fraternity for commerce students, was organized.

College of Medicine

The year 1919 marked the hundredth anniversary of the chartering of the College of Medicine. The centennial was commemorated by an academic procession which marched from the administration building of the General Hospital to the auditorium of the Medical College where the ceremonies were held. The entrance to the Medical College was guarded by a line of medical students with the senior class at its head. The chief foreign guest was Sir Auckland Geddes, the British Ambassador. Other guests were representatives of the Massachusetts Institute of Technology, the Rockefeller and Carnegie Foundations, the Secretary of the Interior, and other distinguished leaders. Dr. Joseph Ransohoff reviewed with a wealth of reminiscent detail the work of Daniel Drake, Christian R. Holmes, and other famous teachers in the Medical College.

A great shadow was cast over the University and the City in January 1920, by the death of Dr. Christian R. Holmes, Dean of the Medical College. As Dr. Stanley Dorst later said, "The history of modern medical education in Cincinnati centers largely around the figure of Christian R. Holmes," who "built upon a rich medical tradition which began under the dynamic leadership of Daniel Drake." Holmes was a native of Denmark. He started his career as an expert draftsman in the locomotive shops of Seymour, Indiana. A respiratory infection caused him to visit Cincinnati seeking medical aid and led to his chance acquaintance with Dr. Elkanah Williams, professor in the Miami Medical College. This led Holmes to study medicine at that institution, from which he was graduated at the age of twenty-six. In a valedictory address to the graduating class of his Alma Mater in 1894, Holmes, in discussing the ideal physician, also characterized himself: "The physician should be discreet in speech and gentle yet firm of manners. . . . He should always be well-poised, calm, and deliberate, but not apathetic; sedate, but not gloomy; cheerful, but not clownish; kind, but not obtrusive; unruffled by trifles, but careful of everything that concerns his reputation."

In Holmes were found in perfect harmony, "breadth of vision, dynamic force, and exceptional capacity for leadership." His absorbing life interest was to make Cincinnati a great medical center. After years of unceasing labor he was permitted to see the foundations for this plan laid in the completion of new Cincinnati General Hospital and the Medical College buildings. In recognition of his work the Carnegie Corporation gave $250,000 to establish a chair in the Medical College in his memory. Dean Holmes, in his will, gave $25,000 to establish a medical journal for the College. Mrs. Charles Fleischmann contributed $100,000 to the Christian R. Holmes Memorial Fund to be used for a Department of Preventive Medicine and Mrs. Holmes gave $3,000 to equip a laboratory for this department. Mrs. Holmes donated the library of Dr. Holmes to the Medical College library; gave $250,000 to the University to endow the Deanship of the College of Medicine; and subsequently gave $200,-000 for the construction and establishment of the Christian R. Holmes Hospital.

At the death of Dr. Holmes, Dr. John Oliver was appointed Acting Dean. He was a man "of entirely different bent from his predecessor." Dean Holmes had seen "the need for a complete overhauling of the medical educational facilities in Cincinnati and the need for new teaching personnel." He was "dynamic beyond description; with little patience for the incompetent." Dr. Oliver was "more suave and deliberate; definitely the educator rather than the contentious reformer, builder, and organizer."

Just at this time Judge Smith, Chairman of the Board of Directors, had a conference in New York with Dr. Abraham Flexner, Secretary of the Rockefeller Foundation, seeking a grant for support of the Medical College. Dr. Flexner told Judge Smith that at that time the Foundation considered the Medical College to be "a Faculty-controlled College" and that they not only took "no interest in colleges so controlled" but would "afford them no support." Upon his return from this trip to New York, Judge Smith told the Board it was "therefore necessary to reorganize the Medical College" if they wanted to get aid from the Foundation.

All the members of the Board agreed to this and "to the necessity for reorganization." Director Otto Renner stated that "in attempting such a reorganization, undoubtedly decided opposition would be encountered and asked each member individually if he realized this, and would be willing to meet such opposition and in spite of it would put the reorganization through." All the members of the Board answered affirmatively. All the members agreed to keep from "publication" and agreed "further that if a new Dean was selected and the reorganization was entrusted to him the members of the Board must and would stand by him."

Subsequently, the General Educational Board of the Rockefeller Foundation contributed $700,000 to the endowment fund of the College and the Carnegie Foundation $250,000. The Carnegie Foundation also contributed $250,000 to endow the Christian R. Holmes chair of surgery, and another $200,000 to assist the College to receive the gift of the Rockefeller Foundation for the endowment fund, which had been made contingent upon the raising of funds from other sources. The Medical College named the chair of biochemistry in honor of Andrew Carnegie because of his interest in the welfare of the College. In 1923, Professor Shiro Tashiro, associate professor of biochemistry, was decorated with the highest scientific honor conferred by the Japanese government, the degree of *Igakuhakushi*, in recognition "of his distinguished contributions to medical science."

In 1921, Colonel Henry Page was appointed Dean of the Medical College. He was a graduate of Princeton and the University of Pennsylvania Medical College. After graduation he spent a short time in general practice and then entered the United States Army. He served in the Spanish-American War and in the Philippines. During World War I he was the head of a large hospital in France and later was in charge of a school for training doctors for war service. He was the first Dean to devote all his time to the College.

It was not long before Colonel Page with his "military background and new ideas" was in trouble. One of the medical professors who had been head of his department for fourteen years was told by Colonel Page that "for his own good and that of the institution he should resign." This same professor had been in trouble before, and both Dean Holmes and Dr. Dabney had recommended his resignation; but the local branch of the American Association of University Professors (AAUP) had come to the aid of the professor and the Board had taken no action. Colonel Page mentioned the fact that the graduating class had drawn up a petition to the Board asking for the professor's dismissal. Colonel Page refused to allow the professor "two or three days to consider the charges brought against him." The professor was told he must either resign or be dismissed. The Board directed President Hicks to investigate the condition of affairs in the Medical College. The local branch of the AAUP investigated the case and criticized Colonel Page for not permitting the professor time to think over the question. The local branch of the AAUP at the same time passed a resolution that hereafter, as a general policy, whenever the resignation of any professor was requested he should be entitled to know the charges brought against him and be allowed an investigation of these charges. The controversy ended when the professor resigned, and a few months later Colonel Page also resigned.

Following the resignation of Colonel Page, Dr. Arthur Bachmeyer, Superintendent of the General Hospital, was appointed Dean. He was an "amazing and skillful organizing technician" who had a "flair for accounting detail and strict operational supervision." Dr. Bachmeyer was the "kindest of men" but a "most exacting" Dean.

The College of Law

The College of Law made significant progress in the period after World War I. The Faculty was enlarged and more of them devoted their entire time to classroom instruction. After the War four of the men on the Faculty gave their entire time to the School and five others, who were practicing lawyers, gave part of their time, each of them spending two hours a week in instruction at the College. Judge Thomas H. Darby was appointed to the Faculty and gave courses in criminal law. Joseph B. Foraker gave his library to the Law College. The tuition was raised in 1919 from $60.00 to $100 a year, and the enrollment rose to 88. The old College building was sold, and there developed agitation to transfer the College building to the University campus. In the meantime the work of the College was carried on in the old Medical College, which was reconditioned for that purpose. Robert C. Pugh served from 1923 to 1926 as Acting Dean of the College.

The instruction became more realistic. A carefully arranged mock murder trial under the direction of Professor Carl C. Wheaton created a sensation and attracted much attention in the local press. In a third-year law class Milton Schmidt, later a prominent lawyer of the City, allegedly made some remarks which antagonized another student, Donald Dilatush. Professor Wheaton ordered Schmidt to appear before the class and apologize. Schmidt did so but repeated his alleged criticism of Dilatush. The latter, enraged, rose from his chair, drew a revolver, and fired point-blank at Schmidt, inflicting a wound in his arm. The entire school was in pandemonium. Someone called the police and a Patrolman O'Brien appeared. Schmidt rose from the floor and fled from the building. Professor Wheaton announced that the whole episode had been prearranged in order to provide a realistic setting for a mock trial. The reporters left in disgust, and Patrolman O'Brien is said to have remarked as he left: "It may be all right, but they'd better not try setting fire to the school to start an arson case."

The subsequent mock trial afforded much hilarity among the student spectators. Judge Walter M. Shohl presided as judge; Carl W. Rich was the attorney for the defense; Edward Meyer, the prosecuting attorney, assisted by Chase M. Davies. Dilatush, the defendant, pleaded not guilty. During the course of the trial the young lady who played the part of Mrs. Schmidt, vainly tried "to remember the address of her husband" until the necessary information was slipped to her by the prosecuting attorney. When she was asked if anyone was in the house when her husband returned on the fatal night he was shot, she replied, "Yes." The spectators gasped when the witness quickly added, "The maid." Professor Wheaton was a witness for the prosecution; but whenever he was asked any embarrassing question, he "shut up like a clam" and laconically retorted "I don't know." After a few minutes of deliberation the jury returned a verdict of "not guilty"; and the trial was concluded.

On October 28, 1925, a new era in the history of the College of Law began with the dedicatian of the Alphonso Taft Hall. The funds for the erection of this building on the University campus were contributed by Charles P. Taft in commemoration of his father, Judge Alphonso Taft, a former member of the Faculty of the Cincinnati Law School and also the fourth chairman of the Board of Directors of the University of Cincinnati.

The dedication program was opened by an academic procession led by the students of the College of Law wearing their robes. Then came the procession of notables led by Chief Justice William Howard Taft and President Hicks, who in turn were followed by the members of the Board of Directors, Deans of the various Colleges, members of the Law Faculty, and prominent visitors. On the platform were the four sons of Alphonso Taft: W. H. Taft, Charles P. Taft, Henry W. Taft, and Horace D. Taft, all of whom were graduates of the Cincinnati Law School. In the audience were Vice-President Charles G. Dawes; Nicholas Longworth,

Speaker of the House of Representatives; "Uncle Joe" Cannon, former
Speaker of the House of Representatives; Chief Justice Carrington; T.
Marshall; former Chief Justice Nichols of the Ohio Supreme Court; and
other notables.

Chief Justice Taft gave the principal address. Home again in the City
of his birth and surrounded by friends who had had a large part in the
upbuilding of the School from which he was graduated fifty years previously, Judge Taft seemed almost inspired. In a comprehensive survey
he traced the history of the organization and development of the Law
School. In his prepared speech Chief Justice Taft gave his views of what
a law school should be. He said an adequate preparation for the law
was one of the important duties of a law school. He held that a thorough general education was necessary for every lawyer. "No man can
sit in a court of justice and not realize how men suffer, how injustice is
done that cannot be remedied, through the ignorance and blundering of
men who have acquired the right to practice law. The interests of society demand that legislation and those charged with legal education
should put up the bars against accepting candidates inadequately prepared." He proposed the expansion of the University to include schools
of mechanic arts, music, and fine arts. That evening at a banquet Chief
Justice Taft indulged in a reminiscent talk interspersed with many
chuckles that delighted his audience and put them in a great good humor.

The following year (1926) Merton L. Ferson began his long, distinguished Deanship of the College. He was a graduate of the State University of Iowa, and had been professor and Dean at George Washington
University and at the University of North Carolina.

In 1927 the Law School began the publication of a quarterly journal
known as the *University of Cincinnati Law Review*. It was the only law
review then published by a law school in Ohio.

The School of Applied Arts

The School of Applied Arts originated in a Department of Architecture.
In 1919, Dean Schneider in a memorandum to the Board of Directors
pointed out the need for a department of architecture in the College of
Engineering and Commerce. Since he had worked as a college student
in an architect's office, Dean Schneider felt qualified to direct such work.
He assured the Board that the department could be built and maintained
from the fees of the students and would not be a drain on the general
funds of the University. The Board approved the project; and in September 1922, a five-year co-operative course in architecture leading to the
degree of Bachelor of Science in architecture was established in the College of Engineering and Commerce.

The course was designed to meet the demand for architectural designers, landscape architects, interior decorators, and industrial designers. Twenty-two students enrolled that fall in the course, which was open to women and men alike. The first year was the same as in all the engineering courses, but in the second year the study of architectural design was begun. In addition to the design course the curriculum included the history of architecture, general history, several courses in architecture, together with special courses in landscape architecture, interior decoration, appreciation of art, and the structural theory of design. The courses for men were on the co-operative basis throughout the five years. Women were in school full-time for the first two years, and at the beginning of their third year could elect for the completion of their course either two years of full-time in the school or three years on the co-operative basis. The first head of the Department of Architecture was Cecil Franklin Baker.

In July 1925, by action of the Board upon the recommendation of President Hicks, the Department of Architecture became the School of Applied Arts, under the direction of the College of Engineering and Commerce. Because of the rapid growth of the School of Applied Arts and the need of the Department of Electrical Engineering for additional space, a new building was erected on the campus. The new building, called Swift Hall, was made possible through the gift of John D. Swift, President of the Eagle-Picher Lead Company in memory of his brother, Thomas Truxton Swift, who had spent several years at the University making an intensive study of lead and its uses. In 1927 two new courses, ceramics and art in industry, were added. By 1929 there were 129 regular four-year students and 206 co-operative students in the School of Applied Arts.

STUDENT ACTIVITIES

Student activities were given a decided stimulus after the War by making compulsory the payment of a student activity fee of $5.00 per year in the Colleges of Liberal Arts, Engineering and Commerce, and Medicine. With the money so obtained, athletics, the *University News,* the *Cincinnatian,* debating, dramatics, and music received well-merited support; and more individual students were able to secure for a small amount greater advantages in extracurricular affairs. About the same time Mrs. Morris L. Bettman and children gave the University $2,000 to create a fund to be loaned upon the recommendation of the Deans to needy and worthy students attending any College.

With its share of the student activity fee allotted to it, the *University News* was able to double its size. Under the direction of Chase M. Davies, who was editor-in-chief of the *University News* in 1920, and of Norman P. Auburn in 1927, the paper became more influential. New student publications appeared. The *Cooperative Engineer* became the official organ of the College of Engineering and Commerce, efficiently guided by Professor C. W. Park. Two new literary magazines, *The Scribe* and *The Retort Literary,* had a short-lived existence. In 1925, *The Cynic,* a humorous magazine, was started, but was suppressed three years later by President Hicks because of its "improper, indecent, and obscene humor."

In 1919 the students gave two performances of *Varsity Varieties* at the Emery Auditorium. It was the most ambitious dramatic event so far attempted at the University. Four years later the University made its debut in the field of original musical comedy with *Fresh Paint,* a three-act comedy with music, presented at the Schubert Theater, in which the entire libretto and music was the product of the students. Frank R. Byers was the dramatic director. The star was Libby Holman, who later became a well-known actress on Broadway. The success of the first venture of *Fresh Paint* led to the formation of a permanent organization, the purpose of which was to produce an annual musical comedy. In 1926 the "Fresh Painters" took to the road Christmas week and played in Cleveland, Toledo, Columbus, Pittsburgh, and Dayton. Such titles as *Lemme Alone, Now I Ask You, Wonderful Me, The Silver Sabre,* and *Lilaine* bring back happy memories to "old grads" of the performances of the "Fresh Painters." The production of *Lilaine* in 1928 was so poor that the disheartened "Fresh Painters" did not try it in 1929. But they were back again in 1930 with *Sitting Pretty, Weigh Anchor, G'wan 'n' Kiss Me* (1931), and *Call Me Comrade* (1933). The "Fresh Painters" appeared again in 1935 and in 1938.

Interest in athletics led in 1921 to the formation of a University band. Ralph A. Van Wye, later professor of co-ordination and editor of the *Flow Sheet,* publication of the Department of Chemical and Metallurgical Engineering, was in charge of the fieldwork and the appearance of the band at all athletic events. During the War, Mr. Van Wye had served overseas as assistant director and clarinetist in the Army Headquarters Band. Student cheering was led by the "incomparable Edward Strietelmeyer." In the same year (1921) a student symphony orchestra was organized as part of a hobby hour activity of the College of Engineering and Commerce under the direction of Karl Wecker, a member of the Faculty of the Conservatory of Music. In February of the following year (1922) the Varsity Art Club was formed due largely to Imogene Wager to stimulate greater efforts in creative art.

The next year (1923) the first annual Homecoming and Alumni Day was held. In 1927 the slogan "Know Your University" was adopted for Homecoming Day, and placards with this motto appeared on the front of three hundred Cincinnati street cars calling attention to the celebration. The citizens of Cincinnati were now aware of the growing importance of the University and were willing to give it more public attention. In 1928 the publicity of the University was placed in the efficient hands of John De Camp who was appointed Director of Public Relations.

On November 14, 1925, the first annual interfraternity Sing was held in the gymnasium as the climax to Homecoming Day. Twenty-three organizations, including independents, locals, and national Greek societies participated. Large silver loving cups were awarded to SAE and Kappa Kappa Gamma, winners of the first Sing. Three years later the Sing was moved to graduation week and was held out-of-doors in the locust grove near the Women's Building. Since 1937 the Sing has been held in the Greek Amphitheater and the Armory Fieldhouse.

In 1920 the flag rush gave way to a mat rush; but the following year this contest became "too rough" when the President of the freshman class and two others were seized and gagged by the sophomores, taken to the Cincinnati Zoo, and put in the monkey cage "to communicate with their equals." In 1925 the flag rush was revived but under more rigorous rules.

The growth of a college atmosphere during the decade of the 1920's was also reflected in the number of new fraternities and sororities organized. Five new fraternities were formed —Pi Lambda Phi (1920), Triangle (1921), Alpha Tau Omega (1922), American Commons Club (1924), and Phi Kappa Theta (1925)—as well as one recognition society, Ulex (1924). Five new sororities were also formed—Alpha Chi Omega and Theta Phi Alpha (1919), Zeta Tau Alpha (1921), Alpha Gamma Delta (1923), and Sigma Delta Tau (1923).

ATHLETICS

In 1918, Boyd B. Chambers was appointed Athletic Director. He worked unceasingly for better teams. He conducted a campaign among the high schools in the vicinity to attract promising athletes to the University after their graduation. He stood for clean sportsmanship. He sharply reprimanded the student body for booing the umpires when they gave decisions against the Bearcats and for applauding when their opponents were penalized. Under his direction in 1919 the basketball season was a financial success for the first time in the history of the University. The games were attended by unusually large crowds. The gymnasium was packed for each game. The track team, coached by Mr. Oliver M. Nickoloff, made a splendid showing during these years. In 1920 the Cincinnati Bearcats shattered an eight-year "voodoo" by defeating the Miami football team by a score of 7 to 0. In 1922, Dr. Morrison resigned as director of Physical Education, and Chambers was appointed to fill the vacancy. George W. McLaren was appointed the new football coach.

The attendance at the football games stimulated a movement to enlarge the stadium. It will be recalled that when the University first entered football in 1885 the team did not even have a field on which to practice, and the athletic association was compelled to rent local fields for the games. In 1895, Dr. Arch I. Carson proposed the construction of a field on the campus in Burnet Woods. It was estimated to cost $4,650. It took five years to raise the sum, and then it was accomplished only with the aid of a $2,000 donation by Mayor Fleischmann. In 1901 work began on the field. No provisions were made for stands, but tiers of seats were laid out on the sides of the surrounding hills. In 1910 the field was named after Dr. Carson who had done so much towards its realization.

The small sections of wooden stands which had been erected on both sides of the field soon proved inadequate. Plans were drafted for a concrete stadium. The original intention was to build the stands in the form of an oval, extending around the playing field. But this plan was abandoned, as such football bowls had proved unsatisfactory because of the lack of air circulation within them.

The funds for the first nine sections of concrete stands were made available by a City bond issue in 1916. Two more sections were added in 1920 from war reclamation funds. The following year Frank Raschig of the Board Committee on Athletics proposed the construction of three more sections. The Athletic Council inaugurated a campaign to get the money by student subscriptions. Chase Davies, a graduate of 1921, and a second-year student in the College of Law, was chairman of the student committee to raise the money to complete the stadium. With men wearing Stetson hats and women wearing "stadium blue" dresses, an effort was made to stir interest in the project. The slogan of the student drive was: "It's yours; finish it." A gridiron was placed in lower McMicken on which a movable football indicated the total as the drive progressed. But as many of the student pledges remained unpaid, the athletic authorities began to despair of finishing the horseshoe for some years when suddenly they found the necessary funds in hand as a result of the following tragic event.

What helped materially in creating an interest in athletics was the inauguration on September 30, 1923, of the first night football game. It will be recalled that in 1909, in order to make it possible for engineering co-ops to play football, Dean Schneider had arranged to have all those who wanted to try for the team put into the same section. By this arrangement—since in those days the co-ops alternated every other week —they would all be in school the same week and at the factory the next. Under these conditions football practice was held in late afternoon in daylight one week and then at night the next week using artificial lights. Accordingly in 1909 a number of arc (or carbon) lights on poles were erected on the playing field, and the football was painted white. In this way the co-ops were able to practice at night every other week.

On November 2, 1921, the system of artificial lighting was improved by the use of incandescent lights for Carson Field. The system was designed by Jack B. Silverman, an engineering co-operative student in the Electrical Department, as his thesis. The construction of the system of floodlighting was done by the Union Gas and Electric Company through the courtesy of Francis H. Healey, Superintendent, Electrical Distribution Department, in collaboration with Professor A. M. Wilson, head of the Electrical Department, and Frank Raschig, chairman of the Athletic Committee of the Board. The system was first energized on November 2, 1921, with floodlights totaling 22,000 watts. An enlarged system was placed in service September 29, 1923, with aggregate rating of 32,000 watts, when the University Bearcats played the first night football game in the United States. Kentucky Wesleyan was defeated that night by a score of 17 to 0. The following year (1924) WSAI broadcast for the first time all the home football games of the University.

On Christmas Day 1923, James Gamble Nippert, center of the Bearcat football team, died of blood poisoning due to injuries received during the Miami-Cincinnati football game on Thanksgiving Day. Early in the second half of the game Nippert was kicked on his left leg, but owing to the mud which covered the uniform he was unable to see the extent of the injury and continued to play until the end of the game. In memory of his grandson, James Gamble Nippert gave the University $250,000 and later an additional $20,000 to complete the University stadium. The grandfather expressed no particular wishes or conditions attaching to the development of the plan but said that he would like to add to the regular stadium "certain dressing rooms, bathrooms, and two fully equipped dispensaries, one for each contending team, so that in case of even the slightest injury to a player the best and most scientific treatment may be administered immediately."

On November 8 of the following year the James Gamble Nippert Memorial Stadium was dedicated. A memorial tablet in the form of a ten-foot figure of a football player was erected at the entrance to the stadium by donations of the students at the University. Carved beneath the figure were Jimmy Nippert's last words: "Five more yards to go—then drop." "The primary object of this athletic field," said the grandfather at the dedicatory ceremonies, "is to develop sound minds in sound bodies . . . . May it always be said that either in victory or defeat, good, clean sportsmanship is the *sine qua non* on the campus of the University of Cincinnati."

With the gift of the Nippert Stadium and completion of the gymnasium and the dormitory, the chief drawbacks to the development of athletics and physical education at the University from the standpoint of purely physical equipment were removed. But there was a growing dissatisfaction on the part of many persons with the standing of the University in the field of athletics, particularly in football. In 1925, Miami defeated the University by a score of 33 to 0. Various civic organizations throughout the City clamored to know "what was the matter with athletics at the University?" The Cincinnatus Association appointed a committee, headed by Victor Heinz, a "C" Club man, to see what could be done to remedy matters. The "C" Club also appointed a committee to study the problem. It was composed of Walter Hyman (chairman), Robert Heuck, Carl Phares, and Charles W. Skinner, President of the "C" Club, an ex officio member.

After five months of exhaustive inquiry the committee in 1926 submitted a confidential report to President Hicks. According to the committee the reason for the lamentable showing made at the end of the 1925 football season was that the teams were the products "of a totally wrong system." They had no doubt that the University could engage "a strong, resourceful, skillful coach, support him with adequate funds and facilities to scout for players" and influence them (with whatever inducements his conscience and the chances of detection and exposure would dictate) to attend the University, "and plenty of games could be won." That was what might be called the old standard. This was "the simple, easy, obvious course to pursue, if winning games was the only object." But such teams were "not of the student body"; they were "merely appended to the student body"; they operated "under a questionable code of ethics"; and they contributed "absolutely nothing to the improvement of the physical well-being and character of the average student nor to the spiritual well-being of the particular student."

The committee were unanimously opposed to the fostering or further development of such a system. They favored the adoption of a system similar to those employed at Harvard or the University of Pennsylvania. They suggested thorough reorganization of the Department of Physical Education and Athletics; placing it in the charge of a capable man; and requiring physical examinations of every student with a view to correcting any of their defects. Such a system would raise "the general level of the physical conditions and athletic ability of the entire student body, and the University could develop its own talent of Varsity team caliber." President Hicks expressed his hearty endorsement of the general policy recommended and declared steps were being taken to put that policy into effect.

A committee of three Board members, Sanford Brown, Edward H. Ernst, and Herbert C. French, was appointed to study the athletic situation. Mr. French conferred with representatives of the "C" Club and other interested groups. After considerable study this committee recommended that a new Department of Physical Education and Athletics be established under a director of athletics appointed by the Board. The control of athletics was taken out of the hands of the Athletic Council and vested in the Board. In the reorganization there were to be two departments in the general field of athletic activity and general health and hygiene. One department was to deal with all problems pertaining to the business phases of athletics and the coaching of all teams. The other department was to devote itself to all problems of health and hygienic instruction. The outcome of these revolutionary changes was the resignation in 1926 of George McLaren as football coach, and in September 1927, the appointment of George Babock as the new coach and head of the Athletic Department. Dr. Lawrence B. Chenoweth continued to be in charge of health and hygiene. Boyd Chambers, having been "eased out," left after the close of the 1928 basketball season.

The poor showing of the Varsity football teams at length aroused the business interests of the City. The merchants awakened to a realization of the great commercial advantages they might derive by aiding in the development of athletics at the University. At the annual dinner of the "C" Club in 1928, Judge Robert S. Marx said that when the businessmen of the City realized what a valuable asset a football team might be to them, by attracting large crowds of out-of-town visitors who would spend large sums of money, they would be more favorably inclined toward Varsity football. He said a movement was on foot to get closer co-operation of merchants, students, and alumni of the University for better support of University athletics. He said that the details of a plan were being worked out in such a way that interested merchants could give summer employment to students, and that means could be found to employ scouts to visit the high schools and induce prospective students to attend the University and try out for the football teams.

The Reverend Frank Nelson, rector of Christ Church and newly appointed member of the University Board, sharply scored the plan which was becoming prevalent in downtown amateur clubs of hiring players from other fields. "There is something else to be derived from athletics besides winning the game," he said. "In fact the greatest recompense comes from fair play and clean sportsmanship, attributes which do not always go to the winning team."

Out of all this agitation there was formed in 1929 a group known as the University of Cincinnati Boosters' Committee, the members of which were appointed by Chase M. Davies, President of the Executive Alumni Council. The purpose of this Committee was to provide a "City-wide movement to promote and develop an interest in clean, wholesome athletics at the University of Cincinnati" and to give the University "an outstanding football team." Chase Davies made it clear that the Committee did "not favor any move to subsidize a University team in any sport." The slogan of the Committee was "Let's go, Cincinnati." There were about eighty prominent civic and business leaders in Greater Cincinnati in the ranks of the original Boosters' Club. As the years passed this organization became a potent force in stimulating interest in athletics at the University.

THE RESIGNATION OF PRESIDENT HICKS

21- 28

In 1928, Dr. Hicks, having reached the retirement age, tendered his resignation as President of the University to take effect February 1, 1929, after a year's leave of absence. During the Presidency of Dr. Hicks the University grew from an enrollment of 3,500 to more than 9,500. President Hicks' chief concern was always to maintain a high standard of scholarship. He was popular with the student body and had the respect and confidence of the citizens of Cincinnati.

During the seven years of the Presidency of Dr. Hicks a number of new buildings were erected. In 1924 the Men's Memorial Dormitory was erected through the efforts of the alumni to commemorate the memory of those students, alumni, and Faculty who had served during World War I. The Invocation and Benediction of these services were pronounced by Rabbi Michael Aaronsohn. In addition to this building the James Gamble Nippert Stadium (1924), the Tanner's Research Building (1925), the Alphonso Taft Hall (1925), and Swift Hall (1926) were erected. Besides these buildings the Lithographic Research Laboratory was founded; the College of Education was reorganized with Dr. Louis A. Pechstein in charge; the School of Applied Arts was established; and the Athletic Department was reorganized with George Babock as professor of physical training and athletics.

The financing of the University was improved during these years by the passage of a bill introduced in the State Legislature by Representative Mary Van Wye, wife of Professor B. C. Van Wye. It empowered municipal universities to charge fees for contingent expenses. Finances were aided also by public approval of a University bond issue for new buildings, to relieve congested conditions at the University.

Upon his retirement Dr. Hicks was given the title Research Professor of Economics and was made a fellow in the Graduate School of Arts and Sciences. Dr. Hicks died on September 7, 1953, in his ninetieth year.

17 Herman Schneider to the Rescue

In the latter years of the administration of President Hicks, the political climate of Cincinnati had changed profoundly. Accumulating public anger against municipal waste and corruption finally brought about a powerful movement for fundamental reform. Earlier revisions of the City's charter had failed to restore honesty and efficiency. In 1925 the people of the City voted decisively for a radically new system of municipal government. Its prime features were a small council of nine members, elected at large by proportional representation, a City Manager in whom full administrative authority and responsiblity were concentrated, and a merit system to remove City employees from politics. It was, perhaps, the most exhaustive and complete house-cleaning any major city in the United States ever made. In the decades subsequent, Cincinnati was to become known across the nation as the best governed of all large cities.

Through the Dabney administration, the University had been amply protected from political interference. But that immunity rested on the personal pledge of George B. Cox, the all-powerful political boss. Under the reform government inaugurated January 1, 1926, the University's independence was buttressed by the elimination of patronage and corruption at City Hall. Inevitably, as a municipal university, it was affected by political forces in the community. The University benefited, consequently, from the new climate of a reform wave intent on honesty and efficiency, backed by strong segments of the business community as well as political groups opposed to the old Cox machine. For thirty years, political control of the City was to alternate between the reform group, made up of Charter Republicans and Democrats, and the Republican organization, which responded to the new climate with many progressive changes, most notably in the caliber of its leaders. At no time from the inauguration of President Dabney onwards was the University to be drawn seriously into the partisan controversies of local politics. The concept of an independent university was achieved, and made secure.

Upon the retirement of President Hicks the Board of Directors elected Dean Herman Schneider Acting President for one year (1928–1929). The Board then appointed a committee to find a suitable person for permanent President. At first they thought of selecting someone within the University for the position, if possible. When this seemed inadvisable they sought a suitable candidate elsewhere. Many names were suggested and several prospective candidates were invited to come to Cincinnati. But the net result of this canvass was that the Board found no one outside the University who measured up to their conception of the requirements and was willing to accept the position. After a thorough investigation the Board came to the conclusion that the Acting President alone fulfilled the requirements they held were essential for a President, but it was well known that Dean Schneider was unwilling to assume the burden of the permanent Presidency.

As Acting President, Dean Schneider had shown that he possessed executive ability "of an extraordinarily effective type." He had demonstrated a "rare and ideal combination of broad vision and practical capacity." So the Board approached Dean Schneider, and at length he reluctantly consented to accept the position. Accordingly, in 1929, Dean Schneider was elected permanent President at an annual salary of $9,000, and at the same time the office of Vice-President in charge of business administration was created. Daniel Laurence was given this title in recognition of the high service he had rendered for many years to the University. The title of Chris Wilkie was changed from messenger in the office of the clerk of the Board of Directors to University auditor and assistant clerk of the Board of Directors.

Within a year President Schneider raised the question with the Board of his continuance in office. Because of his health, he did not feel he ought to be asked to continue. Furthermore, he felt that he was of more value to the University in other lines of activity. It was evident that he wanted to return to the Deanship of the College of Engineering and Commerce. At his request the Board appointed a committee consisting of Messrs. Warrington, French, and Schneider to look for a new President.

Several months after assuming the Presidency, Dr. Schneider submitted to the Board his views on educational policy. Briefly, his policy provided for five major university divisions: (1) the Liberal Arts Division, which should deal with broad fundamental fields of knowledge and should render service to the professional divisions by giving pre-professional training in basic courses to medicine, law, and education; (2) the Economic Division, which should cover the manufacture and distribution of goods; (3) the Human Adjustment Division based on four years of required Liberal Arts work and two years of graduate professional work, including also education and law as separate schools; (4) the Physical and Mental Health Division; and (5) the Fine Arts Division. Furthermore, Dr. Schneider proposed that the work of each division dealing with undergraduate, graduate, and research work be carefully measured and evaluated, and the duplication of courses in the various divisions be eliminated. The Board approved this plan in principle, but the details of the plan were never put into effect.

THE UNIVERSITY UNDER PRESIDENT SCHNEIDER

A number of significant events occurred during the administration of President Schneider in the fields of instruction, research, and administration. In 1929 the medical profession, the College of Medicine, and the City suffered a great loss with the death of Dr. Benjamin Knox Rachford, who might justly be called the "Father of Pediatrics" in Cincinnati. After having graduated from the Medical College of Ohio in 1882, Dr. Rachford took postgraduate work in the physiological laboratory of Professor Gad in Berlin, where he began his work on the effects of bile on the action of the pancreatic juice. His work in this field was epoch-making and a permanent contribution to physiology. Upon his return to Cincinnati, Dr. Rachford became professor of bacteriology in his Alma Mater, subsequently professor of physiology, and finally in 1901 of pediatrics. Dr. Rachford created the Department of Pediatrics in the Medical College— one of the first on this continent. His great service was to little children. He started the Babies' Milk Fund Association which, with the financial assistance of Mrs. Mary M. Emery, was able to establish new clinics and sell the best grade of certified milk to less privileged groups at three cents a quart.

In the same year Dr. William B. Wherry, another distinguished member of the Faculty of the Medical College, was one of two American scientists chosen by the Rockefeller Foundation to inaugurate public health training and research in the graduate department of the new school of hygiene organized by the Philippine government at Manila. Born in India of missionary parents, Wherry received his education in the Middle West. After a brilliant early career as scientific investigator and teacher in the Philippines and the Far West he came to Cincinnati in the fall of 1909 as assistant professor of pathology, in charge of bacteriology in the Medical College. Three years later he became full professor of bacteriology. The following year Dr. Wherry recognized an eye infection of a meat butcher as identical with a disease of California ground squirrels. This led to his discovery of tularemia as a human disease and the finding of the source of his infection in wild rabbits.

Also in these years the Schmidlapp Chair of Aeronautics was established in the College of Engineering and Commerce by the creation of a trust fund by Jacob G. Schmidlapp. In 1930, Jermain G. Porter, after forty-six years as professor of astronomy at the University, resigned; and the following year Everett I. Yowell was appointed Director of the Observatory.

On May 30, 1930, Mrs. Charles Phelps Taft wrote a letter to the Board of Directors stating her intention to give $2 million to establish the Charles Phelps Taft Memorial Fund in memory of her husband. The income from this Fund, she proposed, was to be used "to assist, maintain, and endow the study and teaching of the 'humanities' in the College of Liberal Arts and the Graduate School of the University; namely, the Departments of Classics, Economics, English, German, History, Mathematics, Philosophy, and Romance Languages." Mrs. Taft stipulated in her letter that this Fund should be administered by a Board of Trustees. The original Board of Trustees consisted of Herbert G. French, William T. Semple, Louise Taft Semple, Robert Taft, and Hulbert Taft. In the fall of September 1930, President Schneider, at the suggestion and with the approval of the trustees of the Fund, appointed a Faculty Committee of the Fund to work in conjunction with the Board of Directors and the trustees of the Fund in administering the income of the bequest.

The establishment of the Charles Phelps Taft Memorial Fund had an immense influence in promoting the humanities and in encouraging the scholarly work of members of the Faculty. In its first thirty years (1931–1961) the Fund supported in whole or in part the publication of eighty books, including the results of the archaeological expeditions to Troy sponsored by the University through its Department of Classics under the direction of Professors William T. Semple and Carl Blegen. It brought to the campus and to the community nearly three hundred distinguished visiting scholars and lecturers. It granted 483 fellowships and scholarships to enable outstanding students to continue graduate training. It also granted partial support for four professorships; and made grants to enable Faculty members to spend extended periods of research either abroad or in this country. In that period the Fund expended $650,000 for the enrichment of the University Library.

In 1930, President Schneider established the Basic Science Research Laboratory as a part of the Institute of Scientific Research. George Sperti was placed in charge of it. The functions of the Laboratory were to investigate fundamental laws in all realms of science and to develop applications of their principles.

President Schneider made a number of administrative changes. Three new Deans were appointed: Robert C. Gowdy, Acting Dean of the College of Engineering and Commerce; William Wallace Hewitt, Acting Dean of the College of Liberal Arts; and Marjorie S. Palmer, Acting Dean of Women. The joint control of the College of Education which had been exercised by the Board of Education and the University Board of Directors for a quarter of a century was terminated by an agreement in 1930 under which full control was vested in the University Board.

The construction of several new buildings was either started or completed. In 1929 the University Library, representing an investment of nearly $1 million, was completed, as was the YMCA building adjoining the campus, a gift of the Gamble family. In the same year the Christian R. Holmes Hospital of the College of Medicine, financed by private funds, was dedicated. Further expansion of the University's facilities was assured by the passage in November 1929 of a $1.7 million bond issue for new buildings, including a biology hall, a physics hall, a student commons, shop building, and additions or alterations in other buildings. In the fall of that year announcement was made of the gift of $130,000 by three industrial groups outside of Cincinnati for the erection and equipment of the Charles Franklin Kettering Laboratory for applied physiology.

The next year (1930) was a banner year in the annals of the University, for it witnessed ground-breaking for two important and much-needed additions to the physical plant of the institution. The two new buildings on which construction began were the Wilson Convocation Hall and the College of Education building. A feature of the new College of Education building was a unit known as the Annie Laws Memorial. The Memorial to Miss Laws was made possible as a result of a campaign for $75,000 under the direction of a committee headed by Dr. Frank H. Nelson. Miss Laws was the founder of the Cincinnati Kindergarten Association and from 1912 to 1916 was a member of the Cincinnati Board of Education.

The Cincinnati Alumni Association was very active during these years. The Alumni Council was first organized in 1914 for the purpose of harmonizing and centralizing the efforts of the alumni associations of the various departments of the University. In November 1915 the first number of the *Cincinnati Alumnus* was issued. After a few numbers were issued this publication was suspended for lack of financial support. About 1925, under the leadership of Judge Chester R. Shook, the Alumni Council was reorganized; and since then the Alumni Association and the *Cincinnati Alumnus* have become more active.

One fraternity (Acacia, 1929); one recognition fraternity (Sophos, 1931); and one honorary fraternity (Omicron Delta Kappa, 1932) were organized during these years.

THE COMING OF THE GREAT DEPRESSION

In the fall of 1929 there began a series of stock market "breaks," which reached a climax on October 29. Despite remedial efforts of governmental officials and business leaders, industrial activity continued to decline in 1930. The following year, the depression spread to Europe.

The Evolution of the University Seal

McMicken Hall

First Sections of
Co-operative Students
of the College of
Engineering, 1906

Elijah Slack, 1819–1822, 1823–1836

Philander Chase, 1822–1823

William H. McGuffey, 1836–1839

Thomas J. Biggs, 1839–1845

Thomas Vickers, 1877–1884

Jacob D. Cox, 1885–1889

Henry T. Eddy, 1889–1890,
1890–1891

Howard Ayers, 1899–1904

Joseph E. Harry, 1904

Charles William Dabney, 1904–1920

Frederick C. Hicks, 1920–1928

Herman Schneider, 1928–1929, 1929–1932

Raymond Walters, 1932–1955

Pogue's Studio

Walter C. Langsam, 1955–

Financial crises occurred in Austria and Germany; and finally on September 21, 1931, Great Britain was forced to abandon the gold standard. The abandonment of specie payments by Great Britain was followed shortly afterwards by similar action in a number of countries. The European crisis had immediate repercussions in the United States. The country was in the grip of the Great Depression.

As business conditions grew worse steps were taken by the University in 1931 to meet the difficult financial situation. First, it was announced by the Board that there would be no increase in salaries among the Faculty or the University staff for the new college year. In nearly every instance where a vacancy occurred in the Faculty ranks, it was left unfilled. Wherever possible funds ordinarily used for granting fellowships were diverted to the general fund. In response to an appeal from Washington the proceeds of football games throughout the country were designated for charity. The University-Miami Thanksgiving football game was made a charitable affair, and the net proceeds were devoted to unemployment relief. It was in such a disheartening atmosphere that a new President was chosen and began his term of office.

18 The Searing Impact of the Great Depression

It has been said, and with much truth, that only two events in their history have really shaken the American people—the Civil War and the Great Depression. We have seen in earlier chapters the pervasive and stultifying influence of the slavery controversy and the Civil War on the infant predecessors of the University of Cincinnati. The hardship and retrenchment ushered in by the stock market crash of 1929 and the ensuing slump in business activity and employment were reflected with at least equal intensity in the fortunes of the University. The main responsibility, with its headaches and its onerous decisions, fell upon Raymond Walters, who was chosen on March 7, 1932, to succeed Herman Schneider as President. No matter how inauspicious its beginning, President Walters' administration was destined to be the longest on record, and after the shock of depression had passed, one of immense progress and achievement.

Raymond Walters was born in 1885 in Bethlehem, Pennsylvania, the son of L. F. and Ida (Keller) Walters. To his task as head of the University, Dr. Walters brought a varied experience. He was graduated from Lehigh University in 1907 and received his Master of Arts degree in 1913 from the same institution. Following his graduation from Lehigh University he engaged for four years in newspaper work, serving on the staff of the *Philadelphia Public Ledger*. He then returned to his Alma Mater as a member of the English Department and also as registrar. During World War I, Dr. Walters served as a captain on the executive staff of the Field Artillery Officers' School at Camp Taylor, Kentucky.

In 1921, Dr. Walters was called to Swarthmore College as a member of the English Department. When Dr. Frank A. Aydelotte accepted the Presidency of Swarthmore he selected Dr. Walters as his assistant and later appointed him Dean of the College. In this capacity Dr. Walters took an active part in developing the administrative and educational

274

policies of the institution. He also became executive manager of the Bach Choir at Bethlehem, Pennsylvania, and was active in musical affairs.

He was a member of the editorial staff of *School and Society,* a leading educational journal, and as associate editor reported on educational meetings in all parts of the United States, Canada, England, and Europe. His annual statistical analysis of enrollment in American colleges and universities was a standard work in this field. On the basis of these annual surveys Dr. Walters became known as the "Statistician Laureate" of higher education. As an inspector of institutions of higher learning for the Association of American Universities, Dr. Walters became widely known in the educational world. He was a member of Phi Beta Kappa and later was elected a senator of the united chapters.

Selecting the New President

Early in January 1932, Dr. Walters visited Cincinnati to deliver an addresss before the Association of American Universities. President Schneider was in the audience and later took Dr. Walters to see the University plant. After Dr. Walters had returned to Swarthmore, President Schneider sent him a telegram inviting him to come to Cincinnati to meet members of the Board of Directors. Dr. Walters came, stopping at the Netherland Plaza, which he considered "a very magnificent and a very comfortable hotel." He met four members of the Board—Messrs. Morgan, French, Dinsmore, and Rowe—who comprised the committee on the selection of a new President. Dr. Walters found the interview "agreeable rather than a trying experience."

Upon his return to Swarthmore he reported his experiences to President Aydelotte. Dr. Walters told him that he would not consider an offer from Cincinnati unless Dr. Aydelotte approved as it was near the end of the academic year, and his sudden resignation would make difficult the handling of some administrative matters at Swarthmore. President Adyelotte replied "quite positively that the offer was so unusual that it was the chance of a lifetime." If they offer you "the place, take it," was his command. This advice greatly influenced Dr. Walters in making his final decision.

A few days later Dr. Walters received another telegram from President Schneider asking him to come again to meet those members of the Board whom he had not met on his previous trip. After this visit Mr. Dinsmore, Vice-Chairman of the Board in the absence of Chairman Morgan, telegraphed Dr. Walters that he had been elected as President at a salary of $15,000 a year. His wife, whom Dr. Walters always affectionately called "Bob O'Link," urged him to accept the offer and agreed with him that, in the words of Wordsworth's phrase, "the path lies clear before us." That night Dr. Walters found that it calmed him "to read Wordsworth."

RAYMOND WALTERS: THE MAN

Dr. Walters was forty-six years old when he came to Cincinnati. He was about five feet eight inches in height; broad shouldered and deep chested; with a ruddy round face; black hair that was becoming thin over the top of his head; and always a smile for everyone. One of his best-known qualities was his friendliness to students and Faculty alike. Dr. Walters was a confirmed optimist. He always looked on the bright side, and whenever he had a difficult and disagreeable task to perform he took it in his stride as one of his duties he had to perform as President.

When he assumed office, he was "very humble" about his ability and attainments; but within a year he was fascinated with his administrative duties, and as he recorded in the diary he kept every day, "he was neither overwhelmed nor afraid." Dr. Walters relied heavily on the members of his Board of Directors for advice and guidance, especially on the counsel of the respective Chairmen of his Board, Frank R. Morgan, George H. Warrington, Frank F. Dinsmore, and Renton K. Brodie.

His path as the new chief executive officer in his early years was also made smoother by the assistance of a capable Vice-President, Daniel Laurence, who had served through three previous administrations and was familiar with every detail of the University operations. In the later years of his administration Dr. Walters depended greatly upon the efficient services rendered by Vice-President Norman Auburn; Dean of University Administration, Ralph C. Bursiek; and his loyal, devoted secretary, Mrs. Grace Sales.

Dr. Walters' earlier journalistic experience helped him in presenting his views on University policy to the public. He was a firm believer in freedom of speech and of the press. Before he came to the campus the Board denied the Socialist Labor Party the use of the auditorium during the Presidental election of 1932. In the succeeding Presidential election of 1936, Dr. Walters persuaded the staunch Republican members of the Board to grant permission to President Franklin D. Roosevelt to visit the campus.

Dr. Walters was interested in music and the fine arts and was an enthusiastic supporter of athletics. He paid great attention to the Commencement exercises, insisting that the graduates of each College come forward after the conferring of their degrees to receive their diplomas from the hands of their Deans. He felt that this procedure humanized the whole affair. In 1938 for the first time in the recent history of the University the formal Commencement address was eliminated in order to center attention upon the individual awarding of degrees.

He was a devoted family man and every year on his wedding anniversary he sent "Bob O'Link" a bouquet of flowers. As an administrator Dr. Walters was very susceptible to flattery; and when some of his appointments caused him later trouble, he tried to handle the disagreeable task as tactfuly and justly as he could.

Dr. Walters was an Episcopalian and took an active part in church affairs. Any extra money that Dr. Walters received for lectures he always devoted to charity. He was the first President of the University to invite a Catholic priest (The Right Reverend Monsignor R. Marcellus Wagner) to deliver the Baccalaureate address; and after his retirement, Father Paul O'Connor, President of Xavier University, told Dr. Walters that he would always be remembered "as the citizen who did most to promote good will between Catholics and Protestants of Cincinnati."

1932: A YEAR OF GREAT DECISIONS

Dr. Walters came to the University at the very nadir of the Great Depression. The first meeting of the Board of Directors he attended as President in the fall of 1932 had to take up the distressing business of reducing the pay of Faculty members and of office employees. Believing that at such a time the University should spend money only for strictly educational purposes, he requested the Board to dispense with the elaborate academic pageantry usually arranged for the inauguration of a new college President. The decision to omit a formal inauguration was widely noticed in the news and editorial pages of the nation's press and won general approval.

The problem of the budget occupied his days and "loomed before him when he awakened at night." The work on the budget was often interrupted by five and six interviews a day, many of them dealing with difficult and disagreeable tasks. He was called upon to deliver many talks around the City. He gave as many as seven addresses in five days, and while not fatigued he was compelled to keep quiet for a time in order "to recharge his mental storage batteries." He found his audiences very friendly and came to the conclusion that "appreciation was characteristic of the Cincinnati people in the University and the City." In discussing his educational views he set forth what he considered should be the purposes of a college education: "A university should not be a trade school or a business school. It should be an institution where reason is applied to all ideas and the constant search is for truth that makes men free."

THE BUDGET AND THE GREAT FLOOD

The new administration began operations when the economic depression was having its most devastating effects upon colleges and universities throughout the country. Here as elsewhere many students were forced to drop out of college because of financial troubles at home; and the University income from tuition and fees, from City taxes, and from other sources fell sharply. Dr. Walters and the Board came reluctantly to the conclusion that salary cuts were "inevitable." In October 1932 all employees of the University were notified that there would be a flat reduction of all salaries of 10 per cent beginning in November for the fiscal year 1932–1933. At the same time in the hope of increasing enrollment the University inaugurated what was known as the save-a-year plan by which high school graduates were admitted to the University beginning with the second semester of 1932–1933 instead of having to wait until the following fall.

When some of the University professors in a series of popular lectures gave a critical analysis of economic conditions in the country, a group of Cincinnati businessmen—the Association of Credit Men—requested that the University discontinue the lectures because of their "extraordinary gloomy character." President Walters was "flabbergasted" at this sort of criticism. Never before had the University Faculty been challenged in their interpretation of contemporary economic events based upon careful and impartial study. This was an evidence of the hysterically emotional condition of the country created by the Depression. The public did not want to be told that things might get worse before the Depression was over.

The situation grew worse instead of better during 1933–1934. The deficit grew larger. Dean More suggested that the Board either raise money to meet the deficit or operate during the coming year with an unbalanced budget. President Walters opposed both of these measures. Dean Ferson proposed that reductions, if necessary, be on a graduated scale. The Board decided to install a new accounting system. A firm of expert accountants were called in and after making a study recommended certain cuts in operating and maintenance expenses. A committee was also appointed, composed of Professor Wilbur P. Calhoun, Vice-President Laurence, and Comptroller Ralph W. Miller to make recommendations to the Finance Committee of the Board for the purchase and sale of securities. The Board finally decided to increase the salary cuts from 10 to 23 per cent on a graduated scale. President Walters recommended that the Deans notify those members of their Faculty whom it was no longer possible to retain because of the financial stringency, and inform them that they would be given a leave of absence for the first semester 1934–1935 with one-half their semester salary. Virtually all of the Faculty, however, were retained.

The salary cuts were allotted among the various Colleges; the College of Applied Arts and the College for Teachers suffering the largest reductions. Dr. Walters reported that Dean Pechstein faced the proposed cuts in the Teachers College with "admirable firmness and spirit," and cut his budget $30,000. Dean More accepted the decision for the Graduate School and suggested that non-teaching fellows should carry a substantial teaching schedule. Dean Schneider similarly co-operated and cut his budget for the three schools under his direction $50,000. Chairman Warrington complimented President Walters on performing "three miracles" in getting these Deans to co-operate. The local chapter of the American Association of University Professors approved the policy of the administration in the handling of the budget.

Three of the professors in the College for Teachers who had been scheduled for dismissal, however, requested permission to present their case to the Board. This was done, and the Board voted to retain two of them on a part-time basis. They later appealed their case to the national AAUP. The AAUP suggested a conference with them, and their continuance on more satisfactory terms was worked out. The chairman of the AAUP committee appointed to investigate the case later told Dr. Walters that "after considering the case carefully he regarded the University action as just and the later handling of the case as a model of patience and courtesy."

As business conditions improved in 1935 a small restoration of salaries was made immediately; and in December a substantial additional salary restoration was made, reducing salary cuts from a range of 3¼ per cent to 11¾ per cent for the year. There were joyous repercussions on the campus by this announcement of a restoration of 25 per cent of the total salary cuts. "This is the happiest day I have had in Cincinnati," recorded Dr. Walters in his diary.

To add to the tribulations of the administration, just as the country began to recover from the effects of the Great Depression, Cincinnati had a great flood. The Ohio River passed flood stage (fifty-two feet) on January 18, 1937, and reached a record crest of eighty feet on January 26. This was nine feet above the previous high of 1884. It was not until approximately eighteen days later, February 5, that the water receded below flood stage. During the period of the flood, 12 per cent of the City's area was inundated. Fifty thousand people were driven from their homes. Sections of the City were isolated from each other by backwater from Mill Creek and the Little Miami River. Streetcars ceased running on "Black Sunday," January 24, and did not resume partial service until February 4. The damage done to property was tremendous. There was no panic or hysteria, however, on the part of the public during the emergency.

In common with all City activities the University closed all its departments from January 23 to February 8. The closing was made necessary, because the flooding of the City waterworks and of the generating station of the Cincinnati Gas and Electric Company shut off the supply of water and electricity.

During this period the teachers and students of the University rendered valuable relief services. The five main branches of University activity were: (1) the University helped the Red Cross in assembling clothing at Music Hall; (2) members of the Faculty and students of the College of Medicine and members of the Cincinnati Academy of Medicine inoculated relief workers and others with anti-typhoid serum; (3) the University Short Wave Radio Station, operated by the College of Engineering and Commerce, transmitted communications; (4) the University ROTC units served in various duties throughout the stricken area; and (5) University teachers and students worked at Red Cross canteens and directly in the Red Cross organization; and University women collected relief funds.

Just as the City was recovering from this disaster the nation plunged into a new depression in the fall of 1937. As stocks declined and unemployment mounted, cruel salary cuts loomed up again. Dr. Walters could see no hope of anything less than salary cuts for 1938–1939 of 1⅓ per cent to 18 per cent. "The latter will be my own," he recorded in his diary. "But that is the least of my worries." "I really grieve to think of the hardships that will be brought upon some of our teachers and employees." The Board decided to postpone action on the 1938–1939 budget until June, and finally decided to assure the Faculty and staff that their salaries for the next year would not be below the 1936–1937 scale. This meant a decrease from salaries of the present academic year of 2½ per cent to 4½ per cent, much less than Dr. Walters anticipated. The Board concluded to defer until the fall of 1938 the actual budgeting of expenses against income.

The high hopes entertained in the early part of 1938 about the budget vanished by the end of the year. The world was becoming frightened as the shadow of Hitler lengthened in Europe, and any hopes of better times the next year were to be blasted by the outbreak of another war in Europe in 1939.

NOTABLE UNIVERSITY EVENTS DURING THE DEPRESSION YEARS

During the Depression years four distinguished members of the University family died; two in 1936 (Sanford Brown and Dr. William B. Wherry); one in 1937 (Dr. Max Poll); and one in 1938 (Arthur R. Morgan).

For twenty-nine years Sanford Brown was a member of the Board of Directors. As an undergraduate and as a member of the Board he was closely identified with student and alumni affairs. During his student years he made an excellent scholastic record and was pre-eminent in extracurricular activities. He was President of his class, manager of the baseball team, and manager of the first college annual. He was largely instrumental in obtaining passage of the bond issue for the erection of Baldwin Hall, the Men's Gymnasium, and the Power House. As a memorial to Sanford Brown, his lifelong friend, Herbert G. French, made a gift to the University of chimes which were placed in the Student Union Building.

Dr. William B. Wherry, professor of bacteriology in the College of Medicine, was the distinguished tropical expert who among other things discovered tularemia. For thirty-four years Dr. Max Poll rendered distinguished services as head of the Department of German. He was a sound scholar and an excellent teacher. Dr. Poll was a man of dignified mien. Kindness and gentility permeated his whole being. He was beloved by his students.

Arthur R. Morgan was a member of the Board of Directors for nearly a quarter of a century, and for seven years (1924–1931) was Chairman of the Board. It was during his period as Chairman that plans were laid for the physical expansion of the University. In the building program Mr. Morgan contributed a most valuable share by reason "of his vision and his practical experience."

Three notable anniversaries in the history of the University occurred during these years. With fitting ceremonies in June 1933 the Cincinnati Law School, the fourth oldest law school in the United States and the oldest west of the Alleghenies, celebrated the hundredth anniversary of its founding. The Cincinnati institution could number among its graduates one President of the United States (W. H. Taft); one Chief Justice of the United States Supreme Court (W. H. Taft); one Vice-President of the United States (Charles G. Dawes); four Speakers of the House of Representatives (Milton Sayler, "Joe" Cannon, Champ Clark, and Nicholas Longworth); four Ambassadors (Charles G. Dawes, Edwin F. Noyes, John Stallo, and Bellamy Storer); Chief Justices and Associate Justices of Ohio and other State Supreme Courts; cabinet members; governors; and a host of prominent local leaders of the profession. As one of the founders of the College was Timothy Walker, a graduate of Harvard, it was appropriate that the chief speaker at the centenary was the Dean of the Harvard Law School, Dr. Roscoe Pound.

In accordance with Dean Schneider's wishes, there was no formal celebration in 1936 of the thirtieth anniversary of the establishment of the co-operative system of technological education by the College of Engineering. The closest approach to an anniversary event was the annual program of the "Co-op Day." Dean Schneider prepared a brochure entitled "Thirty Years of Educational Pioneering." It is interesting that the thirtieth anniversary of the co-op course marked the development of a plan to extend the system into the graduate field.

On March 5, 1937, the thirtieth anniversary of the organization of the Graduate School was celebrated. Dean Luther P. Eisenhart of the Graduate School of Princeton was the guest of honor and delivered an address on the meaning and value of graduate study.

A landmark of the University was lost in 1935 when it became necessary to raze the original building located on the McMicken homestead. This building, erected in 1875, housed the classes of the Academic Department until they were moved to McMicken Hall on the campus in 1895. After that it was used by the College of Medicine until the completion in 1916 of the Medical College building. During World War I the building served as a barracks for soldiers of the Student Army Training Corps. Later it was occupied by the College of Law which vacated it in 1925 at the time of the erection of the Alphonso Taft Hall. For a short time during the Depression it was occupied by one of the local welfare agencies. The cost of remodeling it for classroom or rental purposes was so great as to make such action inadvisable.

The following year (1936) the University, with the aid of funds from the Works Progress Administration, constructed a new amphitheater for the Greek games of women students and for other activities. In June of the same year the completion of the Student Union Building was celebrated. President Walters for some years had urged the construction of such a building. He maintained that a city university should provide facilities "to unite its students and to supply them with gracious and civilizing influences." The City Council authorized the issuance of bonds for such a purpose. The total cost of the construction of the Student Union Building of fine colonial architecture and its equipment was $664,-994.49, of which $257,580 was a Public Works Administration grant.

THE COLLEGES IN THE DEPRESSION YEARS

The Graduate School

During the Depression, in contrast to the condition of the colleges and professional schools throughout the country, the enrollment in the Graduate School increased. The quality of applicants for entrance also improved, since many able students graduating from college did not find suitable positions immediately, and so decided to continue their education. The number of applicants for fellowships and scholarships became so large that the Board of Directors, on the recommendation of the Faculty, increased the number of scholarships giving free tuition.

In the fall of 1936 the co-operative system of technological education was extended into the graduate field. Graduate students in co-operative engineering worked on problems in the Basic Research Laboratory. These students worked on a co-operative basis of six months; one student attending the University the first semester of the college year; the other in the second semester; splitting their summers on the industrial job.

Dean Louis T. More of the Graduate School was awarded that year the

Sachs Prize of $500 by the Cincinnati Institute of Fine Arts in recognition of his newly published book, *The Life of Sir Isaac Newton.*

The Faculty of the Graduate School underwent significant changes during these years. The heads of three departments—Professor Burtis B. Breese (psychology), Nevin Fenneman (geography and geology), and Harris Hancock (mathematics)—were retired at the close of the academic year 1936–1937. Professor Breese was a psychologist of national standing and an able and devoted teacher. Professor Fenneman was an internationally known physiographer. He was pre-eminently a teacher who guided and inspired many students. He had a "salty" style, both in writing and conversation. Professor Hancock was a mathematician of distinction and a stout advocate of the study of mathematics and classics as indispensable subjects for culture.

The College of Liberal Arts

There were a number of changes in the College of Liberal Arts during the Depression. In September 1933, Howard Dykema Roelofs, head of the Department of Philosophy, was appointed Dean upon the resignation of Acting Dean Hewitt. The new Dean was a graduate of Amherst College and had taught at his Alma Mater and at the Universities of Michigan, California, and the Leland Stanford. He was an able scholar with the highest educational ideals. He wanted to make the College of Liberal Arts not "just a college" but a "good college." In his opinion the difference between "just a college" and "a good college" was that the latter "did its work well." He held that the ideal of qualitative excellence should be the "major object of both the Faculty and the students of the College."

During his administration the Faculty in May 1935 made the first general revision of the curriculum since 1914. In the new curriculum the unit of instruction was the course, the continuous study throughout the academic year of a single subject with five courses constituting the normal program for the regular full-time student. The emphasis was upon the mastery of a subject rather than the accumulation of credits for graduation. In the junior and senior years the curriculum was organized in terms of a field of concentration with the senior reading course and a comprehensive examination covering the entire field of concentration. Dean Roelofs called the attention of the Faculty to the importance of the fine arts and the desirability of instruction in this field.

In 1936, Dean Roelofs resigned as Dean, owing to administrative pressure, but retained the headship of his department. In the same year, as a result of a request from the student body, the Board established a new administrative post, that of Dean of Men, and appointed to it Mr. Arthur S. Postle, a member of the English Department. To succeed

Miss Simrall the Board appointed (1936) as Dean of Women, Mrs. Katherine Dabney Ingle. She was the daughter of former President Dabney and by her background, academic training, and administrative experience in social welfare and physical education was well equipped for the position.

Upon the resignation of Dean Roelofs, Professor Merton Jerome Hubert, head of the Department of Romance Languages, was appointed Acting Dean. During his administration the effectiveness of the comprehensive examination was improved; a course in music appreciation was recommended; and the establishment of an all-University employment bureau was suggested. During his term of office Dean Hubert won the respect and admiration of his colleagues by his tact and skill in the conduct of Faculty affairs.

In 1938, George B. Barbour of the Department of Geology and Geography, an authority on Asian geology, was appointed Dean. He had a keen interest in the human problems of students.

During these years the College gave courses in training for public service under the direction of Professor S. Gale Lowrie, head of the Department of Political Science. Courses in this field were inaugurated at the University during the academic year 1927–1928. This work was put on a much more satisfactory basis by the grant of $80,000 from the Rockefeller Foundation over a six-year period. One of the graduates of this department was Charles Adair Harrell, later City Manager of Cincinnati.

The College for Teachers

The College for Teachers faced exceptional problems during the Depression years. As a result of the financial situation, the budget of the Teachers' College was scaled to a low figure; the Faculty was reduced; the curricular offerings were scaled down to a minimum; and all extension courses were discontinued. The entire teaching profession was drastically affected by the financial stringency. There was an oversupply of teachers caused by former teachers returning to the profession in search of jobs; many college graduates entered the teaching profession as opportunities for employment were reduced in other fields; fewer women left the profession to get married; and the Board of Education suspended the earning of professional credits for eligibility and promotion. On the other hand there was an increased demand for teachers as the school population mounted and classes grew larger. All these factors disturbed the balance between the supply and demand for teachers.

To meet this situation the College of Teachers made a radical reorganization of its courses and curricula. The programs for undergraduates were reduced and a revision was made of the basic courses offered. On the graduate level the reorganization centered in the development of integrated seminars with divisions covering the major areas of education and the establishment of a system of comprehensive examinations. There was a consolidation of several programs leading to the Master's degree in Education; and the professional degree of Doctor of Education was opened to newly entering graduate students. Dean Pechstein vigorously denied that the College had ever recommended for this degree, as an article in the *Enquirer* claimed, a student who wrote a thesis entitled "Janitorial Methods and the Care of Public Schools."

When in 1936 the College celebrated its thirtieth anniversary, Dean Pechstein called attention to the fact that more than three thousand students had been graduated in three decades since its founding. In his address entitled "A Vision of the Future," Dean Pechstein declared the College still operated on the basic principles laid down by its founders "both educate a person to live and at the same time train him to become a technician as a teacher or administrator." The Depression years represented a trying time for the College for Teachers.

The College of Engineering and Commerce

The co-operative course had its real test during the hard years of economic stagnation. There had always been the question of what would happen to a co-operative course in a severe depression. Dean Schneider had said that at the worst the students could be put on a full-time basis in the school and so be no more badly off than the students in a regular four-year course. The co-operative course had survived the minor panics in 1907, 1914, and 1921, but there still remained the test of a major economic disturbance.

When the panic came in the fall of 1929, the outside work fell off as economic conditions became worse. The lowest ebb of employment of co-operative students of the University was about 50 per cent for a few months in 1932. After that the curve began to go up, haltingly at first, but later with greater acceleration, except during the recession of 1937. Aid furnished by the National Youth Administration was most helpful to the students who had no financial reserves. Many of them were employed by the NYA in some phase of the University's many activities.

Because of the wide geographical range of the outside work, with new rules covering hours of work under the National Recovery Act, the College reorganized its periods of alternation in class work and field work. When the co-operative course was started in 1906 it was decided to alternate the students on a weekly basis. This worked satisfactorily but after a year or so, the biweekly period was tried. This was found better, and after a period of a few years it was decided to try a four-week alternative. The results seemed to indicate that the longer unit was better, and so the College tried out the eight-week alternative. This did not work so well, and so return was made to the four-week scheme. During the Depression all freshmen students attended school full-time for fourteen weeks (September to the Christmas holidays); at the beginning of the second term they began to alternate on a seven-week basis. All the classes above the freshmen alternated on the seven-week schedule. This scheme proved most satisfactory with the Christmas and spring vacations and made three terms of exactly equal periods of work and study. The College has used this seven-week unit since the depression.

Two new courses were begun during these years. In 1934 a new course in business administration was inaugurated, which included courses in English, English literature, history, mathematics, geography, economics, and chemistry, together with a body of specialized material in the commercial field; and four years later Dr. S. B. Arenson of the Chemistry Department inauguarated a novel series of popular lectures on science which were given to a selected group of high school students.

In 1935, George Sperti, Director of the Basic Science Laboratory, and his staff resigned and joined the *Institutum Divi Thomae*, which had been established by Archbishop John T. McNicholas. Explaining his action, Dr. Sperti said that since the Laboratory was completed "much of his time had been taken up with its administrative duties" and that he hoped this freedom would enable him "to conduct theoretical research." The resignation of Dr. Sperti was a severe blow to Dean Schneider; but the Laboratory continued its work under the direction of Dean Schneider, the originator and father of much of its research.

Two of the graduates of the College won national recognition of their achievements. In 1932, Winston E. Kock invented a reedless, pipeless "pipe" organ. Five years later, on May 26, 1937, President Walters represented the University and the City at the dedication of the Golden Gate Bridge at San Francisco. The designer and chief engineer in charge of the construction of this magnificent bridge with "its 4,200 foot span and tremendous towers" was J. B. Strauss, a graduate of the class of 1932. President Walters and Alfred K. Nippert, who was with him, watched the United States Fleet, "consisting of about forty battleships and cruisers and a host of smaller fighting craft, sail majestically under the great span of the bridge."

It had been the ambition of Strauss's college days to build the "biggest thing in the world." He realized his ambition in completing the Golden Gate Bridge. He was "a small man, not more than five feet, three inches, with a magnificent head, noble features, simple of speech and manners."

To commemorate the opening of the Golden Gate Bridge Strauss composed a poem, two stanzas of which follow:

The Mighty Task Is Done

At last, the mighty task is done;
  Resplendent in the western sun,
  The Bridge looms mountain high,
Its Titan piers grip ocean floor,
Its great steel arms link shore with shore,
  Its towers pierce the sky.

On its broad decks, in rightful pride,
The world in swift parade shall ride,
  Throughout all time to be,
Beneath, fleet ships from every port,
Vast landlocked bays, historic fort,
  And dwarfing all-the-sea.

The Evening College

Between 1920 and 1931 the enrollment in the Evening School of the College of Engineering and Commerce increased steadily from 400 to 4,315. The 1931 fall enrollment reached a peak figure of 4,743, although most other evening schools felt the effects of the Depression in 1930 and 1931. In 1933 the enrollment dropped to 3,788, the lowest figure during the Depression. Then it began to rise slowly until by 1938 it was 5,424.

Because of the size of the evening student body and the importance of adult education in the program for a municipal university, the Board, acting on the recommendation of President Walters in March 1938, decided to consolidate and co-ordinate all the evening courses offered in the Colleges of Liberal Arts, Engineering and Commerce, and the School of Applied Arts under one College with Dr. Schneider as Dean and Professor Vincent H. Drufner as Director. President Walters first suggested that the new unit be called the University College, but it was finally named the Evening College.

The new College was the fourth largest evening commerce school in the country. The Faculty was composed of men and women drawn from the Faculties of the various Colleges of the University and from Miami University. Business and professional men with broad experience and training gave courses in the fields of their specialization as lecturers. The College sponsored the previously mentioned course of lectures for the Business and Professional Men's Group; a series of radio talks by members of the University Faculties over the Crosley radio station WLW; and a course of illustrated lectures, "The World At Your Door," by world travelers.

The Evening College was designed to meet the educational need of men and women of Greater Cincinnati who were occupied during the day. For persons under thirty-five years of age the College provided sequential programs of study bearing directly on their daily work. For men and women of all ages it provided opportunities for intellectual enjoyment and self-expression in courses in applied arts and liberal arts and in informal lecture series. Since the College sought to serve a community as a whole, the student body represented a diversity of occupations and professions. The average age of the students in the Evening College was twenty-six, but the range was from seventeen to seventy-five. Almost a fourth of the total number were above thirty years of age. About 85 per cent of those attending were high school graduates, and there were also many college graduates in the student body.

Undoubtedly the most important of the motives which brought men and women to the Evening College was economic. Some wanted to become more proficient in the positions they already had; others to prepare themselves for advancement; and still others, with a background of knowledge and experience, to familiarize themselves with recent technological and industrial developments. Then there were those who were motivated by a desire to develop a hobby or cultural enrichment.

In addition to Delta Mu Delta founded in 1925, another honorary scholarship fraternity was formed in 1933, Mu Pi Kappa, for evening engineering students. Three years later (1936) the first Evening College edition of the *News Record* made its appearance.

The School of Applied Arts

By action of the Board of Directors in July 1935, the Department of Architecture became the School of Applied Arts under the direction of the College of Engineering and Commerce. In addition to the courses offered in architecture and landscape architecture, instruction was given in interior decoration. In September 1927 two new courses were added—one in ceramics, and one in art in industry. In the same year an opportunity was offered for graduate work in applied arts. Two years later (1929) courses for teachers of art were developed.

During the Depression the profession of architecture was severely affected. As a consequence the number of students entering the School to study architecture decreased—as was the case in most schools of architecture in the United States. Young men avoided a field which appeared to offer no opportunity. On the other hand there was increased enrollment in the courses in art in industry. As business grew worse, producers sought new appeals to buyers. The application of art to product design, as in automobiles, refrigerators, containers, and fabrics became a major factor in business competition. Therefore, there was an increased demand for trained designers.

The curriculum of the School of Applied Arts underwent changes during the period of hard times. In 1933 freshmen male students in architecture and landscape architecture attended classes full-time; from January until August they attended every four weeks between the classroom and their co-operative jobs. In all the other courses in Applied Arts male students were permitted to go full-time throughout the course. The following year (1934) all male students attended the School full-time for fourteen weeks; after that they attended on a seven-week basis. All freshmen women also attended full-time for fourteen weeks; after which they could either continue their courses full-time, or go on a co-operative basis.

It was during the Depression years, nevertheless, that the School of of Applied Arts began to win national recognition. The School was admitted to membership in the Association of Collegiate Schools of Architecture and was placed on the American Academy of Rome's accredited list for the prize competition in architecture. A student in the School won the first prize awarded by the American Institute of Decorators for the design of a public room for a hotel, and another student won first place in a contest sponsored by the American Society of Landscape Architects for the design of a country estate.

The College of Medicine

In 1934 the Medical College and the General Hospital became involved in a controversy with the Academy of Medicine of Cincinnati. Dissatisfaction had existed for years on the part of many of the local physicians with certain practices and policies of the College and Hospital. Members of the local profession objected to the private practice of members of the staff of the Medical College and the Hospital. They also criticized the conditions in the General Hospital, claiming that the institution did not give proper care to patients nor to the instruction of internes and students. They also objected to the operation of Holmes Hospital.

In reply to the Academy resolutions with regard to the operation of Holmes Hospital, Mrs. Holmes wrote a letter pointing out that the Holmes Hospital was privately endowed; and denied the accusation that any doctor had been prohibited from practice in the Hospital. The result of this controversy was that on January 22, 1934, the Academy of Medicine adopted nine resolutions. These resolutions might be classified in two groups: (1) those dealing with the activities of the General Hospital; and (2) those concerned with the policies of the Medical College. The most important one of these resolutions stated that "no member of the Cincinnati General Hospital or of the College of Medicine" should be permitted "to carry on private practice excepting under such terms as those of other physicians of Cincinnati." The Academy wanted the Board of Directors of the University to make contracts with all the salaried employees of the College.

At a special meeting of the Board of Directors on February 3, 1934, a committee of eight physicians representing the Academy presented the resolutions adopted by the Academy. The Board voted to investigate the situation. The Board Committee on the Medical College had a conference with Dean Bachmeyer and four Faculty members of the College of Medicine, Doctors Reed, Austin, Mitchell, and Friedlander. After considerable discussion the Board Committee came to the conclusion that it was "clear" in their opinion that "the main attack on the College was not justified."

The Board then held a six-hour session with members of the Medical College and a committee of four local physicians representing the Academy of Medicine. In the estimation of the Board the committee of doctors were unable "to supply substantial evidence supporting their specific charges."

On March 6, 1934, the Board submitted its report. By a vote of 7 to 1 the Board approved the manner in which the College of Medicine was conducted. Lester A. Jaffe was the only director who voted against approval of the report on the ground that the Board had not carefully investigated the case. The report of the Board pointed out that some of the resolutions adopted by the Academy took "in activities of the General Hospital" which were "not within the scope of the Board."

Concerning the Academy resolution that the University make contracts with salaried members of the College of Medicine the Board declared that the University and other universities of high standing throughout the country did not make "contracts with Faculty members in any of their professional and undergraduate colleges" but engaged their services "by appointment." The Board held that the policies of the University in regard to private practice by members of the College of Medicine were "in accord with those of other universities of high standing."

The Academy of Medicine made a tart reply to the report of the Board of Directors of the University. It elaborated on its previous criticism and centered its attack on the Board members. As a result of a meeting between the President of the Academy of Medicine and City Manager Clarence Dykstra the quarrel was settled. Dr. Bachmeyer resigned his position as Dean of the College "in order to devote more time to the increasing demands of the Hospital." Shortly thereafter he left the University and went to the University of Chicago Medical School.

Dr. Alfred Friedlander was appointed the successor to Dr. Bachmeyer as Dean of the Medical College. Under his "positive and dynamic leadership" the College was revitalized. His most outstanding contribution was in strengthening the financial position of the College. Dean Friedlander awakened the friends of the University in the City to the needs of the Medical College. Since it was difficult to obtain large endowments during the hard times, Dr. Friedlander solicited small gifts of money to be expended over a period of from three to five years for specific projects. Funds were thus made available for research, new laboratories, and the strengthening of the personnel of the Faculty. As Dr. Dorst later said: "In the death of Dr. Friedlander on May 28, 1939 (he had previously retired), the College of Medicine sustained a loss which it will not soon recover."

The ranks of the Faculty were strengthened by the appointment of a number of outstanding men. Dr. Marion A. Blankenhorn was appointed head of the Department of Internal Medicine. He had achieved national recognition for his work as "clinician, investigator, organizer, and teacher." He and Dr. T. Douglas Spies won national recognition for their scientific achievement of the study of the efficiency of nicotinic acid in the treatment of pellagra, a chronic disease common in the Southeastern states which affected the skin, the digestion, and the nervous system of its victims. Dr. Lee Foshay was appointed professor of bacteriology and hygiene and attracted international attention by his studies of tularemia and vaccine therapy. Dr. Robert Kehoe and his colleagues in the Kettering Laboratory made many valuable contributions, especially in their studies of lead absorption and lead poisoning.

In 1935 the College revised the curriculum covering the clinical years of the course. Under the new plan students in the latter two years spent almost all their time in hospital wards and in the outpatient dispensary. The value of didactic instruction was recognized, but it was definitely subordinated to clinical work. An elective course in the history of medicine was inaugurated by Dr. David A. Tucker, Jr., professor of the history of medicine. This course was illustrated by photographs, slides, and graphs; and the students were permitted to study some of the older masterpieces of medical literature supplied by Dr. Tucker from his large and valuable collection of rare medical books.

The College of Law

The years of the Great Depression and the New Deal placed a great strain upon the legal profession and colleges of law. The bewildering changes that occurred during these years gave the law schools much concern. The Federal government set up new agencies to deal with banking and monetary problems, to curtail agricultural production, to curb competition and the growth of monopolies, and to grant relief and jobs for the unemployed. The Great Depression and the New Deal created a ferment of ideas and led to the emergence of new economic, social, and political theories. As these revolutionary changes took place, the Faculties of the law colleges began to examine their objectives and aims, the content of their curricula, and the need to raise their standards and the ethics of the entire legal profession.

As a conscientious legal educator, Dean Ferson was deeply interested in trying to correct some of the serious deficiencies in legal education and admission to the bar. He did not think that the present situation, critical as it was, called for "any radical departures" in the curricula of law schools; but he and his Faculty, "while conservative," watched the new experiments "with sympathy and interest." He believed that the legal profession had "a social responsibility"; and that the law school should impart more than "categorical learning." The business of the law school, he thought, was to teach "the technique in the handling of law materials" and develop "social-mindedness," so that its graduates would be "creditable and useful both in professional and public service."

In clear-cut fashion Dean Ferson advocated the doctrine that as the Cincinnati College of Law was supported "largely by public funds and private endowment" it clearly should heed "the need of society for an educated and upright bar." He also thought that because of the growth "in bulk and complexity of law itself," new subjects should be introduced into the already overcrowded curriculum by adding a year to the regular law course. Furthermore, he wanted to "eliminate some of the weak" law schools and raise the standards of admission to the bar.

Steps were taken by the College under the direction of Dean Ferson to realize some of these goals. A course in taxation was added to the curriculum. In 1934 a confederation of the twelve Ohio Law Schools was organized with its objectives "the improvement of legal education in the State of Ohio" and the improvement of the standards for admission to the Ohio Bar. Dean Ferson was the founder of the League of Ohio Law Schools, "although the undertaking would not have been possible without the support of the Ohio State Bar Association's Legal Education Committee and its Chairman, Grauman Marks, of the Cincinnati Bar." The first objective of the League was accomplished when the Supreme Court of Ohio in 1935 abolished the system of law office study which "not only brought to an end an institution of more than one-hundred and fifty years' duration in Ohio but also made the law school the exclusive route to the profession of law."

At the same time the Supreme Court of Ohio revised its rules and made the League of Ohio Law Schools, or a law school approved by the American Bar Association, the accrediting agencies for admission to the bar examination. Newton D. Baker, Paul Martin, and other prominent lawyers of the State rendered valuable service in achieving this. The League's second objective, the improvement of the scope and quality of the bar examination was "effectuated by cooperating with the Board of Bar Examiners and the Legal Education Committee of the Ohio State Bar Association."

The standards of admission to the College of Law were raised during these years. The Board of Directors, on recommendation of the Law Faculty, beginning with the fall of 1937, required three years of college work as a prerequisite to entering the College of Law; and in view of the crowded curriculum Dean Ferson in his report for 1937–1939 recommended that the University should add a fourth year to the course of the College of Law.

Dean Ferson reported that "the ability, industry, and professional attitude" of the students was gratifying. They adopted and strengthened their constitution for handling the honor system; and they organized the first and second year students into case clubs for "the study, briefing, and argument of legal questions. The work of these clubs was to supplement the regular classroom work, and was entirely voluntary."

During the Depression the Faculty suffered a notable loss in the death in 1934 of Judge Thomas A. Darby, who had taught criminal law in the College for fourteen years. The following year Judge Robert C. Pugh died. He had served as Acting Dean of the College on numerous occasions. His place was taken by Professor Harold Shephard, Dean of the College of Law of the University of Washington. Two years later Judge Benton S. Oppenheimer died, after twenty-nine years on the Faculty.

STUDENT ACTIVITIES DURING THE DEPRESSION YEARS

The Depression curtailed student activities on the campus. In order to lighten the student's financial burden the general activity fee was reduced from $15.00 to $10.00 a year. The "Fresh Painters" musical comedy organization was suspended in 1935 by the University Administration because of its inability to remain solvent and its failure to comply with regulations, but the next year it was revived.

A new student spirit manifested itself on the campus. Dean Simrall claimed that the Depression had a beneficial effect upon the undergraduate student. She said there was "a greater seriousness of purpose, a deeper sense of responsibilities, and a more sound and wholesome attitude toward life." A new sorority (Alpha Delta Pi, 1935) and a new fraternity (Alpha Sigma Phi, 1937) were organized on the campus; and Mystic 13 became a chapter of Mortar Board (1932).

Musical organizations flourished during these years. The combined Men's and Women's Glee Clubs made a trip to eastern cities during the spring vacation of 1935. They gained favorable newspaper comment on their stage and broadcasting engagements. The youngest musical activity —choral music—won exceptional laurels. The Oratorio Society composed of some five hundred student and Faculty singers, conducted by Mr. Sherwood Kains, won the honor of inclusion in the 1935–1936 program of the Cincinnati Symphony Orchestra. With the orchestra, the Society gave Handel's *Messiah* in Music Hall on December 20 and 21, 1935.

Activities of the colored students attracted attention on two occasions. In 1934 a delegation of colored students waited upon President Walters and requested the right of Negroes to attend the Junior Prom. The Prom

Committee wisely granted it, and the dance was held with colored students in attendance "without the semblance of trouble." The colored students' society, *Quadres,* was commended for the fine "spirit of philanthrophy" shown by donating the proceeds of its play *Slightly Delirious* for scholarships for needy students.

The only student activities that caused serious difficulty were the college papers. In 1935 the Student Council barred the humorous magazine, the *Stoic,* from the campus. It was succeeded by the *Mad Hatter,* a humorous literary magazine. After several issues this magazine was discontinued because "it did not conform to regularized financial and ethical procedure stipulated by Student Council and the Student Activity trustees." The editor of the *Cincinnati Bearcat* was sharply reprimanded by President Walters for the "unfortunate style of flippancy" and "wisecracking" in which he wrote an article on atheism.

In 1937 there appeared a single issue of a literary magazine called *The Little Man.* Its format was similar to that of the *Reader's Digest.* The next year *The Little Man* changed its name to *The Profile.*

In 1936 the Student Council changed the name of the official college paper at the suggestion of Professor Norwood C. Geis to *The Cincinnati News Record.* For some years the college paper had appeared under the dual title of *The Cincinnati News* and *The Cincinnati Bearcat.* The name *The Bearcat* had been used since 1903; and among its editors had been Louise E. Bentley, Sybel M. Heck, Howard L. Bevis, Lester Jaffe, Chase M. Davies, Frank Byers, Stewart Cooper, and Norman P. Auburn. Part of the week the paper was called *The Cincinnati News;* the rest of the week it was called *The Cincinnati Bearcat.* This caused confusion with the United States postal regulations covering college papers. The change was made because some thought the name *Cincinnati Bearcat* was not in keeping with the dignity of the University. Others, however, objected to the changed title on the ground that it was too formal and not representative of the campus spirit.

In the late thirties a wave of emotional pacificism swept through many American and European colleges and universities. This gesture was viewed with alarm by some people who believed that students were vowing to take no part in any future war. Perhaps it did mean that in some colleges, but a student poll at the University revealed that the anti-war demonstration here was less radical. The student body voted 1,039 to 35 against bearing arms if the United States invaded another country, but 1,060 to 147 were in favor of bearing arms if this country were invaded. Only 353 out of 1,254 refused to bear arms in any war. Although these statistics were a little confusing, they indicated that the local student body did not believe in peace at any price.

More than a thousand students of the University on April 22, 1936, attended an anti-war demonstration in Wilson Auditorium. A feature of the meeting was the taking of a revised Oxford oath which read: "We will not support any war which the United States may undertake with the exception of a war in which there is territorial invasion of the United States."

ATHLETICS DURING THE DEPRESSION YEARS

Next to the budget, the athletic situation at the University caused the most trouble for President Walters during these years. He was an enthusiastic supporter of football as a college sport; but he wanted to keep it on a wholesome basis, irrespective of whether the University teams won or lost. But sports writers of the local press and alumni organizations kept offering gratuitous advice and suggestions on how to conduct athletic affairs, which frequently stirred up more confusion.

The "C" Club strongly advocated the enlargement of the stadium. President Walters and the Board were dubious about the project and resolved that if it were undertaken the University should "assume no obligation, expense, or responsibility." President Walters was strongly opposed to a campaign in the City to obtain funds for it. But, like Banquo's ghost, the stadium project kept bobbing up. Works Progress Administration officials became interested, thinking it would be an advantageous work relief job and offered to give financial assistance. Finally on September 26, 1936, an enlarged stadium was completed and dedicated by a committee of the University "C" Club headed by James Pottinger. This work was made possible by a Federal grant through the Works Progress Administration of $134,182, and a loan of $30,000 guaranteed by the "C" Club, and a donation of $1,000 each by A. K. Nippert and B. H. Kroger. This undertaking increased the seating capacity of the stadium from 11,957 to 23,004 and provided restrooms.

There was also trouble in connection with Negro players on the football squad. A disagreeable problem arose in 1933 when President Walters found out that a contract had been signed to play a game with the University of Kentucky which contained a clause barring any Negro player. President Walters and Chairman French of the Athletic Committee of the Board agreed that Kentucky should be asked to delete this clause, and if she refused the University should ask to be relieved from playing the game. Kentucky declined to delete the clause, and the game was played without the University using one of her best linemen. Two years later Marshall College agreed to play a game with Cincinnati, even though Varsity used a Negro player.

In 1933, Dana King was appointed football coach and Director of Athletics. In that year the Varsity shared the championship of the Buckeye Conference and held it alone in 1934. With the help of the Civil Works Administration and the Federal Emergency Relief Administration, funds for new play fields were developed; and for the first time women students had adequate facilities for hockey and other games.

Because of the criticism of the athletic situation, President Walters notified King in 1935 that he would not be continued the next fall as football coach, but should devote himself exclusively to his work as Director of Athletics with the understanding that the whole athletic setup would be reconsidered. President Walters communicated with Russell Cohen of Vanderbilt for the position as football coach. The Board Committee on Athletics, however, agreed to restrict King to his duties as Director but did not act upon the appointment of Cohen as coach to succeed King. They felt that "for one thing separate action was preferable and second, that more candidates should be considered." President Walters, however, finally persuaded the Board to appoint Cohen as football coach.

In 1937 there occurred the greatest upheaval in the entire athletic history of the University. That year the University football team compiled the worst record, a total of eighteen points, in the history of gridiron activities at the University. Some people were of the opinion that the inferior material of the football squad was responsible for the poor showing. Others were outspoken in their belief that Coach Cohen's style of football had been outmoded and that there was an urgent need for a change if the Bearcats were to emerge from the wilderness of defeat. Perhaps, as one writer of the local press claimed, "too many cooks had been preparing the football broth at the University." There had been clashes of personality and methods in the Athletic Department. The coach had often "been assisted—against his will—by 'downtown coaches' among the alumni." Suddenly in the middle of the season Coach Cohen presented his resignation. His assistant, Wade Woodsworth, was designated as his successor until the end of the season. President Walters was told that the football team had been stirred up "to revolt against Cohen as coach." At the same time Dana King was released as Director of Athletics and M. Charles Mileham, intramural director, was appointed acting Director of Athletics. Then in 1937 a new head coach was appointed—Joe Meyer, former coach at Xavier University. In 1918 the University played a game with Xavier; but antagonism between the two opponents marked the postwar period, and to avoid unruly demonstrations no further UC-Xavier games were scheduled. By 1937, however, there was strong pressure for the University to resume athletic relations with Xavier University. In that year City Councilman James R. Clark urged that the University play Xavier University. But the Board of Directors of the University decided that in view of the reorganization of the athletic department of the University and the appointment of a new football coach it was not advisable "to enter upon athletic relations with Xavier University at that time [1937]."

In 1942, however, for the first time in twenty-four years (since 1918) the University of Cincinnati Bearcats clashed with the Xavier University Musketeers in the gridiron field at the University. No more games were scheduled during World War II between the two institutions because of the War Department ban on soldier-students participating in intercollegiate contests. From 1947, however, the University played Xavier University regularly every year in football.

19   *After Depression, War*

In September 1939 came the shock of another major European war. With the rise of Nazism in Germany and of Fascism in Italy and Japan the war clouds over Europe and Asia began flashing with lightning. It was only a question when the bolts would strike. Collective security died, and World War II was born when Japan in 1931 marched into Manchuria and withdrew from the League of Nations. Two years later Adolph Hitler became Chancellor of the German Reich; Germany withdrew from the disarmament conference at Geneva and left the League of Nations. In 1936 German troops occupied and remilitarized the Rhineland. Two years later Germany occupied Austria and soon absorbed Czechoslovakia. The final crisis arose from the dispute between Germany and Poland over the Free City of Danzig and the Polish Corridor. On August 22, 1939, Germany and the Soviet Union astounded the world by announcing they had signed a non-aggression pact; and on September 1, Germany invaded Poland. Two days later England and France declared war on Germany.

From the outbreak of the War, American public opinion was overwhelmingly in favor of England and France. Hitler's persecution of the Jews and his wanton aggression against independent nations shocked the American public. In all probability the average American of 1939 was more antagonistic to Nazi Germany than the American of 1914 was to Imperial Germany. Nevertheless, at the beginning of hostilities the American people were determined, if possible, to keep the United States out of war. They had to relearn the lesson of 1812 and 1917—that isolation did not give them national security. The Neutrality Act of 1937 was repealed in the hope that England and France who had control of the seas would be able to buy freely the supplies they needed. The astounding victories of Germany in the spring and summer of 1940 at last awakened the American public to the inadequacy of their own military preparedness in case the United States should become involved. The American government began to set up agencies to mobilize the economic resources of the nation for national defense.

The impact of the national defense program was soon felt by the University. In September 1940 the Board of Directors voted to refund tuition and other fees of those who might leave the University on being called to service; and it renewed this offer for the academic year 1941–1942. The Board also voted to grant leave of absence to Faculty members and other members of the staff who were called to national defense service, and assured them that their positions would be held open for them.

At the suggestion of President Walters the American Council of Education approved a plan to extend ROTC basic units in American colleges and universities in the event the United States entered the War. Curricular changes were made in the various Colleges. A course in military medicine was offered as an elective at the College of Medicine. The national emergency focused the attention of the Surgeon General of the Army on the importance of augmenting the supply of physicians in order to meet both civil and military demands. The College of Medicine along with other medical schools in the country agreed to increase the number of students admitted to the freshman class. Responding to the national defense program the College of Engineering and Commerce and the College of Liberal Arts accelerated their scholastic programs. The Engineering and Commerce College made it possible for students to receive their degrees *in absentia*. The College of Liberal Arts waived certain degree requirements for students in good standing who were called into military service.

At the request of the United States Office of Education the College of Engineering and Commerce early in the summer of 1940 undertook a survey of the industrial needs in this area for special training of men in defense plants and extended its engineering technical courses. The Department of Aeronautical Engineering, under the direction of Professor Bradley Jones, helped the Civil Aeronautical Administration expand its program for civilian pilots and carried on a research program at Wright Field, Dayton, Ohio. The College of Engineering and Commerce cooperated closely with the Evening College in developing defense training courses. Dr. Ralph L. Jacobs of the Teachers College was active in the "training-within-industry program" of the Council of National Defense.

Various departments in the University engaged in research directly related to national defense. Dr. Milan A. Logan and his colleagues in the Department of Biological Chemistry in the College of Medicine investigated the production of toxoids from the gas bacillus. Members of the staff of the Kettering Laboratory of the Medical College worked on several problems at the request of the Army. Dr. Eugene B. Ferris, Jr., and Dr. Henry W. Ryder of the Medical College developed special techniques for the study of high-altitude flying. Dr. Marion A. Blankenhorn and Dr. T. Douglas Spies of the same College carried on their significant investigations in the field of nutrition.

Burnham Finney, a University graduate of 1921 and editor of the *American Machinist,* wrote a book in 1941 entitled *Arsenal of Democracy.* This was acclaimed by the press as one of the most accurate pictures of the nation's national defense efforts.

OTHER UNIVERSITY EVENTS OF THE NATIONAL DEFENSE PERIOD

Apart from the programs for national defense, the most important organizational change in the University was the approval in 1940 by the Board of Directors of a petition presented by the Faculty of all of the Colleges establishing a general University Faculty. The purpose of the University Faculty was to make "available to the President and Board of Directors the advice and aid of a co-ordinated academic body." Professor F. S. Rowley of the College of Law was elected the first Chairman of the University Faculty.

In the same year the Board of Directors published a monograph, amplified in 1941, entitled *Historical Sketch of the University of Cincinnati,* written by President Walters. This was the most comprehensive account of the origin and development of the University, its spirit and traditions, which had been written. It reflected great credit upon its author for his meticulous research and interesting style. As a result of this study the Board in 1940 selected two founding dates for the University: 1819, the chartering of its oldest units, the Cincinnati College and the Medical College of Ohio; and 1870, when the University was chartered as a municipal university.

Important changes occurred in the personnel of the Board during the national defense period. On November 30, 1940, George H. Warrington died. He had been a member of the Board for seventeen years and Chairman since 1931. An alumnus of the College of Law, he was deeply interested in all the departments of the University. Besides his active interest in varied civic and philanthropic enterprises Mr. Warrington was a patron of art and music. "No man," declared President Walters, "had a clearer conception of what was truly the scope and work of a university." Frank F. Dinsmore was elected Chairman of the Board of Directors.

To fill the unexpired term of the late George H. Warrington, and for the first time in the history of the University, a woman, Mrs. Jane De-Serisy Earley, was appointed a member of the Board of Directors. Both Mrs. Earley and her husband, Dr. Daniel E. Earley, were graduates of the University. During her undergraduate days she was the first woman sports editor of the University paper, and her husband was a basketball and baseball star. Mrs. Earley was a valuable addition to the Board. Her counsel was sound and judicial, and she devoted her time and energies untiringly to the advancement of all the activities of the University. Soon after her appointment Mrs. Earley began to urge the organization of Friends of the University, which had been previously proposed by Director John Rowe, to solicit funds to aid the University. This later developed into an annual fund-raising campaign for the University.

Five new administrative heads of Colleges were appointed during these years. Shortly after the death of Herman Schneider on March 28, 1939, Acting Dean Robert C. Gowdy was appointed Dean of the College of Engineering and Commerce and Director of the School of Applied Arts. Shortly after the death of Dean Alfred Friedlander on May 28, 1939, Acting Dean Stanley Dorst was appointed Dean. On December 5, 1939, Dr. Frank H. Nelson, rector of Christ Church and for ten years a member of the Board of Directors, died. His work and influence pervaded varied fields of activity in the City and nation, and he contributed especially as Chairman of a Committee on the Teachers College in the reorganization of the College.

When Dean Louis T. More of the Graduate School retired at the close of the academic year 1939–1940, Professor Rodney P. Robinson of the Department of Classics was appointed Dean. Because of illness, Catherine Buckley also retired at the close of the academic year 1939–1940 from the position as Director of the School of Nursing and Health, which had become a separate unit of the University in 1938, and Helen G. Schwarz was appointed Director. On July 31, 1940, Vincent Drufner, Dean of the Evening College, died. It had been due to his vision, sound judgment, and almost limitless energy that the evening work had been raised to a level which ranked it among the foremost evening colleges in the country. To succeed him, Acting Dean Norman P. Auburn was appointed Dean. On June 26, 1940, Professor Benjamin C. Van Wye, who had organized the University's Speech Department in 1907 and was its chairman for thirty years, died. He was known to thousands of Cincinnatians for his reading at Christmas time each year of Charles Dickens' *A Christmas Carol*.

THE UNITED STATES ENTERS WORLD WAR II

The year 1941 closed with a dramatic crisis in the Pacific. Ever since Japan had joined the Berlin-Rome alliance in September 1940, and had announced her intention of creating a "new order in Eastern Asia," there had been increasing tension in American-Japanese relations. The United States showed its opposition to Japan's aggressive policy by extending financial aid to China and finally by "freezing" all Nipponese assets in the United States and stopping all shipments to Japan of gasoline and other sinews of war. While peace negotiations with Japanese envoys in Washington were in progress, Japan made a surprise attack on Pearl Harbor, Hawaiian Islands, on December 7, 1941. This was followed by a formal declaration of war on the United States and Great Britain. The following day Congress declared war on Japan. Three days later (December 11) Germany and Italy declared war on the United States. On the same day Congress responded by a unanimous vote declaring war on both these countries.

The entrance of the United States into the War had profound reactions on the student body. Tense, silent crowds clustered around the radio sets in the Student Union Building and in the Women's Building to listen to the fateful words of the President's war message. It was hard for them to realize that within a quarter of a century after World War I the United States was again at war, but the tone of the *News Record* reflected the national unity which had been created by the electrifying blow of the Japanese at Pearl Harbor. "The decision has been made" editorially commented the *News Record*. "Since the beginning of school we have permitted and encouraged all students to write to the paper commenting upon the actions of the national government. . . . Now, however, the situation has changed; and we must take cognizance of the change by closing our columns to any expressions which might be deemed contrary to the successful prosecution of the war." The editors voluntarily imposed upon themselves a censorship of their news coverage.

IMPACT OF THE WAR UPON THE FACULTY AND RESEARCH

Immediately after the Japanese attack on Pearl Harbor, the Board of Directors, as in World War I, placed at the disposal of the United States government the laboratories and facilities of the University; and it granted leaves of absence to members of the Faculty and other employees. It is estimated that close to two hundred members of the Faculty were granted leaves, most of them entering the armed forces, others taking up research or other duties for government agencies or wartime organizations doing scientific investigation for the government.

The College of Medicine made noteworthy contributions to the war effort. Dr. Albert B. Sabin, Lieutenant Colonel in the Medical Corps, rendered outstanding service in connection with the investigation and control of infectious diseases. His research in the Middle East yielded much information concerning methods of controlling sandfly fever, one of the chief epidemic diseases of the Mediterranean area. He assisted to a notable degree in dealing with this scourge during the Sicilian campaign. He conducted extensive studies of dengue fever which resulted in the preparation of a vaccine. He also collaborated with others in developing a vaccine against Japanese B—encephalitis. Later Dr. Sabin was sent to Okinawa where he supervised the vaccination of more than 65,000 Army and Navy personnel. For his outstanding service he was awarded the Legion of Merit.

Dr. William Altemeier and his associates in the Department of Surgery developed to new levels of efficiency the techniques of immunization; and in co-operation with a subcommittee of the National Research Council, made significant contributions in evaluating "the place of penicillin in the treatment of established infections." Dr. Marion A. Blankenhorn aided by other members of the Departments of Medicine, Psychiatry, Pediatrics, Otolaryngology, and applied Physiology made significant contributions in the field of aviation medicine by carrying out experiments in high altitude flying. Dr. Merlin Cooper and Dr. Frederick Barnes of the Department of Pediatrics helped the Army in "the fight against dysentery." Dr. Howard D. Fabing was Director of the School of Military Neuropsychiatry in Europe. Dr. Lee Foshay was made a consultant to the military service at Camp Detrick, Maryland, where he expanded the scope and intensity of his prewar work on tularemia.

Dr. Robert Kehoe and his colleagues in the Department of Industrial Physiology made many valuable contributions in the solution of numerous problems of industrial hazards. Dr. Frank H. Mayfield was Chief of the Neurosurgical Section of the Percy Jones Hospital, Battle Creek, Michigan; and as the Director of a training school for general surgeons in neurosurgery supervised an extensive program of electro diagnostic tests for nerve injury. Dr. George X. Schwemlein, in co-operation with the United States Health Service, made valuable contributions in the study of the use of penicillin in the treatment of syphilis. Dr. John Romano made a tour of the European Theater of Operations as a member of a committee appointed by the War Department and the Surgeon General's Office to study psychiatric disabilities incident to combat warfare.

During the summer of 1941 the Surgeon General of the United States requested the University of Cincinnati to set up a general hospital unit as it had done in World War I. The new hospital unit received the same number (twenty-five) which the former unit had had in World War I. The 25th General Hospital saw active service in France through the period extending from their landing in Normandy shortly after D Day to the capitulation of Germany in May 1945. It was highly commended for the effectiveness of its service by Major General Paul R. Hawley, a graduate of the College of Medicine of the University, Chief Surgeon of the European Theater of Operations.

Valuable research applicable to the use in the War was also made by many other departments of the University, including the Applied Science

Laboratory (basic science); the Department of Basic Science in Tanning Research; the Department of Lithographic Research; the College of Engineering and Commerce; and the Departments of Mathematics and Physics in the College of Liberal Arts. American military and civilian shoe leather was made 25 per cent more durable than the best pre-Pearl Harbor sole by an oil-wax formula developed by the Department of Basic Science in Tanning Research.

IMPACT OF THE WAR UPON THE CURRICULUM

In order to arrange for Army training courses and to integrate the programs of the various colleges and schools of the University, the Board of Directors on January 5, 1943, appointed an Administrative Committee on War Training Programs. The Administrative Committee comprised Dean Pechstein of the Teachers College, Chairman; Vice-President Laurence; Professor Auburn, Dean of Administration; Professor Brand, of the College of Engineering and Commerce; and Professor Hubert, of the College of Liberal Arts. Working with them as co-ordinators were Dean Barbour of the College of Liberal Arts, Dean Gowdy of the College of Engineering and Commerce, Dean Dorst of the College of Medicine, Professor Lowrie of the College of Liberal Arts, the Comptroller Ralph W. Miller, and the Superintendent of the Building and Grounds Department, William B. Schoelwer.

The War brought drastic changes in the curriculum and teaching methods. To enable men students to complete their undergraduate courses before entering the armed forces and also to permit women to prepare themselves quickly for their professions or a program of national service the courses of study were accelerated in most of the departments of the University. Realizing that the War demanded quick training and early usefulness the College of Engineering and Commerce approved two-year certificate programs on the co-operative plan. The Department of Aeronautical Engineering and the School of Applied Arts gave a course to women at the Goodyear Corporation, Akron, Ohio, to train them for supervisory work in airplane factories. The Reserve Officers Training Corps, under the command of Colonel Sidney Guthrie, who had established the ROTC at the University after World War I, gave basic and advanced training courses.

In February 1943 the University was among 486 institutions of higher learning designated by the Army and Navy and the War Manpower Commission to receive military units. The Administrative Committee on War Training programs negotiated with the War Department for two separate units: the Army Air Force and the Army Specialized Training Program (ASTP). The AAF cadets received instruction in mathematics, physics, geography, history, English, and physical education given by lectures of the Graduate School, College of Liberal Arts, Teachers College, and College of Home Economics.

Four types of programs were set up by the Faculty for the Army Specialized Training trainees: (1) a basic pre-engineering course; (2) advanced instruction in civil, mechanical, and electrical engineering; (3) a foreign language and area course; and (4) an accelerated course in medicine. A small number of Naval students in medicine were enrolled in the University.

With the arrival of the soldier-students the University campus took on the aspects of an Army camp. The varying enrollments of soldier-students reached a maximum of 2,450 in the academic year 1943–1944; most of whom were housed, fed, and instructed on the campus. The entire accommodations of McMicken Hall, Hanna Hall, and Cunningham Hall were evacuated to provide dormitory space for the ASTP students, and eight fraternity houses were temporarily leased for Army use. Professors moved their libraries from their familiar haunts to almost anywhere; steel cots replaced the age-old classroom desks. The soldiers became the feature attraction of the annual Homecoming with the barracks opened for inspection and an exhibition in Nippert Stadium. A soldier ran as a candidate for freshman queen and won the election, conceding the trophy, however, to the coed with the most votes. The outbreak of a scarlet fever epidemic among the soldiers early in January 1944 was the cause for extending the Christmas recess a full week, with semester examinations postponed for civilians.

In February 1944 the War Department announced the ASTP program would be curtailed, and in June it ended. This was due to two factors: (1) the existence of a very large pool of young officers; and (2) attacks made in Washington upon the ASTP program as withholding young men from active service when fathers were being called.

The experience of the Faculty in teaching the army units was similar in many ways to that of those who had taught the SATC in World War I. Some of the ASTP students were very appreciative of the cordial way in which they had been welcomed at the University. Some were thrilled by the fact that they were given an opportunity to attend a university. But as soon as word was received that the ASTP would be reduced, student morale collapsed as it had done following the Armistice of World War I. The Faculty profited as a result of their experience. They learned new techniques of teaching which they found were far better in some cases than the older methods.

THE UNIVERSITY IN THE WAR

University officials tried to keep in touch both with the Army trainees and their own graduates and undergraduates who saw active service in all parts of the world. The letters these students wrote home give an idea of the participation of UC men in the War and their reactions to their varied experiences. A former UC student of the class of 1938, Colonel Paul W. Tibbets, was the pilot of the plane that dropped the first atomic bomb on the Japanese city of Hiroshima. An Air Force lieutenant, who later received the Distinguished Flying Cross, gave vivid accounts of raids over Germany which, he said, "had caused Adolph to age plenty." Some wrote of their experiences in England and France. One wrote of his visit to London: "In order to facilitate my relations with the English I carry a box of cigars with me and distribute them with sagacity. You see cigars cost four shillings (eighty cents) and upwards, so you can imagine how taxi drivers, waiters, ushers, and other public servants react to your generosity."

A medical graduate, a captain with front line troops, "wrote of the great ovations the American troops received as they passed through the small towns of France. Old men would stand at attention and salute, and everybody from the little kids up would shake hands and some of the young gals (they are really pretty here) would kiss you if you weren't on guard. In my open jeep they threw bouquets of roses and in their enthusiasm they threw fruit, and we came close to being hit with ripe tomatoes or hard apples; making it wise to keep your helmets on at all times."

Many of the engineers wrote of their work. "More than a dozen UC men were officers with the 343rd Engineer Regiment which was responsible for the famous Capua Bridge over the Volturno River in Italy. . . . The Bridge was the longest military bridge—375 feet—and was completed in twenty days. Directly responsible for the Bridge was the 343rd's First Battalion, commanded by Lieutenant Colonel Thomas E. Holt, 1927 graduate of the College of Engineering and Commerce. Major William E. Harrison, former College of Engineering and Commerce student, class of 1924, made the design. Soundings were directed by M.Sgt. Charles W. Lippart, former UC Evening College student." Another wrote in a lighter vein: "Now I am an engineer. . . . We build roads, bridges, dams, docks, and other things. We also do a lot of destroying such as blowing up roads, bridges, trees, etc. . . . I like to blow up things. I guess this is part of my destructive nature."

Among the most interesting letters were those written by former medical students. Many of these letters were published by the *Good Samaritan Hospital Staff Bulletin* and by the *Cincinnati Journal of Medicine*. Many wrote of the horrors of war and the knowledge they were acquiring in treating sick and wounded soldiers. One wrote of the battle of Iwo Jima and of how the doctors had had to work "for 36 hours without stopping and treated about 3,000 cases before we got any sleep." Another wrote from Greece and told of the terrible condition of hospitals in that area.

Others mentioned the language barriers they encountered "which ran from French to Arabic and other African dialects." Some commented on the scenery and climate of the countries in which they were located and of their homesickness and their desire to get home as quickly as possible.

There are no definite figures of the number of University men who served on the battlefronts of World War II. A large proportion were officers, for, as President Walters said, "there had been, since 1919, a total of 6,201 UC men enrolled in the Reserve Officers Training Corps at the University who were consequently trained for service as Army officers." Of the 1,400,409 doctors in service during World War II decorated in recognition of meritorious service and gallantry, 6 per cent were from the College of Medicine, according to a report of General George Marshall. These figures were exclusive of the Air Medal and the Purple Heart.

Four UC men held the rank of general in World War II. Two were graduates of the College of Medicine: Major General Paul R. Hawley, class of 1914, who was Surgeon General of the European Theater of Operations; and Brigadier General Leon A. Fox, class of 1912, who was Director of the United States Typhus Commission. The other two were graduates of the College of Engineering and Commerce: Brigadier General Carroll A. Powell, class of 1917, who was with the Signal Corps; and Brigadier General Edward Barber, class of 1924, who was with the Coast Artillery. Rear Admiral Paul Stewart, Surgeon General of the United States Coast Guard, was also a graduate of the College of Medicine.

The only list of casualties of University men in World War II is that published in the UC *News Record* in its V-E Day edition. It reported more than 160 students and Faculty as casualties since D Day eleven months earlier. The lists showed 59 dead, 23 missing, 68 wounded, and 13 prisoners-of-war.

In his address at the V-E Day Convocation, May 8, 1945, Professor William S. Clark, II, of the English Department, quoted the words of Chaplain Gittelsohn at the dedication of the Marine Cemetery on Iwo Jima: "Here died officers and men, Negroes and whites, rich and poor men. . . . Here are Protestants, Catholics, and Jews. . . . Here no man prefers another because of his faith or despises him because of his color."

IMPACT OF THE WAR ON CAMPUS LIFE

Campus life was severely affected by the War. Although Theta Chi fraternity was organized in 1942, many of the social fraternities were forced to suspend operations during the War, as their active members and many of their alumni were called into military service. Active fraternity chapters on the campus sank from sixteen in 1942 to six in the fall of 1943. Eight of the sixteen fraternities in 1942 rented their houses to the University for use as barracks for the Army soldier-students. The Junior Prom was suspended and formal parties were abandoned. For the first time in the history of the University, women were elected both editors and business managers of the *News Record*.

With the entrance of the United States into the War it became extremely difficult to carry on intercollegiate sports. The Varsity football team carried out its regular schedule in 1941 and 1942 and in the fall of 1942 achieved what was probably the best record in the athletic history of the University. However, the Board of Directors decided to omit intercollegiate football in the fall of 1943, inasmuch as all available athletic facilities and staff were required for the military drill and athletic programs of the Army soldier-students, who were not permitted by the War Department to play on intercollegiate teams. The decision to abandon intercollegiate football was followed by a reduction in the student activity fee from $10.00 to $7.50. Basketball and fencing were the only intercollegiate sports carried on in 1943–1944. In 1944–1945 it was possible to foster intercollegiate competition in basketball, baseball, track, tennis, and golf. The tennis and golf teams went through the season undefeated.

OTHER EVENTS DURING WORLD WAR II

Two deaths occurred during World War II that were a serious loss to the University and to the City of Cincinnati. On June 25, 1942, Herbert Greer French died. He had been a member of the Board of Directors for nearly twenty years. He was a prominent industrialist and an outstanding leader in the cultivation of the fine arts in the City. While interested in all phases of the University's work he was particularly a champion of the humanities as represented by the College of Liberal Arts and the Graduate School of Arts and Sciences. His zeal in behalf of the College of Medicine was likewise noteworthy. His love for his Alma Mater found expression in a will that left to the University half of his residuary estate without any restrictions as to use or purpose. Renton K. Brodie was appointed to fill the unexpired term of Mr. French on the Board. On May 11, 1943, Dr. Mont R. Reid, professor of surgery in the College of Medicine, died. He had a national reputation as a surgeon and had made many outstanding contributions in the surgery of the vascular system. His deep interest in his students, along with his high professional standards, made him a singularly valuable member of the Medical Faculty.

A number of administrative changes were made during the War. On the retirement on August 31, 1943, of Daniel Laurence, Vice-President and Business Manager, after forty years of loyal and devoted service to the University, a new office of Dean of Administration was created. The Board elected Dean Auburn of the Evening College to the new office and later added the title of Vice-President. Acting Dean Frank R. Neuffer was appointed Dean of the Evening College. In November 1944, Laura E. Rosnagle was elected Dean of the College of Nursing and Health upon the resignation of Miss Helen G. Schwarz.

One of the notable early achievements of Vice-President Auburn was his conduct of the first successful Emergency Fund Campaign of 1944. This was a plan proposed by Mr. Rowe and Mrs. Earley in a different form, to obtain contributions from local industrial corporations to meet a prospective deficit. To the great delight of President Walters and Vice-President Auburn, Mr. Fred Geier of the Cincinnati Milling Machine Company agreed to serve as Chairman of a Sponsoring Committee. Then to their amazement he told them that the Cincinnati Milling Machine Company would contribute $100,000 to the campaign, one-fourth of the prospective operational deficit. This led other industrial leaders to agree to serve on the Sponsoring Committee, and many of them also made contributions. The First Emergency Campaign produced $406,000, which enabled the University to retain its Faculty and staff during that difficult year when enrollment was limited to women and a relatively few men deferred from military service after the Army soldier-students left the campus.

The whole University family did their best in the war effort. But there is no mistaking the fact that the War seriously interrupted and slowed down the life of learning on the UC campus.

20 The GIs Return, Enrollment Soars

The college year 1945–1946 marked the beginning of a new era in American higher education. Starting moderately in the autumn following the August 1945 cessation of hostilities, the full enrollment in colleges and universities throughout the nation soared to over two million students by the fall of 1946. In line with the national trend the enrollment in the University totaled in September 1946, more than 8,000 day students and more than 8,000 in the Evening College.

The increased enrollment was made possible by passage of the Servicemen's Readjustment Act of 1944, which provided that veterans of World War II might take school, college, or university courses for one year and additional instruction in proportion to their term of service. The Federal government paid tuition charges up to $500 annually and subsistence allowances of $65 a month for single veterans and $90 a month for married veterans. Financial aid was also given for part-time study.

The first year after the War was a difficult and arduous one for the colleges and universities, but it was a thrilling one in the history of the University of Cincinnati. The hundreds of students and scores of Faculty members who came back to the campus were welcomed by the Faculty and non-veteran students, not omitting the coeds. The Faculty were well pleased with the veterans. They were mature, earnest, and capable students. Their war experiences had broadened their horizons. They knew more about the geography and civilizations of distant lands; they were more interested in history and current affairs; they were more alert and industrious. The Deans of the various Colleges of the University testified that the veterans had fewer scholastic failures and higher grades than non-veteran students.

To take care of the increased number of students the University Building Committee arranged with the Federal Works Agency for the shipment from Fort Thomas, Kentucky, and the re-erection on the campus of five two-story frame barrack buildings. The entire cost of dismantling the buildings, trucking them to the campus and their re-erection, amounted to $160,000. All this was borne by the Federal Works Agency under a law passed by the Seventy-ninth Congress which provided for temporary educational facilities for the student-veterans. Some of the married veterans settled in a "Vetsville" group of government buildings in a corner of the campus.

On February 12, 1945, the Board appointed Major Spencer Shank as Director of the Veterans Education Division of the University. Major Shank had been Assistant Dean of the Teachers College before he entered the armed forces. During the War he was Chief of the Education Branch of the Army for the entire European Theater of Operations. He did an excellent job of organizing and administering the entire educational program for ex-servicemen and women at the University. He also had charge of the Guidance Center for counseling veterans which was established by the Veterans Administration in the spring of 1945. Major Shank organized refresher courses and special programs for the veterans.

The veteran enrollment at the University continued to grow until the peak total enrollment of full-time and part-time veterans of 8,129 was reached in 1947. At the Commencement exercises in June 1949, more than 1,200 of the 1,800 receiving degrees and certificates were veterans.

THE KOREAN WAR AND COMMUNISM

Meanwhile the American public gradually awakened to the fact that World War II, like the former War, had not brought about what they had hoped for—peace and security. Allied efforts to negotiate a peace treaty with Germany and Austria were blocked by Russia. The tension between the Soviet Union and the free world increased; and it became still greater in 1949, when the Soviet Union announced it had developed an atomic bomb. As General Omar Bradley commented: "The world has achieved brilliance without wisdom, power without conscience. Ours is a world of nuclear giants and ethical infants. We know more about war than we do about peace, more about killing than about living."

A new and more menacing phase of the cold war was ushered in on June 25, 1950, when the North Korean Army, Russian-trained and equipped, crossed the 38th parallel in Korea and attacked South Korea. The Council of the United Nations, with the Soviet Union absent, unanimously branded North Korea the aggressor and called upon all member nations "to render every assistance" to the United Nations in restoring peace. Two days after the invasion, President Harry S Truman, by virtue of his constitutional authority as Commander-in-Chief, ordered the American air and naval forces to aid South Korea; and three days later he ordered American ground forces to render assistance. For reasons based on international law, President Truman called the participation of the United States in the conflict "a police action, not a war." Thus began the Korean War which lasted for three years and thirty days and resulted in 140,000 American casualties.

The University, like other American universities, was markedly influenced by the hot war in Korea and the cold war elsewhere. Registration at first declined with the passing out of the veteran war crest and later with the further calling up of men to active service for the conflict in Korea. President Truman by executive order subsequently amended the Selective Service Regulations to provide draft deferment for college students of superior scholastic standing or for those who made a high score in a national aptitude test. However, as the Selective Service Director was vague about how many would be deferred, it was almost impossible for the University administration to estimate definitely the size of entering classes in the University. Then with the passage of Public Law 550, which provided that Korean War veterans were entitled to thirty-six months of educational benefits, enrollment began to increase. When as a consequence of the military reverses in Korea President Truman proclaimed the existence of a national emergency, the University promptly made available to the Federal government its scientific, technological, and educational facilities; and President Walters appointed a Special University Committee on Research with authority to proceed in respect to research contributions that might be made to the government by University scientists.

The University also felt the repercussions of the fear of communism which swept over the nation. On February 12, 1950, an article appeared in the Sunday edition of the *Enquirer*, written by James Ratliff, relating to Cincinnatians alleged to be members of the Communist Party. The author claimed that "among the listed members of the Communist Party" were a "professor of the University of Cincinnati" and "several other professors" who were "enthusiastic fellow travelers."

At the suggestion of the Board, President Walters wrote to Mr. Ratliff requesting the names of Faculty members accused of being members of the Communist Party. A few days later Mr. Ratliff telephoned President Walters apologizing "for any embarrassment his article had caused." He said his purpose in writing the article was "1) to serve notice on members of the Communist Party in Cincinnati that they were known; and 2) to arouse public interest in support of legislative action to require oaths for public employees." Mr. Ratliff said that he could give no names as his information was "confidential." However, he assured President Walters that the University professor who held membership in the Communist Party was "not using his position to disseminate propaganda among students or Faculty," that he was "very hush-hush."

The next day President Walters received a communication from the

Parent-Teacher Association of the Annunciation School very critical of the University and its alleged Communist professors. At the suggestion of the Board, President Walters replied. He explained patiently that the University administration shared their "detestation of Communism" and added, though unnecessarily, that "the University never has knowingly employed a party member." But since Mr. Ratliff would supply no names, the University could take "no steps," as it had no name upon which to proceed.

In commenting upon President Walters' answer, the *Post* editorially said: "In this connection, we should not forget that independence of mind—which is not communism—is essential to the health of a university in a free community. A Faculty harassed and hounded if it dares stray an inch from the sharp paths of orthodoxy is not likely to be a Faculty zealous in the pursuit of learning. Academic freedom must be a reality, not a fiction, if truth is to be sought and served."

Shortly thereafter President Walters learned the name of the alleged Communist professor. He was a member of the Faculty of the College of Medicine on the Children's Hospital Staff. Later, Mr. Ratliff at a Senate Committee hearing in Washington identified him as Dr. Samuel Rappaport, who was then in Switzerland attending a scientific meeting. Shortly thereafter Dr. Rappaport resigned and thus relieved the Hospital and the University from great embarrassment.

EXPANSION OF THE UNIVERSITY

Two new Colleges—the Summer School and the College of Pharmacy— were created in the decade after World War II. In 1924 the Board had organized a Summer Session with a director in charge. Under the competent direction of Dean Pechstein and Dr. Gordon Hendrickson, the summer program grew to such large proportions that the Board in 1947 established the Summer School as a separate component of the University. Dr. Spencer Shank was appointed the Dean.

In March 1945 the Board of Trustees of the Cincinnati College of Pharmacy proposed to the University that it take over all the assets of that College and continue to operate the College as a division of the University. A committee of the Academic Deans, consisting of Deans Barbour, Dorst, and Auburn held several conferences with representatives of the College of Pharmacy and finally recommended: (1) that the University and the College of Pharmacy effect an affiliation; (2) that a study of the feasibility of providing two years of the pharmacy curriculum at the University with the last two years at the College of Pharmacy. It was expected that this study would reveal if it were financially desirable for the University and the Pharmacy College to enter into such an agreement. The Board of Trustees of the College of Pharmacy were informed that complete integration of the College with the University would be possible only "if the trustees had a sufficiently large endowment, the earnings of which, added to the normal income of the College, would support the College if it were operated as a College of the University."

Again in 1949 the Committee of Academic Deans rejected a proposal of the College of Pharmacy for complete integration with the University until the College raised an endowment fund—one that would enable the University to support the College in accordance with University standards and the professional standards of pharmaceutical education. The College of Pharmacy was notified that it must have an endowment fund of at least $850,000, but this was later reduced to $625,000. Happily, local pharmaceutical companies and citizens of Cincinnati responded to a solicitation of the College of Pharmacy; and the endowment fund stipulated by the University was attained.

In September 1954 the 103-year-old College of Pharmacy, the oldest institution of its kind west of the Alleghenies, became the thirteenth integral unit of the University; and on November 26 the new home of the College on the University campus, located in a wing of the Biological Building, was formally dedicated. Professor Joseph H. Kowalewski, of the Cincinnati College of Pharmacy, was appointed Dean of the College.

FINANCIAL MEASURES; ENLARGING THE CAMPUS

The progress of the University during these years was made possible by the increase in the tax revenue and by the untiring efforts of the Board to enlarge the campus. The sudden cessation of hostilities, the rapid demobilization of the armed forces, and the consequent increase in student enrollment after the War created serious repercussions in the University's financial and business administration. The University was fortunate in having Dr. Auburn, Vice-President and Dean of Administration, in charge of the financial and administrative affairs of the institution during the postwar period.

The financial dilemma of the University was due to a number of factors. Although the income from tuition and fees reached new high records, the expenses of operation also soared not only because of higher costs but also because the teaching and service staff had to be augmented greatly to instruct the larger student body. The financial problem was aggravated, because, whereas the principal source of income in tuition and fees increased markedly, it accounted only for one-half the educational costs. Meanwhile two other sources of income, in City taxes and endowments, remained practically static. In an effort to increase the University's income, the Board adopted a number of recommendations suggested by President Walters and Vice-President Auburn.

Faced with the prospect of a deficit in 1945–1946 of approximately

$200,000, the Board in June 1945 approved a second fund-raising campaign among industrial and business concerns in Greater Cincinnati. The campaign, under the direction of George D. Crabbs, resulted in 197 industrial firms contributing more than $205,000 to the fund.

Other measures were adopted that increased the tax revenue received by the University. In 1913 the Ohio Legislature had fixed at .55 of a mill the amount which city councils might levy for the support of the municipal universities. But while the city taxes supplied 60 per cent of the University's operating cost in 1913, the tax income for 1945 accounted for only 12 per cent of the operating budget. The first remedial step was taken when the University joined its sister municipalities in sponsoring a bill in the State Legislature to amend Section 4003-11 of the Ohio Municipal Code. This was to increase the amount which the City Council might levy from .55 of a mill to one mill. Governor Frank J. Lausche aided materially in securing the passage of the bill in June 1946. However, this was only enabling legislation so far as Cincinnati was concerned. Before the Cincinnati Council could increase the tax to one mill the city charter had to be amended by a vote of the people.

Meanwhile the Board endeavored to enlarge the campus in order that the University might expand its facilities. In 1945 the Board requested the Park Commissioners to turn over to the University nineteen acres of ground in Burnet Woods. On this space the Board said they wanted to erect a women's dormitory and an armory and field house, the funds for which had been voted by the citizens of Cincinnati in a $2 million bond issue in November 1944.

This was the third time the University had requested additional acreage in Burnet Woods for the expansion of the institution. It will be recalled that the City Council in 1889 had given the University forty-three acres of land in Burnet Woods to enable it to move from the old Mc-Micken homestead. In 1914 the City Council had voted to the University the use of an additional thirteen acres of ground in Burnet Woods. The Board of Park Commissioners at that time had agreed that this extension was "necessary and proper." In 1939 the University attempted to secure a part of Burnet Woods for the location of a parking lot. This second request was rejected, as many residents of the Clifton-Fairview Heights area had objected, and the matter was dropped. In the third request in 1945 for more land in Burnet Woods the Board stressed four points: "First, the University must expand its physical plant to maintain its position as an educational institution; second, the women's dormitory and the armory and field house were essential, and the Burnet Woods area had been earmarked for these sites; third, additional grounds were needed as the present campus was congested; and fourth, the natural expansion of the campus was to the north."

It was natural that the Park Board was reluctant in acquiescing to this proposal. The Park Board was interested in increasing and developing, not decreasing, the City's park area. As a general principle, Cincinnati needed more land in parks, not less.

The University request produced a heated discussion at a meeting of the Park Board and a University committee. One of the Park Commissioners likened the University's request for additional ground to a "gradual encroachment." He pointed out that this was the third time the University had asked for more land. Mr. Dinsmore, Chairman of the University Committee, emphasized that the early planners of the University had not foreseen the day when the University would be one of the nation's leading educational institutions. He gave repeated assurance that the application for ground would take care of the expansion of the University for the next twenty years.

The Park Board, however, rejected the University's plea. The Board held that the use of any part of the remaining acreage of Burnet Woods for other than park purposes could not be justified. The alumni of the University filed a protest on the Burnet Woods decision, and the Board of Directors and the alumni called upon the Park Commissioners to reconsider their refusal. The Park Board finally agreed to give the University Directors another meeting "if they could present anything new" to offer in the Burnet Woods land dispute. Here the matter rested temporarily.

INCREASED TAX REVENUE; THE BURNET WOODS DISPUTE REVIVED

At the November 1947 election, the citizens of Cincinnati by a majority vote of 60 per cent approved an amendment to the city charter increasing the University tax millage from .55 to one mill. This produced an increase in tax revenue for the University from $590,000, or 12 per cent of the 1946–1947 budget, to an estimated $1,206,000 for the 1949–1950 budget, or about 20 per cent of the annual budget.

This increase in city taxes was the most significant financial development at the University in several decades. Until the electorate placed this stamp of approval on the University's service to the community and the nation, the University's tax income had been frozen at 55 per cent of a mill for thirty-four years. The response of the citizens to the University's needs was a source of profound encouragement.

A second increase in tax revenue was effected in 1947 when the administration sponsored legislation in the State Legislature whereby the City Council was required to appropriate for University purposes up to 9 per cent of the local government fund if the University Board so requested. The local government fund consisted of a portion of the sales tax and other taxes which the State returned to the cities by vote of the General Assembly each biennium.

The Board also, at the recommendation of President Walters and Vice-President Auburn, approved a plan suggested by the Alumni Association which permitted an annual fund-raising campaign among alumni and friends of the University. The fund campaign of 1947 was directed by Kelly Y. Siddall and produced over $50,000 in contributions from 2,200 alumni, representing approximately 12 per cent of the University's graduates.

Meanwhile the University took steps to improve the financial condition of its employees. In 1945 the Board voted a cost-of-living increment to the Faculty and staff of $10.00 per month. Three years later salary raises on graduated scales were made possible by the increase in the tax levy. In the same year (1948) the Board adopted a rule making it mandatory for all newly appointed Faculty members to apply for membership in either the City Retirement System or the Teachers Insurance and Annuity (TIAA). It had been compulsory for non-academic personnel to join the City Retirement System. The new rule insured that a larger percentage of the Faculty would provide for their financial security upon retirement.

Also in 1948, through the generosity of a benefactor, the University was given an opportunity of making a new approach to the Burnet Woods project. Mr. Albert P. Strietman, a former University director, offered to give the University eleven and one-half acres of land that he owned adjacent to the Alms Park. The gift was given without restrictions, and Mr. Strietman told President Walters he had in mind the possibility that "the University Board might thereby have a bargaining basis to obtain in exchange acreage in Burnet Woods Park for University buildings."

ACQUISITION OF LAND IN BURNET WOODS PARK

In 1949 the Board of Directors of the University proposed to the Park Commissioners the transfer of seven and one-half acres of land north of Alms Park, a part of the eleven and one-half acres given to the University by Mr. Albert P. Strietman, in exchange for twenty-two acres of the Burnet Woods Park. The twenty-two acres in Burnet Woods the University desired for further expansion was the same general tract it had requested in the spring of 1945. At that time, however, the University had requested approximately nineteen acres. The plan in 1945 was that the University would construct a women's dormitory and a field house there (p. 315). Since that time a men's dormitory had been transferred into living quarters for women and additional land had been purchased east of the campus as a possible location for a field house.

The majority of the Park Board was favorable to the proposal, as it seemed beneficial to the park system. The projected exchange of tracts of land between the Park Board and the University was unmistakably in the public interest. The University could not make effective use of the tract adjoining Alms Park while it would be a real addition to the facilities of the Park Board. The University now wanted to use the site for a building of the College of Applied Arts.

Then it was discovered that an old law provided that exchanges of land or property between divisions of a municipality had to balance the appraised value and any difference had to be made up in money. The Solicitor's office valued the Burnet Woods tract at $110,000. The Alms Park tract was valued at $65,655. The University accordingly agreed to pay $34,345 to the City for the tract of land in Burnet Woods.

After some delay the Park Commissioners agreed to the transfer of eighteen acres of Burnet Woods property to the University for $48,937 and seven and one-half acres of land adjacent to Alms Park. In the meantime the City Planning Commission had sharply criticized the Park Board decision.

The City Council now faced the difficult problem whether or not it would permit the Park Board to transfer the land in Burnet Woods to the University on these terms. This was not a dispute in which all the merits lay on one side. The University argued that the land was needed to meet the growing educational needs of the community.

In the meantime a vigorous opposition had developed. Its spokesmen retorted that the transfer would take one-fifth of the land of the leading park in a growing part of the City already deficient in recreational areas. The twenty-two acres of Burnet Woods, the opponents argued, included many beautiful old trees and a wild flower preserve. Asserting that they too were eager for the University to expand, they asked why it did not go eastward and northeastward of the campus where the City Council had already given land worth $330,000. As for a "last time" pledge, the opposition pointed out the same assurance had been given by the University whenever it wanted a part of Burnet Woods.

In rebuttal the University stated that the location and topography of the land to the east of the present campus was unsuitable for a much-needed Applied Arts building. In reply to this the opponents said that this was a matter of convenience, not necessity, and that the University building plans could and should be altered "to save Burnet Woods."

The City Council decided to turn the matter over to the City Planning Commission for study and to hold public hearings on the matter. After considerable delay, on January 6, 1950, the public hearing before the City Council began on the Burnet Woods proposal. The University had formed an alumni-faculty-student organization under the chairmanship of Ralph C. Bursiek and a group of distinguished Cincinnatians as a Committee for University Development which included former Judge John C. Dempsey; Walter A. Draper, Chairman of the Board of Directors of the Cincinnati Street Railway Company; Lester Jaffe, a former Board member; Mrs. Claude M. Lotspeich, founder of the Lotspeich School; Neil H. McElroy, President of Proctor and Gamble; and George A. Philips, Principal of the Harriet Beecher Stowe School. Judge Shohl was in charge of the University advocates at the hearing. Gilbert Bettman and Judge Dixon were the leaders of the opposition.

In the course of the discussion one of the opponents made the erroneous and slanderous assertion that "it was being said that the University should have all of Burnet Woods because only Negroes from the west side of the City used it." President Walters quickly rose and denied this. Quite properly, Mayor Albert D. Cash requested President Walters to postpone his comment. When the speaker had finished, Gilbert Bettman, chairman of the opposition, apologized before the audience, expressing regret for the speaker's misstatement. Judge Shohl, who was sitting next to President Walters, whispered to him, "You may have been out of order but that was a good stroke."

The City Planning Commission discussed the merits of the exchange of property at length, and after prolonged discussion, by a vote of 4 to 3 reported in favor of the transfer. This report was submitted to the City Council. But the land deal encountered a new delay because the Mayor requested time to study the City's capital improvements. By a vote of 2 to 0, the Mayor not voting, the City Council Committee on Planning and Boundaries recommended the passage of an ordinance authorizing the Burnet Woods-Alms Park land transfer. But action on the passage of the ordinance was delayed again by Councilman Edward N. Waldvogel, who said he wanted to visit the area in Burnet Woods the next Sunday to see for himself how extensively the land in question was used.

Finally on February 15, 1950, the long-drawn-out controversy over the proposed use of Burnet Woods for University expansion was settled when the City Council by a vote of 6 to 3 approved the transfer of eighteen acres of the Park from the Park Board to the University in exchange for seven acres of land adjacent to Alms Park, plus a cash settlement of $46,993. Thus was consummated an important milestone in the development of the University. The Board of Directors at its next meeting extended a hearty vote of "appreciation to the President and Vice-President for their magnificent work in the Burnet Woods cause." In his diary Dr. Walters recorded: "Norman Auburn's contribution to the University's victory was great—only I know how great."

DEDICATION OF NEW BUILDINGS

The same year (1950) in which the Burnet Woods land dispute was settled, a new McMicken-Hanna-Cunningham Hall was erected on the site of the original building. Old McMicken was a beloved University landmark. But, while it suited and represented the University of other days, it was outmoded and inadequate for the needs of the growing and developing institution.

The new McMicken was an attractive brick structure in the Georgian style of architecture similar to that of the Student Union Building, with a Christopher Wren spire, simple and impressive from afar, suggestive of the function of a great university which is the search for wisdom and for truth. It contained 650,000 bricks of Old McMicken; and as a reminder of old days, the traditional lions, Mick and Mack continued to guard the entrance. The building was constructed from funds supplied by the citizens of Cincinnati in a $2 million bond issue approved by them in 1944.

The dedication ceremonies for the new McMicken-Hanna-Cunningham Hall were held on the afternoon of April 28, 1950, on the terrace in front of the building. Vice-President Auburn presided. Mayor Albert D. Cash extended the City's greeting. Mr. Frank F. Dinsmore, Chairman of the Board of Directors, gave the dedicatory address. Mrs. Daniel E. Earley, Acting Chairman, Board Committee on Buildings and Grounds, presented the completed structure "to the entire University family, students, Faculty, alumni, and friends." Mr. William R. Nester, President of the Student Council, responded for the students. In behalf of the University, President Walters accepted the building. Members of the Faculty presented a symposium discussion of *Higher Education and Citizenship at Mid-Century*. An intra-squad football game was played in Nippert Stadium, witnessed by 12,000 spectators.

Two years later, on October 17, 1952, the Alms Memorial Building of the College of Applied Arts was erected on a commanding knoll in Burnet Woods by the trustees of the Alms Estate in memory of the late Frederick H. and Eleanora C. U. Alms through a bequest of $200,000 by Mrs. Alms. The following year, on May 12, 1953, the Herbert Greer French Residence Hall for men was dedicated. This new $1,130,000 building accommodating 408 students was financed by revenue bonds to be retired from room rentals. It was named in memory of Herbert Greer French, a former member of the Board of Directors, who in his will left half of his residuary estate to the University. Two unique features of French Hall were the English Garden and a Browsing Library. The Garden was made possible by a gift from Ralph F. and Bessie E. Rogan as a memorial to Mr. French. The Browsing Library, also a memorial to Mr. French, was the gift of Richard R. Deupree.

In the same year (1953) the Dr. Reed A. Shank Pavilion of the Nippert Stadium and the Armory-Field House were dedicated, both being completed the next year. Dr. Shank was a distinguished surgeon, a graduate of the Medical College, a tireless and effective supporter of everything at the University, especially football, who died of a heart attack while watching the 1953 Thanksgiving football game between the University and Miami. Also in 1953 the Women's Building was renamed Beecher Hall after Harriet Beecher Stowe, author of *Uncle Tom's Cabin*, and a gate was erected at the main entrance to the University.

ADMINISTRATIVE CHANGES

There were important changes of administrative personnel after the War. Illness caused the resignation of Dr. Rodney P. Robinson as Dean of the Graduate School; from 1945 to 1947, Professor Claude M. Lotspeich served as Acting Dean. In the spring of 1947, Professor Hoke Smith Greene was appointed Dean of the Graduate School and temporarily remained as head of the Liberal Arts Department of Chemistry. Dr. Greene received his undergraduate degree from Mercer University, Georgia, and his Master of Science and Doctor of Philosophy degrees from the University of Cincinnati. In 1931 he was an exchange student in Germany and then became supervisor of development and production with the Du Pont Company before he returned in 1934 to the University.

Illness also necessitated the resignation in 1946 of Dr. Robert C. Gowdy as Dean of the College of Engineering and Commerce and Director of the School of Applied Arts. In that year there was a reorganization of this College and its allied School of Applied Arts. The College of Engineering and Commerce became the College of Engineering with Professor C. Albert Joerger as Dean. The former Department of Co-ordination of the College of Engineering and Commerce became the University Department of Co-ordination and Placement with Professor H. Calvert Messinger as Director. A College of Business Administration was created with Professor Francis H. Bird as Dean, and the School of Applied Arts became the College of Applied Arts with Professor Ernest Pickering as Dean. Also in 1946, Dean Merton Ferson retired as Dean of the College of Law, having served with distinction as Dean since 1926. He was succeeded by Professor Frank S. Rowley as Dean.

The following year (1947) Dr. Louis A. Pechstein, who had served as Dean of the Teachers College since 1922, resigned upon the advice of his physician. Appointed to succeed him as Dean was Professor Carter V. Good, who had been Acting Dean for several years. Since 1945, Robert W. Bishop had been serving as Acting Dean of Men upon the resignation of Arthur S. Postle. In 1947, Dr. Bishop was appointed Dean of Men. In 1948, Katherine Dabney Ingle, who had been an excellent administrator, resigned as Dean of Women; she was succeeded by Dr. Lillian Johnson, who had been Assistant Dean. Upon the retirement of Dr. Edward A. Henry in 1951 the Board appointed to succeed him as University Librarian, Professor Wyman W. Parker of Kenyon College.

In the same year (1951) Dr. Norman P. Auburn resigned to accept the Presidency of the University of Akron. He had demonstrated, as the Board said, "an admirable capacity for academic administration, a keen understanding of civic values, and a splendid sense of human relationships." His departure was a real loss to the institution. He was succeeded as Dean of Administration by Ralph C. Bursiek. In 1955, Dean Bursiek was elected Vice-President in addition to his title as Dean of Administration. Under his direction the business affairs of the University were managed efficiently and economically.

Dean Bursiek was a UC graduate, having received his Commercial Engineering degree from the College of Engineering and Commerce and his Master of Arts degree from the Graduate School. He had been a Faculty member of the College of Business Administration. In his student days he had played for three years on the football team and the track team, winning five letters in the two sports. For a newly created position of Assistant Dean of Administration the Board appointed Frank Purdy, a University graduate who had served for several years as Secretary of the University Alumni Association.

The following year (1952) Frank F. Dinsmore retired. He had served as a director for thirty years—longer than any other director in the University's history—and for twelve years as Chairman of the Board. The University had greatly benefited from his "keen discernment and sound judgment," and he had proved himself a "valiant advocate of the true University spirit." Renton K. Brodie, Administrative Vice-President of the Proctor and Gamble Company, was elected Chairman of the Board. Mr. Brodie was a modest, retiring man, and an excellent head of an institution of higher learning because of his own early teaching experience in chemistry, his broad intellectual interests, and his business sagacity.

In the same year Miss Elizabeth Dyer, who had both initiated the College of Home Economics (earlier, the School of Household Administration) and had directed it for twenty-eight years with constant regard for educational and professional standards, resigned. She was succeeded as Dean by Professor Elizabeth D. Roseberry of Purdue University. On the death of Dean Rowley, Professor Roscoe L. Barrows was designated Acting Dean and in 1953 was named Dean of the College of Law.

PRESIDENT WALTERS' MISSION TO JAPAN

At the invitation of the United States Army, Dr. Walters in 1949 visited Japan for three months on an educational mission. He went as an expert in the field of University administration to aid in developing a long-range program of higher education for Japanese college presidents and administrators. Dr. Walters conducted conferences and seminars and gave lectures and addresses before Japanese educators in Tokyo, Kyoto, Osaka,

Hiroshima, Kobe, and Yokohama. He had a conference with General Douglas MacArthur and an interview with Emperor Hirohito. It was a pleasant experience, and an honor for him and for the University.

THE CURRICULUM

After the War, Faculty committees were appointed in each of the component Colleges of the University to study their respective curricula with a view to revising the requirements for degrees and the content of courses. By 1948 all the Colleges had abandoned the accelerated programs.

During the postwar decade the Graduate School of Arts and Sciences introduced new programs of studies leading to the degrees of Doctor of Philosophy in Clinical Psychology and Doctor of Industrial Medicine; evening programs of graduate studies leading to the degree of Master of Science in certain of the physical sciences were instituted. The degree of Doctor of Science was established to meet certain professional needs. In order to meet the needs of high school teachers in the social studies, the Graduate School, in co-operation with the Teachers College, developed a program leading to the degree of Master of Science in Social Studies.

Upon Faculty recommendation in 1953 the name of the McMicken College of Liberal Arts was changed to the McMicken College of Arts and Sciences. The new title was in accord with the recognized practice in other universities. The curricular requirements in the McMicken College of Arts and Sciences were thoroughly revised so that students were permitted to choose programs leading either to a Bachelor of Arts or a Bachelor of Science degree. Both programs provided "studies for breadth in four groups of studies" while retaining "the field of concentration principle."

A noteworthy innovation in the curriculum of the College came as a result of a munificent bequest. In 1946, Miss George Elliston of the *Times-Star* staff died. She bequeathed the residue of her estate, estimated at $250,000, to "the cause of poetry" through the University. A trust fund was created "to establish and maintain . . . a chair or professorship of poetry to promote the study and composition of poetry in such a manner and by such methods as the Board of Directors of the University deem advisable and effective." The dream of the benefactress was realized in 1951 when Dr. Robert P. Tristram Coffin, the New England poet, joined the English Department as visiting professor and as the first holder of the George Elliston Chair of Poetry. Subsequent occupants of this professorship have been John Berryman, Robert Lowell, Stephen Spender, Robert Frost, Peter Viereck, John Betjeman, Randall Jarrell, David Daiches, Richard Eberhart, and John Press. A seminar relating to the United States

324

Foreign Service, under the direction of Professor Harold Vinacke, was established through a gift by Dr. and Mrs. Julian E. Benjamin.

In the College of Engineering the course in general engineering was discontinued, and a course in geological engineering was offered. A Department of Engineering Drawing was organized, and Professor A. H. Knebel was appointed as head. The degree of Metallurgical Engineering was again authorized. In June 1949 two women were graduated in Electrical Engineering, the first time a woman had received an engineering degree. Computer methods and nuclear engineering were also beginning to be studied.

Various changes were made in the content and length of the course in the College of Applied Arts. Outstanding among these was the decision that, since most architectural schools had five-year full-time curricula, the co-operative course in architecture was lengthened to six years. In 1954 the Albert P. Strietman Professorship of Art was established. The first holder of this chair was Professor Jesse L. Paul. On her retirement the following year Professor Reginald Grooms was appointed her successor.

Among the significant advances of the Evening College was the establishment of two degree programs—the Bachelor of Philosophy and the Bachelor of Industrial Management. A second major advance was made in 1949 when the Evening College, in co-operation with WKRC-TV, offered its first television course under the title "UC in the Home" on Sunday afternoons.

Great interest was aroused in the fall of 1950 when for the first time a semester course in Advanced Management for Executives was offered by the College of Business Administration. The course, under the direction of Herbert Koch, was given at the request and with the co-operation of business leaders in the Cincinnati area. The advanced students were young executives of established standing in local business enterprises. The next year the College organized an international project, the British Industrial Management Program, sponsored by the National Management Council and the Economic Co-operation Administration. Seventeen young executives of England, Scotland, and Wales were given training; and this was repeated for a similar group in 1952–1953. Their programs included visits to numerous plants in the Cincinnati area and other parts of the country. In the fall of 1951 the College offered for the first time a two-year certificate program for women on the co-operative basis which was substantially the same as the first two years of the regular five-year co-operative program.

After the end of the War the Faculty of the College of Law re-examined the curriculum and teaching methods for the purpose "of intensifying the training in the older case-law skills and adding training in such newer skills as legal history, drafting, counseling, and law administration."

Under a fund established by Judge Robert S. Marx of the Cincinnati Bar the College was able to bring to the University "notable authorities in the field of law and of political science." The Marx Seminars were conducted each year with notable success.

As a result of a two-year study by the Faculty, the College of Medicine effected in 1951 comprehensive changes in the curriculum which appreciably altered the pattern of the last two years of undergraduate instruction. The College of Nursing and Health revised its curriculum and integrated public health nursing into it. The Teachers College improved its curriculum programs and instructional procedures. The College of Home Economics revised its program to educate women for the home and family and also to prepare them for professional service. Courses in bacteriology, chemistry, and speech were introduced.

In the spring of 1951 the first volume of the monumental *Troy* series, written by Professor Carl W. Blegen and his associates in the Classics Department, was published. These were exhaustive and scholarly reports of the University of Cincinnati Excavations in the Troad.

That year also, Professor Gustav Eckstein of the College of Medicine published his book *Every Day Miracle* which was translated in Germany and Japan. Dr. Eckstein had already acquired an international and national reputation as a result of his publication of the definitive biography of Hideyo Noguchi and other works.

In the same year the College of Medicine conferred the honorary degree of Doctor of Laws upon Dr. Martin H. Fischer, a distinguished colloid and physiological chemist, who had been for forty years Eichberg Professor of Physiology in the University. Not only was Dr. Fischer a distinguished physiologist, but he was also an artist, a man of letters, and for generations of students extending back almost to the turn of the century, their most inspiring teacher.

ATHLETICS

During the War football was suspended, but in the spring of 1945 the Board of Directors reactivated intercollegiate teams. Ray Nolting, Varsity halfback in 1934 and 1935 and later a star pro halfback with the Chicago Bears for ten years, was appointed coach. By 1947 the University was once more offering collegiate competition in football, basketball, baseball, track, cross-country, tennis, swimming, golf, fencing, and rifle.

The University football team was highly successful in the 1946 season. Nolting was named "Coach of the Week" following his team's victory over the University of Indiana, which was considered one of the strongest teams in the country. The same year the Varsity team went on to win eight out of ten games, including a triumph over Michigan State.

After a 13 to 7 victory over Miami, the University received an invitation to play a New Year's game in the Sun Bowl at El Paso, Texas, against Virginia Polytechnic Institute. The invitation, however, precluded the participation in the game of Willard Stargel, a Negro on the Varsity team. Dr. Walters recommended to the Board that for this reason the University should decline the invitation. He declared that the decision of the University should be based "solely on ethical and patriotic principles." By a majority vote of 4 to 3 the Board voted down the recommendation of President Walters. They sincerely "felt that no serious principle was violated" and also thought it was "expedient to accept the invitation" as there was "great local enthusiasm for the game" and it was "the unanimous desire of the team and the coaching staff to play." Since President Walters' recommendation did not relate "to an educational problem or policy" he accepted the Board's decision. Three of the Directors, however, stood with the President "on the question of principle"; but "principle" lost that day to "prestige." The University played the Sun Bowl game without Willard Stargel and won by a score of 18 to 6. The game was won, but something had been lost, too.

Another chapter in the long and colorful, and sometimes turbulent history of football at the University was written in 1948. Plagued by alumni trouble and injuries to the squad, the 1948 season was the most disastrous for Nolting since he had become football coach. In 1948 the Varsity team won 3 games, lost 6, and tied 1. The defeats that sealed Nolting's fate were those to Xavier and to Miami. Xavier defeated Varsity by a score of 13 to 7, and the University after losing to Miami in 1947 by 38 to 7 lost again in 1948 by a score of 43 to 19.

On December 6, eight of the nine members of the Board held a secret meeting in the Proctor and Gamble office of Mr. Brodie to consider the football situation, and as a Committee of the Whole voted against re-engaging Ray Nolting as coach of the football team. This action was taken despite the fact that President Walters, Athletic Director Mileham, and the Faculty Athletic Committee consisting of Vice-President Auburn and Professors Joerger and Bursiek voted for his retention for one year. President Walters warned that the Board decision would be interpreted as meaning "that a coach who did not win games at the University was dropped." Professor Joerger pointed out that the University had had seven coaches in twenty-three years. The opposition against Nolting was led by Dr. Reed Shank, who claimed that Nolting "sometimes lost his temper."

The controversy over Nolting did create a lot of publicity. But as an *Enquirer* editorial sanely pointed out:

If the University of Cincinnati can produce a winning football team, fine. But if it cannot, that fact does not reflect on the institution. . . . Whether football flourishes or languishes at UC, the institution is important for what is taught in its Engineering College, its Liberal Arts College, Medical and Law

Colleges, its Graduate School, and the other departments which caused it to be built. . . . The main business of the University is to educate its students in something other than putting an inflated football over a chalk line.

In the midst of this furor the University announced that Sidney Gilman had obtained a release from West Point where he was line coach and had accepted the position of head football coach at Cincinnati. Gilman had formerly been coach at Miami University where he had made an imposing football record. During the next couple of years the University athletic teams made very creditable records. In 1949 the football team won the Mid-American Conference championship; and the next year was invited to participate in the Sun Carnival at El Paso, Texas. During the same years the Varsity tennis team won the Mid-American Conference championship. In 1951 "the greatest individual sports accomplishment in the history of the University was achieved. Tony Trabert won the National Collegiate Athletic Association Singles Tennis Tournament." In the same year the University Basketball team won the Mid-American Conference championship for the fifth consecutive year, and was invited to compete in the National Invitational Championship Tournament.

In 1953 the University withdrew from the Mid-American Conference, ostensibly for financial reasons, but also because there was a growing demand in certain quarters that the University play stronger teams. The incident which caused the rupture was the adoption of a new regulation by the Mid-American Conference which provided that each member in the Conference should play five games with other member teams. Since the University for a long time had looked to the profits of the football season to help carry the expenses of minor sports, the University requested that this rule be modified, asserting that the local drawing power of several of the MAC members was not sufficient to justify five games at home. When the Mid-American Conference refused to modify the new regulation, the University withdrew from the Conference and began to negotiate with the Missouri Valley Conference.

In 1955 three events of importance occurred in respect to intercollegiate activities. In January of that year Sidney Gilman resigned as coach to accept a similar position with the Los Angeles Rams. For some time there had been criticism of his attitude and methods. George Blackburn, who had earlier served as assistant coach at the University and at the United States Military Academy, West Point, was appointed coach of the football team. In April of that year the National Collegiate Athletic Association (NCAA) placed the University on probation for a year and barred it from national championship tournaments "for violations of NCAA principles, rules, and regulations." The NCAA charged that the University's violations consisted of "offering prospective athletes aid in excess of that permitted by the University and the NCAA, providing transportation for prospective football players to visit the campus during the years 1951 through 1953, conducting an off-campus employment program for student athletes in football and that jobs were arranged for members of the football coaching staff at certain rates of pay." The report also said that neither University officials nor employers were "reasonably diligent in determining whether the work was performed." In reply President Walters issued a statement that "the practices criticized were largely in respect to football under a former coaching staff. When these points were brought to the attention of the University administration and the Board of Directors, immediate action was taken and the practices in question no longer exist." Although the blame for probation rested on the shoulders of a former coach, the blow was a serious shock to friends of the University.

STUDENT ACTIVITIES

The period after the War witnessed a growth of social activities and an increase in social fraternities. Sigma Sigma revived its Carnival, which had originated in the spring of 1940 but had been discontinued during the War. The object of the Carnival was to raise funds for some worthy cause on the campus. In 1949 a new fraternity, Sigma Phi Epsilon, appeared on the campus.

There were seventeen college fraternities on the campus after the War, many of them owning their chapter houses. There were two Negro fraternities and two Negro sororities. The scholastic standing of the college fraternities during these years was good. For two consecutive years, 1949 and 1950, men at the University led the nation in scholastic standing among college fraternities. Only twice in the twenty years between 1930 and 1950 did more than half of the Varsity fraternities fall below "the all-men's scholastic average." In 1954 the first Negro student was pledged to a University fraternity, the American Commons Club. President Walters insisted that the sole criteria for the admission of any student to any of the component colleges should be "scholarship and character" without "respect to race, color, or creed."

The first Religious Emphasis Week was held in the spring of 1947. The purpose of this week was "to foster religious thought and action by presenting in terms intelligible to college men and women the reliance on religious faith in life." The week was marked by an all-University Convocation, and by seminars and discussions on various religious issues. Religious Emphasis Week was sponsored by all the religious groups on the campus and included representatives of the Catholic, Protestant, and Jewish faiths. For many years it has continued to be a highly successful annual event on the campus.

The question of freedom of speech arose twice during this period. In 1947 the University banned a proposed speech by Henry Wallace before a student organization, "Progressive Youth," a discussion group, which was refused permission to use the Annie Laws Auditorium. President Walters said it was a policy "as a municipally-owned institution to refrain from sponsoring or appearing to sponsor partisan political opinion." The *Post* said editorially that in its judgment the decision was "unwise." Of course, Mr. Wallace was a "controversial figure," but how could any university which performed its historic function as a "market place of ideas" rule out "the controversial"? The *Times-Star* editorially upheld the decision. The University was "municipally owned, the property of the City of Cincinnati. For that reason it must remain non-partisan. "It cannot appear to take sides or sponsor one political idea as against another."

President Walters objected to the Mummer's Guild giving a production of *Dark of the Moon* on the ground that it satirized the religious revivals of the "southern mountaineers." The Mummers Guild agreed to substitute another play.

21   *A New Captain on the Bridge*

As it entered the second half of the twentieth century the University of Cincinnati was a large, thriving enterprise, counting 15,000 students, and meeting more fully than ever before the needs of the community and the encircling region for public higher education. It had weathered the storms of war and the postwar financial crisis, had strengthened its tax base, and greatly enlarged its endowment. It had come a long way from the years of struggle, a half-century earlier, when its students were a few hundred, not many thousands. Its place in Cincinnati, its right to public support, its acceptance by the press and political leaders in the City, and its claim to recognition in the world of scholarship, all were assured. The University of Cincinnati was a going concern.

Cincinnati itself was not growing much in this period, limited as it was by surrounding incorporated cities and villages. But metropolitan Cincinnati prospered greatly in the postwar years, reflecting the steadily rising productivity of the great industrial empire along the Ohio River. Situated at the mid-point of the Ohio River, Cincinnati and the neighbor communities clustered about it were ideally placed to benefit by the spectacular development of the "American Ruhr Valley" stretching from Pittsburgh, Pennsylvania, to Cairo, Illinois. Abundant coal, plus low-cost river transport by barge, plus ready access to the major United States markets, set the stage for a host of new industries along the river—aluminum, steel, chemicals, atomic energy, and many others.

Closely linked with the economy of the Valley, through its Engineering and Business Administration Colleges and especially by its famed co-op system, the University of Cincinnati stood to prosper also. Its task was growing rapidly. And although the means of financing the requisite expansion were never easily managed, the University rose to its opportunity and obligation. Lying ahead, and not too far ahead, there was a still greater challenge, commonly known as the "population bulge." The high marriage and birth rates of the period from 1940 on augured massive increases in university enrollments, commencing in the late 1950's and swelling still more in the 1960's. President Raymond Walters had presided with unfailing equanimity over the varied fortunes of the University as it staggered out of depression into better days, as it lived out the tribulations of wartime, and then met the awesome inflow of students in the GI rush after 1945. He could look back with comfort to some hard victories won, and he also could look ahead to formidable new problems—problems that would land, not on his desk, but on that of a successor.

Early in the fall of 1953, President Walters brought to the attention of the Board the fact that he would retire within two years. In view of this he suggested that the Board should start immediately on a program to select his successor. His experience in selecting Deans, he said, had impressed upon him the advantage of having plenty of time to devote to the matter. Mr. Brodie said that it was "characteristically high-minded of Dr. Walters to make this suggestion." Upon the recommendation of President Walters, the Board appointed Judge Walter M. Shohl, Chairman of the Board Committee on Colleges and Schools, the Chairman of a Committee to select the new President. The other members of the Committee were Renton K. Brodie, Dr. Frank H. Mayfield, and Jane D. Earley.

The replacement of Dr. Walters as President of the University was not an easy task. The local chapter of the American Association of University Professors submitted twenty names for the Presidency. Judge Shohl invited the Faculty and the Cabinet to suggest names. The Board Committee held conferences with the Deans and a Faculty Committee. At the request of the Deans, Dean Barrow presented to the Board a summary of the Cabinet's consensus of "Qualifications for President of the University." It was generally agreed that two prime essentials for the Presidency were experience in college administration and scholarship. Lists of over fifty names were submitted to the Board as possible candidates. Personal interviews were arranged with many of these prospective Presidential candidates, and a number of them were invited to the campus for more intensive investigation. When it looked for a time as if a definite decision on the Presidency could not be reached, three of the Deans proposed that Mr. Brodie should be urged to become President for a two-year term. Mr. Brodie, however, positively refused to have his name considered.

After months of careful screening and interviewing numerous individuals, there were two outstanding candidates—Dr. Walter C. Langsam, President of Gettysburg College, and Dr. Norman P. Auburn, President of the University of Akron. Dr. Langsam was approached, and consented to have his name considered. He and Mrs. Langsam were invited to the campus. Finally at a special meeting of the Board on March 17, 1955, Dr. Langsam was unanimously elected President and accepted the office.

The new President had been a successful teacher. He had a national and international reputation as an authority on European history, and he had been President of two small Eastern colleges. He was born in Vienna, Austria-Hungary, the son of Emery Bernhardt and Angela Virginia Bianca (Münz-Kleinert). Before Langsam was a year old, he was brought by his parents to the United States and naturalized through his father. He received his Bachelor of Science degree at the City College of New York and his Master of Arts and Doctoral degrees at Columbia University. He taught history at Columbia University and Union College, and had also been visiting professor at Duke University, Ohio State University, New York University, the University of British Columbia, and the University of Colorado. Dr. Langsam had been President of Wagner Lutheran College, New York, and at the time of his election to the Presidency at Cincinnati, he was President of Gettysburg College. During World War II, Dr. Langsam served in the office of Strategic Services.

From his long association with Columbia University he was familiar with the problems of a large and diversified university. His leadership of two small Eastern colleges had acquainted him with some of the problems he would encounter at Cincinnati in dealing with the component colleges at the University. He came to Cincinnati with years of solid experience in university administration, in which, as it proved, he had talent of a high order.

Dr. Langsam was the author of numerous historical works, and his textbook, *The World Since 1914* (revised 1954 under the title *The World Since 1919*), had been widely adopted by colleges and universities and was a perennial best seller. Despite the pressure of work as President, he was to continue writing in the field of history.

THE MAN

Dr. Langsam was a tall, handsome man, who greeted everyone who entered his office with sincere cordiality. At the time of his election he was an inveterate smoker, occasionally squinting through his own cigarette smoke. He was given to understatement in referring to his own accomplishments. He had a keen sense of humor. He hoped eventually to get to know as many students by first name as possible, but he soon learned that it was impossible for him to become personally acquainted with all the University students. Dr. Langsam had a tremendous capacity for work, and he expected the same of all those associated with the University. He was a dignified executive and by his courtesy and friendliness made the office of President of the University respected by the entire community. He said that he loved to dance, was fond of sports, and that his favorite diversion was "playing classical and semi-classical records at night." He and Mrs. Langsam, a charming woman, were gracious hosts in their home in Clifton, which had been bought by the University and established as the President's residence for the use of future Presidents of the University and their families.

INAUGURATION AND EDUCATIONAL VIEWS

On October 25, 1955, Dr. Langsam was installed in office as President of the University of Cincinnati. It was an impressive and dignified occasion. Three hundred and fifty black-gowned delegates, wearing the varicolored hoods of their schools, marched in the procession in the order of the founding dates of the institutions and societies they represented. First in line were the delegates from the Catholic University of Louvain, Belgium, founded in 1425, and Harvard, founded in 1636. Dr. Harold O. Voorhis, Vice-Chancellor of New York University, gave the principal address.

In his inaugural address President Langsam dwelt upon the duties of an institution of higher learning. "In a sense," Dr. Langsam said, "our students are the unfinished product with which we work, but as someone has well said, they are basic material with a soul. It is our task to fashion this material and to guide it not merely in the pursuit of happiness but in the pursuit of the significant. . . . We must be interested in the emotions as well as the reason of our students, for whereas reason helps us to decide on the means to reach a desired end, it is emotion, more often than not, that determines the end itself."

During his first year at the University, Dr. Langsam amplified his educational views in addresses to the student body. Scholastically, he thought, the University "ought to grow to the point where it could serve adequately the largest number of qualified students." He stressed the importance of a strong Faculty, good equipment, and the maintenance of high standards. A good teacher was one who "knew his subject," was "enthusiastic about it," and was "eager to pass on his knowledge to the students in a way to arouse their interest." A good teacher was characterized "by sincerity" and a "great teacher also by humility." More than in any recent period it was important "to comprehend the need for liberally educated young men and women who possessed a core of basic general knowledge, who understood the principles governing human behavior, and who had themselves established a proper relation with God." He approved of sororities and fraternities when properly managed. He felt that intercollegiate athletics should not be overemphasized, but that they were "important, helpful, and constructive parts of collegiate life." He felt that the editorial policy of student publications should be governed by "one, good taste; and two, certainty of facts."

When Dr. Langsam was asked to characterize the University's personality, he offered the phrase "alert conservatism—conservatism tinged with alertness to progress." And he added, "which I, for one, happen to like." "Conservatism, academically, socially, in every field," he remarked.

RETIREMENT OF DR. WALTERS

On September 1, 1955, Dr. Walters reached the mandatory age of retirement. For twenty-three years, nearly a quarter of a century, he had been at the helm of the University. During his regime, the longest in the history of the University, the number of Colleges had increased from nine to thirteen; the enrollment had risen from 9,522 to 13,361; and the investment in buildings had more than doubled.

Dr. Walters retired, as he said, to a new career of "leisure with dignity" amid the plaudits of a host of admirers; but, within a year, his retirement years were greatly saddened by the sudden death of his beloved wife, "Bob O'Link." Mrs. Walters was a self-effacing, friendly woman with a sense of humor that had endeared her to the members of the Faculty and Faculty wives.

NEW ADMINISTRATIVE PERSONNEL

In the first six years of President Langsam's administration a number of new administrative positions were created. In 1956 a revision of the bylaws and regulations of the Board of Directors created a new office, that of Dean of Academic Administration. Dr. Hoke S. Greene was appointed to the new position.

Three years later (1959) two more administrative posts were created. Dr. Greene became Vice-President and Dean of Faculties. A special fund-raising office was established, and Frank T. Purdy was appointed to the new post of Executive Director of Development.

The following year two more administrative posts were created. In December 1959 the Board established a two-year college to be known as the University College; and in February 1960, Dr. Hilmar C. Krueger became Dean of the new academic unit. A Faculty Committee recommended the establishment of this College. The program of the new College was designed for students who: "1) for personal reasons did not want to enter a four-year undergraduate program; 2) desired a short-term college education related directly to their economic welfare; and 3) wished to make up entrance requirements for a four-year college." It was expected that the University College with its two-year terminal courses in diversified practical fields would be "a major contribution to the solving of the nation-wide problem of over-crowded colleges." In the same year a new office of Dean of Special Services was created, and Dr. Shank was appointed to this position.

At the November 1960 general election an amendment to the city charter was approved which empowered "the City Council to transfer the control of the administration and executive work of the General Hospital from the City Manager to the Board of Directors of the University of Cincinnati, under terms and conditions agreed to by the City Council and the Board of Directors, including the allocation to the University of the City funds already being used for the General Hospital; thereby ending the division of authority between the administrative work now the responsibility of the City Manager, and the medical and nursing services which the Board of Directors is already responsible." As a result of the adoption of the city charter amendment the Board created the office of Vice-President and Director of the University of Cincinnati Medical Center.

On April 13, 1961, Major General Clement F. St. John, commanding general of Walter Reed Army Medical Center, Washington, D.C., was appointed to this position. General St. John was a native of Ohio and a graduate of Ohio State University. During World War II he had served as assistant surgeon in General George Patton's Western Task Force; was operations officer to the surgeon of General Mark Clark's Fifth Army; became surgeon of the First Army at Fort Bragg; and later was surgeon with the United States Army in Europe.

A number of new administrative heads were also appointed during these years. When Librarian Wyman W. Parker resigned in 1956, Arthur T. Hamlin was appointed Librarian. When Dean Joerger retired the next year (1957), Howard K. Justice was appointed Dean and Cornelius Wandmacher, Associate Dean of the College of Engineering.

In 1958 four new administrative heads were appointed. Upon the retirement of Dean Barbour, Dr. Charles K. Weichert was appointed Dean of the McMicken College of Arts and Sciences. The same year Dean Bird retired, and Dr. Kenneth Wilson succeeded him as Dean of the College of Business Administration; shortly thereafter Professor Milan R. Karas was appointed Associate Dean. The Board approved in 1958 a reorganization of the administration of the University's research, and Dr. Fred O'Flaherty was appointed Administrator of University Research in addition to his office of Director of the Tanner's Council Laboratory. The same year the University established a pioneer Institute of Space Science and Dr. Paul Herget, Director of the Observatory, whose work in the field of minor planets and in satellite training had won for him world recognition, was appointed Director.

In 1959, Dr. Campbell Crockett succeeded Dr. Greene as Dean of the Graduate School of Arts and Sciences. In the same year the College of Home Economics became the School of Home Economics affiliated with the Teachers College, and Dr. Emma B. Whiteford was appointed Director.

On September 20, 1960, the University's new FM Station, WGUC, went on the air with the special purpose of "enriching the cultural life of the community," and Joseph Sagmaster became Director of UC Broadcasting. Mr. Sagmaster, a University of Cincinnati graduate, had been executive editor of the *Times-Star;* when that paper consolidated with the *Post* he had become editor of the editorial page of the *Enquirer.* The new FM Station devoted 60 per cent of its programming to good music, offering many cultural programs that commercial stations did not provide.

SPECIAL CEREMONIES AND CELEBRATIONS

A galaxy of leaders in the fields of management, engineering, and designing participated for a week, April 19–25, 1956, in an exhibition of "Education and Industry at Work for Progress" in commemoration of the fiftieth anniversary of co-operative education. By 1956 there were over 3,000 in co-operative courses at the University working in nearly 500 firms, and the co-operative plan of technological education had been adopted by 34 other colleges and universities across the nation. Cornelius Wandmacher was Chairman of the University Committee which planned the observance. Frederick V. Geier, President of the Cincinnati Milling Machine Company, was Chairman of the National Sponsoring Committee. Cyrus R. Osborn, M.E., '21, Executive Vice-President, General Motors Corporation, was Chairman of the Panorama of Progress in which employers of co-operative students gave a display of America's industrial progress during the past half-century. The Herman Schneider Memorial Quadrangle and memorial stone platform, the gift of the Herman Schneider Foundation, were dedicated as a tribute to Dean Herman Schneider, the founder of co-operative education.

The Graduate School of Arts and Sciences celebrated its fiftieth anniversary in March 1957, with appropriate ceremonies. The principal address was delivered by Sir Edward Appleton, Nobel Prize winner and Principal and Vice-Chancellor of the University of Edinburgh, Scotland.

Also in March 1957 the University participated in the centennial celebration of the founding of the Cincinnati Academy of Medicine. Dr. Reginald C. McGrane, College of Arts and Sciences, wrote the centennial history of the Academy, entitled *The Cincinnati Doctor's Forum,* and was elected an honorary member of the Cincinnati Academy of Medicine.

On May 8, 1958, the Cincinnati College of Law celebrated its one hundred and twenty-fifth anniversary. The principal address was delivered by the Honorable Earl Warren, Chief Justice of the United States Supreme Court.

FACULTY RECOGNITION

In 1956, at the invitation of the United States Department of State, President Langsam was the official United States delegate to the Fifth International Congress on Peace and Christian Civilization at Florence, Italy. He then went to West Germany to lecture as United States specialist in history.

In 1955, Dr. Kenneth E. Caster, Graduate School of Arts and Sciences, was named the first recipient of India's new Gondwanaland gold medal. In 1957, Dr. Carl W. Blegen, Graduate School of Arts and Sciences, received the honorary degree of Doctor of Letters from Oxford University, England. In the same year Dr. Margaret Fulford was elected the first woman to be honored with election to the Fellows of the Graduate School of Arts and Sciences.

In a number of significant ways President Langsam recognized the achievements and activities of the Faculty. He raised the salaries of the Faculty to figures comparable to those in other institutions of higher learning in the same category as the University.

In 1960, on Dr. Langsam's nomination, the Board appointed the first Distinguished Service Professor, Dr. Albert B. Sabin, in recognition of his achievements in "alleviating the scourges of such virus diseases as poliomyelitis, Japanese B-encephalitis, and dengue fever." Dr. Sabin's poliomyelitis antipolio live virus vaccine was endorsed the following year by the American Medical Association, was approved in time by the U.S. Public Health Service, and became the accepted means of mass inoculation against polio, in the United States and abroad.

Dr. Langsam also encouraged the recognition of good teaching in the Faculty. In 1961, Dr. Gaylord Merriman, professor of mathematics in the McMicken College of Arts and Science, was the recipient of the first award of $1,000 for excellence in university teaching made possible by the generous gift of Mrs. A. B. ("Dolly") Cohen. The next year (1962) Mrs. Cohen gave two awards of $1,000 each for excellence in university teaching. The recipients were Dr. Gustav G. Carlson, professor of sociology and head of the Department of Sociology in the McMicken College of Arts and Sciences, and Miss Hope D. Warner, professor of history in the College of Design, Architecture, and Arts.

ENDOWMENTS AND CURRICULUM

In 1961 the University received the largest bequest in its entire history for the advancement of learning. The will of Mrs. Louise Taft Semple, who died March 27, 1961, created a $3 million trust fund for the benefit

of the Department of Classics. The will provided that the net income
of the Semple Classics Fund should be used, under the direction of the
trustees of the Fund, "solely for the purpose of promoting the study of
classics" in recognition of the vital part in our civilization of "the spiritual,
intellectual, and esthetic inheritance we have received from the Greek
and Roman civilizations."

The interest in advancing learning during these years was reflected
also in the innovations in the curriculum of the various Colleges. During
the academic year 1956–1957 the Graduate School of Arts and Sciences
for the first time in its history offered off-campus graduate courses. As
noted earlier, the Institute of Space Science was established in the
Graduate School. The McMicken College of Arts and Sciences in 1959
gave instruction in the Russian language and literature.

As a result of elaborate studies conducted by the Faculty of the College
of Engineering, radical changes were made in all the degree programs
and the co-operative education plan was extended to the graduate level
with research programs in engineering and physical science. The degree
programs were modernized by requiring all students to take certain basic
courses in each of the six engineering sciences—mechanics of solids, fluid
mechanics, thermodynamics, heat transfer, electric science, and the nature and properties of materials—and all students were required to take
a sequence of humanistic-social courses comprising 25 per cent of the
total curriculum. In order to co-ordinate and stimulate research among
the students and Faculty, Hans Ernst was appointed Herman Schneider
Research Professor of Engineering to direct graduate study leading to the
master's and doctoral degrees. Basic research fellowships sponsored by
industry were established.

In 1958 the College of Business Administration introduced a graduate
program. The following year the College began offering a regular four-
year program, providing an alternative to the five-year co-operative program.

In response to numerous requests the Department of Architecture in
the College of Applied Arts announced that, starting in 1961, it would
offer an undergraduate co-operative program in city planning. The course
would lead to the degree of Bachelor of Science with a major in city
planning.

In 1957 and in 1959 the College of Medicine brought a visiting professor of philosophy for public lectures under a grant from the John and
Mary R. Markle Foundation. In 1961 the College established a Department of Gynecology.

The names of two departments were changed to describe more accu-
rately the nature of the work done. In 1961 the name of the College of
Applied Arts was changed to the College of Design, Architecture, and
Art; and the name of the Department of Aeronautical Engineering in the

College of Engineering was changed to the Department of Aerospace Engineering. In 1959 a new men's dormitory was named Dabney Hall as a tribute to the late President Charles William Dabney.

In 1962, after prolonged negotiations and a major fund-raising campaign, the College-Conservatory of Music was brought into the University as one of its constituent Colleges. This brought to fruition the hopes of a great number of Cincinnatians, people who cherished the rich musical tradition of their City and who had been disturbed by the obstacles that stood in the way of a fine but inadequately financed music school. This merger held promise of enriching the life of the University, and of restoring the vigor and quality of the College-Conservatory. It was made possible in great part by the decision of the Cincinnati Institute of Fine Arts to assign $1,264,000 of its endowment funds to the University to underwrite the transfer of the College-Conservatory, and in part by the contribution of $1 million by private citizens interested in the furtherance of music education.

ATHLETICS

During these years the University athletic teams made distinguished records and attracted national attention to the University. In 1956, Cincinnati became a member of the Missouri Valley Conference, one of the oldest and strongest athletic conferences in the nation. The next two years the University basketball, swimming, and baseball teams won Missouri Valley Conference championships; and the basketball team in 1956 and 1957 participated in the National Invitational Tournament in New York.

In a unique ruling by the Council of the National Collegiate Athletic Association (NCAA), the University was placed on probation, without penalty, for six months on the ground that UC athletes were paid on co-op jobs and, therefore, were receiving more aid as student-athletes than was allowed by the NCAA rules. President Langsam promptly issued a strong statement questioning the NCAA's position in "publicly stigmatizing the University of Cincinnati by putting it on probation. . . . While the University obviously from time to time may revise its co-operative system for *educational* reasons, it will *not* do so for *athletic* reasons." In October of that year the probationary status was lifted by the NCAA Council. The University and the NCAA agreed "that the co-operative student athlete should receive a commonly accepted amount of student aid prorated on the number of weeks each year in the classroom."

In was during these years that the fabulous Oscar Robertson, under the direction of Basketball Coach George Smith, broke all collegiate basketball records. Sports reporters exhausted their stock of adjectives in commenting on his remarkable co-ordination and uncanny skill with a basketball. The six-foot five-inch "Big O" rocketed into orbit in the 1958 season with a fantastic 56-point debut at Madison Square Garden, "the best individual show ever staged there." After that eye-opener the twenty-year old sharpshooter was "box office" wherever he went. In 1958 he was named collegiate basketball All-American. The University added another thousand seats in the Armory-Field House to accommodate the "Big O's" following, but even then all who wished could not be admitted. When Oscar Robertson graduated in 1960 all the Number 12 uniforms he had worn in his three years playing basketball were officially retired at a special convocation on the UC campus.

In 1960, Edwin Jucker assistant basketball coach, was named Varsity basketball coach to succeed George Smith, who became Director of Athletics. M. Charles Mileham, former Director of Athletics, was appointed Assistant to Vice-President Bursiek, a newly created position. In 1961, William D. Schwarberg was promoted from Assistant to Associate Director of Athletics.

Under the direction of Coach Jucker the University basketball team soared to even higher honors. For four years the Varsity basketball team had captured the Missouri Valley Conference championship, the first time in thirty-four years a member had won four undisputed MVC championships in a row. On March 25, 1961, the Varsity basketball team climaxed its spectacular record by winning the National Collegiate Basketball Championship in the NCAA finals at Kansas City by defeating Ohio State University, the nation's Number One team, in a thrilling overtime game by a score of 70 to 65. The conquering Varsity champions came home to a roaring welcome from students and citizens of Cincinnati.

On March 24, 1962, the University basketball team, under the direction of Coach Jucker, won its second consecutive National Basketball Championship, defeating Ohio State University in a convincing and overwhelming triumph by a score of 71 to 59 before 18,649 spectators at Freedom Hall, Louisville. Tall Paul Hogue with 22 points, and Tony Yates, quarterbacking the team (Tony Yates was elected the new captain of the team, 1962–1963) were the main cogs in the Cincinnati machine. Because this was the second time the University of Cincinnati basketball team had won the championship, Mayor Walter H. Bachrach said the City Council felt "that something had to be done to remember the occasion." On April 12, 1962, the City Council voted unanimously to place signs on University Avenue between Clifton and Scioto indicating that while it was still University Avenue, it was to be "called the Avenue of Champions."

In 1961, George Blackburn resigned as football coach. He was succeeded by Charles B. Studley.

Three new fraternities, Phi Kappa Tau (1959), Sigma Nu Colony (1960), and Alpha Epsilon Pi Colony (1961), were organized during these years.

Public support for the University was enlarged and strengthened in 1962 at the primary election on May 8, when the voters of Cincinnati approved an amendment to the city charter authorizing 2 mills instead of the previous 1 mill of property taxation. This additional mill replaced the previous and somewhat smaller annual grants customarily made by the City Council from revenues of the City payroll-income tax; thus the University was freed from the necessity of seeking annual appropriations from the City Council. The vote authorizing the higher levy was 22,960 in favor of the amendment, 22,444 against. The percentage of University revenues from public sources had been dropping steadily, as the total budget mounted and the tax dollars remained constant. By the amendment of 1962, the percentage represented by tax funds for the year 1963 amounted to some 16 per cent of the total operating budget.

22   *Dreams that Came True*

The people of Cincinnati have always had a deep-seated desire for education. Many of the early leaders of the town were college men and all were eager for the community to have an academy or college. Within two years after Ohio was admitted as a State to the Union and when the population of Cincinnati was less than a thousand, the settlers of Cincinnati petitioned the State Legislature to obtain a college township provided for in the Ordinance of 1787 for the purpose of encouraging education. When they were thwarted in obtaining this, a school association was formed, and the State Legislature was induced to pass a law establishing Cincinnati University the funds for which were to be obtained by means of a lottery.

"Its endowments," wrote Daniel Drake, "were not exactly correspondent to its elevated title"; and Cincinnati University did not last very long. Nor did the Lancasterian Seminary flourish which was later established. But in 1819, due to the tireless energy of the indomitable Daniel Drake, Cincinnati's first great physician, a scholar and an inspiring teacher and lecturer, the State Legislature chartered the Cincinnati College and the Medical College of Ohio, the two oldest units of the University of Cincinnati. Drake wanted to make Cincinnati a great medical center and the institution a great and useful university.

The news of the incorporation of the Cincinnati College was acclaimed by the citizens of Cincinnati. They boasted that in time the institution would rival other seminaries of similar grade in the Atlantic states. They took great pride in the college building, "an extensive two-story brick edifice" with a "colonnade forming a handsome portico" and a fine belfry. A Faculty consisting of three members was secured; and within three years after the College was opened, the first Commencement was held and three students were graduated. But lack of funds and internal friction handicapped both the Cincinnati College and the Medical College of

342

Ohio and they languished. In 1835, Cincinnati College was revived with a distinguished Medical Department, Law Department, Academic Department, and an Observatory, and began operations with William Holmes McGuffey as President. But, again, financial troubles, internal friction, and the coming of a war militated against the establishment of an institution of higher learning in Cincinnati.

Then in 1858, Charles McMicken bequeathed to the Queen City the bulk of his estate to aid in establishing a university that would make Cincinnati a great center of higher learning. It had long been Mr. McMicken's desire to found at Cincinnati an institution "for instruction in the higher branches of learning, except denominational theology." The munificent gift of Charles McMicken laid the foundations of the University of Cincinnati which was chartered as a municipal university by the passage of an act in 1870 by the State Legislature.

The dream of Charles McMicken has come true. The growth of the University has been remarkable. The University of Cincinnati today ranks twenty-fourth in size among the colleges and universities in the United States. The University is composed of thirteen component Colleges—three of which, the College of Medicine, the College of Law, and the College of Pharmacy—are the oldest Colleges of their kind west of the Alleghenies; and affiliated with the University are the Art Academy of Cincinnati, Cincinnati School of Speech and Hearing, College-Conservatory of Music of Cincinnati, and the Hebrew Union College. In 1963, the College-Conservatory of Music became a separate unit of the University under the direction of Dr. Jack M. Watson as Dean. The current net enrollment of the University of Cincinnati is approximately 19,600 students drawn from practically every state in the Union, thirty foreign countries, and most of the continents. Six hundred thousand boys and girls have been given an opportunity to attend college thanks to the gifts of Charles McMicken and numerous other benefactors and the generous financial aid voted by the citizens of Cincinnati to the institution. There are approximately seven hundred full-time members of the Faculty and six hundred lecturers.

The University has become a conspicuous and durable asset of the City. It has become in large measure the City's intellectual and spiritual dynamo. The College of Medicine and the adjacent General Hospital have made Cincinnati a great medical center. The College of Law has contributed notably to the development of an educated and upright bar, locally and nationally. The co-operative system of technological education which originated at the College of Engineering is world famous and has been adopted by some sixty other colleges and universities. The Graduate School and the McMicken College of Arts and Sciences attract students and scholars from all parts of the world in the pursuit of the study of the humanities.

The University of Cincinnati has combined happily two quite distinct yet harmonious concepts of higher education. As a municipal institution, subsidized in part by local taxation, it has had—and has honored—an obligation to provide economical education for a great number of young people of the City and its immediate environs. And it has done so without becoming embroiled in politics, without having to make concessions to the gusts and eddies of political sentiment. At the same time, in conformity with the highest standards of independent universities, it has become the center of a sound and rich scholarly tradition, a place for study and research and writing in realms of thought and experiment for which there never has been a popular demand.

The independence of the University has been preserved and strengthened through the decades by several factors. The directors are appointed for nine-year terms, insulating them in large measure from direct public pressures. The public revenues of the University, to a very large degree, have been provided by a specific property tax levy written into the city charter, enabling the University to operate without a budgetary review by the City Council or other public body and to pursue its course without annual requests for funds. Equally important, there has been established a tradition, with almost the force of customary law, that directors and administrative officers are not to be subjected to political pressures of any kind.

Still another buttress of the University's independence and security is the magnitude of private gifts and bequests. In the years 1952–1962, $31,868,000 were so contributed to the University, either for endowment or operating budget. In 1961 the University of Cincinnati ranked twenty-third of 1,031 colleges and universities of the nation, in the total amount of gifts and grants received. Without such accretions to capital funds and operating budget, the University could not have carved out its important role in scholarly and scientific research.

Through the years Cincinnati has found the University of Cincinnati a productive greenhouse for the nurturing of leaders in both business and politics. In 1957 the UC mark was on the "City Manager, the Director of Public Safety, the two United States Congressmen, the Prosecuting Attorney, the City Solicitor, six members of the City Council, an Ohio Supreme Court Justice, two of the three Court of Appeals Judges, and a large number of the bench in both municipal and common pleas courts." Probably no other educational institution can point to the fact that at one time graduates of the University of Cincinnati presided simultaneously over the principal branches of the Federal government in Washington. The University's influence on the course of Cincinnati's economic life is incalculable. Too numerous to list are the graduates of the University in top-level positions in Cincinnati commerce and industry.

The University has become an increasingly important economic as well as a cultural asset and resource to the City. It is one of the City's most important "businesses." A recent survey disclosed that the wage and salary payments of the University amount approximately to $9 million annually. Supply and equipment purchases and services brought another $1.6 million to Cincinnati industry and business. Research grants and contracts accounted for expenditures of several million dollars. It was estimated that fraternities and sororities at the University spent in excess of $700,000 annually. Parents, friends of non-resident students, athletic contests, professional and scientific conventions and meetings brought by the University accounted for 80,000 visitor days in the City at approximately $20.00 a day. It is estimated that non-resident students, in addition to their tuition and fees, spend between $4–$5 million a year with Cincinnati firms.

It was a Faculty composed of such men as Daniel Drake, Timothy Walker, Ormsby MacKnight Mitchel, Jacob D. Cox, Herman Schneider, Christian R. Holmes, Benjamin J. Rachford, William B. Wherry, and Frank W. Chandler, to mention only a few of the giants of former days, who made possible the realization of the dream of Charles McMicken. The University today is continually searching for top-level men like these, and finding them as year by year more members of the Faculty are elected officers of learned societies and are publishing authoritative works in their respective fields. One thing that attracts these men to the University is that they know they will find at Cincinnati, now as in the past, an intellectual climate and conditions in which a scholar can effectively work. The City of Cincinnati is more and more appreciating that the best investment of its funds is in developing scholars, teachers, scientific experts, laboratory technicians, business leaders, engineers, and doctors in its midst at the University. Increasingly the respective Presidents of the University have won the respect and confidence of the people of Cincinnati; and the Board of Directors have shown themselves competent, industrious, and devoted to the ideal of making the University a leading institution of higher learning.

The future of the University is not without its problems. An institution of 20,000 students, with an annual budget of more than $20 million, if it continues to grow may prove to be "more university" than can be sustained from a tax base of 500,000 people living in the City of Cincinnati. State assistance, in the form of a per-student subvention, may be found a necessary supplement. The three municipal universities of Ohio (Cincinnati, Akron, and Toledo) are educating about 30 per cent of the students enrolled in higher public education in Ohio, but have not been able to draw upon the resources of the State with its 10 million population.

Meantime, a notable record in the annals of American municipal higher education has been made. It has been shown beyond cavil that a distinguished and independent university can flourish in a representative large American city, irrespective of the vagaries of political morality and public opinion. It has been shown that a city university can serve certain practi-

THE UNIVERSITY OF CINCINNATI

cal and urgent needs of the industries roundabout, and at the same time conserve its devotion and achievement in true scholarship.

The administrators, Faculty, students, and alumni of the University of Cincinnati are the custodians of this rich heritage of tradition and high ideals. The future of the University and the enrichment of these dreams rest in great measure in their hands. The ultimate sanction of the University, however, and the final guarantee of its continuing service as a seat of learning must be found in the lust for educational opportunity that has marked the people of the Queen City of the Ohio from the earliest days—from the tireless, irascible visionary, Daniel Drake, to the thousands of unnamed citizens, who in 1962 voted to double their own tax contribution for the support of their University.

APPENDIX I

Board of Directors of McMicken University and University of Cincinnati

Larz Anderson, 1863–1876
William Harvey Anderson, 1910–1914
William P. Anderson, 1885–1889
Brent Arnold, 1893–1904
Norman P. Auburn, 1943–1951
Ward Baldwin, 1883–1890
Louis Ballauf, 1883–1890
Alfred B. Benedict, 1893–1897; 1903–1905
R. M. Bishop, 1861–1870
Robert L. Black, 1938–1948
Eugene F. Bliss, 1899–1904
Renton K. Brodie, 1942–
James Brown, 1882–1898
F. Sanford Brown, 1903–1910; 1914–1936
Gustav Bruehl, 1870–1872
M. L. Buchwalter, 1872–1876
Joseph C. Butler, 1899–1905
John A. Caldwell, 1894–1896
J. P. Carbery, 1883–1886
Archibald Irwin Carson, 1908–1914
Cornelius George Comegys, 1861–1869; 1871–1896
Jacob D. Cox, 1870–1876
Briggs S. Cunningham, 1896–1901
Henry Melville Curtis, 1903–1910
John Davis, 1869–1870
S. S. Davis, 1871–1872
William D. Davis, 1871–1872
W. W. Dawson, 1880–1893
Walter De Camp, 1901–1903
Frank F. Dinsmore, 1922–1953

Ozro J. Dodds, 1875–1880
M. R. Dodson, 1956–
William M. Doughty, 1936–1942
Ernst Du Brul, 1906–1912
Jane DeSerisy Earley, 1941–
Edward H. Ernst, 1925–1932
Francis Ferry, 1870–1876
C. D. Fishburn, 1876–1886
Julius Fleischmann, 1940–1941
Abner J. Frazer, 1871–1872
Herbert G. French, 1923–1942
James N. Gamble, 1902–1908
Fred A. Geier, 1905–1910
Walter Y. Grainger, 1956–1958
Miles Greenwood, 1861–1862
Walter R. Griess, 1914–1919
W. S. Groesbeck, 1871–1872
George Guckenberger, 1908–1911
Henry Haacke, 1876–1893
L. M. Hadden, 1889–1892
M. B. Hagans, 1890–1897
Henry F. Handy, 1859–1861
L. A. Harris, 1864–1866
Frederick Hassaurer, 1874–1875
George Hatch, 1862–1863
John W. Herron, 1867–1870
Frederick Hertenstein, January–May 1914
William H. Hessler, 1957–
Smith Hickenlooper, 1910–1916
Robert W. Hilton, 1911–1923
A. Howard Hinkle, 1893–1894
George Hoadly, 1870–1800

347

G. B. Hollister, 1859–1870
James J. Hooker, 1906–1912
William Hooper, 1871–1872
Samuel Hunt, 1872–1890
Charles Jacob, Jr., 1879–1880
Lester Jaffe, 1930–1940
Frank J. Jones, 1887–1906
G. W. C. Johnston, 1875–1876
Ellis Guy Kinkead, 1903–1908
Rufus King, 1861–1870; 1871–1879
Robert Kreimer, January–May 1914
Oscar W. Kuhn, 1891–1908
Max Lilienthal, 1873–1882
Alexander Long, 1882–1886
J. W. Luhn, 1893–1905
William McAlpin, 1892–1899
Alexander McGuffey, 1870–1878
William McMaster, 1876–1884
J. C. McMechan, 1876–1879
Alfred Mack, 1919–1930
Patrick Mallon, 1877–1883
H. H. Mattox, 1882–1886
Max B. May, 1899–1906
Frank H. Mayfield, 1951–
William Means, 1881–1882
Philip M. Meyers, 1953–
Lewis Mills, 1870–1877
Thomas C. Minor, 1875–1881
Thomas J. Moffett, 1906–1912
R. M. Moore, 1877–1878
Arthur Morgan, 1914–1938
William H. Morgan, 1888–1900
John B. Mosby, 1889–1892
John A. Murphy, 1881–1887
Walter F. Murray, 1932–1951
Frank H. Nelson, 1928–1938
Alfred K. Nippert, 1912–1914
John G. O'Connell, 1903–1906
James B. O'Donnell, 1950–1956
Henry Pearce, 1870–1872
J. B. Peaslee, 1876–1907
Hiram D. Peck, 1878–1884
Elliot H. Pendleton, 1897–1903
Emil Pollak, 1910–1927
William A. Procter, 1899–1906
William M. Ramsey, 1884–1896
Joseph Ransohoff, 1903–1908

Thad. A. Reamy, 1894–1896;
 1902–1908
C. A. L. Reed, 1892–1907
Otto J. Renner, 1914–1922
C. D. Robertson, 1877–1883
J. M. Robinson, 1890–1904
John J. Rowe, 1932–1949
J. G. Schmidlapp, 1896–1902
Arthur W. Schubert, 1953–
Lewis Seasongood, 1870–1883
Edward Senior, 1898–1907
Reed A. Shank, 1942–1953
Walter M. Shohl, 1941–
James D. Shouse, 1948–1956
Amor Smith, Jr., 1885–1888
Rufus B. Smith, 1912–1923
Arthur M. Spiegel, 1914–1915
Edmund K. Stallo, 1890–1899
John B. Stallo, 1870–1875
Thomas J. Stephens, 1882–1883
Robert W. Stewart, 1908–1914
Bellamy Storer, 1890–1894
Erwin O. Straehley, 1915–1932
Albert P. Strietmann, 1938–1947
William Strunk, 1890–1898
G. S. Sykes, 1900–1906
Alphonso Taft, 1870–1876;
 1881–1890
Benjamin E. Tate, 1947–1955
John F. Torrence, 1870–1871
Samuel W. Trost, 1903–1906
Thomas Vickers, 1876–1882
James P. Walsh, 1959–
George H. Warrington, 1923–1940
J. D. Wells, 1885–1891
Emerson F. White, 1886–1892
Frank B. Wiborg, 1901–1904
James Wilson, 1859–1866
Moses F. Wilson, 1884–1891
Obed J. Wilson, 1898–1904
Charles F. Wilstach, 1867–1869
Charles F. Windisch, 1898–1908
John Flack Winslow, 1902–1906
Issac M. Wise, 1882–1899
David I. Wolfstein, 1912–1920
John Woods, 1880–1893
William Worthington, 1883–1889
Thomas L. Young, 1878–1884

APPENDIX II

Chairman of the Board of Directors
of the University of Cincinnati

Rufus King, 1872–1876

George Hoadly, 1877–1878

Samuel F. Hunt, 1878–1880

Alphonso Taft, 1881–1882

Samuel F. Hunt, 1883–1889

Cornelius George Comegys, 1890–1896

Frank J. Jones, 1896–1898

Oscar W. Kuhn, 1898–1903

Frank J. Jones, 1903–1906

Oscar W. Kuhn, 1906–1908

Henry M. Curtis, 1908–1909

Fred A. Geier, 1909–1910

Robert W. Stewart, 1910–1914

Rufus B. Smith, 1914–1923

Arthur Morgan, 1924–1931

George H. Warrington, 1931–1940

Frank F. Dinsmore, 1940–1953

Renton K. Brodie, 1953–

APPENDIX III

Administrative Officers of the University of Cincinnati

Office of the President of Cincinnati College
and of
the University of Cincinnati

Elijah Slack, President of Cincinnati College, 1819–1822

Philander Chase, President of Cincinnati College, 1822–1823

Elijah Slack, Vice-President and then Acting President of Cincinnati College, 1823–1836

William H. McGuffey, President of Cincinnati College, 1836–1839

Thomas J. Biggs, President of Cincinnati College, 1839–1845

(No President of the University of Cincinnati until 1877; but in 1873 George H. Harper, Principal of Woodward High School, was Executive Head of the University)

Thomas Vickers, Rector of the University of Cincinnati, 1877–1884

(No head of the University, 1884–1885; but Henry T. Eddy acted as Executive Head until General Cox assumed office)

Jacob D. Cox, President of the University of Cincinnati, 1885–1889

Henry T. Eddy, Executive Head of the University of Cincinnati, 1889–1890

Henry T. Eddy, Acting President of the University of Cincinnati, 1890–1891

(No President of the University; the Dean of the Academic Faculty, rotating among the faculty acted as Executive Head of the University, 1891–1899)

Howard Ayers, President of the University, 1899–1904

Joseph E. Harry, Acting President until Dr. Dabney assumed office, 1904

Charles W. Dabney, President of the University, 1904–1920

Frederick C. Hicks, President of the University, 1920–1928

Herman Schneider, Acting President of the University, 1928–1929

Herman Schneider, President of the University, 1929–1932

Raymond Walters, President of the University, 1932–1955

Walter C. Langsam, President of the University, 1955–

Office of the Vice-President and Dean of University Administration

Daniel Laurence, Dean of University Administration, 1929–1943
Norman P. Auburn, Dean of University Administration, 1943–1945
Norman P. Auburn, Vice-President and Dean of University Administration, 1945–1951
Ralph C. Bursiek, Vice-President and Dean of University Administration, 1951–1963
Ralph C. Bursiek, Senior Vice-President and Dean of University Administration, 1963–

Office of the Vice-President and Dean of Faculties

Hoke S. Greene, Dean of Academic Administration, 1956–1959
Hoke S. Greene, Vice-President and Dean of Faculties, 1959–

Office of the Vice-President and Director of the Medical Center

Clement F. St. John, 1961–

Office of the Dean of Special Services

Spencer Shanks, 1960–1963

Office of Development

Frank T. Purdy, Executive Director for Development, 1959–1963
Frank T. Purdy, Vice-President for Development, 1963–

Dean of the Graduate School

Joseph E. Harry, 1906–1916
Louis Trenchard More, 1916–1940
Rodney P. Robinson, 1940–1945
Claude M. Lotspeich, Acting Dean, 1945–1947
Hoke S. Greene, 1947–1959
Campbell Crockett, 1959–

Deans of the Academic Department, McMicken College of Liberal Arts, and McMicken College of Arts and Sciences

W. R. Benedict, 1891
E. W. Hyde, 1892
William O. Sproull, 1893–1894
P. V. N. Myers, 1895–1897
E. W. Hyde, 1897–1900
Merrick Whitcomb, 1900–1901
Joseph E. Harry, 1901–1906

Merrick Whitcomb, 1906–1910
Louis Trenchard More, 1910–1912
Frank W. Chandler, 1913–1928
Merton J. Hubert, Acting Dean, 1928–1929
William W. Hewett, 1930–1933
Howard D. Roeloffs, 1933–1936
Merton J. Hubert, Acting Dean, 1936–1938
George B. Barbour, 1938–1958
Charles K. Weichert, 1958–

Deans of the College of Engineering

Herman Schneider, 1906–1928
Robert E. Clyde Gowdy, Acting Dean, 1928–1932
Herman Schneider, 1932–1939
Robert E. Clyde Gowdy, 1940–1946
C. A. Joerger, 1946–1957
Howard K. Justice, 1957–1962
Cornelius Wandmacher, Associate Dean, 1957–1962
Cornelius Wandmacher, 1962–

Deans of the College of Education
(since 1959, the College of Education and Home Economics)

William Paxton Burris, 1905–1922
Louis Pechstein, 1922–1945
Carter V. Good, Acting Dean, 1945–1947
Carter V. Good, 1947–

Deans and Directors of the School of Home Economics

Elizabeth Dyer, Director and Dean of the College of Home Economics, 1914–1952
Elizabeth D. Roseberry, Dean, College of Home Economics, 1952–1959
Emma B. Whiteford, Director of the School of Home Economics, 1959–

Deans of College of Commerce, College of Engineering and Commerce, and College of Business Administration

Frederick C. Hicks, Dean, College of Commerce, 1912–1919
Herman Schneider, Dean, College of Engineering and Commerce, 1919–1928
Robert E. C. Gowdy, Acting Dean, College of Engineering and Commerce, 1928–1932
Herman Schneider, Dean, College of Engineering and Commerce, 1932–1939
Robert E. C. Gowdy, Dean, College of Engineering and Commerce, 1940–1946
Francis Bird, Dean, College of Business Administration, 1946–1958
Kenneth Wilson, Dean, College of Business Administration, 1958–

Deans of the College of Medicine

Daniel Drake, 1819–1822
J. Moorhead, 1825–1827
J. Cobb, 1827–1828 and 1835–1838
Josiah Whitman, 1828–1829
Charles E. Pierson, 1829–1830
Elijah Slack, 1830–1831
James M. Staughton, 1831–1832
Thomas D. Mitchell, 1832–1835
John T. Shotwell, 1838–1842
M. B. Wright, 1842–1843; 1847–1848; 1860–1862; 1864–1866 (part of year); 1867–1869
John P. Harrison, 1843–1844; 1846–1847; 1848–1849
John Locke, 1844–1845
R. D. Mussey, 1845–1846
M. L. Lawson, 1849–1854; 1858–1860; 1862–1864 (died January 1864)
Tom O. Edwards, 1854–1855
J. S. G. Armor, 1855–1857
James Graham, 1857–1858; 1869 (part of year)–1874. Died and replaced by Wright
Theophilus Parvin, 1865–1867. Died and replaced by Wright
Roberts Bartholow, 1874–1879
W. W. Dawson, 1879–1881
W. W. Seely, 1881–1900
P. S. Conner, 1900–1905
Frederick Forcheimer, 1905–1909
No Dean was appointed; E. O. Smith acted as Secretary; 1909–1911
Paul G. Woolley, 1911–1913
Christian R. Holmes, 1913–1920
John S. Oliver, Acting Dean, 1920–1921
Herman Page, 1921–September 26, 1924. First whole time Dean to be appointed
Arthur C. Bachmeyer, 1924–1934
Alfred Friedlander, 1934–1939
Stanley E. Dorst, Acting Dean, 1939–1940
Stanley E. Dorst, Dean, 1940–1962
Clifford G. Grulee, Jr., Dean, 1963–

Deans of the College of Law

Timothy Walker, in sole charge of Law Department of Cincinnati College from 1839 to 1843–1844, with the exception of year 1841–1842 when owing to his illness there was no session
M. E. Currem, 1850–1868
J. Bryant Walker, 1873–1874
Rufus King, 1875–1880
Jacob D. Cox, 1880–1897
Gustavus Wald, 1899–1902
Harlan Cleveland, July 21–August 1, 1902
William P. Rogers, 1902–1916
Alfred B. Benedict, 1916–1917; 1919–1924

Robert C. Pugh, 1924–1926
Merton L. Ferson, 1926–1946
Frank S. Rowley, 1946–1952
Roscoe Lindley Barrow, Acting Dean, 1952–1953
Roscoe Lindley Barrow, Dean, 1953–

College of Nursing and Health

Laura R. Logan, Director, 1916–1924
Phoebe M. Kandell, Acting Director, 1924–1926
Catherine M. Buckley, Director, 1926–1940
Helen G. Schwarz, Dean, 1940–1944
Laura E. Rosnagle, Dean, 1944–

College of Applied Arts and College of Design, Architecture and Art

Ernest Pickering, Dean, College of Applied Arts, 1946–1961
Ernest Pickering, Dean, College of Design, Architecture, and Art, 1961–1963
Harold R. Rice, Dean, College of Design, Architecture, and Art, 1963–

College of Pharmacy

Joseph F. Kowalewski, Dean, 1954–

College-Conservatory of Music

Marjora Shank, Dean-in-Charge, 1962–1963
Jack M. Watson, Dean, 1963–

University College

Hilmar C. Krueger, Dean, 1960–

Evening College

Vincent H. Drufner, Dean, Evening College, 1939–1940
Norman P. Auburn, Dean, 1940–1943
Frank R. Neuffer, Acting Dean, 1943–1945
Frank R. Neuffer, Dean, 1945–

Summer School

Louis Pechstein, Director, 1924–1945
Gordon Hendrickson, Acting Director, 1945–1947
Spencer Shank, Dean, 1947–1960
Robert W. Bishop, 1960–

Dean of Women

Emilie Essel Born, March–November 1901
C. K. Dumbar, 1901–1902
Margaret F. Washburn, 1903–1904
Elizabeth Czarnomski, 1904–1909
Emilie Watts McVea, 1909–1916
Loueen Pattie, 1916–1921
Josephine P. Simrall, 1922–1929
Marjorie S. Palmer, Acting Dean, 1929–1930
Josephine P. Simrall, 1930–1936
Katherine Dabney Ingle, 1936–1948
Lillian M. Johnson, 1948–

Dean of Men

Arthur S. Postle, 1936–1945
Kathleen Ressler, Assistant to the Dean in Charge, 1941–1945
Robert W. Bishop, Acting Dean, 1945–1947
Robert W. Bishop, 1947–1960
William R. Nester, Acting Dean, 1960–1963
William R. Nester, Dean, 1963–

University Library

Harriet Evans Hodges, 1901–1907
Charles Albert Read, 1907–1922
Julian S. Fowler, 1922–1928
Edward A. Henry, 1928–1951
Wyman W. Parker, 1951–1956
Arthur T. Hamlin, 1956–

Directors of the Observatory

Ormsby MacKnight Mitchel, 1843–1859
Cleveland Abbe, 1868–1871
Ormond Stone, 1875–1884
Jermain G. Porter, 1884–1930
Everett I. Yowell, 1930–1940
Elliott S. Smith, 1940–1943
Paul Herget, 1943–

Research Foundation and Scientific Research Laboratories

Fred O'Flaherty, Administrator of University Research; Director, Tanners'
Council Laboratory, 1946–

Registrar and Central Admissions Office

Lelia G. Hartman, Registrar, 1901–1939
Helen H. Burgoyne, Registrar, 1939–1954
Kenneth Varner, Registrar and Central Admissions Office, 1954–1956
Garland G. Parker, Registrar and Central Admissions Office, 1956–

Department of Co-ordination and Placement

George W. Burns, Head of Department of Co-ordination, 1919–1944
Griffith T. Addison, Acting Head of Department of Co-ordination, July–
November 1944
H. Calvert Messinger, Acting Head of Department of Co-ordination, 1944–1946
H. Calvert Messinger, Director of Department of Co-ordination and Placement,
1946–1962
Raymond W. Renn, Director of Department of Co-ordination and Placement,
1962–

Department of Public Relations

Allison Stanley, Director, 1922–1925
John P. DeCamp, Director, 1925–

Executive Secretary of the Alumni Association

Allison Stanley, 1922–1925
John P. DeCamp, 1925–1928
Mayo Hoffman, 1928–1933
Norman P. Auburn, 1933–1936
Samuel O. Beall, 1936–1941
Jack Humphries, 1941–1944
No Secretary for 1944–1946
J. Robert Sutherline, 1946–1947
Frank T. Purdy, 1947–1950
John E. Small, 1951–

Radio and Television Department

Joseph Sagmaster, Director of Broadcasting, 1960–

Index

Format by Mort Perry
Set in Linotype Caledonia
Composed, printed and bound by American Book-Stratford Press
HARPER & ROW, PUBLISHERS, INCORPORATED